The First *Star Trek* Movie

ALSO BY SHERILYN CONNELLY

Ponyville Confidential: The History and Culture of My Little Pony, *1981–2016* (McFarland, 2017)

The First *Star Trek* Movie
Bringing the Franchise to the Big Screen, 1969–1980

SHERILYN CONNELLY

McFarland & Company, Inc., Publishers
Jefferson, North Carolina

Library of Congress Cataloguing-in-Publication Data

Names: Connelly, Sherilyn, 1973– author.
Title: The first Star trek movie : bringing the franchise to the big screen, 1969–1980 / Sherilyn Connelly.
Description: Jefferson, North Carolina : McFarland & Company, Inc., Publishers, 2019 | Includes bibliographical references and index.
Identifiers: LCCN 2019035879 | ISBN 9781476672519 (paperback : acid free paper) ∞) | ISBN 9781476638195 (ebook)
Subjects: LCSH: Star trek (Motion picture : 1979) | Motion pictures—Production and direction—United States. | Motion pictures—United States—History—20th century.
Classification: LCC PN1997.S65932 C66 2019 | DDC 791.43/72—dc23
LC record available at https://lccn.loc.gov/2019035879

British Library cataloguing data are available

ISBN (print) 978-1-4766-7251-9
ISBN (ebook) 978-1-4766-3819-5

© 2019 Sherilyn Connelly. All rights reserved

No part of this book may be reproduced or transmitted in any form or by any means, electronic or mechanical, including photocopying or recording, or by any information storage and retrieval system, without permission in writing from the publisher.

Front cover image © 2019 Shutterstock

Printed in the United States of America

McFarland & Company, Inc., Publishers
  Box 611, Jefferson, North Carolina 28640
    www.mcfarlandpub.com

For Conk

Table of Contents

Acknowledgments — ix

Introduction: The Redefinition of Unwarranted — 1

Prologue: Star Trek—The MacArthur Premiere — 11

1969: THE NETWORK'S KNIFE CARES NOT FOR THE SHOW'S CRY — 25
  Star Trek Dies 25

1970–1972: WHAT'S IN RERUNS IS PROLOGUE — 30
  Star Trek Has Risen from the Grave 30 • The Long Con Begins 31

1973–1974: CHOOSE YOUR TELEVISED PAIN — 37
  Genesis II v. *Planet of the Apes* 37 • The Animated Series Is Pre-Rejected by the Fans 38 • The Animated Series Is Barely Accepted by the Fans 41 • Roddenberry on Tour 44

1975: MAGICAM TO MAKE THE SANEST MAN GO MAD — 49
  Star Trek II Is Announced; Expectations Are Managed 49 • Rumored Redford 53 • *Star Trek II* Is Denounced; Expectations Are Mangled 55

1976: THE WAR WITHIN THE SCRIPT, THE WAR WITHOUT — 58
  Harlan Ellison v. Star Trek 58 • The 743 Speak 59 • The Isenberg Cometh; The Trektennial Begins 61 • Look Now! It's Bryant and Scott 66 • Kaufman Commissioned 67 • A Log … of the Stars! 70 • Enter Eisner 73

1977: THE BATTLE OF THE BINARY STAR TREKS — 75
  Captain Kirk Almost Meets John Galt 75 • Of Cygnans and Spiders; Kaufman Keelhauled 79 • The Fourth Network Awakens 84 • Here We Are Now, Entertain Us the Way We Tell You To 87 • Shatner Says "See Ya Never!" 90 • "Robot's Return" Returns 93 • Roddenberry Ruminates 97 • The New Kids on the Bridge; Whither Leonard? 99 • Collins Conferred; The Fourth Network Sees Its Shadow 103

1978: Into the Luminescent Powerfield I Go 108
Roddenberry Recaps 108 • The Starship of the 1970s Future 110 • Collins Cleaved; Wise Wrangled 113 • Star Trek—The Massive Presser 114 • Magicam Can't, but Abel's Able 119 • To Boldly Pump the Brakes 120

1979: Will You Take My $44M Hand? 127
Star Trek—The Marketing Problem, Part I: The Nerve of Steel 127 • Star Trek—The Marketing Problem, Part II: The Purview of John Askew 130 • Star Trek—The Marketing Problem, Part III: Set Printers to "Tilt" 134 • Star Trek—The Marketing Problem, Part IV: Brrap Brrap Pew Pew! 140 • Star Trek—The Marketing Problem, Part V: Ready-to-Spacewear, Everywhere 144 • Star Trek—The Marketing Problem, Part VI: A Wagon of Trailers Full of Stars 148 • Star Trek—The Manifest Procession, Part I: New York, New Jersey, Pennsylvania and Florida 154 • Star Trek—The Manifest Procession, Part II: Kentucky, Mississippi and Arkansas 160 • Star Trek—The Manifest Procession, Part III: Indiana, Illinois, Michigan and Minnesota 162 • Star Trek—The Manifest Procession, Part IV: South Dakota, Nebraska, Kansas, Utah and Arizona 164 • Star Trek—The Manifest Procession, Part V: Washington, Oregon, Nevada and California 167 • The Shakedown, Part I: Acceleration 170

1980: The Vulcan Goodbye 177
The Shakedown, Part II: Deceleration 177 • One Brief, Shining Sequel Set in … Camelot! 179 • A Moving Analog Image Transferred from a Magnetic Medium 182 • V'ger's Gait 183

Epilogue: Star Trek—The Mathematical Phantom 185

Chapter Notes 193

Bibliography 209

Index 221

Acknowledgments

I am deeply grateful to many carbon-based units for many things. Gene Roddenberry, for starting the whole thing. Susan Sackett, without whose hard work in the 1970s this book would probably not exist, and for graciously putting up with my requests, questions, and general fangirlishness in the late 2010s. Larry Nemecek, David Gerrold, and especially Judith and Garfield Reeves-Stevens for further laying the groundwork. Tim Gaskill and Richard Arnold, for answering questions and pointing me in proper directions. Helena Lukas, for venturing into the Multnomah County Library on my behalf, and for being there even when she wasn't. Rachel Bernstein, Louise Hilton, Kristine Krueger, and everyone at the Margaret Herrick Library for their patience during Hurricane Sherilyn. Michael Monahan, for his Bob Wilkins expertise and for generously supplying research materials. Joan Marie Verba, for writing *Boldly Writing: A Trekker Fan and Zine History, 1967–1987*. The crew of the USS *Mission Bay* (NCC-94158) for taking this wayward Burnham into their fold, and for their understanding when she transferred to Deep Space Potrero. Ensign Perez, for asking what we were all thinking. Vaishali Sinha, for coming in toward the end and assuring me I was on the right path. Kim Cotton, for her editorial assistance, and for always having been on the path. KrOB, for helping me realize "The Fourth Network Awakens" was a better gag than "May the Fourth Network Be with You," for being the only person I know who loves this movie as much as I do, and just for being a good friend. And my brothers John and Jim, for reading their sister's words.

Introduction: The Redefinition of Unwarranted

This is a scholarly history of the Robert Wise film *Star Trek—The Motion Picture*, with an emphasis on the years, months, days, and hours leading up to the movie's initial North American release on December 7, 1979. It will study the many unsuccessful efforts to revive Star Trek following the cancelation of the original television series in 1969, how the 1979 film was marketed and presented to the public, the way that film's massive national release presaged the blockbuster era as now know it, and the unfortunate rise of the "even-numbered rule." Star Trek was a frequent reference point in my previous work of scholarly sparkliness, *Ponyville Confidential: The History and Culture of My Little Pony, 1981–2016*, and while the books share DNA, it is not necessary to have read one to appreciate the other.

* * *

I loved *ST—TMP* when I first saw it in the theater when I was six and a half years old in 1979, and I watched it countless times when it became available on VHS the following year, blissfully unaware that the film was slow and boring and that I shouldn't like it. I was also fascinated by what happened behind the scenes from an early age. While still in elementary school I read, re-read, and re-read again Stephen Whitfield and Gene Roddenberry's *The Making of Star Trek,* and especially David Gerrold's *The World of Star Trek* and *The Trouble with Tribbles,* all of which taught me how to think critically about the pop culture I love. (I read the *Best of Trek* collections because they were about Star Trek, but even at the time I sensed they weren't authentic.)

This is by no means the first book published about this most contentious of Trek films. Susan Sackett and Gene Roddenberry's *The Making of Star Trek—The Motion Picture* and Walter Koenig's *Chekov's Enterprise: A Personal Journal of the Making of Star Trek—The Motion Picture* were both published within a few months of the release of the film, while Preston Neal Jones' 2014 oral history *Return to Tomorrow: The Filming of Star Trek: The Motion Picture* was originally intended to be a *Cinefantastique* double issue in 1980. Star Trek in the 1970s is also covered in some detail in Edward Gross and Mark A. Altman's 2016 *The Fifty-Year Mission: The Complete, Uncensored, Unauthorized Oral History of Star Trek: The First 25 Years.*

However, to the best of my knowledge this is the first scholarly nonfiction work about Star Trek to be based on primary and secondary sources, and to relate the history of the project according to how it was reported on and discussed at the time. For this reason I used very few memoirs as sources, with the main exceptions being Susan Sackett's *Inside Trek: My Secret Life with Star Trek Creator Gene Roddenberry*, Robert H. Justman and Herbert F. Solow's *Inside Star Trek: The Real Story*, Michael Eisner's *Work in Progress: Risking Failure, Surviving Success*, and Dawn Steel's *They Can Kill You, But They Can't Eat You: Lessons from the Front.*

Preston Neal Jones' *Return to Tomorrow* was a valuable resource because the interviews were conducted from mid-summer 1979 through the end of that year during post-production and the initial release of the film. While I highly recommend Gross and Altman's *Fifty-Year Mission* for further reading, I did not use it as a reference because it did not specify when a given interview was conducted, and as is the nature of oral histories, it repeated untrue rumors and treated them as fact. Consider its coverage of Gene Roddenberry's treatment for a sequel to the first Star Trek movie, a story which involved the crew traveling back to an alternate 1963 in which John F. Kennedy wasn't assassinated. The first public reference to it was a 1981 news item in *Starlog*, wherein "a Paramount official (who asked not to be named)" revealed that in Roddenberry's story, "just about the last scene in the story had Spock walking up to Kennedy's limousine and killing him with his phaser."[1]

Speaking as one who has seen the treatment in question, that is simply not true. The considerably more authoritative Susan Sackett debunked the rumor in *The Fifty-Year Mission*, but the way the book was structured, the second-to-last word on the matter was given to Paramount publicist Eddie Egan: "Spock appeared behind the fence and fired the shot and everything returns to normal. Of course, the attitude of the studio was mostly just horror; that you can't make a movie like that. Their thoughts about Gene were 'It's just in bad taste and we don't like you, anyway, so go away.'" This was followed in *The Fifty-Year Mission* by *Access Hollywood*'s Scott Mantz printing the legend, *The Man Who Shot Liberty Valance*-style: "Boy, what a mess. Paramount was wise to toss it to the side in favor of the greatest Trek movie of them all, *The Wrath of Khan*."[2]

There is so much to unpack in that statement—such as the false dichotomy that the second Star Trek movie would have been either "Spock kills Kennedy" or the Nicholas Meyer film as it was released to theaters in 1982—but the point is that the printing of legends which replace the facts is in the nature of oral histories, and human memory is tricky enough when those memories are being formed, let alone when being recalled decades later. A prime example of this is an interview with William Shatner on the website IGN in 2017 for the 35th anniversary of what Mantz called "the greatest Trek movie of them all." After acknowledging that he doesn't remember many details from the time period, Shatner goes on to state a number of demonstrably false details, such as the sequel only having been made because "the wife of the owner of the studio, whose name I'm trying to remember, said to her husband that Star Trek is so good, you've got to do it again. And he said, the gentleman who owned the studio, not even head of the studio, owned it, we've got to do it again." This itself is a variant on an apocryphal story Shatner told at the 1979 *ST—TMP* premiere about how that film only got made because the studio owner Charles Bluhdorn's daughter Dominique told him to make it. In addition to getting his vaguely sexist anecdotes confused—women sure pester!—Shatner told IGN that after every Trek movie, "they burned the sets, that was it. There was no reason to store them, because there was never gonna be another movie. So they burned them … and they kept burning them right up to Star Trek VI, as far as I know." What Shatner knew in 2017 didn't go far at all, considering that his participation in the fourth film was contractually predicated on him getting to direct the fifth film. This notion that the sets were burned after every film can be disproved by *watching* the films—the Enterprise sets in the second and third films are clearly the ones built for the first film with a few cosmetic changes, and the Bridge in the sixth film is unmistakably that of the fifth film with fresh paint—but the statement went unchallenged by the interviewer.[3]

Which brings us to David Alexander's *Star Trek Creator: The Authorized Biography of Gene Rodenberry*. That so much of the book is an info-dump of Roddenberry's letters and files with no acknowledgment of their frequent inaccuracies and inconsistencies made me trust it as a reliable secondary source, since Alexander was clearly happy to just get as many of the Great Bird of the Galaxy's thoughts out into the world as he could. Among them was a letter Roddenberry sent to a Paramount executive sometime after June 1986 in which Roddenberry described the Klingons as having been "invented by an episodic writer when he ran into 'last act problems.' They were never considered very imaginative but those of our writers who tended toward bad guys/good guys 'hack' scripting loved them dearly." The "episodic writer" to whom Roddenberry referred was Gene L. Coon, who was also the producer of the show by that point after Roddenberry had changed to executive producer. Coon invented the Klingons in the episode "Errand of Mercy," and rather than being a solution for the final act, they were mentioned in dialog within the first sixty seconds and were the focus of the episode. Regarding those writers who tended toward "hack" scripting featuring good guys and bad guys, the next two episodes to feature Klingons were "Friday's Child" and "The Trouble with Tribbles," written by Dorothy Fontana and David Gerrold respectively. The latter is one of the most beloved episodes of any Star Trek series, and Roddenberry would soon bring on Fontana and Gerrold to work on *The Next Generation*, though they would each leave acrimoniously by end of the first season.[4]

A few sentences later in that same letter, Roddenberry wrote that when the second movie's producers "began seeking bad guys for their film story ... the Klingons volunteered. Having by then adopted a policy of rarely interfering with the film producers and directors, I simply made my feelings known but never carried my belief beyond that." Setting aside that Roddenberry's own rejected story used them as the enemy, the Klingons were not the bad guys in the second movie. In the first movie they were only seen from afar in the first five minutes and have no interaction with the *Enterprise* or Starfleet, and in the second movie they're only seen from afar in the first five minutes and don't actually exist in the movie's world, being make-believe elements of a training simulation.[5]

In the letter quoted verbatim by Alexander, Roddenberry continued that "in the succeeding movie, *Star Trek III*, the Klingons stayed on and many people, including some right here at Paramount, began assuming that was what Star Trek was basically about. By the time of release of *Star Trek III*, I had become alarmed that over-emphasis on Klingons might be harming the property. These movies turned too often to 'tried and true' (read *simplistic*) Klingon villainy rather than making use of the myriad alternatives that science fiction offers."[6]

The truth is that the third film is the first in which the Klingons interact with the main characters or do anything villainous, but according to Roddenberry's letter, the result of this non-existent "over-emphasis on Klingons" was that "interest in *Star Trek* was visibly declining and my office was encountering statements of disappointment from the most respected of fans and science fiction writers, their concern being that *Star Trek* seemed to be deteriorating into a two-dimensional "'good guys vs. bad guys' space opera." Those "most respected of fans and science fiction writers" go unidentified by Roddenberry, probably because they didn't exist. However, an argument has been made by the least respected of fans that the success of the second movie had a deleterious effect on the creativity of the franchise as films in later decades attempted to recreate its "villain seeks revenge" dynamic, particularly 2002's *Star Trek: Nemesis*, 2009's *Star Trek*, 2013's blatant *Wrath* retread *Star Trek Into Darkness*, and to a lesser extent 2016's otherwise superior *Star Trek Beyond*. But at the time it was written, before even the Klingon-heavy *Star Trek V: The Final Frontier* in 1989 or *Star Trek VI: The Undiscovered Country* in 1992, Roddenberry's letter suggests that he had paid little attention to the films he was criticizing, and he figured no one else would, either.[7]

    This was also the case with the films he was praising, as he went on to write that the fourth Star Trek movie "changed the whole picture. That very talented production team (many of which also made *Star Trek* movies II and III), sensed the stagnation induced by Klingon over-emphasis and came up with an entirely different kind of story which ignored Klingon villainy in favor of a story closer to *Star Trek*'s origins ... and the difference this has made is already visible." While it is true that director Leonard Nimoy has said *Star Trek IV: The Voyage Home* was always intended to be a far lighter film than the third, that "it was time to really lighten up and have a good time, kick up our heels and do a caper," he at no point hinted at this being due to "stagnation induced by Klingon over-emphasis," probably due to the Klingons having only been emphasized once to date. In the February 1986 *Starlog*, *Star Trek III* writer and producer Harve Bennett explained that the Romulans were the villains in his original script, but director Nimoy "felt that the Klingons were more exciting, more theatrical," while "a sampling of mail also indicated that the fans wanted to see Klingons." The fans' desires to see Klingons in the third film may have had to do with their virtual absence from the first two movies beyond the first five minutes of each—and much like in those first two films, the Klingons only appear in the beginning of the fourth film, though during those first ten minutes a Klingon ambassador swears vengeance on Admiral Kirk for the events of the third film. For the duration of the fourth film the crew of the recently-destroyed USS *Enterprise* use a stolen Klingon Bird-of-Prey, a ship which figured prominently into the marketing of what would go on to be the second-most beloved and highest-grossing of the Trek films as of 1986 (without adjusting for inflation). All of this suggests that Gene Roddenberry's weariness about seeing Klingons on the big screen was not shared by the general public, probably because they'd only seen them at length in the third film.[8]

    But David Alexander took Roddenberry's description of the problem of the "outdated preoccupation with the Klingons" at face value in *Star Trek Creator*, writing that Roddenberry "partially solved the problem in *The Next Generation* by making the Klingons allies and putting one on the bridge of the Enterprise." In doing so, Alexander praised Roddenberry for solving a Klingon-fatigue problem which did not exist. But that's fair, since as an authorized and ever-so-slightly-fawning biographer, Alexander did his job of reporting things Roddenberry said and did, usually without comment, and with no evident sign of whitewashing—and that's why the reprinted documents in Alexander's book were treated as reliable sources for this book.[9]

However, the aforementioned books only provided a a small amount of material for this one. My intention was not to simply repeat conventional wisdom and popularly-held beliefs about Star Trek, but to tell a new history based on the facts as they were recorded at the time, many of which have been difficult to find until they were digitized and made available to the public. As such, the majority of the research for the book was done using ProQuest databases, the *Variety* Archives, Google Books, the Internet Archive, Newspapers.com, and by digging through papers at the Margaret Herrick Library at the Academy of Motion Picture Arts and Sciences in Beverly Hills. Appropriately enough for a project as massive as *ST—TMP*, I gathered enough research material for two books; the work of scholarly sparkliness you currently have the good taste to be reading will be the first.

* * *

Some words about titles, and a historiography of the unmade Star Trek projects which as of 2018 are commonly referred to as *The God Thing*, *Planet of the Titans*, and *Phase II*. In the interest of telling the story of the first Star Trek movie as closely as possible to how it happened, I will not be referring to the projects by those aforementioned names, for all the early attempts at creating a Star Trek feature film were either called *Star Trek II* or *Star Trek—The Motion Picture*, and the unmade series was only called *Star Trek II*. (Roddenberry's fondness for the title *Star Trek II* is further hinted at by it being the name of his sailboat in the 1970s.)[10]

Susan Sackett wrote in the August 1977 *Starlog* that "Gene is now completing his novelization of the original Star Trek movie script (the one Paramount rejected) tentatively titled 'The God Thing.'" This appears to have been the first reference to the story by that name, but just the never-completed novelization, and only "tentatively." In her memoir *Inside Trek*, Sackett would later recall that "following the studio's rejection of this script, Gene began writing it as a novel, calling it *The God Thing*." But there is no indication that the film would have been called *The God Thing* had it been produced, and the story Roddenberry turned in to Paramount and which is currently in the collection at the Margaret Herrick Library—and which I have seen with my own eyes—is titled *Star Trek II*, not *The God Thing*.[11]

Introduction: The Redefinition of Unwarranted

Susan Sackett and Gene Roddenberry's *The Making of Star Trek—The Motion Picture* was published in February 1980 by the Paramount subsidiary Pocket Books, as all the best non-fiction tomes about Star Trek are. Sackett wrote of the television series that "at first it sounded like the name of a bar of soap: *Star Trek—Phase II*," but "fortunately, the *Phase* part was dropped," and going forward the series is only referred to as *Star Trek II* in that 1980 book. In his 1986 *Star Trek Compendium* from Pocket Books, Allan Asherman referred to the series by the discarded soap name of *Star Trek—Phase II* referenced in Sackett's book. This may have had something to do with the fact that in 1982 Pocket published Asherman's authorized *The Making of Star Trek II: The Wrath of Khan*, so he would have had an early interest in distinguishing between the unmade series and the Nicholas Meyer film, which was already in the process of being sanctified.[12]

In the 1992 *Star Trek: The Next Generation Companion* published by Pocket Books, Larry Nemecek referred to the unmade 1978 television series as *Star Trek II*. Published in November 1994 by Pocket Pooks, J.M. Dillard's *Star Trek: "Where No One Has Gone Before": A History in Pictures* referred to the unmade 1975 movie—which "soon evolved from TV series to a modest-budget $3 million movie"—as *Star Trek II*, and Roddenberry's rejected story as "The God Thing." Dillard did not refer to the subsequent unproduced feature film written by Chris Bryant and Alan Scott and to be directed by Philip Kaufman (now commonly referred to as *Planet of the Titans*) by any specific title, though she did call the subsequent aborted television series *Star Trek II*, and the first revised and updated edition of Larry Nemecek's *Next Generation Companion* printed in May 1995 continued to refer to the unmade 1978 series as *Star Trek II*.[13]

Published in October 1995 by Hyperion, Leonard Nimoy's *I Am Spock* referred to Roddenberry's "first draft of a movie script" as *The God Thing* and the unmade television series as *Star Trek: Phase II*, and Nimoy did not mention the Kaufman film. But the first Pocket Book references to *The God Thing*, *Planet of the Titans*, and/or *Phase II* as the official names in a work solely about Star Trek appears to have occurred in Judith and Garfield Reeves-Stevens' *The Art of Star Trek*, published in November 1995. The Reeves-Stevenses wrote that "Roddenberry delivered his script—*The God Thing*—in August of [1975]" to Paramount's president Barry Diller, who rejected it, and that the script later written by Bryant and Scott "was titled *Planet of the Titans*, and ultimately it, too, was rejected by Paramount." They also wrote that "in 1977 Paramount decided to produce a second television series, appropriately titled STAR TREK: PHASE II." The series was next referred to as *Star Trek:*

Phase II in Herbert F. Solow and Robert H. Justman's *Inside Star Trek: The Real Story*, published by Pocket Books in 1996.[14]

This title became retroactively canonized in the 1997 publication by Pocket Books of the Reeves-Stevens' *Star Trek Phase II: The Lost Series*, a fascinating and highly recommended history of the unmade series, referred to throughout merely as *Star Trek Phase II* without the colon used in *The Art of Star Trek* and *Inside Star Trek*. They also referred to the Roddenberry and Bryant/Scott scripts as *The God Thing* and *Planet of the Titans* respectively, names which stuck. And while the series was referred to colloquially as *Phase II* throughout the text of the book *Star Trek Phase II: The Lost Series*—hereafter referred to in this book as *The Lost Series*—there are hints of the original title throughout, including in a reprint of the Writers/Directors Guide, which was titled *Star Trek II*. The title *Phase II* was codified for good in 2001 with the short documentary *Phase II: The Lost Enterprise* released on the *Star Trek—The Motion Picture: The Director's Edition* DVD. Curiously enough, the final revised and updated edition of Larry Nemecek's *Next Generation Companion* in 2003 slipped through the revisionism cracks and still referred to the unmade 1978 series as *Star Trek II*.[15]

None of this is meant in any way to criticize the Reeves-Stevenses or anyone else involved in documenting the history of Star Trek, for the franchise's history is confusing enough without having to sort through multiple properties with the same name like so many early Peter Gabriel records. I also work as a librarian and thus fully understand the importance of a naming standard, and it's compounded by the 1982 film *Star Trek II: The Wrath of Khan* being considered by many people who are not myself to be the greatest Trek movie of them all. As a result, it makes perfect sense that Paramount would want to make sure the words "Star Trek II" only ever refer to that fine if slightly overpraised movie to avoid further confusion. This confusion is so pernicious that many of the scripts and documents for what would have been the first Star Trek movie are classified in the Margaret Herrick Library as being production material for *The Wrath of Khan* due to them being labeled *Star Trek II*; similarly, since Gene Roddenberry titled his treatment for what would have been the second Star Trek movie *Star Trek III*, it can be found at the Herrick among the production material for *The Search for Spock*.

In the interest of telling the story as closely as possible to how it happened, this book will embrace that confusion, and only refer to those properties by the names they were known by *at the time*. The primary exception is that the 1966–1969 NBC series will be referred to as *Star Trek I* as was Gene Roddenberry's wont in the 1970s, hence his revival attempts being titled *Star Trek II*. The 1973–1974 NBC animated series will be referred to as *Star Trek:*

Introduction: The Redefinition of Unwarranted

Animated, and the movies will most often be referred to by their director and/or their chronological placement: *The Motion Picture* as the Robert Wise film, or the first film; *The Wrath of Khan* as the Nicholas Meyer film, or the second film; *The Search for Spock* as the third film; *The Voyage Home* as the fourth film; and *The Final Frontier* as the fifth film, or the William Shatner film. The sixth film, Nicholas Meyer's *The Undiscovered Country*, is beyond the scope of this book.

Regarding how names will be emphasized, specific properties are italicized, but Star Trek as an overall concept or franchise is not. For example: "*Star Trek II* would have been a revival of Star Trek and a direct sequel to *Star Trek I*, and it evolved into the first Star Trek movie, *Star Trek—The Motion Picture*." When quoting sources I've made every effort to retain their original typographical style, which is why in many of the quotes STAR TREK will be written in what is now considered shouty all-caps.

* * *

Covering the entirety of the 1970s, this volume is divided into years (or groups of years) from 1969 to 1980, with a particular emphasis on the days March 28, 1978, and December 6 and 7, 1979. *The First Star Trek Movie* presupposes a familiarity with the theatrical version of *ST—TMP*, available on DVD, Blu-ray, and various streaming services at the time of this writing. (The 2001 *Director's Edition* is outside of our scope.) Yes, I know, it's slow and boring, but if you've made it this far into the Introduction, then it would behoove you to devote two and a quarter hours to watching the film. That said, I will not be overly concerned with the actual content of the first Star Trek movie, or its famously troubled principal photography. The story I'm telling is less about the stone and more about its ripple.

Or, to put it in relativistic terms that I *totally* understand or else I wouldn't use them, the story I'm telling here is less about the specifics of the event and more about its light cones—especially its past light cone—and the massive impact it had on the spacetime of 1970s pop culture. Besides, with one exception those production woes have been covered at length elsewhere. (Again, I highly recommend Preston Neal Jones' *Return to Tomorrow* for the nittiest of the gritty.)

The one exception, and thus the other major omission, is the person known as Persis Khambatta, and her character of Ilia. Her life story, with a focus on her experiences making the Robert Wise film and how it affected her career, will be the subject of this book's companion volume, which will follow in a few years from this same publisher. (Or maybe even from Pocket Books! But probably not.)

And in the interest of full disclosure, here's my personal ranking of the first five movies: (1) *Star Trek III: The Search for Spock.* (2) *Star Trek—The Motion Picture.* (3) *Star Trek IV: The Voyage Home.* (4) *Star Trek II: The Wrath of Khan.* (5) *Star Trek V: The Final Frontier.*

This then is the epic journey to the first Star Trek movie, and the true story of how the human adventure began. Don't be afraid.

Prologue: Star Trek—The MacArthur Premiere

Robert Wise was making short work of the *hors d'oeuvres*.[1]

He had always been a nervous eater, and he was more nervous now than before any previous premiere in his storied career. It was Thursday, December 6, 1979, just a few hours until the black-tie, $100-per-person world premiere of *Star Trek—The Motion Picture* at the MacArthur Theater in Washington, D.C. This screening for Wise's film had been announced in August 1979, and Paramount was holding a cocktail party at the swanky, recently-opened Four Seasons hotel in Georgetown, where most everyone involved with the film was staying on the studio's dime. For as much money as the Mountain had spent on the film, the charges for the rooms and/or their ransacked minibars would be negligible.[2]

Wise was legendary for keeping his cool under duress, and watching him stress-gorge on vittles was making Susan Sackett lose her own appetite. A former schoolteacher who had been hired as Star Trek producer Gene Roddenberry's secretary in August 1974, Sackett had been involved since the beginning—or earlier, depending on what point in time you declared to be the beginning. In addition to seeing a rough cut of the live-action footage *sans* music or effects in October 1979, she'd watched the answer print a few days before the MacArthur premiere. Like so many other things about the film, that answer print was late, originally due to be completed in mid-November.[3]

Beyond the mysterious cabal at the MPAA who had rated the film "G" the day before yesterday, only about a half-dozen other people had seen the movie so far, including composer Jerry Goldsmith, director Wise, and his editor Todd Ramsay. Otherwise, the first people on Earth to see the most-hyped film of 1979 would be the 850 souls at the MacArthur Theater, approximately one for every theater the film would be opening in the next morning. Wise had been told that he absolutely had to deliver the finished product to the lab at Metro-Goldwyn-Mayer by midnight on Friday, November 30, but he was still dubbing in the soundtrack at 2:30 a.m., and viewing composite reels at 3:00 a.m. He returned at noon on Saturday to fix a problem in the sound negative, reviewed the backup sound at six that evening, and finally stepped back and let the printing of the reels begin. A few days later he visited Stage 12 at MGM, which Paramount had rented so they'd have somewhere to lay out the few thousand containers which held several thousand reels of freshly-minted film. Of those completed prints, 360 began shipping on Monday, another 300 went out on Tuesday, and the rest had gone out on Wednesday.[4]

Taking no chances with their investment, Paramount gave each of the cans an additional lead seal, and upon arrival exhibitors were instructed to report back any evidence of tampering with the closely-inventoried and only somewhat-toxic lock. They applied further pressure via a letter which warned that should a piracy case develop with the movie, and a subsequent FBI investigation were to connect a given theater with that case, the Mountain would make use of all legal remedies available to punish the exhibitor. The letter also recommended that the theater manager hold a staff meeting to emphasize that every security measure would be required from anyone who so much as breathed near the print. Paramount would later send undercover operatives working with the MPAA's film security office out to theaters, offering big money for copies of the film to see how long it would take for a bootleg to appear on the market.[5]

For the MacArthur Premiere, Wise protected his ever-so-premature baby by bringing the print on the plane the night before and keeping it locked in his hotel room. In and of itself, hand-delivering films was nothing new for Wise. In January 1941 while editing Orson Welles' *Citizen Kane*—the greatest film ever made as of 1979, and it still is as of 2018 in spite of the British Film Institute having displaced it with Alfred Hitchcock's *Vertigo*, which isn't even Hitchcock's best film let alone the best film by anyone ever, but that's a matter for another book—Wise had flown with a work print for sixty hours in a blizzard to a private preview screening for RKO executives and attorneys at Radio City Music Hall. During production on *ST—TMP*, Wise spoke highly of Welles when prompted, and hired his former boss to narrate the teaser trailer.[6]

Wise had personally brought prints to two premieres of his own pictures in more recent decades, but of the 38 films in his 35-year directorial career, this was the first to not have any test screenings. The MacArthur projectionist had picked up the print earlier that day, so there was nothing Wise could do now except deal with the sense of gnawing dread that the film was not ready for mass consumption. It needed more work, a shakedown cruise, or at least previews with an audience—just a few more weeks to see all the elements put together in order to figure out what worked, and what didn't.[7]

But the premiere date of December 7, 1979, had been etched in stone ever since Paramount sent out bid letters to theaters on December 8, 1978, the furthest in advance a film had ever been optioned for bidding, let alone for a movie which was still in principal photography. The letters came with a promotional packet which contained as much information as Paramount was able, or at least willing, to reveal. The theaters were given until December 28, 1978, to place their bids, several hundred had done so, and now the rubber was about to meet the road. The picture was going to be consumed *en masse*, and it bore Robert Wise's name. Sure, it was tied with Gene Roddenberry's producer credit, which was contractually required to come before Wise's director credit, hence them sharing a title screen with Roddenberry's name on top, while official Paramount press materials awkwardly referred to the film as "'STAR TREK—The Motion Picture,' a Gene Roddenberry Production—a Robert Wise Film." (Wise and Roddenberry's shared title screen was not as much of an indication of equal collaboration as the screen Welles shared with cinematographer Gregg Toland had been on *Kane*, to put it mildly.) But there was a real possibility that this could prove to be less like Wise's 1965 triumph *The Sound of Music* starring Julie Andrews, and more like his 1969 misfire *STAR!* starring Julie Andrews. At least those had Julie Andrews, and Wise would later look back on *STAR!*'s reception as his biggest disappointment, since he considered it to be a better film and a greater achievement than it was given credit for. (This was not an opinion he would hold of *ST—TMP*.) *STAR!* had also been his last film to be released as a roadshow, but those days were long gone; *ST—TMP* would immediately go into release at popular prices, and nothing could be done to stop it.[8]

Meanwhile, final preparations for the premiere were underway at the MacArthur Theater. Located in the Palisades neighborhood of Washington and designed by famed theater architect John J. Zink in the Art Moderne style, the single-screen, 1,000-seat movie palace was completed in 1946 for a then-hefty $125,000. The first film shown was the Errol Flynn vehicle *Never Say Goodbye* on Christmas Day, and after a few years as one of the classier second-run theaters in town, in the early 1950s the MacArthur morphed into an arthouse which primarily showed British comedies, from lowbrow favorites such as the *Carry On* series to the higher-class Ealing Studios pictures starring Alec Guinness. (The MacArthur was also just a few miles from the Uptown Theater where on March 31, 1968, the second of a handful of disastrous preview screenings for *2001: A Space Odyssey* had resulted in Stanley Kubrick trimming 19 minutes of footage *after* his film's official premieres in New York and Los Angeles a week later.) This wasn't the first time in recent memory the MacArthur had hosted a high-profile premiere; President Carter had attended Hall Bartlett's *The Children of Sanchez* a few months earlier. But even the logistics of protecting a sitting President, such as installing special phone lines, weren't as much work as was being put into the premiere of this movie based on a long-canceled television show.[9]

At four in the afternoon on Thursday, December 6, a work crew from Superior Carpets put down $2,000 worth of red carpet in front of the theater, while spotlights and other illumination were provided by R & R Lighting. Both companies had provided these services for Pope John Paul II's visit in October, and security and crowd control in the form of police barricades and 16 officers was provided by the Mayor's Command Post, a local government advisory group which coordinated the response to disasters such as floods and riots. Neither seemed outside the realm of possibility, between the December rain and Paramount's Vice President of Promotion and Publicity Ed Kalish's prediction that anywhere from 3,000 to 6,000 fans would show up. The KB theater chain's general manager Paul Kershner was even prepared to let fans camp out in tents outside the theater, but the earliest anyone got there had been a young man from New Jersey who arrived around 1pm on Thursday, and that was only because he was confused about what time the event started. But he did get to witness ushers Steve Wright and Phil Maggio spending over an hour putting the words WORLD PREMIERE STAR TREK THE MOTION PICTURE on the marquee, complete with a gap between the words "Trek" and "The" to stand in for the erstwhile em-dash that was part of the film's official title. (The colon-and-subtitle standardization for franchise pictures was still a few years off.)[10]

Kershner kept plenty busy even without campers, supervising the street closure and the washing of the pavement. Nor were any stones being left unspruced inside, as the MacArthur's terrazzo floors were mopped and the chrome was shined, an additional candy counter was installed, and a dozen palm trees gave the lobby and its tasteful rose-colored marble panels that extra bit of ersatz Hollywood pizzazz. As for the presentation of the hitherto unseen movie itself, the chief engineer of Samuel Goldwyn Studios had flown in from Los Angeles on Wednesday and stayed until past midnight to work on the sound system, while film editor Todd Ramsay checked the theater's acoustics, and shiny new lenses were installed on the projector.[11]

On the 35mm projector, to be precise. The intention had always been to release the film in both 35mm and 70mm, and many of the upgrades Robert Wise made to the Bridge of the *Enterprise* were so it would stand up to the scrutiny of 70mm exhibition. But it had become apparent by mid–November that just producing enough 35mm prints for December 7 would be tricky enough, and there was no way the more challenging 70mm prints were going to happen in time, never mind any promises which may had been made to the exhibitors. It was less of an issue for the MacArthur, which was already equipped for 70mm projection, and that it was going to be a 35mm print meant one less variable. It was far more annoying for exhibitors who made the costly upgrade specifically for this movie. In addition to the $1.25M for the guarantee to show the movie at their eight other theaters in California, Nevada, and Utah, the Ray Syufy company spent $32,000 to convert the Century 22 B theater in San Jose to 70mm, and advance tickets were on sale at the local BASS outlet.[12]

But it wasn't just major exhibitors plunking down large sums for the film. Apple co-founder Steve Wozniak was such a fan that he had three dozen videotapes of *Star Trek I* episodes even though they weren't yet commercially available, but he was also still smarting from not getting to see *Star Wars* or *Alien* on their respective opening nights, so he paid over $3,000 for 691 seats at $4.50 each for the Robert Wise film's opening night at the Century 22 B as well as a few other nights. Woz then turned around and sold about half of them to Apple employees for $10 each, so never let it be said that his partner Steve Jobs was the only capitalist between them.[13]

* * *

The MacArthur Premiere was a benefit for the National Space Club, which was originally founded in 1957 as the National Rocket Club. Proceeds from the Premiere would go toward the Club's educational programs which provided opportunities for youth to pursue careers in the United States' space program, the future of which was looking rosy. The screening would be followed by an equally exclusive reception at the Smithsonian National Air and Space Museum.[14]

The evening's chairman was former Club president Larry G. Hastings, who had been a Star Trek fan for about as long as it was possible to be such a thing, having been involved in the organized efforts to save *Star Trek I* from cancellation a decade earlier. It didn't hurt that the club had honored Gene Roddenberry in March 1979, considering that shortly after said honoring it was decided that of the more than 40 organizations which had made similar requests, the Club would be the only beneficiary of a premiere screening of the Robert Wise film. The closest any of the others came was the John Thomas Dye School in Los Angeles, which Roddenberry's son Eugene attended; there would be a fundraiser screening at Mann's National Theatre in Westwood, that wouldn't be until the morning of Saturday, December 8. When the film opened on December 15 in London, the 8pm showing at the Empire Theatre Leicester Square—the only venue it would play before opening in the rest of the country on December 20—was a fundraiser for MAGNUM, which raised money for developmentally disabled children. Though they'd raised money through various events over the years, MAGNUM's secretary declared that "a Charity Premiere of the film Star Trek is probably our most exciting, and hopefully our most popular to date!"[15]

It was an additional score for the National Space Club that the December 6 Premiere would be held on their home turf of the United States' capital. Gene Roddenberry had decided *where* the premiere would be, though not *when* it would be, that being one of so many decisions which Paramount's Vice President of Motion Picture Production Jeffrey Katzenberg and President and Chief Operating Officer Michael Eisner had taken out of his hands. Roddenberry assured the fans he would have preferred the premiere to be a much bigger event which more of them could have attended, but it wasn't lost on him that the involvement of the National Space Club and the Smithsonian gave Star Trek a halo of respectability it might not have had in more traditional movie cities like Los Angeles or New York. Rumors even swirled among fans that Washington, D.C. Mayor Marion Barry had declared December 6, 1979, to be "Star Trek Day," which was far from the most outlandish rumor about the film over the past decade. Barry did show up at the afterparty at the Smithsonian, though he said he wasn't a Trekkie because he was a little too old. (His proclivity for, shall we say, more "adult" activities wouldn't become known for some years yet.)[16]

Still, had the premiere been at a more traditional venue such as Mann's Chinese Theatre in Hollywood or the V'ger-sized Radio City Music Hall in New York, Roddenberry could have invited more than just ten fans. Among those ten fans were Shirley Maiewski, Barbara Wenk, Jacqueline Lichtenberg, Alice Asherman, Nancy Kippax, Bjo Trimble, and Kay Johnson, who'd received their invitations from Roddenberry not long after the MGM lab had started cranking out the prints. Like everything else involved with the movie, you hurried up and waited, and then had to sprint.[17]

* * *

It may have been the official world premiere, and the only one attended by the cast and crew of the film, but the MacArthur event wasn't the only Paramount-affiliated *ST—TMP* shindig happening on December 6, 1979. In Phoenix, Arizona, the Mountain worked with radio station KRUX to hold a "Sensational Disco Trek" at the spacious Circles Records. More than 800 people showed up to a dance hosted by KRUX personality Bob Melton, where in addition to a "space light-show" there were hundreds of prizes given away, including shirts, belt buckles, and a trip for two to the see the model of the

Enterprise at the Smithsonian National Air and Space Museum—long after the party attended by the cast and crew was finished, of course.[18]

This was to promote a film they wouldn't be able to see until the next day, while Columbia Records' $8.98 soundtrack LP—the actual circle that would be sold at Circles—was originally scheduled to be released on December 10 but wouldn't hit stores until a week and a half later. Jerry Goldsmith had finished writing and recording the score in late November, and by the MacArthur Premiere the publishing company Charles Hansen Music and Books had made the sheet music and folio available to schools and music stores, along with promotional displays for the latter. Hansen also created marching band arrangements so the theme could be played at high-profile events such as the Rose Bowl, but that was all the way away on New Year's Day. In the shorter term, the score's copyright owner Famous Music was including the theme in their holiday promotional push: when calling MOR radio stations to encourage them to play "Silver Bells" in December, Famous suggested the stations play Goldsmith's Star Trek theme, and those which agreed to would receive promotional spots. As for stores like Circles, the regional branches of CBS Records—which released the soundtrack on Columbia Records, because that's just how vertical integration rolled in 1979—were supplying vendors with promotional aids such as mobiles, posters, album slicks, standees, and in some cases, trailers. Some branches were also arranging showings of the film, though none before Friday, December 7.[19]

*   *   *

Some of the fans invited to the MacArthur Premiere were 15-minute celebrities beyond the tribe. University of Massachusetts at Amherst bookstore clerk Shirley Maiewski was the chairperson of the Star Trek Welcommittee, which answered questions for newcomers and helped fans connect. Maiewski was affectionately known as "Grandma Trek," in spite her being only one year older than Gene Roddenberry, who was never called "Grandpa Trek." If anybody truly deserved to be called Grandma Trek, it was Roddenberry's 81 year-old mother, who flew in from Los Angeles on Wednesday with her son to the attend the premiere, because that's how mothers show their pride in their children's accomplishments. The Roddenberry matriarch had been part of a contingent of about thirty Angelenos which included her grandson and her daughter-in-law, as well as cast members DeForest Kelley and Nichelle Nichols, and Jeffrey Katzenberg, who was proudly wearing a yellow satin jacket with the name of the film on the back.[20]

For Shirley Maiewski's part, though she hadn't been an extra in the film like Bjo Trimble or David Gerrold, she was one of the few fans invited to visit the set. That she had been invited to the MacArthur Premiere made it onto the national airwaves via Paul Harvey's *News and Comment* earlier that week, a broadcast which gave DeForest Kelley many warm fuzzies. It was like a dream come true every step of the way for Maiewski, from being met at the airport by Roddenberry associate Richard Arnold and Maiewski's own Star Trek Welcommittee partner Kay Johnson, then riding with them on the Metro subway to the Mayflower—the hotel where Trimble and her other friends were staying, the kiddie table to the Four Seasons—and finally being interviewed by *CBS News* at the Smithsonian afterparty, having been recommended to the network by Arnold and Sackett as someone who would best represent the fans. Maiewski already knew *that* was going happen, as in the preceding weeks a CBS crew had ventured into deepest Massachusetts to shoot footage of her at home and at work. She had to pay her own expenses, because heaven forbid Paramount spring a few thousand more dollars for plane tickets and accommodations for fans after spending $44M on the film, but that wasn't going to be a dealbeaker. She was still invited to the Four Seasons pre-show reception as part of the greater Paramount entourage, though Maiewski, Arnold, and the others were warned beforehand that they were not to speak to the press about Robert Abel and Associates, the effects house whose sacking back in February was one of the reasons why work on the film had only been finished (well, abandoned) less than a week before its premiere.[21]

But Maiewski, Trimble, and the several other imported fans were the exception, and most had to settle for being outside. In nicer weather Paramount's prediction of 3,000 fans and onlookers might have come true, but the crowd was kept down to less than 400 by the drizzle, which Sonni Cooper of the William Shatner Fan Fellowship would later describe as "a cold east coast wetness which must be experienced to be appreciated." Cooper also suspected that being kept out in that wetness instead of being allowed into the theater for the premiere resulted in some of the bad reviews from the attending press. It certainly couldn't have helped, even if as the stars began arriving the drizzle was so brightly lit it looked like snow, adding a faux winter-wonderland touch to the already surreal evening. Among the only members of the press who were actually allowed into the screening were from the magazine *Starlog*, which had given the film three and a half years of free publicity since its first issue in 1976, and even then *Starlog*'s presence was by the grace of the MacArthur, not the Mountain. Which is not to say the press were prohibited from going inside and seeing the movie, so long as they coughed up the $100 for the ticket, as the *Chicago Tribune* did for Gene Siskel. When asked how local critics could review the film before it opened, Paramount's notoriously cranky Chicago publicist Sherman Wolf snapped that they could use their passes on opening day—a deliberate non-answer considering that going on opening day was by definition *not* before it opened, and most theaters in Chicago and elsewhere would not honor passes during the first few weeks of the film's run, if ever.[22]

Some fans outside the MacArthur were in Starfleet uniforms, though dedication couldn't be judged solely on what is now called cosplay. Among those in civilian attire was Teresa Gallagher, who had driven from Annapolis with her father and her camera. Though she had no club affiliation, Gallagher watched *Star Trek I* religiously, viewing even the episodes she didn't like until she knew them by heart. (By that metric she's a bigger fan than the writer of this book, who has watched "Plato's Stepchildren" maybe twice, if even that many times.) And just as not all the fans in the crowd were in costume, not everyone in the crowd was a fan; some of the onlookers were from the Our Lady of Victory School next to the theater, including an 11 year-old who managed to strategically block Gallagher's camera. Most of the students hadn't even known the premiere was happening until they saw all the commotion, which was also the case with the onlookers still carrying their grocery purchase from the Safeway across the street.[23]

Not at all happy about the arrangement was Jan Cox, president of the Virginia Association for Star Trek. Many people from both VAST and their sister organization Battleforce arrived in costume, and yet they were being kept behind the ropes like so many Gideons. Didn't Paramount know they would be there? Who was this event for if not the fans who kept the spark of the show alive after cancellation? And VAST wasn't the only local group attempting to strike while the iron was hot: the Washington Science Fiction Association looked into the possibility of booking a "theater party" at the MacArthur for a viewing, but were unable to secure a group discount.[24]

Members of the Star Trek Action Group in the UK were similarly unable to buy bulk theater tickets for the Robert Wise film's premiere showing on Saturday, December 15, so they did the next British thing and booked the 400-seat-capacity Cock Tavern on nearby Great Portland Street for a private function starting at 3 p.m., and extended the invitation to all Star Trek fans whether or not they'd attended the premiere 12:30 p.m. showing. There was no age restriction, just a 20p admission to cover the hire charges, and if enough people stuck around they could keep the room until 10:30 p.m. But the day-drinking wouldn't be limited to after the film; the group planned to meet outside the Empire Theatre at 11 a.m., then possibly go to a nearby pub or café, and return to the theater by noon.[25]

* * *

As the limos began arriving at the MacArthur in Washington on the evening of December 6, the press were on the north side of the red carpet and the fans were on the south. But one dues-paying member of both WSFA and VAST had made it closer than most fans: Nancy Handwork from Fairfax, Virginia. Clad in a blazing-white uniform she'd sewn herself—leaving her two children, also wearing her handmade uniforms, back behind the rope—Handwork managed to talk her way onto the red carpet, where she had direct access to the stars. She was armed with small white gift boxes and a business card, and wasted no time giving one of each to George Takei when he and Grace Lee Whitney emerged out of the first limo. Legendary for his fan-friendliness, Takei accepted it graciously, and both he and Whitney (who did not receive a Handwork gift) waved and offered Vulcan salutes to the fans assembled to the south, while also doing their due diligence for the professional photographers to the north. Next to arrive were Nichelle Nichols and Walter Koenig; Nichols seemed a bit apprehensive and pulled away a moment after Handwork embraced her and kissed her cheek, but Koenig was more receptive, even opening the lid to look in the box. (What Koenig saw has been lost to the sands of time.)[26]

The crowd reception was more subdued when Stephen Collins and Persis Khambatta arrived; as one fan said aloud, "That's just the new guy. I want to see Spock." It was a sentiment Collins could appreciate, since he had never been able to shake the feeling of being an outsider during production, and it didn't help that his character was underdeveloped at best. He did, however, do the Vulcan salute upon request from the crowd, and Khambatta made eye contact with a doppelganger: Darla Powell of the VAST-adjacent group Battleforce, who was dressed as Khambatta's character of Ilia complete with a bald cap. Khambatta smiled and pulled at her hair—her honest-to-goodness, real hair, which most people had never seen—and Powell called out, "You look good with hair!" Without missing a beat, Khambatta replied, "You look good bald!"[27]

Next to arrive at the MacArthur were DeForest Kelley and James Doohan. They accepted Nancy Handwork's gifts with the skill of people who'd interacted with awkward fans at many conventions over the years, both even giving her a peck on the cheek. The rest of the fans, to ensure that the people they'd come to see would look in their general direction, started sporadically yelling "Over here!"[28]

The crowd was unimpressed by the arrival of *hors d'oeuvres*-stuffed director Wise and his wife Millicent, to the extent that they did not ask the couple to look in their direction, and Handwork let them pass. But the fans owed more than they realized to Millicent, who had convinced her husband that a Star Trek movie couldn't happen without Leonard Nimoy as Spock, and thus she had more than earned her appearance in the film as a member of the *Enterprise* crew in the Rec Deck scene. The crowd was far more excited when Majel Barrett and Gene Roddenberry arrived, and Handwork promptly moved in on them, though Roddenberry got distracted by the many familiar faces behind the barrier, shaking many hands and kissing one of them.[29]

As Barrett and Roddenberry tried to make it inside, they were stopped every few feet by reporters asking the usual questions, such as how Roddenberry accounted for the popularity of Star Trek and whether he was feeling déjà vu. To the latter point, he let his weariness show through: "Yeah, it's wild, it's … it almost went on too long, y'know." Regaining his composure, he gestured to the fans and said, "But the marvelous point about it is that we're able to recognize these folks here, who ten years ago … some of them bring us kids now who are college students when they started—they say, 'Here are the new Trekkies.'" As though channeling Roddenberry's anxieties, the reporter followed up with, "Can this go on and on and on?" Evading the question expertly, Roddenberry replied, "What I hope goes on and on is the belief that we're all one people on planet, and it's time for us all to get together, and go on to the next step of the adventure, which is out there somewhere."[30]

After Barrett and Roddenberry, the biggest fish arrived. The first was Leonard Nimoy, who graciously accepted Handwork's gift, and was smilingly non-committal to reporters' questions about the film, beyond saying that he was proud that it wasn't just a cash-in on *Star Trek I*'s popularity. Shatner was corralled by the reporters before Handwork could speak, but she was standing *right next to him*. A reporter asked him a question he'd already been asked countless times over the years, and would for many more years to come: "Why do you think the series is so popular?"[31]

"I think these people … love the people in the show, I guess—I really don't know. I'm kind of in awe of the whole thing myself. In fact, I'm a fan!"[32]

Beaming, Handwork said, "Thank you," and Shatner turned and smiled at her. This was her moment! It was happening! Asked by a reporter if he'd seen the movie yet, Shatner replied, "No! Nobody has seen the movie except the brass at Paramount, so we're just as excited to see it as everybody else. Thank you very much!" As Shatner started to move away he glanced back in Handwork's direction, and she seized the moment. Like Mr. Bernstein trying to give a distracted Charles Foster Kane a trophy from the 467 employees of the *New York Inquirer* welcoming him home, Handwork handed Shatner the box and said, "This is from the Virginia Association of—"[33]

"I can't," Shatner said, taking the box and turning away from Handwork, whose moment ended. As Shatner worked his way through the phalanx of reporters, the calls of "Over here! Over here!" turned into a full-on chant. Though Nimoy and Kelley had been willing to sign autographs, Shatner stuck to the no-autograph rule he'd initiated during the conventions, explaining, "If I sign one autograph, I'll have to sign them all and they're waiting for us inside. Thanks for coming. I'm looking forward to the movie."[34]

Among the political figures there to see the movie were three of Ethel Kennedy's children—who were handing out "Kennedy in '80" buttons for free, unlike the $1 the MacArthur was charging for the "I'm a Trekkie" buttons—as well as Colorado Representative Patricia Schroeder and her daughter Jamie, Louisiana Representative Lindy Boggs with her grandson, and Carter White House aide Anne Wexler. A government figure with a direct connection to the film itself was its Technical Advisor, Jesco von Puttkamer from NASA. Von Puttkamer had been personally invited by his hero Wernher von Braun to work at NASA's Marshall Space Flight Center in 1962, and much like how von Braun had found fame through his association with Walt Disney, von Puttkamer was now doing the same with Gene Roddenberry. A fan of *Star Trek I* since he first saw it in NASA's nadir year of 1971, von Puttkamer was introduced to Roddenberry in 1975 by the Smithsonian's Assistant Director of Aeronautics, and he spoke at a Star Trek convention in Chicago later that year, after which Roddenberry started making the politically delicate arrangements necessary for von Puttkamer to moonlight for Paramount. By the time von Puttkamer appeared at a New York convention in late 1976, his involvement with what was then going to be Philip Kaufman's *ST—TMP* had become public knowledge.[35]

Scheduled to begin at 7 p.m. EST, *Star Trek—The Motion Picture*, a Gene Roddenberry Production—a Robert Wise Film started about fifty minutes late. Before it did, current Space Club president John Lent welcomed the attendees, and pointed out that he himself had not yet "seen the film we're about to enjoy." Shatner next took the stage, where he thanked optical effects specialists Douglas Trumbull and John Dykstra, "the geniuses who gave it the epic quality I've heard so much about," which resulted in nervous laughter from the Paramount representatives. Also present was composer Jerry Goldsmith, who in the long run would be far more responsible for the film's epic quality, but nobody knew that just yet. Shatner added, "I also wanted to thank Charlie Bluhdorn's daughter. If she hadn't said, 'Daddy, make me a picture,' we wouldn't have had a movie." Though there was no question that Dominique Bluhdorn was a fan, how the film came to be was far more complicated than just a daughter pestering her father, but Shatner was too much of a raconteur to let the truth get in the way of a good story.[36]

The lights finally went low, and the opening strains of Jerry Goldsmith's

"Ilia's Theme" began. When the lights came back up a little over two hours later, the film they had just watched would be opening as it was across the nation in less than twelve hours; the first showing in New York would be at 9am, and every hour and half-hour thereafter it would begin unreeling somewhere across the nation, all day long, and many theaters would be holding midnight showings on Friday and Saturday. This was it. This was what was would be out there on 850 screens, and the reaction to the premiere of the first Star Trek movie at the MacArthur Theater was not unlike the reaction to the premiere of Susan Alexander Kane's opera *Salammbo* at the Chicago Opera House in the first Orson Welles movie: great anticipation at the start, worn down to a weary smattering of applause at the end.

1969: The Network's Knife Cares Not for the Show's Cry

Star Trek Dies

The first Star Trek movie almost happened before the first Star Trek series. After NBC rejected the pilot "The Cage," producer Gene Roddenberry approached its star Jeffrey Hunter in 1965 about shooting more scenes to extend it to feature length. But Hunter refused, and the idea languished.[1]

Star Trek I's future on NBC had been wobbly since its premiere on September 8, 1966. On January 29, 1969, *Variety* announced it was going to be bounced around the schedule, its fate intertwined with *The Jerry Lewis Show*:

> Paramount TV's "Star Trek" series on NBC-TV will depart the web April 11, and return eight weeks later in a new slot, the 7:30 by the Jerry Lewis series.
>
> Program changes upcoming also involve the British-made series, "The Saint," which replaces "Trek" in its Friday night slot starting April 18.
>
> Lewis show winds its season run on the web April 15, and will be replaced by eight weeks of specials. "Trek" then returns to the air, going into that time period beginning June 10. Possible preemptions for other specials may alter the dates involved slightly.
>
> Decisions have not yet been made on renewals of "Trek" and Lewis for next season.[2]

When the decision was made, it was reported with little fanfare toward the end of a February 12, 1969, *Variety* article about changes in the three networks' schedules: "Definitely out are Jerry Lewis, 'Star Trek,' and midseason's 'My Friend Tony' (Andy Williams probably replaces), and iffy at this point are 'Outsider,' 'Jeannie,' 'Get Smart' and 'Adam-12.'" The final episode of *Get Smart* would be broadcast in May of 1970, and though it never developed as strong a following as *Star Trek I*, its feature film adaptation *The Nude Bomb* would arrive in theaters five months after the Robert Wise film.[3]

The March 12 *Variety* reported that an "important off-web package for fall will be Paramount Television's 'Star Trek'—sci-fi hour from NBC-TV. There are 79 episodes in the bundle." This must have been especially bittersweet for the subset of fans who read the trades, considering that the 78th of those 79 episodes, "All Our Yesterdays," wouldn't be broadcast until March 14. With one episode left to burn on NBC, Paramount ran an ad in the March 24 *Broadcasting* urging the reader to "Take Off with Star Trek!" Featuring an illustration of the *Enterprise* and stills of Shatner, Nimoy, and Kelley, the ad clumsily bullet-pointed the show's virtues[4]:

> STAR TREK now available for syndication.
> A space breakthrough in the audience response barrier.
> Acclaimed by over ten million science-fiction oriented fans.
> STAR TREK seventy-nine episodes of constant quality.
> Now being seen in over sixty-five countries around the world.
> STAR TREK starring William Shatner as Capt. James Kirk, Leonard Nimoy as Mr. Spock and DeForest Kelley as Dr. McCoy.
> PARAMOUNT TELEVISION…on the move![5]

The still of Nimoy was from the episode "Spock's Brain," nobody's idea of quality, but it *was* taking off. The series was on offer at the concurrent National Association of Broadcasters convention, and on March 26 WOR-TV purchased both *Star Trek I* and *The Dick Van Dyke Show*—the latter for more than $2,000,000, and in 1969 dollars!—as part of what appeared to be a "big shakeup in the fall schedule." Those two shows were also purchased in April by Kaiser Broadcasting for their newish UHF station WKBF, and *Variety* described the *Dyke* purchase in particular as "an indication of how much the Kaiser U's are willing to spend to build the band."[6]

The Trek purchase had been in the works for some time. According to Herbert F. Solow and Robert H. Justman's *Inside Star Trek: The Real Story*, at some point in 1967 after Gulf and Western's July purchase of Desilu, Kaiser's President Dick Block met with the head of Paramount Domestic Syndication to express interest in purchasing *Star Trek I*. It seems *Twilight Zone* fan Block had been talked out of purchasing *Zone* some years earlier, and he wasn't about to make the same mistake with *Trek I*. It was still on in 1967, so it was a handshake deal in which Block offered to buy the syndication rights before it was canceled. When the show was finally canceled and the paperwork was signed in April 1969 there would be 79 episodes, though had the show been canceled after the second season it still would have gone into syndication on Kaiser stations with just 55 episodes.[7]

The final first-run *Star Trek I* episode "Turnabout Intruder" wouldn't air until June 3, 1969—in the former *Jerry Lewis Show* slot, where it would remain for the summer reruns—and it wasn't worth the wait. Considering that the fanbase was known to be primarily female, and that women such as Bjo Trimble had helped keep the show alive with letter-writing campaigns, to end the series with an episode about how women are unfit to be starship captains was a dick move at best. And not only was the food terrible, the portions were small, according to the *New York Times*[8]:

> Switchboard operators at the National Broadcasting Company reported a flood of calls last night from television viewers complaining that the program "Star Trek" was interrupted for about 10 minutes for a report on the New Jersey primary election. One of the operators said the callers were particularly incensed that the report went on only 15 minutes after the polls closed at a time when the returns were very sketchy.[9]

The show continued to sell no matter how much luster it lacked toward the end. It was picked to replace *Doctor Who* on the BBC a few weeks after the NBC broadcast of "Intruder," and a few months before its syndication run began in the Colonies. The first episode broadcast on the BBC was "Where No Man Has Gone Before" on July 12, in black and white.[10]

On July 16, some six weeks after the broadcast of the final first-run episode of *Star Trek I* and four days before the Apollo 11 moon landing, Paramount ran an ad in *Variety* with a model of the *Enterprise* orbiting Earth and the hackneyed headline "Star Trek is Out of this World," a layout only slightly redeemed by a modern-looking lowercase Helvetica typeface. The ad boasted that the ARB Network Program Analysis of Spring 1968 (while the third season was in production) had revealed "that in the 61 domestic markets, Star Trek had a share of 30 or more. The average share of Star Trek for these markets was 39.5. Star Trek was seen by 11% of all women in these 61 markets; 13% of all women under 50; and 11% of all men." Part of the lore of *Star Trek I* is that if only NBC had been looking at the demographics of the viewership rather than the raw numbers, they wouldn't have canceled the show. But the Mountain knew who was watching, and they used those numbers to implore stations to pick it up for syndication.[11]

United States stations doing just that were often but not always the newer UHF channels owned by Kaiser or otherwise, including WATL in Atlanta (weekends), WKBD in Detroit (weekends), WGN in Chicago (Monday-Friday 6:30), KDNL in St. Louis ("primetime across the board"), WTTV in Indianapolis (Monday-Saturday 6:30 p.m.), WKBF in Cleveland (Monday-Friday 6:30 p.m.), metro in New York (Monday-Friday 6:30 p.m.), WKBS in Philadelphia (Monday-Friday 6:00 p.m.), KTVU in the San Francisco Bay Area (Monday-Friday 6:00 p.m.), WTTG in Washington, D.C. (Monday-Friday 4:00 p.m.), and WKBG in Boston (Monday-Friday 8:00 p.m.). KTVU was the first to schedule *Star Trek I* at 6pm opposite the evening news, and showed them uncut and in original NBC broadcast order, with an accompanying voiceover announcing the exact time and date of said NBC broadcast. By October 8, 1969, Paramount's Vice President of Global Syndication reported the show had been sold in 50 markets across the country.[12]

Star Trek I proved its value from the start. Stations owned by Kaiser Broadcasting kicked off their fall programming with a *Dark Shadows* imitation called *Strange Paradise* on September 8, but low ratings resulted in it being pulled from all Kaiser stations except Detroit after two weeks. In the September 24 *Variety*, Kaiser's "broadcast boss" said they were "fortunate" to have "'Star Trek' on the shelf, which eased the shift." The Kaiser UHF Group had officially moved *Strange Paradise* from the early evening to daytime or morning slots by October 8, and "rearranged schedules to replace it with the off-web 'Star Trek.'" The off-web series was doing well for WPIX in New York; the last half-hour of its 6:30 p.m. broadcast on Monday, October 6 pulled in a 7 rating, which wasn't quite as good as *The Dick Van Dyke Show*'s 8 rating on WOR or *I Love Lucy*'s 14 on WNEW, but certainly better than the 3 rating of the network news on WABC, and the combined ratings of WPIX, WNEW, and WOR "gave the three independents a greater share of the audience" than the networks. WNEW was one of the Kaiser stations which had been carrying *Strange Paradise*, and in the October 8 *Variety* Bill Greeley described WPIX's *Trek I* broadcasts as "grabbing all ratings honors," though now WNEW looked to be "in strong comeback" with *McHale's Navy, Lost in Space,* and *Lucy*. By October 22, *Trek I* on WPIX was tied in the ratings with WNBC's *Huntley-Brinkley Report*. Less than six months after the final NBC broadcast, a November 5 *Variety* article about a pair of packaging agents included *Trek I* among a list of "hit series of some quality," and mentioned Gene Roddenberry as a producer known for "classier product." Some stations were late to the game, such as WPGH in Pittsburgh not picking up the show until December 6 to be shown on the weekends.[13]

In anticipation of their official switch to color programming on November 15, 1969, both the BBC and ITV in Britain began test broadcasts in mid-October, and the first color broadcast of *Star Trek I* was "The Corbomite Maneuver" on October 16. The episode "Arena" was broadcast on the day of the official switch, along with other programs such as *Dixon of Dock Green, High Adventure,* and *Match of the Day*. By mid-December, London Weekend Television started showing *Bonanza* late on Saturday afternoons to directly compete with *Trek I* on the Beeb. Having run for more than ten seasons by that point, *Bonanza* was a successful television series by any possible definition, but now it was merely a weapon in a foreign ratings war against a show which barely lasted three seasons.[14]

The worst year in Star Trek's history should have been 1969, what with *Star Trek I* being canceled after a so-so season, and yet it ended on a triumphant note as it beat another off-web show which was incontrovertibly more successful during its network run. According to the December 31 *Vari-*

ety, WOR's 7 p.m. broadcasts of *The Dick Van Dyke Show* in New York were only receiving a 6 rating compared to *Trek I*'s 10 rating on WPIX. They were both getting soundly trounced by *Lucy*'s 12 rating on WNEW, but *Star Trek I* had initially been produced at Lucille Ball's studio Desilu, so that's only fair. It should be remembered that all this happened within six months of the broadcast of the final new episode on NBC. That *Star Trek I* was a major hit in syndication has always been baked into the mythology, but the fact that it happened so fast—and that the wheels had been turning since before the series was canceled—tends to be overlooked.[15]

1970–1972: What's in Reruns Is Prologue

Star Trek Has Risen from the Grave

The Independent Television Corporation ran a two-page ad in the January 14, 1970, *Variety* trumpeting the ratings of its show *The Saint*, which replaced *Star Trek I* on NBC on Fridays in April 1969. The ad included two charts of statistics from the Nielsens, one of "Ratings and Shares" and the other of "Audience Composition" of *The Saint* "Vs. Recent Off-Network Hour Series" for the four-week period of June 30 through July 27. *Trek I* was among the shows listed in the latter chart, with Total Homes at 5,190,000; Total Persons, 9,370,000; Men 18–49, 1,400,000; Women 18–49, 1,670,000; and Total 18–49, 3,070,000.[1]

It was a bit of a fudge since during the four-week period in question *Star Trek I* was still in repeats on NBC, yet the ad traded on its known success in syndication. Taking the numbers at face value, what's fascinating is the show was only broadcast twice during the reported period: "The Savage Curtain" on July 1, 1969, and "Spock's Brain" on July 8, and the next two scheduled broadcasts were pre-empted, one of which was for a special on the Apollo 11 moon landing.[2]

The February 18, 1970, *Daily Variety* reported that WCKT in Miami had started programming *Star Trek I* on Saturdays at 5 p.m., while Paramount ran a full-page ad in the same issue with the clunky, first-draft headline of "Star Trek ratings orbit on any heading"—better than "out of this world," to be sure, though both ads used the same photograph of a model *Enterprise* orbiting Earth. The ad extolled what a powerhouse the show was according to "ARB, November 1968, 1969," including the ratings being up 44% in Minneapolis-St. Paul, 30% over the lead-in in Providence, the share being up 31% in Las Vegas, and "Adult viewers up to 50%" in Greensboro-Winston-Salem. It is worth regarding with awe Paramount's chutzpah in declaring, "Remember that series which was canceled less than a year ago because fewer and fewer people were watching it and the network didn't want to spend any more money on it? Well, *you* should totally spend money on it now because more and more people are watching it!"[3]

It did have the advantage of being true: after their initial weekly run of *Trek I* ended in December 1969, the BBC resumed broadcasting it in April 1970, WGN in Chicago began showing it in August on weeknights at 6:30 p.m. alternating with *Lost in Space*, and in September WPIX in New York moved it closer to prime time at 7:30 p.m. According to the September 16 *Variety*, other major markets which picked up *Trek I* for the new season were WKBG in Boston (7:30 p.m.), WKBF in Cleveland (7:30 p.m.), WTCN in Minneapolis-St. Paul (5:30 p.m.), KTNT in Seattle (6:00 p.m.), WALT in Atlanta (10:00 p.m.), WKBS in Philadelphia (6:00 p.m.), and WKBD in Detroit. (According to *Inside Star Trek*, WKBS got the highest ratings of all the Kaiser stations.) More significantly, it was listed along with 52 other shows on a chart compiled by TelCom Associates of "the carryover syndication series from the past season, and even earlier ones, many of them in new firstrun cycles." TelCom took pains to establish that the list was of "the market-by-market programs that are in active circulation nationally at the moment, by TelCom's survey of station usage," and that the shows "obviously do not represent everything in the syndication vaults." In addition to "skipping feature film packages, TV specials, one-time-only programs, or program series that are still available for syndication ('My Little Margie,' for instance), but not really potent syndie items at this time." Even bigger shows like *Ben Casey* weren't listed because "it is not significantly in circulation as are the other which are carried here, and that the key word for was '*active*'" (their emphasis).[4]

Star Trek I certainly was active, and soon a similar slogan would rise: Star Trek Lives.

The Long Con Begins

Though Gene Roddenberry would always fight the perception of *Star Trek I* as a kids' show, the kids those days did enjoy it. On Sunday, January 31, 1971, NBC affiliate WMAQ in Chicago broadcast the documentary *If the Mind is Free*, in which Leonard Nimoy visited St. Mary's Center for Learning in Chicago, which was teaching a course about *Trek I*. (Intended as a fundraiser for the school, the film is not commercially available, but a print is stored in the Saint Mary's High School and Center for Learning records in the Special Collections at the University of Illinois at Chicago.) On February 10, *Variety* ran the results of a poll in which children were asked which shows they preferred; of syndicated programs, *Trek I* came in at number 12 between *McHale's Navy* and *The Dick Van Dyke Show* among children six to eleven years old, and at number six between *Dragnet* and *McHale's Navy* for teens twelve to seventeen years old.[5]

Meanwhile, television stations continued using *Trek I* as counterprogramming for (presumably) grownups. The February 17, 1971, *Variety* listed WKEH in Dayton among roughly two dozen primary ABC affiliates across the county who chose to show syndicated programs in the evening rather than the network news, though only WKEH was showing *Trek I* in particular. As part of a beef with United Kingdom, in April the Pakistan Television Corporation withdrew BBC and ITV shows and replaced many of them with programs from the United States; according to *Variety*, out of the 21 foreign-to-Pakistan programs scheduled for that quarter, 13 of them were "yank vidpix series" including *Trek I* and *Bewitched*. In-mid June, *Variety* reported that in Buffalo, New York, "High school and college students who clamored for return of 'Star Trek' to WGR-TV got their wish this week," as *Trek I* replaced *The Big Valley* at 5 p.m. on weekdays.[6]

According to the ARB Syndicated Program Analysis released around early August 1971, *Star Trek I* came in at no. 8 of the 268 shows in syndication at the time, with a total of 83 stations and 69.6% national coverage with some 5,610,000 viewers. The top show was *This Is Your Life*, with 142 stations and 89.4% national coverage, and more than 10,500,000 viewers. The year 1971 was a strange time, but it was also the year Star Trek proved it was here to stay—inasmuch as it was anywhere at all.[7]

* * *

The first Star Trek convention was held over the weekend of January 21–23, 1972 at the Statler-Hilton in New York. Organizers Al Schuster, Joan Winston, and Elyse Pines initially anticipated no more than 300–400 attendees for what was known as the Star Trek Lives! Convention, but by Wednesday, January 19 they'd received over 700 pre-registrations, and more than 2,000 people attended. A late addition to the proceedings, Gene Roddenberry spoke on Saturday afternoon and made a vague reference to the possibility of a new Star Trek movie, either theatrical or for television.[8]

Available that weekend was the February 16 edition of the bi-weekly horror newspaper *Monster Times*, an issue "dedicated to every aspect" of Star Trek and printed in advance to be sold at the convention[9]:

> You see, we figured that the STAR TREK CON was such a nifty idea, that we put out this special issue in honor of it. However, as our distribution schedules go, some of you readers will be reading this in your (few) spare moments at the hectic TREK-

CON, as this ish is made specially available to you there, whereas the rest of you have purchased your copy after the convention, at your local newsstand.[10]

Among the attractions listed at the con were "an exhibit of authentic STAR TREK props and costumes," as well as the costume of Klaatu from *The Day the Earth Stood Still*, "which is relative to STAR TREK in that Klaatu was portrayed very much like the Vulcan, Spock—a man of peace and logic. And was promptly killed by the U.S. Army." At the time, it was unfathomable that *The Day the Earth Stood Still* would become related to Trek in another, more direct way when its director Robert Wise would eventually helm *ST—TMP*.[11]

The *Monster Times* predicted that at the con, "Trekkie-eyed fans and fanatical-eyed Trekkies (girl STAR TREK groupies)" would "partake in zealous idolatries and ecstacies." What collective name the fans would adopt was in flux and would remain so for decades, through this reference to Trekkies as an overtly feminine term could speak to why it was later considered offensive to some, since many fandoms—even those which are predominantly female—often try to avoid any hints of distasteful femininity.[12]

Editor Chuck McNaughton also printed what he called "an unverified rumor" which arrived at press time about a revival, explaining that the *Monster Times* considered it "worth printing as news even though we have no way of proving it true":

> It seems that such a public clamor is still buzzing over STAR TREK, what with letter, STAR TREK-CONs, people contacting NBC and Paramount for stills, etc., that optimistic rumblings are being made among many People in Charge of Making Big Decisions, that putting STAR TREK back into production would be neither impossible nor unprofitable. If such a decision were made, and should the Enterprise be pulled out of moondust caked dry-dock and again be set adrift in the Galaxy, this would be the first time in the history of network television that it would have happened.[13]

Which was not strictly true, considering that in addition to having been a successful television-to-movie adaptation in 1954, *Dragnet* returned to television in 1967 and ran for four seasons. *Dragnet* had been more successful from the start and it was far less expensive to produce, but it still accomplished two feats Star Trek had great difficulty pulling off over the next decade, though the hype surrounding the Robert Wise film would often emphasize how unprecedented Trek's return allegedly was. McNaughton was one of the first to express reservations about the potential quality of a revival, wondering whether a new show could "keep the same high standards of writing, continuity and special effects as the first season," warning that *Monster Times* would "support a resurrection of STAR TREK if the producers and the networks would try to regain the show's early high standards. Otherwise, forget it." He brushed off the problem of the cast having difficulty finding other work due to their strong identification with Star Trek: "In another year, all the old STAR TREK crew should have gotten over the typecasting problem, anyway be recognized as competent actors and actresses, and find work elsewhere." Because it's as simple as that.[14]

Though tied in with the convention, it's still not insignificant that the second issue of the publication which called itself "The World's First Newspaper of Horror, Sci-Fi and Fantasy" was devoted to Star Trek, though McNaughton promised in the editorial that in the next issue they'd return to their "regular newspaper programming, with Giant Bugs on the Munch." And thus the Monster Kid era began to give way to the Star Kid era, often kicking and screaming.[15]

When the *Monster Times* returned its primary focus to hungry bugs of unusual size in May, the Star Trek Association for Revival (S.T.A.R.)—"an association dedicated solely for Star Trek's revival"—released the first issue of its newsletter *Star-Borne*. In addition to referring to the fans as "STrekfandom," they also suggested that "now is the time to revive the 'Save Star Trek Writing Campaign,'" citing the renewal of *Star Trek I*'s third season as being largely due to "the written response NBC received." Meanwhile, the series was doing great on the BBC, where its repeats on Wednesday nights during prime time were garnering ratings similar to its original Beeb broadcasts.[16]

In order to get the show revived on NBC, *Star Trek I* writer and producer Dorothy Fontana encouraged further letter-writing in a letter of her own dated June 22, 1972, and printed in the June/July *Star-Borne*:

> Paramount has not committed itself to any answer on renewal of the show. But they continue to reveal interest in "off the record" meetings. Our friends at the studio tell us they are enormously impressed with the quantity (and quality) of fan mail they continue to receive. The possibility seems to be slowly developing of a STAR TREK feature movie for theatrical release, aimed at becoming the NEW STAR TREK television pilot. We know for certain their researchers are attempting to estimate the number of fans who could be counted on to buy an admission ticket to such a movie.[17]

Fontana also wrote that "NBC still expresses great interest in doing STAR TREK in some form," and both the network and Paramount "continue to receive a great deal of mail and have had to assign secretaries to the sole job of answering it." The return of Star Trek may well have happened then, but Roddenberry put the kibosh on it because NBC requested a new pilot. As he told the July 5, 1972, *Variety*, "I felt, as did Paramount, that we already had 78 in the can." Those 78 were still going strong across the country; WKBS in Philadelphia, which began running it at 6 p.m. weekday nights in 1969, started showing them again in original broadcast order in September, while WENY in Elmira, New York started broadcasting it at 7 p.m. on Sunday nights.[18]

Fontana next wrote in the September/October *Star-Borne* in reference to a *TV Guide* article that "the possibility of a STAR TREK movie for television has been raised. There is also the possibility for a STAR TREK movie for release in motion pictures houses. No decisions have been made on either of these proposals, and we are still awaiting word." She asked the fans to continue expressing their "enthusiasm to NBC and Paramount Studios for STAR TREK's return in some form," and that their "loyalty may be the deciding factor in the final decision." Well, *among* the deciding factors, given Roddenberry's refusal to shoot a new pilot episode.[19]

The November/December 1972 *Star-Borne* included a lengthy report from the Detroit Triple Fan Fair held at the Hilton on Thursday, October 19 through Sunday, October 22. A comics-oriented convention which had been held sporadically since 1965, the 1972 Fair was a joint effort with Al Schuster, chair of the Star Trek Lives! Convention, with Gene Roddenberry and Majel Barrett as major guests.[20]

On Thursday night following a Marx Brothers Festival (*Duck Soup, Horse Feathers, A Day at the Races*, and *At the Circus*), Fontana presented the inaugural showing of the "infamous" Star Trek Blooper Reel. Roddenberry was interviewed by WWJ-TV on Friday morning, discussing "STAR TREK conventions and the very good chance that STAR TREK has to return as a movie for theatrical release." David Gerrold spoke on Saturday afternoon about his upcoming books *The World of Star Trek* and *The Trouble with Tribbles*—the latter of which would include a footnoted argument as to why the Blooper Reel was legally problematic—and was followed by a speech from Roddenberry, which according to *Star-Borne* "mainly concerned the renewal of STAR TREK, and the problems involved. He discussed the fact that STAR TREK might return as a major motion picture possibly similar to the PLANET OF THE APES movie series, the probabilities of the original cast, and the kind of changes that might occur if STAR TREK returns."[21]

In that same issue, the editors reported that Roddenberry verified at the convention that there was now "only one major obstacle" preventing the return of Star Trek: "PARAMOUNT STUDIOS is still obstinate, but weakening. Because of this, more pressure must be brought to bear on the studio now. We must accelerate the letter writing campaign now." Like Bing Crosby singing about war bonds, fans who'd already done their part were chided for their complacency: "If you have already written, write again. One letter a week is not that impossible a task. Get your friends to write PARAMOUNT— even your enemies. Let's bury PARAMOUNT in a still greater avalanche of letters."[22]

As it happened, burial in an avalanche was a key plot point in Roddenberry's new project, *Genesis II*. The December 19 *Los Angeles Times* reported that Alex Cord had signed to portray a NASA scientist "who becomes the first human guinea pig in his own project experimenting with suspended animation," only to become trapped in an accident and regaining consciousness "when an anthropological party burrows through an avalanche of rock and discovers him in AD 2133." The brief article ended by noting that *Genesis II* was "Roddenberry's first TV project since his Star Trek series." Perhaps unsurprisingly, during production it was known around the Warner Bros. lot as "Son of Star Trek."[23]

1973–1974: Choose Your Televised Pain

Genesis II v. *Planet of the Apes*

Part of the reason *Genesis II* was to be Roddenberry's first television project since 1969—even beyond the financial and critical failure of the 1971 Roger Vadim film he wrote and produced, *Pretty Maids All in a Row*—was that Roddenberry claimed it was too painful to be near a television after *Star Trek I* was canceled. As the story goes, it wasn't until he and Barrett were playing golf in the Bahamas during the summer of '72 that he realized he missed working, and over the next six weeks he wrote the script for the 90-minute *Genesis II* pilot as well as outlines for 17 episodes. Roddenberry also insisted to the *Los Angeles Times* that there was "not a chance" of Star Trek ever returning to television, again raising the possibility of a *Planet of the Apes*-style movie series. Besides, he was still "darkly angry" about the way Star Trek had been treated by NBC, up to and including their impertinence in asking for a new pilot. (It's almost as if "The Omega Glory" or "All Our Yesterdays" didn't guarantee an automatic green light.)[1]

The February 19, 1973, *Monster Times* picked up on the *Genesis II* story, and as was the freewheeling layout style of such papers, immediately above it was a single sentence: "Is it true that 20th Century just sold PLANET OF THE APES to television?" The placement of that line would prove prophetic, as Roddenberry would later blame the *Planet of the Apes* television series for *Genesis II* not getting picked up: "CBS had it penciled into their schedule. Fred Silverman had seen *Planet of the Apes* and he thought the monkeys were so cute that he cancelled doing *Genesis II* and decided to go for the monkeys." During a Stanford lecture, he claimed that he was asked to add apes "or baboons or orangutans or something" to *Genesis II*, and that "a junior executive came up with one of those great front office suggestions" in the form of a talking dog.[2]

The pilot of *Genesis II* was broadcast on March 23, 1973, and the newspaper advertisements mentioned that it was "by the creator of 'Star Trek'" without including said creator's name. Cecil Smith's fair-to-"meh" review lamented that *Genesis II* wasn't up to *Star Trek I*'s standards, while being one of the rare times the burgeoning fanbase was described in a positive light: "The basic idea really interests me more than Roddenberry's Star Trek. And Star Trek had so profound an effect on much of the country—much of the best of the country, I may add—that another series from his fertile imagination would seem to me an immense asset to the sterile world of television." Before describing what the show was even about, Smith noted in the third paragraph that the character played by Mariette Hartley had two belly buttons, and that "after seeing them, I don't think you will ever feel the same about a one-navel girl." That he prioritized the female character who is different in a subtle way—either by having more or less than the usual amount of a common body characteristic—presaged much of the coverage of the Robert Wise film, which treated Ilia's baldness as the most remarkable, gotta-see-it-to-believe-it thing ever.[3]

It's difficult to say how the history of Star Trek would have played out had *Genesis II* been picked up as a series. Roddenberry might not have been compelled to continue struggling to resurrect Star Trek had any of his non-Trek projects been a hit, through one of the 17 unused episode outlines he wrote for *Genesis II* would eventually evolve into the Robert Wise film. According to Susan Sackett in *The Making of Star Trek—The Motion Picture*, "Robot's Return" involved a "twenty-mile-in-diameter space vessel" which arrives at "22nd-century Earth" from a moon of Neptune in order to "learn more about the holy home of the Creator, NASA." Had it been filmed for *Genesis II* Roddenberry may not have later resurrected the story for *Star Trek II*—but then again, he never had a problem recycling stories and character ideas even within the same universe, let alone between them.[4]

The Animated Series Is Pre-Rejected by the Fans

The issue of the *Monster Times* with the *Genesis II* tidbit hit the stands on the final day of Al Schuster's 1973 Star Trek Lives! Convention in New York. As reported in the March/April 1973 *Star-Borne*, Dorothy Fontana gave a speech that day in which she attempted to drop a truth bomb.[5]

> I'd like to talk about STAR TREK, past, present and future, and I don't know whether you're going to like what I have to say. I hope that you will see it the same way I do. STAR TREK past is past. It's nice that we can keep it alive like this. You have a beautiful memory of it and can see it in reruns. But it is past.[6]

She then spoke about its present and possible future:

Herb Solow, the gentleman with Oscar Katz who was instrumental in bringing STAR TREK on the air, had a contract at WARNER BROS. and is trying to work it so that he could do an independent picture of STAR TREK hoping that perhaps is salesmanship abilities would be able to sell it as a movie. That failed.[7]

Star-Borne did not report whether that subtle burn on Solow's salesmanship abilities got a laugh, though Solow told a different story in *Inside Star Trek*: Roddenberry called him in 1973 and said Paramount was only interested in making a film if Roddenberry wasn't the producer, since he had bad buzz after his inability to rein in director Roger Vadim on *Pretty Maids All in a Row*. Roddenberry's proposed story was a premise from a rough draft of the 1964 *Star Trek I* writer's guide titled "The Cattlemen," about a carnivorous species whose unusually symbiotic relationship with its cattle is telegraphed in the title. Though Solow felt the story would need to be rewritten because it was gross and unpleasant, he nonetheless pursued it with Paramount until Roddenberry demanded more money for the script than the studio was willing to pay, and the project fell apart. It was almost as if, deep down, Roddenberry didn't want to do Star Trek anymore. (Almost.)[8]

Back to Fontana's speech:

> We have asked you to write and you have. PARAMOUNT has been inundated. NBC changed its mind and asked PARAMOUNT "Please could we do the show?" PARAMOUNT said "No."[9]

After making it clear Paramount would not be swayed no matter who was involved—whether it was original series producer Gene L. Coon, writers David Gerrold and Margaret Armen, or Fontana and Roddenberry themselves—she revealed that Paramount had been swayed[10]:

> Just Wednesday (February 14) Gene called me here and said that the deal has been completed to bring STAR TREK back as an animation ... as a cartoon. The only reason Gene would allow that to be done is that he has full creative control. Which means, he will run it.
>
> He has personally chosen the animation house. It is a good one. It is FILMATION. The show will probably go on the air sometime in the fall (Saturday mornings, NBC). However, Gene intends that its intelligence, its science, its stories, will be as good as STAR TREK was originally.[11]

Gene Roddenberry wrote in a letter to Leonard Nimoy on March 27, 1973, that he and Filmation felt "that both kids and adults would respond strongly if it is presented as STAR TREK and not as a moronic kiddies version," though his longer game was "to get Paramount to do a feature release motion picture with the original cast."[12]

> If we were to do this, find the right theatrical level story, produce it properly, I see no reason why it could not do as well as PLANET OF THE APES and spin off a whole

series of releases. Can you imagine boarding the old Enterprise again with adequate budget, feature story latitude, top director and all that? I cannot imagine many things more enjoyable and satisfying.[13]

Less enjoyable and satisfying to Roddenberry was dealing with the fans, which he considered a necessary annoyance:

> Perhaps this helps explain to you why I have continued giving attention to fan mail, conventions, clubs, and all that despite the fact that they can be more tiresome and time consuming than they sometimes warrant.[14]

That *Star Trek: Animated* would become a thing was confirmed in the next day's *Variety*, which observed that the network's focus was cartoons based on live-action shows, hence the other two big premieres being *The Addams Family* and *Emergency Plus Four*. Though Fontana had insisted Roddenberry would have "full creative control," he was listed as the "Creative Consultant," while William Shatner was the only confirmed cast member. By April 18, Leonard Nimoy, DeForest Kelley, Majel Barrett, and James Doohan had officially joined the cast, with Fontana, David Gerrold, Samuel Peeples, Stephen Kandel, and Margaret Armen writing scripts, and Roddenberry now listed as the "Executive Story Consultant." (As it happened, "Executive Consultant" would be his credit on the four *Star Trek* films produced between 1982 and 1989 before his 1991 death.)[15]

Filmation's Lou Scheimer told the May 1973 *Monster Times* that Gene Coon had been signed, though this would be complicated when Coon passed away in July. The item also dropped a bombshell which went against the core of fandom entitlement, past and future, and which would continue to be part of the myth up through the eventual release of the Robert Wise film six years later[16]:

> The revival of STAR TREK as a television series is seemingly NOT in response to the tremendous STAR TREK movement across the country. It is, rather, just one of many live-action programs now being converted to animation. Among others which are being slated for fall syndication are animated versions of MCHALE'S NAVY, I DREAM OF JEANNIE, THE ADDAMS FAMILY and EMERGENCY![17]

Sadly for Ernest Borgnine fans young and old, *McHale's Navy: Animated* did not come to pass. But six weeks after the cast announcement had been made for *Star Trek: Animated*, Nichelle Nichols and George Takei were officially hired, thanks to Leonard Nimoy doing the right thing. As he revealed in 1977[18]:

> I was told that they wanted me to do the voice of Spock, and that all the other actors were signed to play their roles; to do their voices. And when I arrived for the first recording session, I discovered that somebody had found a way to save a few bucks and the way to save it was to use the face of Nichelle Nichols as Lt. Uhura, and to use

the face of George Takei as Sulu, and not use them to come in to do their voices. To get somebody else to save some money so they wouldn't give George and Nichelle the job. I refused to do any more until they were hired, and they were hired.[19]

By early July 1973 *Trek I* costume designer William Ware Theiss was announced as "special consultant," though his name wasn't listed in the final *Animated* credits, and it was presumably an acknowledgment of the use of his *Trek I* costume designs.[20]

Meanwhile, that month's *Monster Times* included a reprint of a coupon which had been recently run in the *New York Post*:

> **STAR TREK FANS**
> If you enjoyed The Star Trek
> Series, and would like to see it
> back on Television, you can
> bring it back by signing this Coupon.
> THE UNDERSIGNED URGENTLY REQUESTS...
> 1.) The Production of a New Star Trek Series
> 2.) Resumption of Star Trek Re-runs in Local Stations.[21]

The urgent undersigner was encouraged to mail it to the "T.V. Viewer's Committee," the provided mailing address for which was (as of September 2017) a lovely two-story home in suburban New Jersey.[22]

The Animated Series Is Barely Accepted by the Fans

There were two significant premieres during the first week and a half of September 1973. The second, both chronologically and in terms of importance, was the debut of *Star Trek I* on KMPH Channel 26 in Fresno, California at 5 p.m. on Monday, September 10. The future author of this book was just shy of three months old, and *Trek I* would run from Monday-Friday at 5 p.m. until some point after which your author was able to start forming memories, by which time it was dropped back to 9 a.m. on Saturday morning. She still remembers waiting excitedly for it to start on many of those wasted mornings, only to be statistically disappointed at least one-third of the time because she'd waited all week for something she'd immediately turn off like "The Paradise Syndrome" or "Mudd's Women."[23]

The other premiere was a show intended to be on Saturdays: *Star Trek: Animated* on NBC on September 8. (Whether or not *Animated* was what inspired KMPH's program director to eventually move young Sherilyn's favorite live-action show to the Saturday morning gulag will probably never be known, but she still takes it a little personally.) As had been suggested in the May 1973 *Monster Times*, *Star Trek: Animated* was just one of many animated adaptations of live-action properties which premiered within a remarkably overstuffed two hours: *The Amazing Chan and the Chan Clan* on CBS and *The Addams Family* on NBC at 9:00 a.m.; *Emergency Plus Four* on NBC at 9:30 a.m.; *My Favorite Martians* on CBS, *Butch Cassidy* on NBC—unrelated to the George Roy Hill film—and *Lassie's Rescue Rangers* on ABC at 10:00 a.m.; and finally, *Jeannie* on CBS and *Star Trek: Animated* on NBC at 10:30 a.m.. Another notable debut that morning was the redoubtable *Super Friends*, which would run until the 1980s, while the male lead on *Jeannie* was a young Mark Hamill, who sang that show's theme song in character. William Shatner reprised his famous "Space, the final frontier" intro voiceover for the opening of *Star Trek: Animated*, so for a brief period in the fall of 1973, the voices of both Luke Skywalker and Captain Kirk were being broadcast simultaneously on two different channels every Saturday morning. (All things on the mycelial network are connected.)[24]

In the September *Monster Times*, Mark Evanier ruminated that while the cartoon could surpass the live-action series in some ways, such as "no patently-fake studio-created alien landscapes," it was unlikely that "any animated product could ever satisfy the most zealous 'Trekkies.'" Evanier was reasonably skeptical about how some of those zealots "would like to (and are trying to) take credit for the 'revival' of 'Star Trek'…but it would seem that all of the petitions, letter-writing and holy crusades had little or no bearing on the decision to do the animated series. Saturday morning TV always goes in cycles and, this year, the trend is to resuscitate shows that have done extremely well in syndicated reruns."[25]

The other side of the "Yay, it's because of us!" coin was the "Boo, it's not exactly what we wanted!" backlash, which was already underway:

> At the recent Star Trek-Equicon in Los Angeles speculation ran the full spectrum from delighted anticipation to utter dread. A few Trekkies are so utterly horrified by the prospect of the animated series that they are already readying petitions to protest its very existence. Like many of the crusades mounted at the time of STAR TREK's cancellation, these crusades reek of paranoia and of a total ignorance of the economic and practical aspects of network programming. (I can recall being asked to affix my John Hancock to a scroll demanding, in no polite terms, that STAR TREK be immediately revived as a two-hour-a-week series. That would be enough to put Gene Roddenberry in his grave and start him spinning!)[26]

(The early 1970s Star Trek fandom may not have been the first to engage in such gnashing of teeth and/or reckless petitioning—fans of Margaret Mitchell's novel *Gone with the Wind* got there first during pre-production on the Selznick picture—but for certain it was not the last. For more on the subject, see my previous book *Ponyville Confidential*.) For their part, *Star-Borne* praised *Star Trek: Animated* in an editorial in the September/October issue following the broadcast of the third episode on September 22, 1973. Margaret A. Basta wrote that "there is much to praise about this new ST," in spite of the 22-minute time limit "there are moments in every episode that I've seen so far where the personalities of the characters come across," and most importantly, "this show is still STAR TREK" and "we are glad to have it."[27]

But they weren't resting on their laurels.

> Obviously though, STAR CENTRAL doesn't intend to just stop with the animation. A STAR TREK with live actors which will probably be a movie, is still the goal that we are aiming to achieve. However, we do not think that there is any cause for certain people to condemn the animation because the only thing that they will settle for is Leonard Nimoy in the flesh. It is more than likely that if a ST movie is made, not all of the original actors and actresses will be in it. It seems impossible to ever expect ST to return the way it once was. Those days are dead though not gone. But the ST of the future could become even better, if all goes well.[28]

Sadly, all did not go well for *Star Trek: Animated*. It exhausted its run of 22 original episodes in October 1974, and in March 1975 NBC announced that the show would not be returning for the 1975–76 season, a decision they stuck to even when the episode "How Sharper than a Serpent's Tooth" won *Animated* the Daytime Emmy for Best Children's Series in May. Roddenberry's feelings about the series were always mixed, and the Emmy going to Filmation's Lou Scheimer and Norm Prescott couldn't have helped.[29]

What was unknown then was that in aesthetic terms, *Star Trek: Animated* would be as close to *Star Trek I* as any revival would ever get. It further speaks to how quickly *Animated* would be forgotten that during the mad rush among fans after the release of the Robert Wise film to name *Trek I* episodes that the movie reminded them of—usually "The Changeling" and "The Doomsday Machine," with less frequent references to "The Immunity Syndrome"—nobody brought up the *Animated* episode which was broadcast right before Basta wrote her editorial, "One of Our Planets is Missing." Written by frequent *Trek I* series director Marc Daniels, it involved a large cloud of incredible destructive power heading toward a populated planet. The *Enterprise* enters the cloud, which they soon discover is a living entity, and communication with said entity is established via Spock performing a mind meld. (Kirk also sets the *Enterprise* to self-destruct, a subplot that was filmed and then edited out of the theatrical release of the Robert Wise film.) This episode is in many ways closer to what the Robert Wise film would eventually be than the oft-cited *Trek I* episodes, but in spite of having been broadcast just six years before the release of the film and *Animated* still being in syndication in December 1979, I couldn't find any examples in my research of fans pointing out the similarities, perhaps because to do so would have been to acknowledge the show's existence.

Roddenberry on Tour

As *Star Trek: Animated* continued to be underappreciated (give or take its eventual Emmy), *Star Trek I* continued to do well, being carried by 106 stations in the United States by the end of 1973, and up to 111 by April 1974. The possibility of a movie was also back on deck: according to the May 1974 issue of the Star Trek Welcommittee's newsletter *A Piece of the Action*, Roddenberry announced at Equicon '74 in April that he was negotiating a "a revival of live-action Star Trek," though no contracts had been signed "since several details are yet to be resolved." Among those unresolved details were "whether the film would be shown in theatres or TV; after the original movie, there would be a possibility of a TV mini-series." He also stated that "every effort would be made to get the original cast."[30]

During a Q&A at the University of New Hampshire on April 25 which was transcribed in the June 1974 *Star-Borne*, Roddenberry said that Paramount "would like to consider bringing STAR TREK back on the air," and that he was into it conditionally:

> I told them I was willing to discuss it as long as we are not discussing a cheapie rip-off of STAR TREK, so they can cash-in and make some fast money on the fan enthusiasm. The way I would discuss doing it would be if we made it as a feature-length, feature release motion picture with adequate budgets to rebuild the Enterprise, the bridge, and all of the things and do them right. I think have convinced them that there are enough fans that would go to a feature. With all that done, and if it's done well, and I'm satisfied that we aren't going to make a rip-off, then yes, I would be very happy to go into a weekly production. So cross your fingers. It would be fun if we would do it. I'd say if we make the feature it's two years away...[31]

Roddenberry's feelings about going into a weekly production would vacillate in the years to come, but as for whether the full cast would be involved in a movie or television series, he was cautiously optimistic while getting in an odd swipe at Leonard Nimoy: "I think for the movie the original cast would be easy, for a television show a lot would depend on what they were doing at the time—what their commitments were ahead—what they would work for. Leonard Nimoy, when he started the show was really an unknown as a co-star, and he spends on clothes today what we paid him for the first few episodes." After the laughter subsided, he continued: "I'd love to do it with the original cast if at all possible, but we had better hurry as the years have a way of sliding by." The way the years slid by would end up being largely ignored in the Robert Wise film.[32]

Walter Koenig spoke at a Star Trek convention being held in connection with the Houstoncon comic book convention on June 23, and according to the July 1974 *A Piece of the Action*, he "mentioned that ST revival is possible and that Roddenberry is currently negotiating with Paramount," though "even if decisive steps are taken now, it would not be possible for the show to come on until the Fall of 1976." The September *A Piece of the Action* included a letter from Dorothy Fontana to the zine's publisher Helen Young, dated August 15, 1974[33]:

> Official news on a ST movie you can print: from GR to me as of 8-7-74. Paramount is now negotiating definitely on a movie. They are discussing at least a million and a half dollar budget. Gene is insisting they use the original actors in their previous roles unless, of course, the actor is contractually unavailable or does not want to return (that's up to the actor, naturally). There would be name guest stars. Gene would do the script and probably insist on producing. At this moment, NOTHING IS SIGNED OR DEFINITE—but the first steps are finally being taken. Thanks to the letters of fans, I might add.[34]

The zine further elaborated that at the recent Discon II in Washington, D.C., Fontana indicated that "if the project were to be instituted as Mr. Roddenberry wishes, it would be a 90-minute theatrical film," and "no consideration is currently being given to producing a tailored-for-television film."[35]

* * *

At the New York Waldorf on September 10, 1974, Paramount unveiled their new Magicam system, in which the images from two cameras—one focused on performers in the foreground, and the other on a miniature set in the background—were combined into a single image. Paramount's President Frank Yablans said Magicam could reduce set costs from $300,000 to the neighborhood of $12,000 to $15,000, using their recent (and unsold) pilot for a *War of the Worlds* television series as an example. Though Paramount predicted it would eventually be used in features, in the short term it was seen as more viable for television. Among the consultants on the Magicam process was Douglas Trumbull, who worked on the effects for *2001: A Space Odyssey* and directed 1972's *Silent Running*.[36]

Not present at the Magicam unveiling was Gene Roddenberry. Speaking in the far less posh environs of a non-air-conditioned gymnasium at the Miami-Dade Community College North Campus on September 24, he assured the audience negotiations were progressing on the Star Trek movie. And possibly not just a movie, as the "Trek Talk" section of the October 1974 *Monster Times* reported that a fanzine had ran an item stating that "STAR TREK is slated to return as a feature-length live-action TV series."[37]

> At present, the deal is still in the negotiations stage, with Paramount saying that it will return ST to TV if a network will take a 13-week gamble on the project. In addition to this startling news, plans for a feature-length STAR TREK film are also being made and stand an even stronger chance to reach fruition than the proposed series. The original STAR TREK cast has already been contacted for possible reinstatement in the crew of the Enterprise, and chances are good that all will be available for the movie and all, with the possible exception of Bill Shatner, would be willing to return to the series as well.[38]

That same month, *A Piece of the Action* ran excerpts from a letter from Susan Sackett, quoting Gene Roddenberry, to the Star Trek Welcommittee's Shirley Maiewski:

> The status of the STAR TREK theatrical film has gone from fair to good.... Negotiations are currently underway between our attorneys ... my major consideration is that we do it right with a film budget adequate for the proper rebuilding of sets, props, costumes, and so on ... the acquiring of all these things out of a film budget makes more likely a possibility of STAR TREK's return to Television ... the next hurdle will be the story outline or possibly the full screenplay, at which time Paramount would then estimate the cost of making the film and determine whether or not anticipated revenues merit the risk of that amount of money.... If all went well, then Paramount would consider several possibilities, First, I think, would probably be the pros and cons of making a series of STAR TREK motion pictures as was done with Planet of the Apes. I think Paramount Television would also, at that time, be considering whether STAR TREK should return to television in is original hourly form or whether it might best return as several ninety or one hundred twenty minute television Movies of the Week each year. Of course, all of this is speculation at this time...[39]

Roddenberry continued to make the college rounds. After speaking at Sangamon State University (now University of Illinois at Springfield) in November 1974, he was interviewed by the underground newspaper *SunRise*, and the interview was later reprinted in the June 1976 issue of the zine *Star Trek Today*. Exactly when the interview took place is uncertain, but it was likely around November 6, when *Variety* reported that "the addition of 10 stations to the lineup for syndie use of Paramount TV's 'Star Trek' boosted total user stations to 130," with the latest stations being WATU in Augusta, KBAK in Bakersfield, WJZ in Baltimore, WDAY in Fargo, WHAG in Hagerstown, WHBQ in Memphis, WJAR in Providence, WTVR in Richmond, WJCL in Savannah, and WKBN in Youngstown. Elsewhere in the world, *Star Trek I* had become the longest-running series on Turkish National Television, and it was one of the few shows from the United States to be broadcast in Argentina, though it was beat out in the ratings by *Kung Fu*.[40]

In November 1974, it was believed a new Star Trek would take the form of a series of made-for-television movies. Asked by *SunRise* how it would be different than before, Roddenberry acknowledged that "Star Trek has become something of a legend, and legends have a way of looming larger in people's minds than reality." If they made the show the same it had been before, Roddenberry mused, "the fans would be very disappointed. That's one of the reasons we decided we didn't want to make another series of hour shows; we weren't sure that we could do it that much better. However, by going to movies (for TV) we've got longer scripts, we can probe more deeply into the characters. We have longer to prepare them we can afford better directors." Asked if time will have moved on for the crew and if there would be new technology, Roddenberry skipped the question about the crew and focused on the technology, which would later be one of the most common criticisms leveled at the Robert Wise film. "I doubt if we can improve on matter-anti-matter propulsion power, the transporter and that sort of thing," the great futurist speculated, adding that they were going to work with NASA and JPL to try to "jump ahead" with the instrumentation. Asked if Spock would continue on as a character if Nimoy refused to reprise his role, Roddenberry replied, "I'd rather not. I think it'd hurt us if we had to. If we did, I think we'd go with the actor who played Sarek, Spock's father." (When Nimoy declined to reprise his role in the aborted *Star Trek II* television series, a new Vulcan character was created, but it's fascinating to imagine Sarek actor Mark Lenard playing Spock.) Roddenberry's prescience always had the accuracy of a stopped clock, but when asked if he could imagine any resolution or end-point for Star Trek, he was on the money: "I never conceived of that. If it goes as it's going and becomes a sort of pop classic, like Sherlock Holmes or Tarzan, I think it could be revived over and over, with new characters."[43]

But that was at some unspecified point in an uncertain future. In the here and now, the fans wanted any Star Trek revival (like the animated one they were largely ignoring) to have the original cast. But untraceable rumors were beginning to spread that the characters *would* be recast, so in 1974 a fan named Carole Brownell founded an organization called Save the Star Trek Cast. In addition to referring to the fans collectively as "Star Trekkers," Brownell promised that "S.T.S.T.C. will not print rumors, no matter how strong and any information we do put out will be able to be checked." The source for this checking was Gene Roddenberry himself, who at the time was considered to be the true definition of reliable, and he encouraged the fans to continue writing letters to Paramount. Brownell boosted that signal, and made it clear who Star Trek truly belonged to[42]:

> You all read it! Letters, letters, letters. Let's keep up the pressure and help G.R. to get us back our Star Trek.
> Not Paramount's Star Trek, OURS!⁴³

The same dedication to grassroots fan outreach which resulted in Roddenberry's community college gymnasium speech on a humid September night in Florida led him to call the editor of the *Monster Times*, a conversation which was discussed the December 1974 issue. It was not the first time that Roddenberry had called the editor, a conversation having been referenced in the *Times*' Star Trek-heavy Collectors' Issue No. 1, published sometime in 1973 (and in which fans are referred to as "Star Trekkers"). In both instances Roddenberry had said Paramount balked at reviving the show due to the sets costing $750,000 to rebuild, too expensive for a series but possible for a movie, the script for which Roddenberry was working on as of December 1974.⁴⁴

Around that same month, the eleventh issue of the UK-based Star Trek Action Group's same-named newsletter reported that "Paramount is talking of spending at least 1.5 million dollars" on the movie. That issue also stated that Paramount's new president Barry Diller was "unaware of the intense interest in the show" since it was his predecessor Frank Yablans who had "received the thousands of letters."⁴⁵

> Therefore, we must impress him with a large amount of mail! Negotiations between Mr Roddenberry and Paramount were progressing but not finalised when Mr Diller took office, and Mr Roddenberry states that it is now vital that Paramount receives letter regarding the movie, the more the better. So write NOW to Mr Barry Diller.... Be polite, sincere, and legible ... and remember to plug the original Star Trek cast, all of whom have indicated an interest in doing their original roles again.⁴⁶

And so began the latest avalanche.

1975: Magicam to Make the Sanest Man Go Mad

Star Trek II Is Announced; Expectations Are Managed

By the end of January 1975, *Star Trek I* was being shown on 137 stations across the United States, 49 of those were in the top 50 markets. By late February it was up to 142 stations, though it was still hovering at only 49 of the top markets.[1]

Speaking at Rice University in Houston on January 22, Roddenberry told the assembled crowds that after suffering "a year-long deluge of mail demanding a Star Trek motion picture," Paramount "has finally cried 'enough,'" and "we're now finishing negotiations for a full-length wide-screen Star Trek motion picture" to be shot "with the original cast." In a lecture at the Rensselaer Polytechnic Institute in mid–March, he reported that the negotiations had been completed, and the original cast would be appearing in the film that was definitely going to happen. *Variety* confirmed on March 19 that Star Trek "will be brought to theatrical screens in a feature film version by Paramount and Gene Roddenberry's Norway Productions Inc." Roddenberry would write the script after completing negotiations with the original cast—while seeking "10 celebs for cameos"—and the film would be made "entirely in Hollywood using Par's Magicam process." The piece also noted that in addition to the 142 domestic stations, Star Trek was seen in 47 countries, while voting for "'Trek'ophile" as the fan demonym.[2]

The Rice University and Rensselaer Polytechnic Institute speeches were referenced in the March *A Piece of the Action* regarding potential subject matter for the film, many ideas of which were supposedly brought about by fans requesting information: "He has been thinking about bringing people up to date on the past history of the Enterprise, showing how it was built in space, and how each character became part of the Enterprise crew; also something more on the mating cycle of Vulcans—whether or not it would be strictly every seven years or Spock's human blood would alter it." The only element of this to make it to the final product was the *Enterprise* being rebuilt in space. (Roddenberry's 1976 record *Inside Star Trek* would pick up the not-at-all prurient thread of Spock's sex life.)³

A letter from Roddenberry dated March 26 appeared in fanzines including but not limited to the May/June 1975 *Archives' Log*. He apologized for it being a form letter, since "I am certain you understand that I must necessarily seclude myself for the next two or three months while writing the STAR TREK film script," but he was taking time out from the seclusion to "dispell the flurry of potentially harmful rumors which have accompanied the announcement of the motion picture version of STAR TREK." After thanking the fans for their fannishness, and praising their diversity as "an exciting spectrum ranging from bright ten-year-olds to college presidents and statesmen," he set out to manage the expectations of the fans and their potential participation in the making of the film. This was addressed in the first of many "facts regarding the STAR TREK motion picture"⁴:

> a. The motion picture will be written and produced by myself. No director will be set until the script is completed, budgeted, and a start date estimated. No staffing from outside the entertainment industry is contemplated for this particular production. Paramount has, however, begun to understand the importance of STAR TREK fan organizations and they will receive special consideration in the release of information and in any other kind of publicity-promotion efforts.⁵

After assuring the reader that negotiations were underway to obtain all the original cast pending availability and "other reasonable career considerations" such as "the handling of their role in the script," he addressed casting rumors:

> d. No other actor is being discussed or has even been considered to replace Shatner, Nimoy, or any other of the television cast members. Rumors of my disliking or not wanting to work with any television cast member are totally false.
>
> e. Also totally false is the rumor that there has been discussion or even consideration of dropping any of the secondary actors in order to pay higher salaries to the series stars.⁶

Something similar had happened on *Animated* when Roddenberry chose to not rehire Nichelle Nichols, George Takei, and Walter Koenig, but other than Chekov's absence, that wasn't yet common knowledge. On the topic of casting, he next announced what would be one of the most peculiar aspects of the first attempts at a Trek film:

> f. Since the cast of a motion picture is generally much larger than that of a television episode, Paramount has encouraged me to consider the use of ten or so film "name stars" in guest and cameo roles. The purpose is simply to broaden the box office appeal of the production and in no way is this a plan to diminish the role of the importance of the original STAR TREK television actors.⁷

Considering that one of the major criticisms of the Robert Wise film was how little most of the cast got to do, it's difficult to fathom how this might have played out. The plan for "10 international celebrities in cameo roles" was also mentioned in the introduction of the Roddenberry interview in the July 1975 *Monster Times*, and in the winter of 1976—by which point the film had a new executive producer and two scriptwriters, none of whom were Gene Roddenberry—*Cinefantastique* reported that the picture "may call for as many as ten cameo roles." In an interview in the March/April 1977 *Star Trektennial News*, the executive producer who was not Gene Roddenberry said the cameo idea had been whittled down to "two major roles that we hope to attract theatrical quality stars to be in," one male and one female, who along with Shatner and Nimoy "will be the four major stars of the movie." Considering how much Roddenberry enjoyed positing himself as a misunderstood artist besieged by idiotic network and studio executives, it's surprising that he went along with what in another context he might have referred to sarcastically as "one of those great front office suggestions."[8]

Though Roddenberry established in Section A that fan organizations would "receive special consideration in the release of information," in Section G he made it clear there would be no favoritism, mostly:

> g. In promoting and publicizing a motion picture, no arrangements will be made which give precedence to any particular fan organization over another. Every effort will be made to treat all STAR TREK fans and fan groups equally. Where efficiency and speed is a factor, information may occasionally be aimed at the larger groups and/or toward a convention currently in progress but only under an agreement that these parties will disseminate that information to other fans as quickly and as broadly as possible.[9]

He further promised that the production would use as many of the original show's staff as possible "within limits of the film story direction, budget, and efficient staffing procedures"; that there would be no news about the "nature or direction" of the film's story until it was finalized; fan mail should continue to go to Paramount, not himself; and that no fans should call his office, please. With all those restrictions and admonitions in place, he ended the letter on an up note: "Yes, it lives!"[10]

On or around April 8, Roddenberry granted a telephone interview with the *Monster Times* which would run in the July issue. The introduction listed some planned developments which laid out Roddenberry's obsession with making Star Trek as state-of-the-1970s-art as possible, an obsession which resulted in some of the Robert Wise film's more glaring aesthetic issues—such as that most troubling of compound adjectives "stretch-knit."

> For one, the USS Enterprise will be updated to conform to new aero-space designs. New instruments like digital readouts and new controls will be added to the bridge

and other control areas. The uniforms will be redesigned with new, stretch-knit materials not available when the original show went into production. The entire film will be produced in Magicam, the fantastic new miniature set process which will cut set costs in half.[11]

In the interview itself, Roddenberry spoke highly of Magicam, which would "greatly increase the number of sets we can have. It's almost limitless in scope." A bit more limited in scope was the script, which was mostly in his head and wouldn't be on paper until that August, but he had other things to do[12]:

> I have to redesign the Enterprise. We gave the first model, the eleven-footer, to the Smithsonian. I also have to redesign the costumes, controls ... it will be quite a task.[13]

In addition to the Herculean, entirely solitary labor of redesigning the ship from scratch, he revealed he was considering a prequel based on viewer questions:

> People have always asked me, "Gene, how did this whole United Federation thing get started. How did they meet, how did the Enterprise get built ... what was the beginning of it all like?" I have been toying with the idea of making the feature film start with the early days of the crew in Starfleet and bring them up to the point where we first met them in the series. We'll see how it goes.[14]

The story he would eventually write—and which would be rejected by Paramount—was not a prequel in any way, so this may have been intentional misdirection. Either way, it foreshadows the vogue for *Star Trek* prequels which would take the form of the television shows *Star Trek: Enterprise* (2001–2005) and *Star Trek: Discovery* (2017–) and two feature films, J.J. Abrams' 2009 *Star Trek* and 2013 *Star Trek Into Darkness*. Justin Lin's 2016 *Star Trek Beyond* would be the first property since *Star Trek: Animated* to take place during the *Enterprise*'s original five-year mission, albeit in a different timeline.[15]

Roddenberry claimed a feature film had been in the works ever since *Star Trek I* had been canceled: "I didn't know if we could resuscitate it as a feature or a series. I guess the feature may enable us to get the series back on the air if it shows a good boxoffice return to our 'friends' at the networks." And if it did get back on the air, "I can tell you that I won't see it as a series of hour shows. I would expect the magnitude to be that of a series of Movies of the Week ... a 90-minute or two-hour mini-series like COLUMBO. The old hour format is not suitable anymore." Roddenberry would hold fast to his opposition to Star Trek returning as a weekly, hour-long show—until the opportunity arose for it to return as a weekly, hour-long show, first unsuccessfully as *Star Trek II* in 1978, and then with considerable success as *Star Trek: The Next Generation* in 1986.[16]

In May 1975, Roddenberry moved his office out of his home and into the old *Star Trek I* digs in Paramount's Building E, which had been garishly redecorated red, white, and blue by *Love, American Style.* (1975!) According to that month's *A Piece of the Action*, Paramount had sent a somewhat patronizing postcard to the fans[17]:

> "Dear Trekkie, Thank you for the interest you have shown in STAR TREK. By now you have probably read in the papers that we are planning to make a movie of your favorite series. We suggest you check your local papers for information regarding the progress of this production. We will certainly let you know if there are plans to continue the series in the future. We do appreciate your continued interest in the STAR TREK souvenirs and collectibles. Keep on Trekking! Live long and prosper, The Crew of the Enterprise."[18]

The issue also quoted from Paramount's press release that the movie would be written by Roddenberry, who was currently negotiating with the original cast to play their roles, and that it had been "announced by Robert Evans, Paramount Executive Vice-President in charge of world-wide production." Did Evans neglect to mention this career high point in his otherwise highly entertaining memoir *The Kid Stays in the Picture*? You bet your ass he neglected to mention it.[19]

Rumored Redford

Star Trek I was still going strong; *Variety* reported on July 9, 1975, that the series was "currently licensed to 140 stations"—which was down two from the 142 stations in March, but that the current licensors including "49 of the top 50 markets." Renewal orders had recently been received from WHEC in Rochester, New York, KTVK in Phoenix, WOI in Ames-Des Moines, Iowa, KPTV in Portland, Oregon, KRIS in Corpus Christi, KXTX in Dallas-Ft. Worth, WLWI in Indianapolis, WBMG in Birmingham, WICZ in Binghamton, New York, WQAD in Moline, Illinois, and WNYS in Syracuse.[20]

An ad by National Telefilm Associates in the August 6 *Variety* bragged that *Bonanza* was "America's champion in family entertainment," and that it continued to "beat the competition" such as *Dinah*, *The Mod Squad*, and *Star Trek I* "in many markets," citing the N.S.I. TV reports from May 1975. Since *Bonanza* completed its fourteenth and final season in 1972, the ad promised that fifty new, first-run episodes were now available.[21]

Published around that same time by people outside the continental United States who were disappointed that new, first-run episodes of Star

Trek weren't going to be available anytime soon, *Star Trek Action Group* #13 reported that the movie should begin shooting about January or February of 1976, and that Roddenberry had said "with so much more room for scope, many hitherto unanswered questions (How the crew were picked, what life on Earth is like etc.) will be answered," while George Takei said "Sulu will at last be given a first name!" Which settled that Takei would be Sulu, but the casting of larger roles were allegedly up for grabs: "There have been strange rumors that Robert Redford will play Spock … the rumors coming from people in a responsible position who should know better (or not print them at all.) Anyway, the truth is that Robert Redford will NOT play Spock!"[22]

Unknown until 1980 was that the person "in a responsible position" was Roddenberry himself. In *The Making of Star Trek—The Motion Picture*, Susan Sackett wrote that "there was never a question as to who would play Captain James Tiberius Kirk, although a Roddenberry joke about recasting the part with Richard Burton in the center seat (and Robert Redford as Mr. Spock) got out of hand, and at one point the Burton-Redford costars were actually reported in a TV newscast!"[23]

Star Trek Action Group #13 also included an open letter from Gene Roddenberry which had a far more casual tone than the previous bullet-pointed missive, and addressed that pesky, impossible-to-trace Robert Redford rumor which had come out of nowhere.

> The script is progressing, and is about half way through the first draft. I am hoping to complete this rough draft within a month or so. A beginning date depends, of course, on Paramount's attitude towards the script, the availability of the right director, and many other things. We plan to do a good deal more with our script than we were able to do for television. Some of you may find the theme of our story quite controversial. We also plan to show a bit of our conception of Earth, something never revealed on the TV series.
>
> Some of you have probably heard rumors that Robert Redford is playing everything from Spock to Nurse Chapel! One local TV station even announced that he had been signed to play Spock! I would like to dispel all of these rumors. The script is being written to include EVERY member of the cast, AND WE PLAN TO USE AS MANY OF THE ORIGINAL TELEVISION CAST AND STAFF AS ARE AVAILABLE. Hopefully, this includes all of them. Although William Shatner will have his own TV series by then, it is fortunately a Paramount series, and Paramount can no doubt make him available. As regards Shatner's attitude towards the movie, when asked at a Convention in Michigan State University in May whether or not he would play Captain Kirk, he replied, "I AM the Captain!"[24]

By the time these letters and interviews were published they were somewhat moot, insofar as they were regarding a film to be written by Roddenberry.

Star Trek II Is Denounced; Expectations Are Mangled

The *Star Trek II* story which Roddenberry submitted to Paramount on June 30, 1975, was rejected in July. As related by Susan Sackett in *The Making of Star Trek—The Motion Picture*, many elements found their way into the Robert Wise film, including an "emaciated, bedraggled" Spock meditating on Vulcan, and being disrupted by "something about to happen to Earth and to his old friend Jim Kirk." (That he was thinking of Kirk in particular was also an aspect of Roddenberry's novelization, though the Wise film suggests Spock was only sensing V'ger.) Meanwhile, in Roddenberry's *Star Trek II* the *Enterprise* is being refitted in orbit above San Francisco when "a huge Object, one thousand times larger than a starship" is detected heading toward Earth, where "people are beginning to receive mental impressions of a returning God." Led by now-Admiral Kirk, the reassembled Enterprise crew heads off to intercept the alien[25]:

> The Object turns out to be more than just a vessel-it is a computer form so advanced it is a living entity itself. However we discover that this God they've worshipped is actually the Deceiver, the computer-programmed remains of a race who were "cast out" from their dimension and into this one.[26]

Sackett later recalled that "after a few parlor tricks, such as restoring Lt. Sulu's amputated legs, many of the crew begin to believe that this being may indeed be a deity. In actuality, it is a powerful machine with confused programming (a favorite plot device Gene would use many times), arriving at Earth thinking it is a messiah. Only Kirk remains steadfast in his disbelief." It ends with what may well be the last fight scene Roddenberry would write for use on Star Trek: "Kirk inevitably goes one-on-one with the Entity, whose Christlike image dissolves into patterns resembling 'The Great Deceiver,' as Gene put it." Sackett also noted that this story included a variation on the transporter accident eventually shown in the Wise film, as well as Starfleet Headquarters being in San Francisco, and McCoy being drafted into service.[27]

Back to *The Making of Star Trek—The Motion Picture*:

> At the end, Kirk wins out, the entity returns to its other dimension, and the Enterprise crew is left with a gift-they return to Earth and discover that the "Deceiver-God" entity had made them a gift of time in which they are suddenly younger and are now returning from their first five-year mission.[28]

The basic framework from "Robot's Return" of a massive object threatening Earth is present here, though rather than the object searching for its Creator, it is now it is claiming to be Earth's Creator. But most peculiar is the notion of the crew being younger at the end, appearing as they would have at the end of the first five-year mission; heaven only knows how Roddenberry thought such a thing could be pulled off. (Again, it's almost as though he didn't really want to do Star Trek anymore.)

Roddenberry had written in his June 1975 open letter that some fans "may find the theme of our story quite controversial," and Sackett later wrote in *The Making of Star Trek—The Motion Picture* that Paramount rejected the *Trek II* script due to Roddenberry "iconoclastically asking what if the God of the Old Testament, full of tirades and demands to be worshipped, actually turned out to be Lucifer. If so, was the serpent's offer of the Fruit of Knowledge actually a gift from the real God?" That Roddenberry's vision of a utopian 23rd-century Earth included movie theaters which still showed 20th century skin-flicks may not have helped matters, either.[29]

Paramount spent the rest of 1975 looking for a *Star Trek II* story by someone who wasn't Gene Roddenberry, and they must be given credit for specifically speaking to established science fiction writers. John D. F. Black (who penned the *Star Trek I* episode "The Naked Time") and Robert Silverberg both wrote story outlines, and after Paramount rejected them, other writers who were invited to pitch ideas and were subsequently rejected included Ray Bradbury, Ted Sturgeon, and Harlan Ellison. (Oh, Harlan. We'll get back to him.) Sackett informed the editors of *A Piece of the Action* on December 5, 1975, that both Roddenberry and Paramount "are actively conferring with half a dozen top, well-known science fiction writers. Roddenberry is meeting almost daily with various writers and executives, having story conferences to decide on the finest possible story. They expect to be in pre-production perhaps as early as February. Gene is hopeful the film will be released in late 1976."[30]

Sackett and Roddenberry were soon feeling confident enough to launch a newsletter, *Star Trektennial News*. As Sackett wrote in the first issue of *Trektennial*, which didn't come out until May of 1976 and was somewhat confusingly numbered #13 to maintain continuity with Roddenberry's previous newsletter, *Inside Star Trek*:

> What is STAR TREK II? In case you've been stranded on Rigel V for the last year, that's the working title of the STAR TREK MOVIE!
> As this is being written (mid–December) negotiations are going smoothly, and Paramount Studios is working in conjunction with Gene Roddenberry to obtain a workable story concept. There have been several top sci-fi writers contacted, and while no one has yet been signed, we should have a script perhaps as early as February. Once the final draft of a script is accepted (and Gene will most likely supervise the writing), pre-production will then get underway.[31]

She quoted a personal assurance from Roddenberry:

1975: Magicam to Make the Sanest Man Go Mad

"I have made a commitment to the fans and to myself that when we make a STAR TREK movie, it will be STAR TREK. This means that I'm waiting for a guarantee that in producing the motion picture, I can exercise the same kind of creative supervision that I exercised in creating and producing the television show.... I want some guarantee that we will not end up with something like CAPTAIN KIRK MEETS GODZILLA, and if that delays the movie for the time being, I hope STAR TREK fans will agree with my stand."[32]

So "Captain Kirk Meets Godzilla" was out, but what a difference a few syllables make: four years later in *The Making of Star Trek—The Motion Picture*, Sackett would describe Roddenberry's original *Star Trek II* story as "Captain Kirk Versus God."[33]

* * *

As *Star Trek II* returned to development hell in the latter half of 1975, *Star Trek I* was continuing to do boffo business on the tube. By July it was playing in 50 countries outside the United States, including beginning its fourth highly-rated run in primetime on the BBC, and by October it was up to 150 stations within the United States.[34]

One of those stations was the Bay Area's early adopter KTVU, home of the beloved regional horror show *Creature Features*, whose deceptively milquetoast host Bob Wilkins was a proud *Star Trek I* fan. On September 24, 1975, he hosted a documentary called *The Star Trek Dream*, which looked at both the series and the local conventions. Though bemused by the latter, he was still far less condescending than most mainstream coverage of Star Trek fans. (Or any fans of any franchise—for more reading on that subject, I again recommend *Ponyville Confidential*.) Broadcast at 8 p.m., *The Star Trek Dream* tied *Little House on the Prairie* on NBC in the Nielsens with a 14 rating and 25 share—a remarkable achievement that Wilkins wasn't too humble to mention on the air on *Creature Features*.[35]

If KTVU was able to both broadcast and celebrate Star Trek, other local stations weren't so lucky. Though KQED in San Francisco had the highest Nielsen ratings of any public broadcaster in the country, producer Joe Russin had never been able to find a solid lead-in for his news program *Newsroom*. He unsuccessfully tried to get the station to acquire *Star Trek I*, but had to settle for standard PBS fare such as Lowell Thomas specials. Those were good, but then again, nobody was making *The Lowell Thomas Dream*.[36]

1976: The War Within the Script, the War Without

Harlan Ellison v. Star Trek

Gene Roddenberry soon teamed up with writer Jon Povill to create another *Star Trek II* story. In a treatment dated January 19, 1976, Spock has again left Starfleet, and thoughts of Kirk send him back. The main thrust of the story is that six years after Spock returned to Vulcan, there was "an energy shimmer" one day, and not only did nobody know who Spock was—not unlike the *Star Trek: Animated* episode "Yesteryear"—but, "incredibly, two hundred years of intercourse with Earth were wiped out." Povill would later call Paramount's rejection of the treatment "justifiable," because in its form at that time "it was not a film worth doing." (On the copy of the treatment stored at the Margaret Herrick Library, Gene Roddenberry's name is crossed out on the cover. Interpret that as you will.)[1]

Neither of the *Star Trek II* stories were mentioned when DeForest Kelley, James Doohan, Walter Koenig, and Harlan Ellison were guests on *Tomorrow with Tom Snyder* on February 4, 1976. Snyder pondered whether reviving Star Trek might destroy "the myth and the legend," to which Kelley replied: "We have the gamble with the motion picture where we did 79 episodes, there's gotta be one episode in there that everybody's going to like, but when you come out with one shot on the movie, not everyone is maybe going to like the movie." He was more correct than he could have known. Snyder suggested the movie was a calculated risk, and Koenig agreed that while everybody believed its success to be a foregone conclusion, the only problem was that "if they decide that because it's a feature film as opposed to a television show they have to change the thrust of it in some way, make it monsters and huge battle scenes, something that you can't get on television, you may distort the entire feeling of the show." Kelley then said: "I think it needs a storyline, something on the order of the crew encountering Christ in space, and finding out that Christ is actually Lucifer—Satan." There was laughter, and whether or not Kelley was aware that he'd just described the basis of Roddenberry's rejected story is unknown, but it certainly looked like he came up with the most absurd idea he could think of off the top of his head.²

Kelley had expressed the problem all the writers had been encountering: the story wasn't "big" enough. Harlan Ellison went into more detail on *Tomorrow*, telling one of many versions of the pitch meeting that have surfaced over the years:

> Roddenberry called me in—you know, he was really desperate to call me in ... we came in and we thought up an idea. Paramount keeps saying to them, no matter what plot they offer, it's not big enough, it's not big enough. In one of them we destroyed the universe, we thought that was big enough—no, it wasn't big enough. I have a meeting with the guy from Paramount, the guy who's the liaison, he's the interface between the great powers ... we get a story, it's a super-duper story, Gene and I work it out and it's all solid. So in comes this tumtum from the head office, and he's going to listen to it. We explain the whole thing to him. It's complex but it's fascinating, it goes back to the dawn of time and parallel species that grew up with humankind, and so on. When we get all done, he sits there and he goes, "Hmmm. You know, I was reading von Däniken, and y'know the Mayan calendar is the same as our calendar. Why don't you put in some Mayans?" We said, "Um, Mayans?" "Yeah, why don't you put in some Mayans? That's terrific!" We tried to explain to him that there were no Mayans at the dawn of time. He didn't understand that.³

For another Ellison telling of the story, track down Stephen King's 1981 nonfiction book *Danse Macabre*. It's good stuff.⁴

The 743 Speak

Harlan Ellison wasn't the only one with ideas about what the first Star Trek movie should be. In March 1976, Carole Brownell of Save the Star Trek Cast sent out a poll which asked the fans what *they* wanted *their* Star Trek movie to be like, and she received 743 responses. According to Bjo Trimble, Brownell sent the results to Roddenberry, who in turn handed them to Paramount's executives, which couldn't have possibly helped the cause. If only 1 in 100 fans took the time to fill out the poll and mail it back in, that would still only represent 74,300 people, which wouldn't be close to enough to justify the expenditure of the film.⁵

Of those who did respond, 208 said they were between the ages of 10–15, 180 between the ages of 16–20, 141 between 21–30, 59 were over 30, and 150 declined to state. The number of respondents affiliated with a fan club was 479, and 264 were not. Regarding what kind of story they wanted to see, 393 chose "action/adventure," 174 chose "drama," 37 had no preference, 33 chose "comedy," 21 chose "romance." 291 said they wished to see the *Enterprise* crew emphasized, 197 said alien cultures, 90 chose science and technology,

37 chose Earth culture, and 44 had no preference. It's notable that while Gene Roddenberry was making it clear around this time that the original cast would be returning, his vision for the film primarily involved incorporating advances in science and technology as well as visiting 23rd century Earth, none of which were priorities for these particular fans. Among the polled fans, 380 said they wanted the film to take place during a second five-year mission, with 192 choosing later in the first five-year mission, 72 choosing "many years later," a mere 40 choosing before the first five year mission—in essence, the prequel idea that Roddenberry had been talking about—and 50 having no preference. The number of fans who agreed that the movie should be "controversial" was 408 while 285 did not, and 50 had no preference. Though Roddenberry had written in his 1975 open letter that "some of you may find the theme of our story quite controversial," referring to his since-rejected "Captain Kirk Versus God" *Star Trek II* script, those 408 respondents would still get their wish for a controversial Star Trek film.[6]

Another controversy among fans was how much pressure to put on Paramount. In an exchange from the Trek Roundtable section of the fanzine *Trek: The Magazine for Star Trek Fans* later reprinted in the 1978 book *The Best of Trek*, reader Judy Lee Goldenberg wrote:

> In your editorials (*Trek* No. 3), you urge fans to write to Paramount about the Trekfilm. Well, at the February committee con here in NYC, various people, including the Great Bird himself, told the audience not to write to Paramount. The film is definitely on schedule to be made, Paramount has committed $$$$ to the production and construction of sets, props and costumes are underway. (This was confirmed by Jimmy Doohan on May 9.) If people continue to write to Paramount asking dumb questions like "When are you going to make a Star Trek movie?" the bigshots will get mad and impatient at Gene to finish a script, and no one wants that, do we?[7]

Trek No. 3 was published in 1975, and the committee con in question was the Star Trek Lives! Convention held in February 1976. The March 1976 issue of *A Piece of the Action* gave the start date of the movie as July 15, 1976, and it also included a statement that "letters from fans urging that Paramount do a *Star Trek* movie are not considered necessary at the moment."[8]

But the editors of *Trek* were having none of this wait-and-see nonsense, and while it's unclear exactly when the letter from Goldenberg and the response from the editors was printed, it was most likely later in 1976.

> At this late date, it has become a question of us no longer just wanting a Star Trek film, it is now imperative that one be made if the momentum of Star Trek fandom be kept going. Jimmy Doohan told us in March that the film was scheduled for July. George Takei told us in June that it was scheduled for September, but had just been moved back to November. Are we going to be stalled back to the point where the bigshots can say that the audience isn't around anymore, and scrap the project? We say keep writing.

Let everyone concerned know that we, the fans, are beginning to get mad and impatient at them. Then maybe we will see our movie sometime before 1978.[9]

No franchise can exist without fans, but it is often in the nature of fans to behave as though that all things surrounding the property are for the glory and edification of themselves, and that their desires and their own propagation should take precedence. Hence it being "imperative" that the film be made to ensure that the "the momentum of Star Trek fandom" keeps going, and that the foot-stomping must continue until the fans are given what they want—"maybe we will see *our* movie sometime before 1978"—for the sake of the organized fandom's own continued existence. Star Trek fans may have been one of the first to adopt this solipsistic attitude, but they weren't the last. (Yep, it's all in *Ponyville Confidential*.)

The Isenberg Cometh; The Trektennial Begins

In an interview with Associated Press writer Bob Thomas which ran in many newspapers on March 23, 1976, Roddenberry's weariness with the whole process shone through: "Sometimes I wish I could walk out the door and leave 'Star Trek' behind." This was both due to the frustrations of the constantly-collapsing revival and the pressure of the cult of personality which had bloomed around him, as it always must around creators of popular properties: "I'm not a guru and I don't want to be. It frightens me when I learn of 10,000 people treating a 'Star Trek' script as if it were scripture. I certainly didn't write scripture, and my feeling is that those who did were not treated very well in the end." As for what he did write, he said the reasons Paramount rejected his *Star Trek II* story were "not clear" but "may have concerned a religious theme in my treatment," and that he still expected to maintain creative control even though the Mountain was in the process of trying to find another writer. The budget was to be at least $5M, Paramount was still hoping to land cameos by top stars, and if the feature did well Roddenberry expected Star Trek would return to television. "I would hope that it would take the form of occasional films in the long form. I don't think I could face the insanity of another weekly 'Star Trek.' As you may recall, at one time or another every member of our staff was in the hospital for exhaustion."[10]

By the end of March, the first Star Trek movie was moved from Paramount's theatrical department to the television division. Story ideas from writers including Chris Knopf, Howard Rodman, Will Loren, and Howard Burke were rejected before the movie was returned to the theatrical department in April.[11]

Two significant events occurred in May 1976. The first was head of Paramount Barry Diller calling Jerry Isenberg, the head of the Jozak Company. As Isenberg would tell Susan Sackett in January 1977, "[Diller] asked me if I was familiar with STAR TREK. The project wasn't going anywhere, and was it something I would be interested in taking on? My job was to be the person responsible for getting the picture made, and in that area the responsibility was to make Gene happy and make Paramount happy, to sort of reconcile the differences, whatever they might be." His prior science fiction experience included producing the 1972 television movie *The People*, executive-produced by Francis Ford Coppola and starring William Shatner and Kim Darby, who played the title character in the *Star Trek I* episode "Miri." Isenberg's lone theatrical film was a 1973 documentary about 1950s rock and roll called *Let the Good Times Roll*, which arguably made him less experienced at producing narrative feature films than Roddenberry, who had at least co-written and produced Roger Vadim's *Pretty Maids All in a Row* in 1971. (Then again, like most Vadim films it was rather vile, and did not lead to another feature-producing gig for Roddenberry.) Isenberg described his job as putting the various elements of producing a motion picture together and "making sure they're all in harmony with each other," while ensuring that Roddenberry as well as the screenwriter and the director all "have as much room and freedom to do what they do best." He described the movie as just an expression of the property that was Star Trek, "but there are myriads of books, licenses on clothes, games, records, fan clubs, conventions, speaking tours and so on. My kids' happiest day is when they put on their Spock shirts and go walking off to school. That may be commercialism; but on the other hand my kids are pretty happy wearing their Spock shirts." As far as the commercialism went, however, Isenberg suggested that the existing merchandising program should be stopped, or at least slowed down and studied, a sentiment with which Roddenberry agreed.[12]

The second significant event in May 1976 was the release of the first issue (#13) of *Star Trektennial News*, with Sackett's already-outdated news about *Star Trek II* from the previous December. Also in the post that month was the latest edition of the Lincoln Enterprises catalog, the *Star Trek* memorabilia mail-order company founded and run by Majel Barrett. The *Trektennial* newsletter was duly promoted[13]:

> This is the STAR TREK Official National Fan Club! Keep up to date on your interstellar communications because WE'RE MAKING A MOVIE—"STAR TREK II." Our editor is Susan Sackett, Gene Roddenberry's personal secretary. How close can you get to the source! No more listening to rumors! You will have the news first hand—every step of the way! The project is beginning to move very fast so don't miss any of it! Includes 6

bi-monthly issues of an informative and easy-to-read newsletter, special offers to members, and on the spot interviews with on and off screen personnel.[14]

The fans (and therefore customers) were praised for their efforts in making the movie happen at all:

> On September 8, 1976, it will be 10 years since STAR TREK was first viewed by the public on NBC. Today, 10 years later, STAR TREK is bigger and stronger than ever, thanks to your loyal support. To answer your most frequently asked question: YES—There will be a big budget STAR TREK feature motion picture. The working title is "STAR TREK II" and yes, all of the original cast have expressed their desire to recreate their original roles. Gene Roddenberry will again produce his classic creation. This movie is a reality because of your enthusiastic efforts to bring back STAR TREK. Paramount has heard you loud and clear![15]

In the June 1976 *Star Trek Today*, Jim Meadows presented a roundup of the available information about the film's status, including what may be one of the first public descriptions of Roddenberry's 1975 *Star Trek II* story:

> Originally, Gene Roddenberry was going to write the script, and he did so. The script, by all reports, took place after the Enterprise's five-year mission, with the show regulars in different walks of life (Kirk holding down a military desk job, McCoy as a veterinarian, etc.). The plot involved bringing the regulars back together in a newer and bigger starship to battle a creature that claimed to be God. That, evidently, was the script Paramount turned down last summer.[16]

Meadows reported that there had been "a struggle between Roddenberry and Paramount over who had control of the movie," and that according to the zine *Locus* "at one point last October that Dick Silber was 'currently in charge of production' of the Star Trek movie," but "apparently, Gene Roddenberry is still very much in at this date." Given the understandably imprecise way information was disseminated among zines, "Dick Silber" is probably Richard Zimbert, who is referenced in *The Making of Star Trek—The Motion Picture* as being Paramount's "senior vice president in charge of motion picture business affairs" at the time, and the book includes an April 1976 letter from Roddenberry in which Zimbert is addressed as "Dick."[17]

Star Trek Today also said "the film's budget has been announced with figures of 3 million dollars from one source, and 5 million at another," describing them as "typical figures for a major production," and reported that Magicam had been "dropped as a method of filming the Star Trek movie" since "the process is not going to be as cheap as Paramount hoped."[18] (Paramount's Magicam subsidiary itself would go on to work on the models for the Robert Wise film, however.) The April 30 issue of *Locus* is quoted as listing the first Star Trek movie's director as Jud Taylor, who directed five episodes of the unloved third season of *Star Trek I*. While Roddenberry often said that they would try to get as many of the original production staff as possible, there is no other evidence suggesting that Taylor or any *Trek I* director was ever in the running to direct the film. More's the pity, since "The Corbomite Maneuver" helmer Joseph Sargent had recently directed what is now considered one of the best films of the 1970s, *The Taking of Pelham One Two Three*, while Taylor's imaginative direction of "The Mark of Gideon" and "Let That Be Your Last Battlefield" allowed them to rise above their scripts.[19]

Most significant in the Meadows article is the final paragraph, regarding a speech Roddenberry gave at the University of Nebraska on April 7, 1976:

> Gene Roddenberry predicted the Star Trek movie would be released in the summer of 1977, possibly coming in the middle or near the end of a glut of science fiction features now in production or scheduled for same; many of them have budgets much higher than the ST movie. The success or failure of these other films could have a big effect on the release date of the Star Trek movie, and on its box office appeal.[20]

On the day Roddenberry gave that speech, George Lucas began filming what was then called *The Star Wars* at EMI-Elstree studios in England after two and a half weeks of shooting in Tunisia. It's fascinating to speculate how history would have played out differently had the first Star Trek movie opened in the summer of 1977 head-to-head with the first Star Wars movie. It may well have been the end of Star Trek as we know it, and Roddenberry wasn't wrong about how the success of *Star Wars* would figure into the eventual production of Robert Wise's *Star Trek—The Motion Picture*, though not as much as it's usually given credit for.[21]

In *Star Trektennial News #14*, dated June 1976 but presumably written sometime before May, Susan Sackett confirmed July 15 as the start date pending the existence of the non-existent script. New executives at Paramount, some of whom "might even be considered fans," were currently "considering several story ideas and by the time this reaches you, they will probably have made a decision on one!" (If at all possible, please imagine Ron Howard speaking these words: "They didn't.")[22]

A fan asked in the letters section whether "in the making of 'Star Trek II' will Mr. Roddenberry be following the material in the 'star fleet technical manual' and blueprints?" Sackett replied that "No, they will not be followed in the movie STAR TREK II," and that while Roddenberry agreed that there were "some fine things done in" Franz Joseph's *Star Fleet Technical Manual* and the *Star Trek Blueprints*, they were "solely the inspiration of the author," and had Roddenberry been consulted, "he would have had a great deal to add on his own (being the creator of STAR TREK)."[23]

For sure Roddenberry was the creator of Star Trek, but the *Enterprise* was largely the work of one Matt Jeffries. Asked what he thought of Franz

Joseph's *Star Trek Blueprints* by Susan Sackett in *Star Trektennial News* #15, Jeffries fought to keep in check his annoyance with both the existence of the book, and fans not realizing it was only the work of other fans:

> The set of Blueprints that I saw two years ago ... he's a marvelous draftsman. He did a hell of a job of drafting, and that's what the heck it is. He took what we had and added to it based on what we had ... he merely expanded ... he invented like mad. As much as I hate to admit it, I got thoroughly peeved over the whole thing, because he did take the design work that somebody else had done and built on it. We're talking about another generation of fans, and they pick this thing up and all of a sudden it says STAR TREK and it's gospel. And it isn't, because what didn't actually come out of what we did is a pure fabrication that's happened since then. I got narrow-minded and thoroughly peeved over the fact that there was no mention of what he used as a base to build upon.[24]

It is the official position of *The First Star Trek Movie* that Matt Jeffries had every right to be peeved. The Franz Joseph books were what is now known as "fanon," meaning material that is not taken from the source property but is nonetheless accepted by the fans who created it as being, to use Jeffries' all-too-accurate word, gospel. When the 2012 *My Little Pony: Friendship Is Magic* episode "The Last Roundup" established a name for a background character who had previously gone unnamed, it sparked debate among a small fraction of the viewers regarding what it meant for the fan fiction which had already been written. Further hell broke loose among that subset when Hasbro later changed the character's name. (Can you read all about that truly stupid incident in *Ponyville Confidential*? Oh, maybe.)

Setting aside that the terms weren't in common use yet, further evidence that the distinction between canon and fanon was already blurry came in *Trektennial* #15 when another fan asked, "will the Class I Dreadnought, Destroyer/Scout Class and the Transport/Tug Class be in the movie 'STAR TREK II?'" Sackett responded not by pointing out that they were not obligated to use material created by the fans, but rather that to use that particular material would go against Star Trek's philosophy: "It's a bit early yet to say, but most likely not, especially the Dreadnoughts and Destroyers. Gene Roddenberry is against violence for violence's sake, and hopes to have an imaginative, exciting film, not just another 'battle against the Klingons' television-type episode." This was one of the earliest examples of Roddenberry's belief that there had been an epidemic of *Star Trek I* episodes in which the Klingons were the villains—though as it happened, the Klingons were to be among the villains in Philip Kaufman's soon-to-be-unmade *ST—TMP*.[25]

In her *Star Trek II* update in that same action-packed issue, Sackett wrote that the production had been assigned "STAGE 16, THE LARGEST STAGE ON THE PARAMOUNT LOT!" Construction had not yet begun and the July

15 start date would not be met, though Roddenberry was "now hoping that cameras will start rolling late in October." In his interview, Jeffries pulled no punches about the time estimates for the thing.[26]

> Any idea they're going to get the thing on camera July or August is so asinine I wouldn't think the second time about discussing it. In all honesty, to get that thing ready to go on camera by September, you are not going to get the quality thing that Gene is after. Nor are you going to get the quality thing that's going to match up with what STAR TREK is supposed to be.[27]

Which turned out to be one of the primary issues with the Robert Wise thing: the production was too rushed to be of an especially high quality. History sometimes repeats itself before it happens in the first place.

Look Now! It's Bryant and Scott

The increasingly quixotic search for a film worth doing soon resulted in a major production shakeup. In the August 1976 *Star Trektennial News*, Sackett responded to a fan asking for clarification regarding a number of issues, including that "several sources" had said the film would cost five million dollars:

> Part of what you've heard is accurate. The movie will have a five million dollar budget!
> Here's the latest to date (mid–June at this writing):
> Final contracts between Gene Roddenberry and Paramount Pictures were officially signed on June 4. This means that we are now ready to begin preproduction. The actors' contracts are still being worked out, but we are close to signing both William Shatner and Leonard Nimoy. Once preproduction gets underway, we hope to have cameras rolling within six months. The earliest this would be is mid–November. Release now seems likely for summer of 1977. We have once again returned to the movie division of Paramount for executive supervision. This seems best to GR. And Gene is again meeting with writers, looking for "the" script![28]

(Exactly when Shatner and Nimoy were signed is uncertain, but DeForest Kelley's contract was dated August 25, 1976.) The search for "the" script took yet another turn on August 10 when President of Paramount's Motion Picture Division David V. Picker formally announced that Jerry Isenberg was replacing Gene Roddenberry as Star Trek's executive producer as part of an exclusive theatrical *and* television deal with Isenberg's Jozak Company. Roddenberry would stay on as producer, while Chris Bryant and Allan Scott were being brought over from England to write the script. Best known for Nicolas Roeg's *Don't Look Now*, Bryant and Scott began writing an eight-to-ten page outline on August 16 for a fee of $12,500, a mere drop in the film's then-proposed budget of $7.5M to $9M.[29]

As Scott would later tell *Starlog*, what he and Bryant wanted to create was "a really terrific mindfuck! I think that is something that you can do in movies that you often times cannot do in television. If you can really blow people's minds with this movie, then it will be successful." (Because he was speaking in 1977 during Academy Awards season, he reflected that they had hoped to "touch on the emotions in that sort of visceral feeling that sends people to see movies like *Rocky*.") The August 11, 1976, *Daily Variety* noted that "work will begin on the redesign and construction of a new Enterprise, to reflect the advances made in space technology since the original spaceship was designed nearly 11 years ago," and that while the ship would retain its original design, the new version would be "more sophisticated, complex and imaginative than could have been afforded on a TV budget." And though the official announcement was made on August 10, 1976, George Takei had hinted at it on August 7 while being interviewed for *KPIX Eyewitness News* at Space-Con 2 in Oakland, telling Bill Hillman that "There's going to be a feature film made, there's a contract between Paramount and Gene Roddenberry, and I think some official announcements are imminent … they've asked us not to speak before they do."[30]

Kaufman Commissioned

Though the producers and writers were squared away, there was still the issue of a director. After a roster of candidates including Francis Ford Coppola, Steven Spielberg, William Friedkin, Robert Wise, and George Lucas all proved to be either unavailable or unwilling to direct the as-yet-unwritten film, fate came in the form of what Sackett described in *The Making of Star Trek—The Motion Picture* "a young, handsomely bearded director named Phil Kaufman." Kaufman had recently directed *The White Dawn* and *The Great Northfield Minnesota Raid*, both of which were manly films about manly men doing manly things of the sort which appealed to a manly man's man like Roddenberry, but it was Kaufman who found his way to Star Trek. (Much would be made of Kaufman's beard, which was still a novelty in 1976.)[31]

When Andrei Tarkovsky's 1972 science fiction film *Solaris* was finally distributed in the United States in 1976, it premiered at the Bridge Theater in Kaufman's home of San Francisco on July 14. Kaufman later told the *San Francisco Chronicle* that while *Solaris* was intellectually stimulating, he found the visuals unimaginative and felt the film failed to sustain emotional tension, which inspired him to call his agent and say he wanted to direct a science fiction film. Speaking to Susan Sackett in an interview in the May/June 1977

Star Trektennial News, he recalled that his agent told him "they were looking for a director for STAR TREK and asked if I would be interested. I said I would definitely be interested; he contacted Gene Roddenberry and Jerry Isenberg, we had some meetings and some conversations and I was fortunate enough to be put into this position." In a *Starlog* interview with Mick Garris in 1978, Kaufman revealed that initially Paramount wanted to do "a small, three-million-dollar rip-off, cashing in on the phenomenon. In the six or eight months that I was involved, it was raised to ten million."[32]

Kaufman told Susan Sackett in 1977 that while he was always "interested to a degree" in *Star Trek I* and had watched it while it was on, "I was not a 'trekker' or 'trekkie,' really; I was just interested in it." He described one of the primary issues he was facing in shooting the film to be the need to give it "feature dimension, which is not just a screenplay problem but also a problem of shooting the film with scope"[33]:

> In the feature we've got to remember that it's going to be up there on a big, huge screen and people in a sense are going to be inside the movie rather than looking at it on a small tube, and there's a big difference as to how people respond in a theatre. They want to see more atmosphere, they want to see more backgrounds and so forth. On a television screen you can cut to a close-up and it really fills the screen—you can go back and forth, close-up to close-up. In a theatre that technique generally doesn't work quite that well. You have to use close-ups, but people want a sense of place, a sense of mood and atmosphere.[34]

The lack of interesting backgrounds and atmosphere would be a common complaint about the *mise en scène* of the Robert Wise film, being drab people in drab costumes doing drab things in drab surroundings. (I say this as someone who has deep love for the film, so much so that she's writing two books about it.) Kaufman went on to predict many of the issues that would bedevil Wise's movie even beyond the production design, particularly in pursuit of a film which the fans could "proudly compare to any science fiction film that's been made, including *2001*":

Philip Kaufman at Paramount in 1977, reading *The Animal Kingdom.* **Originally printed in** *Star Trektennial News* **no. 21, May/June 1977 (Susan Sackett).**

They take a LOT of time, a lot of energy and you're able to shoot very little each day, which burns up your energy. Sometimes you have a lot of energy and you can just barrel forward when you're working with actors, but when you're stopping and waiting for an effect to be projected—front screen, rear screen, or you're shooting knowing that there's a matte going to be put in there, or the camera has to be anchored in a special way, often the actors are somewhat restricted because there's an effect going on in the background and that gets very tedious.[35]

In addition to the technical challenges, he had ideas for the film's philosophical bent, later telling the *Chronicle* that the film represented an opportunity to explore the mystery and sense of the occult in the exploration of space, though he clarified that he didn't mean the "occult" as portrayed in horror films like Brian De Palma's recently released *Carrie*.

There is a form of the occult that searches for truth and doesn't search for it by logic, but by intuition. Sometimes by art. By whatever ways are the opposite of logic ... the occult in films is often a vehicle to convey the horrors of the unknown, but I'm interested in the search for the wonders and mysteries of the unknown—which I find more exciting than terror.[36]

It was something Kaufman had explored in *The White Dawn*, describing it to Sackett as having "a certain amount of fantastic things and mysticism in it, such as the shamanistic practices and rituals." He would later describe *Dawn* to the UK magazine *Starburst* in sci-fi terms[37]:

In the way we photographed it, we felt it was science fiction. The landscape. Three guys whose space vehicle, which happened to be a whale boat, crashes on this shore of this other-worldly place. The opening was a black and white prologue which suddenly turns into colour—which in turn is almost monochromatic anyway because all you see are these black figures on a white landscape. Then, they encounter strange creatures, dressed in furs with little bone goggles, speaking other languages. In a sense it's not just Americans—it's earthlings, as we know them, trying to communicate with these other beings.[38]

Watching *The White Dawn* now, it does have a sense of mystery and mysticism, and the sound design alone is enough to make one pine for Kaufman's *ST—TMP*. In terms of performances, *Dawn* doesn't get mentioned much in the context of the Warren Oates *oeuvre*—it was released within months of both Monte Hellman's *Cockfighter* and Sam Peckinpah's *Bring Me the Head of Alfredo Garcia*, and tends to not be as well-remembered as them— but he Oateses up the film something fierce, while an only half-facetious argument could be made that Heath Ledger's screen persona was inspired by Timothy Bottoms' performance as the sensitive Daggett. And when Roddenberry and Isenberg decided to hire Kaufman, it probably didn't hurt that *The White Dawn* began with a Captain's Log.

A Log ... of the Stars!

The Trektennial summer also saw the debut of a magazine which would be deeply associated with Star Trek for years to come, and without which this book would have a considerably shorter bibliography: *Starlog*. Originally intended to be a one-off as was the fashion in those days, the first quarterly issue hit the stands in June. The one-off went unpublished, both because of legal issues surrounding it being titled *Star Trek*, and as editor Kerry O'Quinn later wrote, because many distributors told them "there are a few fanatic Trekkies out there but not enough to justify a national newsstand magazine," which was also among the reasons the movie was having such difficulty getting off the ground.[39]

In "Star Trek: Past, Present, and Future" in *Starlog* #1, David Houston wrote that "the movie (title undecided) is to be written and produced by Gene Roddenberry," and that it was still being proposed as a theatrical release which would itself launch a series of television movies: "Just considering the popularity of the *Planet of the Apes* movies, one *Star Trek* film could beget a whole string of them. Or at least—through being a box-office smash—engender that proposed movie-of-the-week series for television." Of the number of potential storylines, "one possibility involves the early years—when the Enterprise was first built and launched and the original crew, back at the Space Academy, was first selected. Another concerns an outer-space quest for the nature of God. But as of our press time, no final decision has been made."[40]

But for now in the pre–Star Wars era, *Starlog* put Star Trek and its creator on an unshakeable pedestal. Peak Roddenberry Gushing occurred in *Starlog* #2 in September 1976 with Kez Howard's "Two Men in One: Gene Roddenberry," which starts off by calling Roddenberry "an unusual man who can preserve his vision and moral sense—when all about him are losing theirs—and an even rarer man who can develop the skills that allow him to share his vision with others." Howard wrote that Roddenberry received several hundred pieces of mail per month, expressing admiration "for *Star Trek*, for *Genesis II*, for *The Questor Tape*s, for whatever tales of excitement and imagination he is or has been connected with." (Like *Genesis II*, *The Questor Tapes* was a pilot episode which failed to go to series; Roddenberry told the *Monster Times* in 1975 *Questor* had been "shelved when NBC wanted to make many drastic changes," because "it just wouldn't have been the same idea I presented.") A breakdown of the mail wasn't provided, but it's reasonable to assume far more of it was for *Star Trek I* than the little-seen *Genesis II* or *The Questor Tapes*. Howard further described Roddenberry as an "inventive, intelligent, courageous man," and ruminated on how it's easy "both to congratulate the man and to wonder in dismay why there are so few like him." Why aren't you more like Gene Roddenberry, dear reader? It is dismaying to consider that *you* don't have what the caption of a picture of Roddenberry, standing in a macho pose with a tobacco pipe jutting adventurously from his mouth, described as the "love of adventure" which took him "from being a pilot to the Los Angeles police department to producing for television." Howard concluded that the creation of Star Trek required "a man whose inner life was not a battlefield—whose intellect and sense of adventure were not in conflict. It took a renaissance man."[41]

In truth, Roddenberry had made it clear in recent interviews how deeply in conflict he was about Star Trek continuing to define his life and career—but Renaissance man or not, Roddenberry's stock in the pages of *Starlog* had nowhere to go but down with the ascendancy of George Lucas and the film which would become Lucas' own source of lifelong conflict. The first reference to the latter two was a news item a few pages earlier in that same issue which quoted unspecified critics who hailed the film as "everything in science fiction you've always wanted to see on the screen but knew no one would ever put there." So little was known about the film that Mark Hamill was still listed as playing "the film's starring role, Luke Starkiller," and the budget was listed as $8 million, though the cost of the optical effects would inflate the budget to $11 million. The Robert Wise film would eventually have a bigger budget than initially expected due to its effects, but on a much larger scale.[42]

While *Star Wars* may have been hyped as everything a *Starlog* reader always wanted to see in a movie—and those possibly apocryphal critics weren't wrong about that demographic's response to the film—an article about the still-grounded Trek film which followed the gushing Roddenberry profile began by stating that "surely there's no more anxiously awaited event in the sci-fi world than the *Star Trek* movie." Through no fault of *Starlog*'s, much of the information in the article was already out of date by the time the issue hit the stands, a phenomenon hereafter referred to as the Wormhole Effect, in honor of the sequence in the Robert Wise film. For example, it was stated that Roddenberry was currently deciding on a single "skillful and highly experienced screenwriter" in the event that Paramount rejected Roddenberry's latest treatment, and that the $5M movie "will show considerable improvement in the effects department, thanks to Magicam," which had already been dropped by that point. The movie had already been in a constant state of flux, but as the rate of change continued to increase it would prove impossible for *Starlog* to keep up, even when it switched from being published quarterly to eight times a year by issue #4.[43]

As for the news that Roddenberry was looking for a single screenwriter, *Starlog* #2 hit the stands in September 1976, and the team of Chris Bryant and Allan Scott had been announced as the new scriveners in August. To be clear, this is *not* a criticism of *Starlog* or any other outlet for not being able to keep up with such minutiae, considering that the people in charge of the minutiae could barely keep up.

But Paramount was feeling confident, thanks in no small part to the name of the United States' first space shuttle having changed from *Constitution* to *Enterprise*. Though the change occurred after a letter-writing campaign by Star Trek fans, correlation is not causation, and the Associated Press reported that President Gerald Ford had overruled NASA officials because he was "'a little partial to the name *Enterprise*,'" since he'd "served in the Pacific aboard a Navy ship that serviced an earlier aircraft carrier of that name."[44]

But the possibly coincidental naming of certain pieces of 20th century spaceflight technology was enough to convince Paramount to run a full-page ad in the September 21, 1976, *New York Times*, featuring large white text against a background of space with a repeating image of the Federation starship USS *Enterprise* between each paragraph.[45]

> Welcome Aboard.... Space Shuttle Enterprise
> Paramount Pictures and the thousands of loyal fans of Star Trek are happy that the United States of America's new space shuttle has been named after Star Trek's starship, The Enterprise. (It's nice to know that sometimes science fiction becomes science fact.)
> Starship Enterprise will be joining the Space Shuttle Enterprise in its space travels very soon. Early next year, Paramount Pictures begins filming an extraordinary motion picture adventure—STAR TREK.
> Now we can look forward to two great space adventures.[46]

A lovely thought, but the promised "extraordinary motion picture adventure" would be nowhere close to beginning filming early in 1977. There was some cause for optimism when the ad ran, however, as Paramount accepted Bryant and Scott's treatment on October 8, 1976. Later that month, Roddenberry sent the writers a memo assuring them their fifteen-page story "was styled so excitingly that the holes and discrepancies which worried you and us were hardly visible." This was followed by nearly ten pages analyzing those holes and discrepancies.[47]

Starlog #3 hit the stands on November 23, 1976, and it reported that "in a departure from his earlier plans" as discussed in *Starlog* #2, "Gene Roddenberry presently has two English writers developing the screenplay for the proposed full-length *Star Trek* feature movie," with Philip Kaufman as director. Regarding Scott, Bryant, and Kaufman lacking science fiction experience,

Starlog assured the reader that "Roddenberry, serving as the film's active line producer, will have a strong hand in the film's final content." Elsewhere in that issue, a report from the Bi-Centennial-10 Convention held September 3–6, 1976 at the Statler-Hilton Hotel in New York announced that NASA Aerospace scientist Jesco von Puttkamer would be the technical advisor to Roddenberry and Paramount for the movie. At the same convention, William Shatner told the assembled crowd—many of whom were sitting obediently cross-legged at his feet, Instamatic cameras in hand—that his contract for the film included the "potential of *Star Trek* as a series again," but that Leonard Nimoy hadn't yet signed on: "Don't tell anybody, but Paramount Studios has been ripping us off to such an extent that it's humiliating. I've suffered the humiliation graciously, but he has got his back up, and that is really the difference between us. So he's socking it to them a little, and God bless him. He'll be in it."[48]

Exactly when Nimoy would be in it was still anybody's guess. Philip Kaufman spent two weeks around the closing of the year in London, where he worked with Ken Adam and Ralph McQuarrie on designs for *Star Trek— The Motion Picture* and talking with others who'd worked on *2001: A Space Odyssey* and *Star Wars*, while also finding time for a side-trip to Paris to talk with La Cinémathèque Française's Henri Langlois about showing *The White Dawn*. Fresh off of *Star Wars*, McQuarrie's redesign of the *Enterprise* felt much more like the George Lucas film's Star Destroyers than Matt Jeffries' ship from the *Star Trek I*, and it's easy to imagine further accusations of being a cash-in had the designs been used in Philip Kaufman's *ST—TMP*. The concept models built from McQuarrie's design were never intended to be filmed but nevertheless appeared onscreen twice: according to *The Art of Star Trek*, they were photographed in 1991 as part of the Starfleet armada destroyed by the Borg in the *Star Trek: The Next Generation* episode "The Best of Both Worlds, Part II," while the back end of a McQuarrie starboard nacelle is far more visible at 12:26 in the third Star Trek movie as the *Enterprise* approaches its berth in Spacedock. *Star Trek: Discovery* creator Bryan Fuller confirmed that the USS *Discovery* was inspired by the McQuarrie design, so in this writer's headcanon the docked ship in the third Star Trek movie is the ol' *Disco* herself, by now under the command of Captain Michael Burnham.[49]

Enter Eisner

Things were percolating on the television side at Paramount: in mid–October, they sold *Star Trek: Animated* into syndication to WPIX, KTLA in

Los Angeles, WFLD in Chicago, KTVU, WDCA in Washington, D.C., WKBD, WKBS, and WLVI in Boston.[50]

On October 27, 1976, Barry Diller announced that Michael D. Eisner, formerly ABC's Senior Vice President of Prime Time Production and Development, would take over Paramount's newly-created position of President and Chief Operating Officer on November 15. Eisner would be responsible for all divisions other than motion pictures. The biggie was television, a field with which Eisner was intimately familiar after ten years at ABC; the network's president Fred Silverman praised Eisner and his contributions to their current programming success.[51]

It was a programming success Eisner hoped to repeat for Paramount. To that end, in December 1976 Paramount purchased the Hughes Television Network, which was described in the *Los Angeles Times* as not having a set lineup of station like ABC, CBS, and NBC, but rather was "experienced in providing national interconnectedness for special events—mainly sports but occasionally entertainment programs." Most importantly, it included "a contract for the use of the RCA Americom satellite to carry 1,800 hours a year of the network's transmissions." No less significant was that Paramount's new programming could be offered to both independent *and* currently network-affiliated stations.[52]

Eisner and Diller's plan was to begin with a single night of programming per week and add more over time, but it was Paramount's Chief Financial Officer Arthur Barron who had the killer hook: kicking off with a new one-hour version of their brand-name franchise, Star Trek. Exactly when Barron made this suggestion is unclear, but work continued apace on Kaufman's *ST—TMP* as the machinations continued to machinate behind the scenes.[53]

1977: The Battle of the Binary Star Treks

Captain Kirk Almost Meets John Galt

Paramount was still selling *Star Trek: Animated* in the first post–Trektennial year, and by late January the series was being broadcast in 30 markets. Roddenberry spent much of that month touring his *World of Star Trek* show, and during an appearance at the Houston Coliseum he told the audience that the naming of the Space Shuttle *Enterprise* was not his idea, nor did he think it was a good one: "I thought that Earth's first space ship should have a generic Earth name, not that it should be specifically United States, and certainly not a military name." A more immediate concern was that the movie still didn't have a story. He busted out his favorite irradiated straw-reptile when told the several thousand people in the Coliseum, "we found it was harder to fit a story to a large-screen movie when we already have the characters and all of the conditions, and have to fit a story to them, than if we had done an original. I could have had a movie out by now if I had been willing to settle for something like 'Captain Kirk Meets Godzilla.'"[1]

It is unlikely that even the most clueless of studio executives had suggested such a thing—just licensing the character from Toho would surely have been prohibitive—but the Bold Visionary Surrounded by Idiots was Roddenberry's self-perpetuating mythology, and few assembled that night would have known that his own rejected idea had been Captain Kirk meeting a 'zilla-free God. In the November/December 1976 *Star Trektennial News*, Susan Sackett wrote that Bantam Books was planning to publish Roddenberry's novelization of his rejected *Star Trek II* script "sometime next year," and there was a "good chance" that Chris Bryant and Allan Scott's script would be novelized. Neither book came to pass.[2]

Roddenberry assured the assembled Houston masses that the *Enterprise*'s basic configuration would remain the same, but since science had "jumped ahead ten years in time from when we originally started, he could promise a more sophisticated *Enterprise*, and are seeking the cooperation of every scientific lab in the country to be sure it is absolutely right." This was another exaggeration—*every* scientific lab in the country would be a long shot at best, even with the hedged bet of simply "seeking their cooperation"— while the obvious yet unasked question was, "absolutely right" compared to *what*? Modern science had only recently managed to put humans on the moon, let alone hundreds of people on a ship capable of lasting for years and traveling faster than light, propelled by inventions as yet unimagined. Even setting aside that everything was going to be limited to what they could afford to put on screen, the notion that the film could possibly get 23rd spaceflight technology "absolutely right" was Roddenberry hyperbole at its most hyper.[3]

Though the film was nowhere close to being made, the January 1977 *A Piece of the Action* reported via Susan Sackett that Stephen Whitfield, credited co-author of the 1968 *The Making of Star Trek*, was now working on *The Making of Star Trek II*. By the end of the year, in the November/December 1977 *Star Trektennial News*—which would be Sackett's final issue as editor—she announced the book would be titled *The Remaking of Star Trek*, that she would write it herself, as she did the eventual *The Making of Star Trek—The Motion Picture*, notwithstanding Roddenberry's grabby co-credit.[4]

Speaking to Jerry Isenberg in January 1977 for an interview which would eventually run in the March/April *Star Trektennial News*, Sackett asked if one the difficulties in getting the movie made was that "no television show has ever successfully been translated to a motion picture format." Isenberg did not reply, "no, because television shows have been made into successful movies before," but instead agreed that the not-actually-unprecedented nature of the project was a big problem, and then gave his take on why the studio had yet to accept any of the story ideas so far.[5]

> What has stopped the movie is that every time you've gotten a good story, it looked a lot like the television series, and the studio sort of said, "Tell why should we put × millions of dollars into something that looks like a big episode?" So what we have had to do is come up with a story that is STAR TREK and doesn't look like a television episode of STAR TREK.[6]

It was the elemental conundrum which the eventual Trek movies would never entirely escape. As I write this, the Star Wars movies are caught in a wicket no less sticky: they're either accused of being too much like the original films (*The Force Awakens*) or not enough (*The Last Jedi*), whereas the ones that don't feel like Star Wars at all yet have lots of ships blowing up tend to be applauded most by young males (*Rogue One*). For that matter, it's an issue the prequel series *Star Trek: Discovery* would wrestle with in its first season.

Isenberg highly doubted Star Trek would return to television if the movie was successful, since "the STAR TREK property is probably the best property that lends itself to sequels that I've ever seen," and that he "would like to see, by the time I'm an old man, 10, 12 STAR TREK movies out there, maybe 15 STAR TREK movies, every year or two." Mr. Isenberg is still with us in 2018, and setting aside that he had nothing to do with the thirteen movies that have come out thus far, his wish came true.[7]

In the January/February 1977 *Star Trektennial News*, Sackett wrote that while "no one has yet been officially signed to date," they anticipated "getting all the original crew back," and "it seems likely that production will begin in the early summer of 1977." More significantly, this was when she announced that the title, "according to the latest here at Paramount, is 'STAR TREK—THE MOTION PICTURE.'" One-third of the script had been written to date, and Bryant and Scott hoped to have it finished by January. In addition to watching *Star Trek I* reruns every night and reading the scripts as well as fan reference works as such as Bjo Trimble's *Star Trek Concordance*, they were immersing themselves in non–Trek science fiction.[8]

> Their reading list is as valuable to them as it is impressive: "Science Fiction Today and Tomorrow"—an anthology; "The Starmaker" by Olaf Stapledon; "Childhood's End" by A. C. Clarke; "The Third Eye" by T. Lobsang Rampa; "The Morning of the Magicians" by Louis Pauwels and Jacques Bergier; "The Virtue of Selfishness" by Ayn Rand; "The Black Cloud" by Fred Hoyle; the Edgar Rice Burroughs "Mars" series, plus others too numerous to mention.[9]

Scott would later tell *Starlog* that while Burrough's *Mars* books were "close to the feeling we wanted to achieve—in a certain part of the story," Stapledon's *The Starmaker* was "the book that stands out the most," being "a remarkable piece of imagination." (During production of "The Cage" a decade prior, writer Samuel Peeples had loaned Roddenberry a copy of Olaf Stapledon's *Last and First Men*, since future history was a particular interest of Roddenberry's.) However, if Ayn Rand's *The Virtue of Selfishness* made the cut of books worth mentioning, one can't help but wonder what some of those too-numerous-to-mention titles might have included, let alone how Rand's collection of objectivist essays could possibly fit into Roddenberry's utopian vision. Then again, philosophical consistency was never his strong suit.[10]

Since Bryant and Scott were writing a screenplay, movies were also screened:

> Motion picture research included screenings of "2001-A Space Odyssey"; "Forbidden Planet"; "Silent Running"; "The Day the Earth Stood Still"; "Solaris"; "Futureworld"; "Logan's Run"; "When Worlds Collide"; "The Man Who Fell to Earth"; "The Shape of Things to Come"; "The Time Machine," and "Village of the Damned." (Phil Kaufman, our director, has read and viewed all of the above too, and according to Chris Bryant, "His apartment is littered with sci-fi.")[11]

It's possible that one of the factors resulting in the collapse of the Bryant and Scott script was the mixed messages sent by this very research. It's difficult to find films that vary in tone more than *The Man Who Fell to Earth* and *Things to Come*—presumably the 1936 William Cameron Menzies film, judging from Sackett's use of the full title of the H.G. Wells source novel—let alone both *Futureworld* and the inspirational-for-Kaufman *Solaris*. Gene Roddenberry would use this same "watch all the science fiction things" approach a decade later during the development phase of *Star Trek: The Next Generation*, which may have factored into the unevenness of that show's inaugural seasons.[12]

Scott also told Sackett that between Gene Roddenberry and Philip Kaufman, the latter of whom he described as "stimulating and deeply committed to the kind of movie we think STAR TREK fans (and non-fans, if there are any) will want to see," he and Bryant received "enough input for 79 full-length movies. So let's hope the first one works!" This large degree of input from multiple sources was likely compounded by another factor, as a "source close to the production" described to Preston Neal Jones as he was researching his *Cinefantastique* article about the Robert Wise film, though it wouldn't be printed until *Return to Tomorrow* in 2014: "Paramount gave control of the film to Jerry Isenberg, Gene Roddenberry and Philip Kaufman—all simultaneously, all without notifying the others that anyone else had control. So, all three of them were walking around like they were in charge of the movie, and, in the confusion that resulted, nobody had control of the movie."[13]

Chris Bryant (above) and Allan Scott (below) working on the script for *Star Trek—The Motion Picture* at Paramount in 1976. On the wall behind Scott is a "Welcome Aboard ... Space Shuttle Enterprise" ad from the September 21, 1976, *New York Times*. No pressure! Originally printed in *Star Trektennial News* no. 19, January/February 1977 (Susan Sackett).

Of Cygnans and Spiders; Kaufman Keelhauled

Space-Con 3 was held on February 11–13, 1977 at the San Francisco Civic Auditorium. The Master of Ceremonies was Bob Wilkins, whose special *The Star Trek Dream* had aired on September 24, 1975, and its followup *Star Trek: The Superstars—The Superfans* more recently on January 30, 1977. Susan Sackett appeared at Space-Con 3 on Saturday along with screenwriters Allan Scott and Chris Bryant and director Philip Kaufman to discuss *Star Trek— The Motion Picture*, though only Sackett's name was promoted in the marketing due to nobody knowing who the other three people were.[14]

A convention report in the fanzine *Bellerophon* described "the Script Writers—whatever their names are" as standing on the stage "with their hearts on their sleeves looking quite embarrassed as they tried to satisfy rampant curiosities without revealing a damn thing about the plot of the film." That same person also used the word Trekkie, then added parenthetically that they meant Trekkie "in the worst sense of the word."[15]

Looking back on it in 1993, Kaufman recalled that the assembled fans were not excited by his presence.

> I was at this gathering, a kind of Trekkie convention, and to introduce me they "beamed me down to the stage," using all this sparkling dust to create the effect. The audience was dressed up as characters from the show: You know, feelers on their heads, things like that. And they introduced me as the man who would direct the first "Star Trek" movie. One of the Trekkies said to a friend—my wife was sitting next to them so she heard it—"Oh, God, couldn't they have gotten somebody better?"[16]

It may have been Kaufman's first Trek convention, but it wasn't Bryant's. He'd attended the Puget Sound Star Trekkers Convention II held on January 29–30, 1977 at the Olympic Hotel in Seattle. There Bryant ran into Harlan Ellison, who later recalled Bryant saying, "you're Harlan Ellison and I can see that you're a very wise man—because you were smart enough not to get involved" with the Trek movie. "Yeah," Ellison replied. "I don't envy you the job."[17]

An only slightly more enviable job on the eternally troubled production than that of its writer was that of production manager, and Terry Carr signed on in late February, fresh off Dino DeLaurentiis' *King Kong*. By the end of the month, Paramount was spending $7,000 a week in payroll to people other than Bryant and Scott, who fulfilled their contractual obligation to deliver a first-draft script for *ST—TMP* on March 1. Though their script had been rejected by the time of their going-away party on March 18 in the rapidly expanding Star Trek offices in Paramount's Building E, by all accounts spirits were high. It was understood from the beginning that theirs would not be the final draft, hence Bryant and Scott leaving behind a bottle of Anacin with a note reading, "To the writer: Take no more than 48 a day. The dosage may be increased if the director's in town." That next writer would be the director, Philip Kaufman.[18]

Neither Bryant and Scott's full treatment nor script have received a legitimate release—nor are they stored in the Margaret Herrick Library, to this writer's disappointment—but Susan Sackett gave a detailed summary of their story in *The Making of Star Trek—The Motion Picture*. Briefly, while the Enterprise is rescuing the survivors of a doomed Federation ship, Kirk gets a zap to his head which results in him stealing a shuttle and disappearing into an invisible planet. Spock resigns from Starfleet, and the refitted Enterprise gets a new Captain named Gregory Westlake. Returning to the place where Kirk disappeared, they discover a planet which appears to be the home of the Titans, "a lost race with super technology." This occasionally-invisible planet has also been discovered by the Klingons, and is on the verge of falling into a black hole. With the help of a reluctant Spock, the *Enterprise* finds a regressed, wild-man Kirk on the surface, and that the Titans have been replaced by the nasty Cygnans, who board the ship. The *Enterprise* then heads into the black hole to destroy the Cygnans (though whether under the command of Kirk or Westlake is unclear), and the ship re-emerges from the black hole at Earth at the Dawn of Man, whereupon they realize that the *Enterprise* crew had been the Titans. (Meaning the Titans' mysterious, partially-invisible planet had been Earth all along?)[19]

Sackett described the problem with the script as being that it "had received input from so many people—Jerry Isenberg, Phil Kaufman, Gene Roddenberry, as well as the two writers—that it bore little resemblance to the original story that had been approved back in October. It was a script by committee, and therein lay its trouble."[20]

Though she would continue writing *Star Trektennial News* for a few more issues, Sackett began a column called "Star Trek Report" in *Starlog* #6, which went on sale on April 19, 1977. *Starlog*'s editors described Sackett's column as a response to "the constant requests for updated information on the *Star Trek* movie and other Trekfan data." In addition to featuring possibly the first appearance of the title *Star Trek—The Motion Picture* in a traditionally-distributed publication, the frequently asked questions Sackett answered in the inaugural column were "Who Is Writing the Movie?" (Bryant and Scott); "Has Anyone in The Cast Been Signed?" (not yet, though "there are parts being written for two new leads, a male and a female, and we will have major motion picture stars for these new characters"); "When Will Production Begin?" (assuming Paramount approved Bryant and Scott's March 1 script, shooting would start in August 1977 with a planned release date of July 4,

1978); "Why Is It Taking So Long to Get This Film Going?" (the primary reason being that "the successful translation of a television show to the motion picture screen has never been accomplished," and though many TV shows had been based on movies, "the reverse process is something unique to the industry"); and "Will There Be Many Changes in The Enterprise Sets?" ("the exterior will be the same familiar Enterprise," she exaggerated, while adding that the interiors would be bigger and "greatly updated to reflect new scientific concepts," and that in spite of the popularity of Franz Joseph's *Star Fleet Technical Manual*, "don't look for any ships of the Dreadnought Class in the film").[21]

In an April 28 *Los Angeles Times* article by Ronald Soble which opened with the astonishingly condescending admonition to "simmer down, Trekkies," Bryant said their script was rushed at the end due to an unrealized threat of a writer's strike, while Isenberg agreed that "the biggest problem with the script is the second half." (The second half of the script would also prove to be problematic during the production of the Robert Wise film, largely due to that half not existing.) For his part, Roddenberry told Soble that the script would have been produced immediately had it been "just another sci-fi film," but "capturing the flavor of the Star Trek characters and the type of plots that would work around them takes precision writing that may have to go through several revisions with different sets of writers." In other words, according to Roddenberry, the way to fix the script's problems would be to rewrite it by committee.[22]

On the verge of closing a deal that week for "a major rewrite" of the script by a committee-of-one in the form of director Philip Kaufman, Isenberg told Soble he was planning to bring in "a whole design and special effects crew" in June, and a budget would be based on their plans. Paramount would then have until September 20, 1977, to greenlight the film, and if so, production would begin in November or December in hopes of a Christmas 1978 release. And while it wouldn't be possible to give an exact budget until the designs were made and the contracts were signed—Nimoy's commitment to perform on Broadway in *Equus* that fall was cited as a concern—Isenberg estimated that "it will run from $8.5 to $10 million," marking the first moment the (proposed) budget entered the double-digit range. The whole business of cameos by international stars had long since been dropped, but Kaufman's film may have had at least one international star in a non-cameo role: Toshiro Mifune as the primary Klingon antagonist. Of all the great what-ifs of the Kaufman *ST—TMP*, that may well be the greatest.[23]

* * *

Philip Kaufman has long been reluctant to discuss his script, and not without cause. In the halcyon days of January 1977, he told Judy Stone of the *San Francisco Chronicle* that it was being kept secret because "so many people all over the world are so passionately curious about it," while he told the UK magazine *Starburst* in 1979 that he still didn't want to go too much into it "because they're going to rip it off, and I believe that I still own that story." Kaufman had every reason to be gun-shy about revealing his ideas, especially by 1979: when his film *The Wanderers* was announced as the first release from Orion Pictures, it was beat into the theaters by a rush of other films about gangs—none of which had been announced prior to *The Wanderers*—including Walter Hill's cult classic *The Warriors,* and a less-well-remembered Robby Benson vehicle called *Walk Proud*. The latter was directed by Robert Collins, who has something else in common with Philip Kaufman beyond directing a 1979 film about gangs: he had the first Star Trek movie yanked out from under him when Paramount changed their mind about the format.[24]

Asked by *Starburst* for a hint regarding a prior statement that his script was "largely built around Spock," Kaufman revealed a bit more detail[25]:

> Well, it was a mystery. An *Enterprise* mystery—the crew of the *Enterprise* had disappeared and only Spock was left. Only Spock had a memory hidden deep in his mind as to what had gone wrong. Spock filled with shame. Returns to Vulcan. Large Vulcan sequences. A woman arrives who is going to explore his mind and take him on an adventure through time and space, to beginnings and endings. It was really a love story exploring Spock's human and in-human sides.[26]

But not a love story lacking in spectacle. By the time he was working on his version of the story, plans were already being made to shoot in London on Pinewood's James Bond stages. There, Bond production designer Ken Adam was working on the sets, Ralph McQuarrie had moved to London in February 1977 to work with Adam, and Kaufman himself planned to move to London in mid–June, where he would take full advantage of Adam and McQuarrie's talents.[27]

> The opening shot, for example, was going to duplicate the original bridge of the Enterprise, which you only saw one side of on television. We were finally showing you the reverse of that—Kirk walking from off-camera and swinging around and showing you this eleven-story ship that was beneath them, with 430 people working. Hence the big stage at Pinewood. We needed that to construct something of the awesomeness of that spectacle.[28]

Speaking to Preston Neal Jones in the months following the release of the Robert Wise film, Jon Povill described Kaufman's take as being "in a sense, based on the Bryant and Scott script" but still not Star Trek[29]:

[Kafuman] had Kirk and the crew battling these ugly creatures that zap you and rob the serotonin out of your brain and take your intellectual abilities. The idea was that these creatures were the inheritors of this incredible Foundation Three technology. This planet had been the home of the titans with capacities far beyond anything human—like V'Ger's planet in the final script we did shoot, in a sense. After the race of titans had died of attrition, these people had come and taken over the planet but had become corrupted by its tremendous power. They were huge, ugly, spider-like things, and, in the Kaufman version, eventually Kirk stabs them with a sword from underneath, and this is how he gets rid of them. As you can gather from this, Star Trek was not there at all.[30]

Perhaps not, but in the much-loved second film Kirk would go on to vaporize the defenseless Ceti Eel the moment it left Chekov's ear, which isn't very Star Trek either. In any event, Kaufman's script was officially rejected by Gene Roddenberry and Paramount for not being Star Trek on May 8, 1977, but there were other forces at work. As Kaufman told *Starburst* in 1979[31]:

There was a new little unit of guys who have subsequently disappeared from the earth, known as The Fourth Network boys. They had arrived at Paramount and the guys that were running Paramount had come out of television themselves, and so they were interested in this idea of creating, fundamentally, an entire new American TV network. They looked around, looked high and low, for a scheme to start this new network off on a high level. They spotted this program that was doing so well in syndication reruns.

And at some high level meeting—another pow-wow, after I'd been given the go—a battle raged between the feature film people at Paramount and the Fourth Network boys. And the Fourth Network boys walked off with Star Trek... with the bleeding head of Star Trek. Or whatever part of it was bleeding.[32]

Kaufman had just pulled an all-nighter to solve certain story elements that had been troubling him when he received the call that the film was off. He went to the studio and argued that he'd seen footage from his friend George Lucas' upcoming movie and it was going to be a very big deal, but Paramount brushed him off. Isenberg wrote a memo which correctly predicted that *Star Wars* was going to be at least as big as *Jaws*, but the Mountain's counterargument was that no science fiction film had ever grossed more than *2001: A Space Odyssey*'s box office of $19 million, and therefore *ST—TMP* wasn't worth the risk.[33]

Leonard Nimoy found out about the cancellation of the Kaufman film when he called Jerry Isenberg on or around May 11, 1977, just before Nimoy left for New York to begin rehearsal on *Equus*. As he later told the Star Trek America convention in September[34]:

That was the day on which he told me that Paramount had decided not to go ahead with the movie. I was shocked. I really felt that it was on the track that it was going to work and was looking forward to being involved with it. I asked him why, and he told me at that time, that as far as he could see, the intention was to go to a series instead. So be it.[35]

The Fourth Network Awakens

Three months after Paramount purchased the Hughes Television Network, they were ready to make it public: on March 30, 1977, they announced they would use those facilities to distribute original programming which, per the April 1 *Los Angeles Times*, "probably will compete in prime against ABC, CBS and NBC." Eisner was coy about what form that programming would take, other than that it would be "of the first-class, highest entertainment programming quality that the audience has grown to accept from a first-class program service," and that "it will not be inexpensive, game show, talk show, access show kind of material." Acknowledging that Paramount was still "six to eight weeks away" from getting specific about what that first-class, high-quality programming would be, he promised that "I think you will find that the commitment of dollars as well as the commitment of time and energy will make the venture and the importance of the venture evident to everybody." Certainly, nothing promises first-class quality like using the words "commitment" and "venture" twice each in the same sentence, for that is a promise of quality of which, as classes go, is in the first.[36]

Two significant things happened on May 25, 1977, which was a day shy of being almost exactly eight weeks after Paramount's Hughes announcement. The first, with which the date will forever be associated, was the release of George Lucas' *Star Wars*. The other was a *Los Angeles Times* article by Lee Grant titled "Trek from TV to Movie to TV," which in addition to having a far less snotty tone than her colleague Soble's "simmer down, Trekkies" article the month before, announced that "Paramount was now committed to a weekly Star Trek TV show that will be distributed on a syndicated basis." In truth, the May 24 *Daily Variety* had the scoop that on May 23 Paramount's Vice President and overall television poobah Richard Frank had disclosed the Mountain's intention to pour $35M into three hours of programming one night a week which would include a new Star Trek series, but the *Times* was read by a lot more non-industry people than *Variety, Daily* or otherwise. Though the influence of the George Lucas film on the eventual production of the Robert Wise film has been blown out of proportion, that the most widely-read announcement that Star Trek would not be a movie came out on the same day *Star Wars* was released is still too delicious a syzygy not to acknowledge. (So, consider it acknowledged.)[37]

Michael Eisner told the *Times* that the decision against making a feature film came about because "we felt Star Trek lended itself better to 52 hours a year of entertainment rather than one two-hour movie." As was his tendency, Roddenberry burned the bridge before it was built, telling the *Times* that the Paramount suits "don't really care about Star Trek." He didn't care either, but they'd still better invite him back over that bridge: "They want formula TV and don't understand what Star Trek really is all about. They think anybody can come in and make it. When they decide to do it properly, I'm available. In the meantime, I don't want to have it dominate my life. There are other things."[38]

It goes to show how much things were in flux that even though his script had been roundly rejected and it was known Paramount was planning to produce a series instead of a movie, Philip Kaufman was still able to get a meeting with Paramount on Friday, June 3 to argue against the canning of his movie. *Star Wars* was a genuine phenomenon by that day, on the verge of grossing $5.2M and showing no signs of slowing down, though at the meeting Kaufman pointed out that while they could both be classified as a "space opera," Trek had a "different orientation." As he told the *Chronicle*, Star Trek "was more tied in with scientific projections. It was much more of an adult show. The characters were more involved with each other, and it had a more dramatic situation. We were arriving at a powerful, provocative, mind-bending kind of thing." The argument did not change Eisner's mind, even though by Kaufman's estimation Paramount had already spent somewhere in the neighborhood of a half-million on the movie.[39]

New Hollywood credibility was the least of the Bluhdorn-led Paramount's concerns at this point, but one of the great shames of Kaufman being expelled from Star Trek was his association with George Lucas and Steven Spielberg, who first had huge hits with non-sci-fi films but were now about to put their stamp on the genre for good. Kaufman's friendship with both men was a known quantity; in her *San Francisco Chronicle* profile of Kaufman on January 7, Judy Stone wrote that "when Lucas, Kaufman, and Steven Spielberg, who is completing 'Close Encounters of the Third Kind,' get together, they offer a model for interplanetary deportment as they genially swap information on each other's space probes."[40]

Though Michael Eisner said Paramount was committed to a new Star Trek series, that had been all the way back on May 25, a day nobody realized that anything had changed. On June 15, by which time it was clear that everything had changed, *Variety* reported that in addition to dropping the movie, Paramount "may also scuttle an alternate plan of doing a new TV series," though "Trekkies hope" that *Star Wars* "may change that thinking." Or maybe they wouldn't scuttle it, since another article in that same issue confirmed that when Paramount's "one-night network" began in April 1978, "the programming would open with a revival of the sci-fi series, 'Star Trek' (especially appropriate with the current success of the feature film, 'Star Wars')."[41]

Most things don't happen at all, but when they do, they all happen at once: on June 17, 1977—the end of the week that Kaufman had originally planned to move to London to work on *ST—TMP*—Susan Sackett read a Paramount press release at Space-Con 4 at the Los Angeles Convention Center which confirmed that not only would the new series definitely for sure go into production that fall f'reals, but "negotiations have been concluded between Gene Roddenberry and Paramount Television for his services as executive producer of the new Star Trek series." (Writing about Space-Con 4 in *Starlog* #9, David Houston noted that "*Star Trek* has dominated every con STARLOG has attended, but this time, *Star Wars* merchandise won hands down and *Star Wars* events came in a fairly close second.")[42]

Marking a level of hyperbole which would remain at a fever pitch until the critical and popular reaction to the Robert Wise film deflated it hard, the press release quoted Paramount President Gary Nardino that the Mountain felt "we are making television history with this renaissance of the Star Trek series," which was further described as "perhaps the most legendary of all television series." Paramount's Vice President Richard Frank also described the series which would have been known as *Star Trek II* had it been produced as not only "the foundation for the new Paramount Television Service"—that is, a fourth network to compete with ABC, NBC, and CBS—but as a representation of "our commitment to provide fresh programming to a discerning viewing public." All things on the mycelial network are connected: in early May 1977, William Shatner had starred in the television miniseries *Testimony of Two Men*—based on the novel by the literary giant Harold Robbins—itself a failed attempt by Universal to launch a fourth television network called Operation Prime Time. It had been partially developed by Frank while he was the President and General Manager of KCOP, before being hired by Paramount to develop *their* new programming service in March.[43]

Thanks to the Wormhole Effect, information and promotional material continued to appear for the Kaufman film even after it had been officially shuttered. Going on sale the day before Kaufman's final attempt to convince Paramount to make his version of *Star Trek—The Motion Picture*, *Starlog* #7 featured a promo shot of a TIE Fighter shooting at an X-Wing on the cover, and the headline promised a "Preview of the Spectacular New Science Fiction Movie: STAR WARS." It was now a preview of a film which had been released eight days earlier and had almost certainly been seen at least once if not twice by the magazine's core audience, while Sackett's "Star Trek Report" was about the Kaufman film and included an interview with Allan Scott and thus was already outdated. Again, this is not a criticism of anyone involved; it was simply not possible for the publishing apparatus of the time to keep up with the constant changes, nor was it unreasonable of *Starlog*'s editors to hope the information available by the print deadline wouldn't be out of date by the time the issue hits the streets.[44]

Here We Are Now, Entertain Us the Way We Tell You To

Also published around that time was issue #8 of *Trek: The Magazine for Star Trek Fans*, which included the results of a poll from issue #7. The editors were vague about the exact number of responses, but they did admit to being surprised "when literally hundreds of responses to our poll began pouring in!" so we can generously deduce the number was at least in the upper three-digit range. *Trek*'s editors promised those literally hundreds of readers who took the time to respond that "since a new TV series is now in preparation, the results are being forwarded to Gene Roddenberry and his staff to help them implement any changes and refinements in the forthcoming shows." Fans never change, as this sort of "If we tell the creators what we want then they will make it happen because it's what we want" thinking only became more pronounced in later decades. (As a matter of fact, I *do* go into no small amount of detail about it in my previous book *Ponyville Confidential*, thank you for asking!) In both the original June 1977 article and its reprint in the book *The Best of Trek* in April 1978, the *Trek* editors trumpet the self-proclaimed diversity of the fans, calling themselves "such a diverse lot" and calling said diversity "the most outstanding characteristic of Star Trek fandom," but even with foreknowledge of their outstanding diversity, "some of the answers still surprised and delighted us."[45]

Not surprising was "The City on the Edge of Forever" being the most popular *Star Trek I* episode, a mantle it holds to this day. More surprising to modern eyes is "The Trouble with Tribbles" coming in fifth after "Amok Time," "Journey to Babel," and "The Menagerie." "Tribbles" did beat out "Shore Leave," "Balance of Terror," "The Enemy Within"—the only episode on the list to feature an attempted rape onscreen, so that's something—"The Naked Time," and "Mirror, Mirror." Notable for its absence is "Space Seed," considering the rapturous, "this is what we were waiting for all along!" response to the Nicholas Meyer film.[46]

While the editors admitted to being surprised that neither Uhura nor Sulu received any votes for favorite Star Trek character, they did not point out that the two major characters ignored by the totally-diverse fanbase were not white, though they did wonder, "where were all the 'Uhura for Captain' button wearers?" Where, indeed. It should be noted that Yeoman Janice Rand, who only appeared in five episodes—and was only raped or otherwise molested in two of those, not that anyone's keeping track of such things—tied with Scotty and Chekov for 2% of the vote.[47]

Another significant question was the favorite villain. Most popular was Harry Mudd from "Mudd's Women," "I, Mudd," and the *Star Trek: Animated* episode "Mudd's Passion" with 25% of the vote. The Romulan Commander from "Balance of Terror" came in second with 14% and Trelane from "The Squire of Gothos" third with 11%, and the Klingons Kor and Kang from "Errand of Mercy" and "The Day of the Dove" respectively at 7%. The remaining 34% "was just about equally divided between the Horta, the Keeper, Koloth, Khan, the Theleb, Dr. Simon Adams from 'Dagger of the Mind,' and the Romulans and Klingons in general." Khan as a character didn't make much of an impression on the fans, though the actor fared a little better: Ricardo Montalban received 10% of the vote for male guest star, after Mark Lenard (35%), William Campbell (13%), and a tie between Roger C. Carmel and William Windom (11%).[48]

Looking forward, 80% of the respondents said "nay" to whether the *Star Trek: Animated* characters Arex and M'Ress should be included in the first Star Trek movie, resulting in "the only question on the poll to which there was a clear and resounding mandate." At the time the poll was released in early 1977, it was unclear to the fans (and everybody else) whether Trek would return as a movie, television series, or both, hence the next question not referring to a movie but a series: "When Star Trek returns, should the series take up where it left off, or should the intervening years be accounted for?" Only 54% of the respondents wanted the intervening years accounted for, while "most fans simply stated that they just wanted the show back on the air and couldn't care less when it began." To the question "Do you think that the regular characters should die, marry, or otherwise undergo major changes?" 57% were against any changes taking place, though "almost every vote—regardless of whether the voter was in favor of change or not—said that they definitely did not want to see any of the major characters die." And that was that! At least until a major character died in a film which the fans would call the greatest Star Trek movie ever. (There is no evidence that *Butch Cassidy and the Sundance Kid* screenwriter William Goldman was ever under consideration to write the first Star Trek movie, but he would have been perfect, if only because his famous axiom about Hollywood sums up the search for a story: Nobody Knows Anything.)[49]

Whatever else happened in the first Star Trek movie, the editor made one thing perfectly clear: "A warning of sorts to Gene Roddenberry: You had better not make the Star Trek movie without William Shatner as Kirk and Leonard Nimoy as Spock. If you do, then you will lose about half your audience!" Grrr! The question of whether the characters should change at all was addressed in a slightly more measured, if unrealistic, way[50]:

> When discussing at what point in "Star Trek time" the series should be picked up, things are always likely to become hot and heavy. Fans are about evenly split on this question, and good arguments are available to each faction. And this question logically ties in with whether or not there should be major changes in characters.
>
> If the time passage (and the age differences in the actors) is accounted for, then there would and should be changes. Ten years is a very long time, and it would be absurd to assume that the entire crew remained exactly as they were.
>
> No less an authority than Gene Roddenberry himself has advocated accounting for the passage of time in his original script for the movie. And there were major changes in each and every character in that screenplay.
>
> However, if the time difference is written into a new series format, it very well could destroy the delicate balance and chemistry of personalities which made Star Trek so successful. This is also an excellent argument for not having the characters change in any major way.[51]

Fans never change: one of the major backlashes against 2017's *The Last Jedi* was that the character of Luke Skywalker had changed too much since his last appearance in 1983's *Return of the Jedi*, having aged and become a hermit as a means of dealing with the traumas he'd experienced over the decades. That Luke didn't immediately return to his badass lightsaber-wielding ways in *The Last Jedi* was met with anger and disappointment by fans who were bored by such namby-pamby things like "character development" or "the passage of time." Again, fans want things the way they remember them—but not too much like they remember them.

The *Trek* editors reiterated that they sent the results of the poll to Roddenberry, and their recommendations were thus:

1. Use stories which are superbly well written, containing elements of drama, action, humor, and a subtle message.

2. Feature Kirk and Spock prominently, but use the extraordinary chemistry between the regulars to full advantage.

3. Mark Lenard, Roger C. Carmel, Joan Collins, and Jane Wyatt should be featured prominently.

4. Change the ship's equipment only to make it more believable and efficient.

5. Use yourself and D.C. Fontana to fullest advantage on the scripts.
6. Do not have Arex and M'Ress in the movie.
7. Have the intervening years accounted for, but have no major changes in the regulars.
8. Avoid any resemblance at all to "The Children Shall Lead."[52]

It speaks to the entitlement on display that they could have believed that these recommendations, based on "literally hundreds" of responses, would be seen as useful or influential. Did they think that it wouldn't have occurred to Roddenberry to use "superbly well written" stories until he saw the recommendations? (Dorothy Fontana was not involved with the eventual Robert Wise film, nor was she available to work on the *Star Trek II* series, as she was under contract to the *Logan's Run* series at the time.) Or that it would be remotely possible to feature all four of those guest stars "prominently?" Coincidental to this poll, Mark Lenard and Jane Wyatt would appear in the films—Lenard in the first as a Klingon and then as Spock's father Sarek in the third and fourth, while Wyatt had an all-too-brief cameo in the fourth as Spock's mother Amanda. More baffling is the demand to feature Joan Collins prominently, considering her character died in 1930s New York in "The City on the Edge of Forever."[53]

But, like the heart, fans want what they want.

Shatner Says "See Ya Never!"

What William Shatner wanted was not worlds different: for Paramount to, as the saying more or less goes, either defecate or vacate the receptacle. A week and a half after the July 15, 1976, start date came and went, Shatner was interviewed by Bob Wilkins at a March of Dimes tennis tournament. It wouldn't air until *Star Trek: The Superstars—The Superfans* on January 30, 1977, by which point everything had changed, but at that moment in time—shortly before Isenberg took over the project—Shatner said the movie was a definite go: "It's going to be made. I've signed a contract, I've been partially even paid, and when a studio partially pays you, they put their film where their money is. So it's going to be made in the winter … the exact date hasn't been established because the exact script hasn't been written. Which comes as shock to you and to me, but they had to wait until they signed the cast members, which they have done," with the exception of Leonard Nimoy. But with or without Nimoy, "At this moment, there's no question that the film will be made."[54]

Asked what he thought would happen to the "Star Trek cult" when the for-sure-to-happen movie was made, Shatner prefaced his response by disclaiming that his guess was no more or less valid than anyone else's, then guessed that "if the movie is successful, which I think depends on whether it's good, it will start another whole movement, and it may result in a series of movies like the James Bond movies, which is a possibility if it's really good box office, if it really hits. If it's a mediocre hit, it then might become another [television] series. If it's a failure, everybody will tuck it away." Wilkins observed that the timing was right, what with *Logan's Run* and *Futureworld* in the theaters, though that spate of science fiction movies gave Shatner pause: "My fear is that we won't catch it at its tail end." Little did they know; three weeks earlier, publicist Charles Lippincott had presented a promotional slide show at Westercon for *Star Wars*, which was still filming in England at the time of this interview.[55]

Bob Wilkins interviewed Shatner again nearly a year later on June 18, 1977—the day it was announced that *Star Trek II* would be the flagship of the Paramount Television Service—but Shatner's faith was considerably diminished thanks in no small part to *Star Wars* having been made first. Describing himself as a fan of *Star Trek I*, he said he would have liked to have seen a movie: "Well, unfortunately, the studio Paramount couldn't get their act together fast enough, so the movie has been canceled—and with the advent of *Star Wars* taking off in America to such a degree, we must hear shots ringing out every so often as you pass by Paramount Studios." Asked if he felt that the first Trek movie could have found the success currently being enjoyed by Lucas' film, Shatner had thoughts.[56]

> No question! *Star Wars*, as entertaining as it is and as marvelous fun as it is, is just that—it's just fun, it's just special effects, it's cartoon time! We could have had, if *Star Trek* had come out a year ago, if they'd started work on it a year ago and come out now, we could have had equally good special effects. Special effects is an art, but there are people who do that kind of thing, and we would have come up with a better story, I think, and characters. So, *Star Trek* could have been *Star Wars*. Now, they're saying it's going to be a television series to be put on what Paramount Studios is calling their fourth network.[57]

In addition to being uncertain about the potential success of a fourth network, including namechecking his own non-network-launching *Testimony of Two Men*, Shatner said he hadn't yet made up his mind "whether I want to be in Star Trek again. There are a lot of questions involved, the not the least of which is going back ten years and recreating it."[58]

Shatner's frustration and ennui were reflected in an interview excerpt published in *Starlog* #8, which due to the Wormhole Effect was outdated by the time the issue went on sale on July 14, 1977.

WILLIAM SHATNER: "I've given up on the Star Trek movie."

(The following is a timely excerpt from an exclusive interview with Mr. Shatner which will appear in the next issue of STARLOG.)

"An interesting situation has happened with the Star Trek movie. A year ago, Paramount came to me and said, 'There's a log jam here; nobody wants to sign until they see a script, and there can't be a script until you guys sign because we don't want to commit to all those millions of dollars without having some members of the cast. So with some negotiation and a little faith, I said, 'Okay, I'll sign' ... and they paid me some money for signing the contract. Now it's a year later ... and they said to me, 'We're not going to renew the contract you signed last year.' As far as Paramount is concerned, it's an open ballgame now. I find myself in the position of being let go!

"So I have said, 'As far as I'm concerned, the Star Trek movie does not exist for me.' I'm going off and doing my own thing—which includes Broadway, record albums, films.... I've given up on the Star Trek movie."[59]

It was printed as a sidebar in Susan Sackett's also-outdated "Star Trek Report," which she called *Susan Sackett's Complete Guide to the Rise and Fall and Rise and Fall and Rise and, etc., of the Star Trek Movie*. (This writer will forever be in debt to Ms. Sackett for having created *Susan Sackett's Complete Guide to the Rise and Fall and Rise and Fall and Rise and, etc., of the Star Trek Movie* in the first place, as it was indispensable in the research and writing of this book, which could have been titled *Sherilyn Connelly's Complete Guide to the Rise and Fall and Rise and Fall and Rise and, etc., of the First Star Trek Movie*.) *Starlog* was able to acknowledge the Wormhole Effect, as the next page included as-up-to-date-as-possible information culled from a telephone call to Sackett just before the issue went to press[60]:

"Rona Barrett came on the air and said something that was totally false—her statement about a two-hour TV-movie now in the works is totally false." (The movie has not been officially cancelled, but the studio has made an alternate offer to Gene.)

"There will be a fourth major network. Paramount has purchased the old Hughes network and they would like *Star Trek* to be a part of it—to be a fall series. They will be preparing fifteen to twenty programs over the next two years. This is one of the possibilities that Gene is considering. He's also going to be putting out a flyer to our fan clubs to solicit the opinions of our fans." (The flyer will list all of the various possibilities—movie, TV mini-series, etc., and ask that you circle your choice.)

Fans are requested to "Continue writing to Paramount. Let them see how much you want Star Trek back—in whatever form—under Gene Roddenberry's control. They would go ahead and do it without him if he didn't want to do it the way they wanted it. They wouldn't do a halfway decent job, but it could happen because they own it." So the idea is to let the studio know that *Star Trek*'s fans want the show's creator, Gene, to be in charge of any *Trek* project to be produced.[61]

(Five years later, a Star Trek project with minimal Roddenberry involvement would be released, and most fans would tell you that not only did Paramount do a halfway decent job, it's the best Trek movie ever. This writer would not tell you that, but most fans would.) My research failed to turn up any examples of the flyer, but if it did get sent out, the chances of it seriously influencing Paramount's decision-making process were slim to laughable. And as for Rona Barrett's "totally false" statement about a two-hour TV movie, it was only false in the sense that it wasn't the only thing in the works at the time—but it was by far the most important thing.

"Robot's Return" Returns

The assignment to write that most important thing was first given to Alan Dean Foster, author of the popular *Star Trek: Animated* novelizations, who was taken under consideration as a *Star Trek II* writer by July 8, 1977. (Also hired that month were original series veterans Matt Jeffries as technical consultant, Jim Rugg as special effects designer, and Joe Jennings as art director.) Given a copy of the *Genesis II* "Robot's Return" treatment and splitting his time between Los Angeles and his mountain retreat in Big Bear, Foster turned in a seventeen-page first draft retitled "In Thy Image" on July 31.[62]

Famed in Star Trek legend is a production meeting which took place on August 3, 1977, the attendees of which included but were not limited to Michael Eisner, Gary Nardino, Gene Roddenberry, Jeffrey Katzenberg, Terry Keegan, and Robert Goodwin. Keegan was the Senior Vice President for Creative Affairs of Paramount Television, and since July of 1976 Goodwin—formerly the assistant Senior Vice President of Television Production Arthur Fellows—had been the Director of Program Development for Playboy Television Productions, which kept him on the Paramount

Robert Goodwin (above) and Harold Livingston (below) at Paramount in 1977 during pre-production on *Star Trek II*. Originally printed in *Star Trektennial News* no. 23, September/October 1977 (Susan Sackett).

lot as a liaison with Keegan. Goodwin had the single hippest credit of anyone involved with the project: he once wrote for the Credibility Gap, a comedy troupe which boasted Harry Shearer and Michael McKean.[63]

Also in the post-meeting memo loop were Arthur Fellows; Eisner's Vice President and Executive Assistant Bob Boyett, who had formerly been a television executive under Eisner at ABC; and novelist Harold Livingston, who had been Executive Story Editor for the Paramount TV series *Future Cop*, which ran for six episodes that spring. Like Livingston, Goodwin had been on the lot for a while, having been first been hired in 1976 to work on other television projects for Paramount via their recent acquisition of Playboy Enterprises. On August 22, 1977, Harold Livingston and Robert Goodwin were announced by Roddenberry as the show's producers, but as of August 3 they weren't yet part of the official crew.[64]

With the support of Eisner and Barry Diller, Richard Frank had put Katzenberg—whom Eisner would later describe as "focused, driven, and relentless"—in charge of making the two-hour movie. According to the post-meeting synopsis memo, while the suits were focused on that movie, Roddenberry was taking the longer view.[65]

> Roddenberry expects within the next two weeks to have 8–10 writers working on episode stories. Presently 4 writers working on the two-hour concept.
> Our prime concern must be the two-hour show for two reasons: (1) the opening of the series; and (2) enormous amounts of worldwide potential in the first return of Star Trek. February 1st answer print date is vital, and the film must be superb.
> Roddenberry's feeling is that the more story ideas we can get in work, including series episodes, the more we will have to choose from to include in the two hour feature. For this reason all writers are working on cut-offs, with intention to give best material to top established writer.[66]

For a project which was turning and pivoting so quickly, this was the crucial pivot:

> [Michael D. Eisner] not concerned about writing costs, agreeable to whatever is necessary to insure best possible script "even if it takes a hundred or two hundred thousand dollars."[67]

Not only was it a considerable bump from Bryant and Scott's $12,500 fee to write an eight-to-ten page treatment in August 1976, August 1977 marks the moment in time in which money was no longer an insurmountable barrier in the production of the first Star Trek movie. From here, the budgetary untethering truly began, culminating in the $44M price tag for the Robert Wise film. But the numbers being bandied about at the meeting were only for that first two-hour television movie, which was considered far more important than any episodes which may follow:

MDE stressed February 1st delivery date and concern that story must be firmed up quickly to allow sufficient pre-production. Fellows reports pre-production already under way, construction in progress but subject to delays for lack of competent personnel.

Roddenberry at this point cautioned, "We'd be kidding you if I didn't say we have some problems on the February 1st date, but we're hoping to overcome them," to which Eisner responded, "If the two hour script is good enough, three million." He made clear he is not encouraging extravagance but concerned that we meet target date and the film be "visually fabulous," with a writer who can make the characters come alive, with a terrific director and a terrific story.[68]

Sure, there was still a series and that fourth-network hoohaa, but those were secondary considerations to having a movie which didn't suck come February. According to the synopsis, Eisner was "enthusiastic about story concept as described," though Roddenberry wasn't fully on board.[69]

Roddenberry again questioned February 1st urgency; at which Eisner revealed he is trying to make commitment abroad to generate money on this property before it goes to TV; date is crucial, as is quality of the film. He made clear there is only one priority at Paramount: Star Trek February 1st, big time movie; and has given full approval on money needed to move quickly to attain the goal. Specifically he will approve up to $3 million budget "on these conditions: terrific director, terrific writer, Nimoy and Shatner." Consideration must be given to series (projected deliver in March) but cautioned against allowing series problems/ deadlines to affect the two-hour film. Approval given to put 13 scripts in work now.[70]

Eisner was willing to spend up to $3 million to make a good television movie, or roughly twice as much as had been originally planned for Roddenberry's theatrical *Star Trek II* a few years earlier. Even accounting for inflation, the whipping of which was such a concern that decade, it was the highest vote of confidence Paramount had ever given Star Trek. Eisner was concerned that a director hadn't been nailed down, and Terry Keegan told him he was waiting to hear back about Gary Nelson, and he had a meeting scheduled for the next week with Robert Collins as a backup if Nelson fell through. Nelson did fall through, though he bounced back well enough, directing another big-budget science-fiction epic which would open the week after the Robert Wise film in 1979: Disney's *The Black Hole*.[71]

This was the basic concept for the *Star Trek II* pilot which gave Eisner such confidence:

Kirk is aging, and the *Enterprise* is being totally rebuilt after many years of service, incorporating the latest technological advances and designed to serve as a model for future Star Fleet ships. Kirk has been assigned a desk job in charge of the project.

At the far edge of the galaxy, approaching fast, an enormous spaceship threatens Earth-it's already destroyed several ships in its path. The new *Enterprise* construction finished but only in the initial testing stages, is the only ship with the capability of meeting this threat.

> The new, younger Captain of the *Enterprise* (now the youngest Captain in the Star Fleet) is reluctant to take up an untested ship, and insists that Kirk be in command, by virtue of his experience and intimate knowledge of the ship and crew.
>
> Spock is sought and found, but is incapacitated or otherwise unable to actively participate. Kirk insists he be replaced by another Vulcan, as he has accustomed himself over the years to the unique thought processes of the Vulcan and feels this could be of critical importance in emergency situations.
>
> A young Vulcan is found (introduced by Spock?) and subjected to much criticism and resentment from the crew, who are under the impression he has usurped Spock.
>
> The Enterprise goes up, with the young Captain second in command to Kirk, and finds itself unable to control the intruder. Not until the story is half over do we become aware that this is not an invasion by aliens but by a totally new and unique life form, actually a machine—an intelligent entity with the capacity to synthesize biological forms (swarms of poisonous bees which turn out to be mechanical, etc.) possibly to the extent to synthesizing a humanoid adversary.
>
> At some point the *Enterprise*'s computer joins forces with the machine but this is not understood—crew thinks it is malfunction of the new system, to the point of extreme jeopardy.
>
> By some brilliant quirk of the Vulcan thought processes, our new Vulcan saves the day, the *Enterprise*, and Gene Roddenberry's reputation.[72]

(Roddenberry: never not the center of the universe, if he had anything to say about it.) How much confidence did it give Eisner? Speaking to *Starlog* in 1987, Robert Goodwin recalled that Eisner "slammed his hands on the table and said, 'We've spent four years looking for a feature script. This is it! Now, let's make the movie.'"[73]

The Reeves-Stevenses would later write in *The Lost Series* that Eisner was specifically talking about a feature film, because only Eisner knew the Mountain had already given up on the Paramount Television Service. They imply that this revelation came from Robert Goodwin, who told them that by the time of the August 3 meeting Paramount had "decided to do the two-hour movie with the original cast and use it as a pilot, which they would auction to the three networks, trying to sell it as a series to either NBC, CBS, or ABC."[74]

A week after the August 3 meeting, *Variety* reported that Paramount had sold the *Trek*-and-a-movie package to Metromedia stations in Los Angeles, New York, Washington, D.C., Cincinnati, and Minneapolis. (They also quoted Roddenberry that in addition to updating the scientific aspect, the new series "will reflect what is happening," "the dialog will be more realistic and crisp today," and that "we will talk even more boldly about sex, politics and religion—if it makes an interesting story comment.") It's likely Paramount was already feeling disillusioned about the whole endeavor, but if the plan was to cut their losses by selling the series to an existing network, they passed up an opportunity to do so; in late September, industry sources told *Variety* that NBC tried to buy *Star Trek II* "to scuttle Paramount's planned fourth-network operation," and the Mountain was evidently tempted to sell because the only pilot they'd managed to squeak out in the 1977–78 season was *Mulligan's Stew*. (That at this moment you're probably thinking "Wait, *Who's What* now?" demonstrates how well that show fared.) But Paramount not selling *Star Trek II* when they had the chance combined with Goodwin's revelation not surfacing until 20 years later—and it not being corroborated by the contemporaneous historical record—makes it a little suspect. As such, *The First Star Trek Movie* will proceed under the premise that the Paramount Television Service remained a gleam in the Mountain's eye until the end of October 1978. Uncertainty will only continue.[75]

Roddenberry Ruminates

In August, Sackett sat down with Roddenberry for an interview which would eventually be excerpted in the September/October and November/December 1977 issues of *Star Trektennial News* as well as in *Starlog* #12 in January 1978, by which time the Wormhole Effect had rendered it obsolete. The *Starlog* introduction acknowledged that while Gene was given full creative control over the new series, after *Star Wars* and *Close Encounters of the Third Kind*, "Paramount once again changed its corporate mind. The TV series was shelved and *Star Trek II* was changed into a feature-length film. That—as of this moment—is where it stands."[76]

Roddenberry's weariness about the entire process again shone through. Asked about the "everybody thinks they're the one in charge" clusterfuck of Kaufman's *ST—TMP*, Roddenberry wasted no time in comparing himself to George Lucas:

> Good movies are made almost invariably by one person carrying the enthusiasm and the vision of it into completion. This is the way George Lucas made *Star Wars* over three years of struggle. He fought hard because he had the vision of what he wanted.[77]

Gene Roddenberry on the phone at Paramount in 1977. Originally printed in *Star Trektennial News* no. 23, September/October 1977 (Susan Sackett).

In fairness to Roddenberry—and setting aside Lucas' legendary dissatisfaction with the version released into theaters in 1977—it was not yet widely known what a tremendous role people who were *not* George Lucas played in making *Star Wars* a cohesive film. As established in the Lucasfilm-produced documentary *Empire of Dreams* included on the 2004 release of the *Star Wars Trilogy* DVD, Twentieth-Century Fox President Alan Ladd, Jr.'s enthusiasm for the project was almost stronger than Lucas', even though Ladd admitted that Lucas' screenplay "made no sense in any way, shape, or form." The documentary makes it clear it was the vision of editors Marcia Lucas, Richard Chew, and Paul Hirsch which turned the "unmitigated disaster" of the assembly cut into the highly entertaining film it became. Even beyond the sonic contributions of John Williams and Ben Burtt, or the optical effects of the nascent Industrial Light and Magic, so much of what makes *Star Wars* watchable is thanks to the work of Chew, Hirsch, and a Lucas whose first name was not George. Sometimes, it takes a committee.[78]

Asked by Sackett if he would rather have done a movie, Roddenberry said, "I'd like to do both a movie and new *Star Trek* television episodes. Maybe we'll still do that in the end. Perhaps it will work just as well or better to do the new *Star Trek* television series first." So, whatever happened in whatever order would be fine with him. Further pressed by Sackett as to whether that meant he believed a Star Trek movie would still happen, he replied that if it was "still a viable, exciting property after the TV series, I see no way that a movie would not be made. It's a very logical and likely thing to do."[79]

But when asked how having "creative control after being ignored by the studio" was affecting his attitude toward *Star Trek II*, he truly expressed his pain.

> A major concern of mine was that the two years of bad treatment by the studio would affect the enthusiasm with which I entered the television project. Knowing that the worst possible thing I could do was to try to do a television series dragging a corpse of anger, defeats, and double-crosses behind me, I went to a place I have down the coast and spent two weeks there sort of communing with myself, analyzing everything that had happened; analyzing just how badly I wanted to do the television series; what would be the best way to do it, what would be the best attitude. And I succeeded in really putting the abortive two years of the movie behind me. I came back to the studio and announced to all of the executives that as far as I was concerned, it was "Day One," and I was going into my office Monday morning with excitement and enthusiasm, doing the best *Star Trek* television series that I could conceive of, that I would not carry into it any of the angers or disappointments and other things which would, in my opinion, have destroyed freshness and enthusiasm.[80]

When asked if he'd had a change of heart after several years of saying that he would never again do a weekly Star Trek series, the man who regularly fed rumors to the media and then chastised that media for repeating those rumors admitted he was prone to speaking in absolutes which couldn't be taken at face value: "I've said at the end of a golf game or a tennis game, 'I'll never play that game again either!'" Speaking of faces, he acknowledged that there would be some new ones:

> A new *Star Trek* requires that. Also, there's no way to avoid the fact that everyone on *Star Trek* is 10 years older. We cannot have our landing parties go down with all or most of the people in them within 10 to 15 years of social security. We have to see some bright, young, new characters in addition to the old.[81]

The Robert Wise film would avoid the fact that everyone was 10 years older, and the bright, young, new characters—both portrayed by actors who were within a year or two of 30—would not survive the final reel. Meanwhile, the bright, young, new characters of Dr. David Marcus and Lieutenant Saavik introduced in the second film would be either killed off or written out of the story in the third and fourth, and completely forgotten by the fifth film.[82]

The New Kids on the Bridge; Whither Leonard?

Alan Dean Foster turned in his second revised draft of "In Thy Image" on August 24. It was still Spock-free, though a few days later when the touring company of *Equus* left Los Angeles, Nimoy stayed behind to begin talks with Paramount about returning.[83]

Gene Roddenberry took his *World of Star Trek* show to the Capital Centre in Washington, D.C., on August 29. According to the *Washington Post* he said *Star Trek II* was in pre-production with filming scheduled to begin in November and "with completion in February of a two-hour, made-for-TV [movie] to be televised in the spring or fall of 1978," itself the first part of a "13-hour, $7-million package being readied by Roddenberry of Paramount, which will offer the series to independent stations on a 'Star Trek II' network." (It's unlikely that if the network had happened it was ever going to be called anything other than the Paramount Television Service—Michael Eisner and Richard Frank eschewed the word "network," which they felt conjured up different meanings for different people—but it being called the Star Trek II network is a lovely thought all the same.) During a slideshow which revealed "some of the preliminary construction and preparation work on the new series," he said there would be an increased emphasis on visuals including the use of "laser science" and holography, and that Paramount was "firmly committed to spending upward of half a million dollars on each of the one-hour episodes." But even with the new series launched by a television movie, he hadn't given up on bigger-screen dreams: "Roddenberry believes that a feature-length motion picture of Star Trek will be made after the television commitments are completed." Meanwhile, those new episodes would include at least two new characters: "Xon (pronounced Zon) a pure Vulcan science officer," and "a woman alien, Ilia," promised to be "as startling as anything you've ever seen on TV."[84]

While Nimoy remained a no-go for *Star Trek II*, ergo Xon, Roddenberry told the audience that he "got off the phone four days ago with Bill Shatner (who portrayed Captain James T. Kirk) and we had a 'telephone handshake.' I believe he is coming back (in the role)." Wormhole Effect: five days after the Roddenberry's August 29, 1977 speech, *Starlog #9* was published, including Shatner's full interview from earlier that year (first excerpted in *Starlog #8*) in which he said, "As far as I'm concerned, the Star Trek movie does not exist for me. I'm going off and doing my own thing."[85]

Early to mid–1977 William Shatner can hardly be blamed for thinking that was the case, though in Susan Sackett's "Star Trek Report" in the same issue as the Shatner interview, she wrote that "Paramount has said nothing about recasting *Star Trek*, and we are going to try to get all of the original regulars back." As for who would be writing the show, in addition to hoping to "get scripts from top science-fiction writers, including some from many of the original writers on the old series," Sackett revealed that they "have quite a number of outlines on file, having been rejected for potential movie scripts as being more suitable for television episodes." It's uncertain which of the unused *Star Trek II* movie concepts by non–Roddenberry writers in 1975 were seriously considered, if any. Of the writers known to have pitched ideas to Paramount—John D.F. Black, Robert Silverberg, Ray Bradbury, Theodore Sturgeon, and Harlan Ellison—Sturgeon alone had an episode chosen by Story Editor Jon Povill for the *Star Trek II* series, a lightweight and only mildly sexist comedy titled "Cassandra" which was unlikely to ever have been considered as a feature script.[86]

* * *

Uncertainty had been the hallmark of the Star Trek revival from the start, and all that was certain in early September 1977 was *Star Trek II* would be the most expensive television series ever attempted, and it wouldn't be due to Leonard Nimoy's salary.[87]

The August 28 *Washington Post* article about Roddenberry's speech reported that "Attempts to entice Leonard Nimoy ... have not met with any success," and that "Nimoy has refused all offers to return to the role." Either not mentioned by Roddenberry in his speech or not re-mentioned by the *Post* was that Nimoy had been in a legal battle with Roddenberry and Paramount for quite some time, and also unmentioned was that they'd never actually asked Nimoy to return. As Nimoy told the audience in a surprise appearance at the Star Trek America convention on Saturday, September 3, 1977: "At no time did Paramount contact me and say, 'We are changing our minds, and are interested in doing a television series—would you care to be involved or how do you feel about that?' No conversation whatsoever." (Doing her part to quell the masses, Susan Sackett reportedly told the audience at that same convention that Paramount was "doing everything short of offering him the captain's chair to get Nimoy sign on.") But all the fans knew was that he wasn't returning, and combined with what Nimoy later described as the "enormous mistake" of naming his 1976 autobiography *I Am Not Spock*, he received hate mail on a daily basis. Nimoy read an example at the convention, bleeping the expletives as necessary[88]:

> "Dear Nimoy. Good for you. Do not return to STAR TREK. I heartily approve your pretensions to stardom. I look forward to your wrecking the greatest show of all time with your (bleep) tactics. Big man, big money, big book I AM NOT SPOCK. Really fantastic. We will all cheer when you and your fellow star, William Shatner gut the Enterprise of her Captain and Executive Officer next season. You (bleep).
>
> Why the hell should the (bleep) series go on now, if you are going to kick it in the groin before production even starts. You and career can take two running leaps straight into hell. We made you, and we will unmake. So you're not Spock, uh? The one slimy character of the 60's to be in the hall of fame along with Matt Dillon and Lucy Ricardo when everything else about television is lost to memory fifty years from now. The one bloody character that became an icon to a generation. Well creep, I've got news for you. As long as you live, you will only be known as Spock, Vulcan hero to a planet of youth, and that will be OK with me."[89]

(Technology progresses, but fans never change—and for more on the subject I once again humbly suggest my book *Ponyville Confidential*, available in both print and electronic formats.) The letter was signed, but Nimoy did not reveal the writer's name, though he did hint that it was a man (no comment) and expressed puzzlement that they were slamming Shatner: "I don't know why he's attacking Bill. He's negotiating in good faith with the studio, and I think it's going to work out." Work out it did: on Tuesday, September 13, Paramount announced via the *Los Angeles Times* that "William Shatner will return in the starring role of Capt. James Kirk in Star Trek II, a new version of the science-fiction series for Paramount Television." The new producers would be "R. W. Goodwin and Harold Livingston," and filming was scheduled to begin in November with Gene Roddenberry as executive producer. Wormhole Effect: the news of Shatner's September hiring was an

"As we go to press" sidebar in Susan Sackett's "Star Trek Report" in *Starlog* #10, which went on sale on October 18.⁹⁰

George Takei spoke at TerraCon in Liverpool the weekend of September 10, where he said that Shatner was definitely signed on for *Star Trek II*, but Nimoy was iffy because of reasons. As reported in the October 1977 *Star Trek Action Group*:

> At the moment it seems that there will be 3 new characters (George said that Paramount insisted on three new younger characters)—a full blooded Vulcan, Xon, a Human and an alien woman. George's comment was that she was to be "Singularly sensually orientated; voluptuously orientated. Not only is she round all over but even her head is round and bald. So, a sexy bald woman…" The name Gene originally planned for the Human was Decker, until it was suggested he might be the son of the other Decker—so that name may be changed.⁹¹

Decker's name was of course not changed, and whether or not this character was meant to be related to Commodore Matt Decker from *Star Trek I*'s "The Doomsday Machine" would depend on when the question was asked. In her report on the production of *Star Trek II* in the November/December 1977 *Star Trektennial News*, Susan Sackett noted that "he's not supposed to be related to Matt Decker," and that "the name was purely a random choice." When answering a fan query about the Robert Wise film's Decker's parentage in *Starlog* #24 in mid–1979, however, Sackett wrote that while there was nothing about it in the script, "Gene did have this in mind when he created the character, and I believe you will see certain father-son similarities of character and integrity." (I must stress that in pointing out these inconsistencies, I am in no way criticizing Ms. Sackett, for whom my respect knows no bounds. It's hard enough for me to keep track of all this with forty years of hindsight and late-2010s research and database technology, so I can scarcely imagine what it was like for her to keep track of all this nonsense on paper when it was changing daily.) And while "Doomsday" writer Norman Spinrad is presumably responsible for creating the character name of Matt Decker, the Willard / Matthew Decker confusion also speaks to Gene Roddenberry's lack of imagination for male names, combined with his fondness for the hard K sound, hence Pike, Kirk, Decker, and Riker; minus that particular consonant, see "Dylan Hunt," the name of his lead from *Genesis II* and its rewrite *Planet Earth*, and which was later recycled for the posthumously produced *Gene Roddenberry's Andromeda*.⁹²

Willard Decker wouldn't be cast for another six months, but on September 15, 1977, Paramount President Gary Nardino wrote a memo to Gene Roddenberry saying Nardino had learned from the William Morris Agency that Barry Manilow was a "bona fide 'Trekkie,'" and that "it's possible he would love to do a cameo in the two hour film," if such a thing could be arranged. With the debatable exception of Melvin Belli in the *Star Trek* episode "And the Children Shall Lead," this may well be the earliest known instance of a celebrity actively wanting to be involved in *Star Trek*—give or take Nardino's hedging that it was merely possible that Manilow would want to do it—but certainly not the last. The most high-profile example of successful stunt-casting was Whoopi Goldberg as Guinan on *Star Trek: The Next Generation*, while Robin Williams had expressed interest in appearing on that show. (The role Williams was to play was ably filled by Matt Frewer.) The most famous of roles which didn't happen was Eddie Murphy in the fourth film, and Tom Selleck had also expressed interest around that same time. Harve Bennett called Selleck more than once to offer a role as a Klingon, but Selleck was either tied up with his series *Magnum, P.I.* or shooting other films while that show was on hiatus.[93]

Collins Conferred; The Fourth Network Sees Its Shadow

One of the most important aspects of any production is setting deadlines, and meeting those deadlines is equally important. But deadlines had had a way of coming and going throughout the previous half-decade, with projected start dates of *Star Trek II* and *ST—TMP* passing unheeded. Harold Livingston's first draft of his "In Thy Image" screenplay was due on October 4, but not delivered until October 21. Later reprinted in *The Lost Series*, it's interesting as much for how it's different from the Robert Wise film as for how it's similar. Though the focus is primarily on Xon and Kirk butting heads, individual characters get more to do, and while the navigator Lt. Ilia still gets kidnapped and replaced by a machine, she and Decker survive to the end. The third act is almost completely different, and it again ends with a plot point that was used in the *Animated* episode "One of Our Planets is Missing," in which showing the unstoppable alien force pictures of life of Earth is enough to convince them to not kill all humans. Though Arex and M'Ress are not present, there is a reference made to life-support belts, a technology first introduced on *Animated*.[94]

By this point it was known that "In Thy Image" was being produced as a feature, though not a standalone feature, since a blueprint of a hospital bed monitor dated November 9, 1977, was labeled as for a "Feature & Series." The monitor was not used in the Robert Wise film, but it does appear in the Nicholas Meyer film: two of them are strewn haphazardly in the *Botany Bay*, nowhere near hospital beds yet still turned on, and they can be later be seen in the *Enter-*

prise Sickbay, in closer proximity to hospital beds but still just kind of there as futuristic decoration, though one receives a rather loving close-up in Meyer's director's cut. Part of the second film's legend is that it was a great movie made for a fraction of the cost of the not-great first film, yet the detail which often gets left out is that Meyer didn't have to start from scratch. If he and producer Harve Bennett had been required to build everything from the ground up—well, it probably still wouldn't have cost as much its predecessor, but the second film's production values would have been far lower without the shoulders of its unloved behemoth of an older sister to stand upon.[95]

The same day the hospital bed monitor blueprint was dated (November 9, 1977), word broke that there may not be a Paramount Television Service for *Star Trek II* to run on. In an article titled "New Star Trek Debut Postponed," the *Los Angeles Times* reported that Paramount acknowledged "there currently is not enough advertising money available to support the project," and its current April launch would be pushed back to September at the earliest.[96]

> Paramount's plans call for offering a three-hour block of expensive original TV programming one night a week for subscribing stations to air during prime time in competition with the fare offered by ABC, CBS and NBC. New episodes of Star Trek, with William Shatner again portraying Capt. Kirk, will comprise one hour and first-run TV movies will make up the other two.
>
> Richard H. Frank, president of Paramount Television Distribution, said the delay is disappointing but does not forecast the collapse of the whole project before it gets off the ground. Production on Star Trek will begin as scheduled in a few weeks and work is proceeding on the movies too, he said.[97]

The movies Frank referred to were the first-run TV movies which would follow *Star Trek II* on Saturday nights, but work was proceeding on what was to be the Robert Collins feature film, though the intended November 15 start date came and went. On November 18, a film directed by a friend of Philip Kaufman's (and which would eventually share much of its production crew with the Robert Wise film) opened at Pacific Theatres' Cinerama Dome. Word around town was *Close Encounters of the Third Kind* was spectacular, and Collins could start to feel his $8 million Star Trek movie slipping away. As he later told *Starlog*[98]:

> Roddenberry and I went down to the Pacific Theater and sat down for what I think was a noon performance. We came out, both pretty blown away by *Close Encounters*. I turned to him and said, "Well, there goes our low budget special effects." After *Star Wars* and *Close Encounters*, you couldn't do low budget special effects anymore. That meant a whole new way of thinking and a whole reorganization of the production and concepts. They needed a great deal more money and time, and there were only a few people who could do it.[99]

The same week Collins and Roddenberry had their minds blown by the visuals of *Close Encounters of the Third Kind*, an audience at the Hollywood Bowl had their ears blown by "Music from Outer Space: A *Star Wars* Concert" on November 20, just shy of six months after the George Lucas film been released. Conductor Zubin Mehta led the Los Angeles Philharmonic Orchestra in music from *Star Wars* as well as copyright-free selections from Holst's *The Planets*, embellished by smoke, fireworks, and green laser beams. Before Mehta's set, however, the other star attraction appeared: William Shatner, who read D. H. Lawrence's "Whales Weep Not" and excerpts of H. G. Wells' *War of the Worlds*, to a background of synchronized tape effects.[100]

Undeterred by what *Close Encounters* forebode, Robert Collins continued working on his version of Star Trek, as did others: among the teleplays listed as in production in the November 23, 1977, *Daily Variety* was "Worley Thorne, 'Home' seg of 'Star Trek II.'" *The Lost Series* included a synopsis by Thorne titled "Are Unheard Memories Sweet?" though whether it's the same story as "Home" is unknown. (In the February 1978 *Famous Monsters*, the "latest news" on Star Trek was that "a TV segment called 'Home' was being planned for the fall of 1978" but was probably going to be shelved in favor of a movie; in all likelihood, the source for the information was the November 23 *Daily Variety*.) By the end of November 1977, Robert Collins submitted in a draft of "In Thy Image" which combined elements of dueling rewrites by Gene Roddenberry and Harold Livingston, the friction between whom was already legendary during this early stage of production. In a memo about the Collins draft dated December 1, Povill brought up some important issues which would ultimately be held against the Robert Wise film. Unlike most everyone else on the production, Povill was looking at it from the point of view of a fan who was intimately familiar with *Star Trek I*, which set him apart from Roddenberry in a crucial way. As Collins later recalled, "Gene would often say about the script, 'This isn't Star Trek.' One could argue that it may not be Star Trek, but it's good and at the same time you had to realize that on a personal level, he was wrapped up in it. His whole way of defining himself was involved with the series and with this project." So while Roddenberry was the arbiter of what was and was not Star Trek, his grasp of what *Star Trek I* had once been was not great, and he never truly grokked how closely the fans studied it, and that inconsistencies—or, to neologize, overconsistencies—would leap out at them.[101]

This became clear in an interview with Don Shay in the Spring 1979 *Cinefantastique*. Discussing the changes to the shape of *Enterprise*, such as raking back the engine pylons or altering the bulk of the saucer, Roddenberry commented, "Nobody's likely to get up there with a ruler and see the difference, but I think it just looks better." If he'd been paying any attention to how

Star Trek fans operated, he would have realized that was in fact exactly the sort of thing they did, hence the existence of Franz Joseph's unauthorized yet bestselling *Star Fleet Technical Manual* and *Star Trek Blueprints*, and fans demanding that the ships from those books appear onscreen. But such close readings of other people's works wasn't something Roddenberry himself would have done, so it didn't occur to him that other people *would* do it.[102]

In his December 1 memo, Povill noted that while the script attempted to represent V'ger as an incredibly intelligent and complex living being, "if we wish to avoid comparisons to Nomad (from the episode 'The Changeling') we must see evidence of this intelligence and complexity that go beyond its mastery of technology." Considering how many critics of the Robert Wise film noted its resemblance to that *Star Trek I* episode, this warning went unheeded. Povill also noted that Decker made a reference to his father having died "ferrying a tug," in spite of the fact that "somewhere along the line I thought it had been mentioned that Decker's father would be the Commodore Decker who died in the 'Doomsday Machine' episode." That particular tug-ferrying reference would not make it into the Robert Wise film, but it still spoke to the character's underdevelopment, which like so many other issues with the film could have been cleared up with a simple line of expository character dialogue. (Some such lines were scripted, filmed, and subsequently cut from the theatrical release.) Written between May and August of 1977, the *Star Trek II Writers/Directors Guide* described Decker's background as "all service: his father, his father's father were all Academy graduates, Starfleet officers of flag rank."[103]

Such character details were taking a backseat to the visuals, however, and by the end of the year Eisner had increased the budget from $8M to $15M. In a column written in December but not published in *Starlog* until March 2, 1978, due to the Wormhole Effect, Susan Sackett reported that Paramount hoped the increased budget would allow the Star Trek movie to "surpass both *Star Wars* and *Close Encounters of the Third Kind* in both quality and impact," and that the start date had been pushed back to March 1978. This would allow more time for "planning of effects, modifications of sets and miniatures to accommodate filming in 65mm (5mm are taken up by soundtrack to equal 70mm), complete story-boards, better electrical wiring on the bridge set, script revisions and polishing." Magicam as a filming process was off the table, but its namesake company had been tasked with building the models, and Sackett wrote that down Magicam way, "eight gifted technicians and engineers are combining their talents and utilizing the additional time to build an elaborate drydock for the *Enterprise*, which promises to be visually spectacular." As for the *Star Trek II* series, its fate was "still uncertain, although things look good for the series after release of the movie."[104]

They were looking good enough that a potential series was written into the contracts, according to a memo from Hoyt Bowers to Howard Barton dated December 8, 1977, with the subject "De Forest Kelley / Series/ Feature Deal Memo." Under the header "A Feature Picture Agreement as follows," to work on a picture titled simply "Star Trek," Kelley would be paid "$45,000 for five (5) weeks plus one (1) free week plus one (1) free day for looping," with the start date "between 3/1/78 and 4/1/78 on a 30-day notice." Under the section "Series Conditions," Kelley's Series Holding Fee was described as "upon payment of $5,000 we have a Series Hold until 5–15–79 with option at that time to pay $7,500 for additional option until May 5, 1980." The name of the series was listed as simply "Star Trek," though next to it the words "The Motion Picture" were added by hand. (It's odd to put the handwritten addendum next to the series title rather than the movie title, but that may also go to show how punch-drunk everyone was.) While the Feature Picture Agreement section was written like a thing that was for sure going to happen, the language for the series was more tentative and made frequent use of the word "conditions"; notably that the series conditions "if exercised" would be $8,500 per episode for the first 13-episode season, and $9,000 for "all shows produced" in the second season, $9,500 for the third, $10,250 for the fourth, $11,000 for the fifth, and $12,500 for the sixth.[105]

That things were inexorably heading toward a motion picture can be seen in the screen tests of a still-in-progress Engineering set shot from mid-to-late December. Filmed in 1.85:1 widescreen rather than the boxier 1.33:1 television ratio, they looked like what they were: a midpoint between the aesthetics of *Star Trek I* and *ST—TMP*. It was clearly the same physical location used in the Robert Wise film, but the door was red, one of the actors wore an original Starfleet uniform, and though clearly far less expensive than the mechanism in the finished film, the warp engine was a bright yellow which Sackett would describe in *Starlog* #12, and overall it had a warmth the final version lacked by design. Again, it's just a screen test of a set which was far from finished, but it now promises so much, a tantalizing glimpse at a Trek never to be.[106]

On December 28, it was reported on *Daily Variety*'s front page that production on the Star Trek television movie had been postponed for about two months to be retooled into a theatrical film, a decision attributed to the financial success of *Star Wars* and *Close Encounters of the Third Kind*. The budget was estimated to be in the area of $5M to $6M, all the regulars except for Nimoy had signed, and Roddenberry was said to be rewriting the script—though no mention was made of a director.[107]

1978: Into the Luminescent Powerfield I Go

Roddenberry Recaps

Gene Roddenberry kicked off 1978 by sending out a letter dated January 6 to the fan clubs. It began with an assurance that "the news is generally good" before attempting to summarize the history of the revival thus far, starting with the original plan two and a half years prior to make "a medium cost film to be shown in motion picture theatres," the sets for which would in turn "make Star Trek's return to television much easier and much less expensive." But when "the movie script which I wrote was rejected," the project went into limbo, followed by "very discouraging months" in which fan enthusiasm finally convinced Paramount "they would probably sell enough tickets to make a Star Trek film a reasonable gamble." Without naming names, he described the unmade Philip Kaufman film[1]:

> The Star Trek motion picture project was revived. An experienced motion picture executive was brought into the picture; I was to produce under his supervision; experienced motion picture writers and a director was selected. For a while, the project seemed very alive again and included even a scouting trip to England to investigate studio facilities where a film called STAR WARS was then in production. But although the renewed STAR TREK film project attracted a group of talented professionals, somehow the chemistry did not work; the motion picture professionals could not get a STAR TREK film going.[2]

In Roddenberry's retelling, the Paramount Television Service was not the reason Kaufman's *Star Trek—The Motion Picture* was scrapped, but the savior of Trek overall, as "Paramount had become interested in starting a new television network, and it was decided to use STAR TREK as their 'flagship show.'" And it was a show they were willing to devote resources to.[3]

> Paramount committed a considerable amount of money to these scripts and to a staff to supervise their preparation. Even more money was spent to design and construct entirely new, larger and more sophisticated starship interiors on stage. Paramount also ordered the designing and making of new costumes, phasers, and other STAR TREK props and paraphernalia.

During all this, STAR WARS happened. And it was a real happening—both in audience excitement and theatre tickets sold. On top of this came news that another large science fiction film called CLOSE ENCOUNTERS OF THE THIRD KIND might be equally successful. Interest in STAR TREK started to snowball, and the Studio asked me to improve the quality of the two-hour television movie so that it would be shown also in theatres in foreign countries where the fan phenomenon was also being felt strongly. Meanwhile, the sets for the STAR TREK television movie were almost ready, the costumes were being completed, the props were approved and under construction.[4]

All of those sets and costumes and props, many but not all of which would go unused in the Robert Wise film, would be added into the final budget. Roddenberry further wrote that in October 1977, Paramount "became concerned that a made-for-television STAR TREK was bound to suffer" in comparison with the Lucas and Spielberg films, so the studio decided to commit their resources to making Star Trek "a major wide-screen motion picture to be shown in theatres all over the world." He promised that the rumors of Star Trek being shelved again were greatly exaggerated, and that as of January 6, 1978, "we are awaiting the Studio's final 'go ahead.' Since the Studio has already invested several million dollars, it looks like it will finally happen this time. On stage, first class Star Trek sets, costumes and paraphernalia are ready for the motion picture and will be standing there—beautiful and ready—for still further Star Trek production."[5]

Star Trek II was thus downgraded to "still further Star Trek production" following what Roddenberry believed was the still-not-quite-greenlit motion picture, though sequels were considered a more likely result if the film did well. Work continued on *Star Trek II* scripts all the same, and on January 20, Jon Povill sent Roddenberry a memo titled "Final Writer's Status Report" regarding the status of eight of the scripts, at least one of which had been turned in that day, and three of which "will be in toward the latter part of next week." Povill calculated that including "In Thy Image" they would have "eleven hours of script," and that "if the series were to start shooting tomorrow, we would be in very nice shape indeed. Under the circumstances, however, it should be good to know that if and when there is a go-ahead on it, we have a stockpile of existing scripts in hand." The writers were being paid to work on scripts which were increasingly unlikely to ever be filmed, and obscene amounts of time and money being spent on things that would never be committed to celluloid would become a running theme throughout the production of the Robert Wise film.[6]

But if as *The Lost Series* suggests it had been decided the Paramount Television Service was not to be by August 3, 1977, Paramount was holding fast to the idea in public as late as March 1978. The fourth-network concept was expected to be a hot topic of discussion at the forthcoming Association of Independent Television Stations (INTV) convention, and Richard Frank told *Variety* in the January 25 issue that not only were the *Star Trek II* sets ready to go, "over 30 two-hour movie scripts have come in," and that Paramount planned to put the three-hour, Trek-plus-a-movie package back on the market come April.[7]

The Starship of the 1970s Future

Starlog #12 went on sale on January 17, 1978, three days before Jon Povill's status report on the television scripts he probably suspected wouldn't ever be filmed, and the issue was nearly torn apart by the Wormhole Effect. In addition to including Susan Sackett's "Star Trek Report" written before the Paramount Television Service was publicly postponed on November 9, it included the lengthy and now heavily-disclaimed interview she'd conducted with Gene Roddenberry in August. On the facing page from her column was a David Hutchison article about the changes to the *Enterprise* to make it "state-of-the-art." Here and elsewhere, a great deal of attention was paid to how the sets and props were now "practical," meaning when a cast member pressed a button, things hap-

An unidentified person sits on the Bridge during construction in mid–October 1977. Originally printed in *Starlog* no. 12, March 1978 (Susan Sackett).

pened in response. "This new development will force the actors to have a more natural manner of dealing with the equipment, since as they throw a switch they will have to wait to see if the proper indicators light up to show properly functioning machinery." So, a light switch by any other name.[8]

Other elements were pie-in-the-sky ideas which almost certainly couldn't have been achieved on the budget of either a series or a movie at the time, such as how one section of the Bridge "incorporates a large glassy hemisphere which will be rigged with cross-hairs to aid enemy targeting," which became the far more toned-down weapons console operated by Chekov, the operation of which remained fuzzy onscreen due to the Wormhole Effect. (The Wormhole Effect caused by the imbalance of the warp engines in the Robert Wise film, not the Wormhole Effect that caused news such as this about *Star Trek II* to be outdated by the time it reached print.) "Background viewers on the bridge will suggest futuristic instrumentation by specially produced laser-light displays and computer animation," and many of those viewers "will be running continuously, indicating the operational status of the ship and its position in space." In the Robert Wise film, this was reduced to film loops being projected onto small, impractical oval screens from behind the set, the inherent dimness of which resulted in the often-murky cinematography of the Bridge scenes.[9]

Hutchison's source for these details is unclear. Some of it may have been active disinformation from Paramount, though it's easy to picture Gene Roddenberry reclining at his desk, rattling off these ideas as they came to mind, such as "the main view-plate has been removed. Visual communications will be achieved via large 'holographic' projections suspended in the area in front of the captain's chair. Additionally, it will no longer be necessary for officers to come in person to the conference room, but will be able to 'attend' via a 'holographic projection.'" Reading it now, this sounds not unlike the holograms in the Star Wars universe, though their use for two-way communications wouldn't be established until 1980's *The Empire Strikes Back*. After a brief experimentation in the 1997 *Star Trek: Deep Space Nine* episodes "For the Uniform" and "Doctor Bashir, I Presume," this sort of holographic communication wouldn't be a part of a Trek series until *Discovery* in 2017. *Star Trek II* could have possibly pulled it off with the use of Magicam, had it not been abandoned as an optical effects system. (For Star Trek, at least; Magicam was used to some extent for Carl Sagan's shot-on-video *Cosmos* series in 1980. As it happens, when producer Adrian Malone took on *Cosmos* in 1979, he visited Douglas Trumbull during post-production on the Robert Wise film, and Malone "damn near fainted" when Trumbull told him the effects would cost $24 million.)[10]

On the same page in *Starlog* #12 was a "Trek Update" sidebar in which the magazine once again tried to compensate for the Wormhole Effect, reporting Paramount's announcement that "the first two-hour episode of *Star Trek II* will be produced as a feature film for theatrical distribution," and that the original November 28 start date had been pushed back to March to allow extra time to complete the sets. And while the *Star Trek II* premiere had been pushed back to the fall of 1978 before the Paramount Television Service itself fell into oblivion, "Producer Gene Roddenberry and Paramount currently do not foresee Star Trek returning to television on a weekly basis until one year after the theatrical release of *Star Trek II*."[11]

When that theatrical release would be was still up for grabs, but work on the *Enterprise* sets didn't falter, nor did Roddenberry's conviction that fans wanted those sets to have functioning buttons. February 1978 was perhaps the time of *ST—TMP*'s greatest flux, which is saying a lot, but also the time in which much of how the *Enterprise* would operate going forward was nailed down in a forty-four-page document created by graphic designer Lee Cole titled *Enterprise Flight Manual*. It provided instructions for all the major controls on the Bridge, Engineering, and Sickbay, the logic being that since the controls were practical, it was necessary for the cast to know how they quote-worked-unquote. That main cast was not yet to include Leonard Nimoy, as the Science Station controls are described as being for "Xon or subordinate." And while there are a few elements not included in the final product, a close study of the first three motion pictures shows that the controls as they existed in February 1978 were for all intents and purposes the final product, though some cosmetic changes would be made to accommodate both the story and aesthetic needs of the second and third films, which disregard Cole's *Flight Manual*.[12]

Ten years later, production designer Joe Jennings acknowledged that the sets were far more complicated than they needed to be.

> The Enterprise's bridge was designed to go into series, so we were designing it to be all things to all people. As a result, all of the devices were practical and worked off proximity switches. You didn't have to touch the board, but simply had to reach toward it and whatever effect you were tripping would show up on the board. We were asked to design a set that would function for at least three years of shows, so we were being much more sophisticated than perhaps we would have been were it just a feature film. Then, you only build things that operate properly.[13]

On the subject of things which operated properly, Robert Goodwin had contracted Paramount subsidiary Magicam in September 1977 to build the models for "In Thy Image," specifically the Klingon ship, V'ger, the orbital drydock, and the space-office complex, while the *Enterprise* herself was being built by Don Loos of Brick Price Movie Miniatures. Come December the people at Magicam began to sense things were changing when the television production was put on hold, and it was confirmed in January 1978 when—as Magicam's chief model builder Jim Dow later described it—an entourage from Robert Abel and Associates "came roaring through our shop informing us that there was no way in hell that any of the things we had built could be utilized for a feature. It all had to be scrapped." Magicam's models were put into storage, and Abel and Associates functionally took over the production, though since Magicam was a Paramount subsidiary, the Mountain decided to keep them on as well.[14]

The building of the feature-film *Enterprise* model was moved from Brick Price back to Magicam, though Abel's Richard Taylor would take the lead in redesigning the ship. Working with Taylor was newcomer Andrew Probert, who had been recommended to Abel by Ralph McQuarrie when McQuarrie, who had done a considerably more radical redesign of the *Enterprise* for Philip Kaufman's *ST—TMP*, was busy with *The Empire Strikes Back*. Probert was a Star Trek fan from way back, having written a seven-page letter to Gene Roddenberry in 1972 full of suggestions for *Enterprise* upgrades should Star Trek return. He became one of the rare fans who got to see their fanon become canon.[15]

Collins Cleaved; Wise Wrangled

As the *Star Trek II* pilot "In Thy Image" morphed into *ST—TMP* and the budget increased from $8 million to $20 million, Robert Collins realized his own number would soon be up. It was just matter of when and how it would be handled, which turned out to be "soon" and "not well."[16]

> The writing was on the wall. I was a television director who hadn't done a feature film at that time. It was evident that they were going to hire somebody who had done a feature and was used to working with big budget special effects. Paramount wasn't brave about such things, so I called up Jeff Katzenberg and said, "You're going to replace me, right?" He said, "No, Bob, never. Take my word for it, Bob. Trust me."[17]

In reality, negotiations with Robert Wise were underway by March 2, 1978, without the direct involvement of Gene Roddenberry, who had spoken with Katzenberg but had not been included in the memo chains regarding the Wise deal. If Roddenberry was out of the loop then Collins was nowhere near it, save for one little detail Paramount overlooked: Wise and Collins had the same agent, who informed Collins that he'd received an offer for Wise to replace Collins on the picture. Collins again called Katzenberg, who insisted they weren't going to replace him, though when Collins pointed out that he and Wise shared an agent, Katzenberg backpedaled to Collins being the first choice if Wise passed. Collins later reflected, "I laughed about that for a while. I knew it would happen sooner or later, but I was more angry about the way it happened. I could understand them wanting someone else when the budget escalated, but I wish they would have been nicer about it and said, 'Look, these are the facts of the situation.'" Collins bounced back soon enough: by mid–May 1978, he'd signed on to direct *Walk Proud* at Universal.[18]

The Robert whose surname was neither Collins nor Wise turned out to be just as out of the loop as Roddenberry, and soon exited the project of his own accord. Wise was accustomed to producing the films he directed, so Robert Goodwin was offered and subsequently declined the position of associate producer. He wasn't about to return to a title which he'd moved past a decade earlier, especially for a film he reckoned would be in production for at least two years.[19]

If not longer, since at the National Association of Television Program Executives (NATPE) convention in early March, Richard Frank insisted that the Paramount Television Service—complete with a new Star Trek series and original, non-Trek television movies—was still definitely going to happen. The Trek sets had been built, there were now 50 movies developed, and 58 television stations covering 65% of the United States were raring to go, with another dozen ready to hop on board. The only thing holding them back, he said, was "advertiser caution."[20]

There was less caution on the marketing side, as Paramount's Vice President of Merchandising and Licensing Richard Weston was already planning tie-ins for not only the Star Trek movie but *Oliver's Story* and *Heaven Can Wait*. Put another way, Weston was setting a fuse which would be lit the following year—a metaphor that works for many other aspects of the film as well.[21]

It may have been unclear whether a new Trek series was going to happen or was ever likely to have happened, but as of Friday, March 24, it was clear there would be a movie. Less clear was who would direct it, and whether Leonard Nimoy would be in it. A Paramount spokesperson told the *Los Angeles Times* that day, "as of this moment, Nimoy is not in the picture," but that they hoped Nimoy would be on the dais for a press conference scheduled for Tuesday, March 28. The *Times* also noted that "it appears to be an open secret that Robert Wise" would direct the film from a Gene Roddenberry screenplay.[22]

Star Trek—The Massive Presser

And so it came to pass that on Tuesday, March 28, 1978, *Star Trek—The Motion Picture*, a Gene Roddenberry Production—a Robert Wise Film starring William Shatner, and, yes, f'reals, Leonard Nimoy, was officially and incontrovertibly announced at a press conference held in Paramount's Cafe Continental. Setting a precedent which would hold true through the film's release, Paramount spared no apparent expense: the actual press conference part was preceded by a brunch catered by the high-end Beverly Hills eatery Chasen's, including eggs benedict, grapefruit-stuffed papayas, and all manner of pastries. The overall color scheme was a seasonally appropriate green and yellow, with a daffodil centerpiece at each table—bursts of color which stood in prescient contrast to the aggressively monochromatic palette of the eventual film.[23]

Paramount declared it the largest press conference ever held at the studio, featuring the most varied press presence. More than 300 people attended, with 11 television crews including ABC, NBC, CBS, and the Canadian Broadcasting Corporation, 23 radio reporters, 21 magazine writers, 35 photographers, as well as the domestic wire services and reporters from almost three dozen foreign countries. Sci-fi, horror and fantasy publications were well-represented, with attendees including *Starlog*'s David Houston, *Famous Monsters of Filmland*'s Forrest J. Ackerman, David Gerrold writing for *Galileo* and *Locus*, Bjo Trimble under the auspices of *Isaac Asimov's Science Fiction Magazine*, Larry Niven for *Science Fiction Review*, and Jim Wnoroski for pulp magazine publisher Myron Fass. Also present were illustrator Mike Minor, writer and filmmaker Don Glut, and author William Rotsler, who would go on to write tie-in books for the second and third films.[24]

In front of a large mural featuring a Minor painting of the *Enterprise* as Matt Jeffries had redesigned it for *Star Trek II*, and the words "Star Trek" rendered in an art deco-style typeface, stars William Shatner, Leonard Nimoy, DeForest Kelley, Walter Koenig, Nichelle Nichols, George Takei, Majel Barrett, and Grace Lee Whitney faced the press. Of the new *Enterprise* crewmembers from "In Thy Image," the character of Xon had been eliminated at actor David Gautreaux's suggestion (or at least with his blessing) when Leonard Nimoy had returned to play Spock, while Decker had not yet been cast. This left Persis Khambatta as the only bright, young face on the dais.[25]

Michael Eisner, Barry Diller, and the biggest of bigwigs Charlie Bluhdorn were present, with Eisner doing the talking. Declaring that it would be the most important film of 1979, albeit one that Paramount hoped would be at least as financially successful as *Star Wars* and/or *Close Encounters of the Third Kind*, he understated that "it has taken patience and time" for the first Star Trek movie to be made. According to *Daily Variety*, this was how he summarized the development history[26]:

> The metamorphosis was said to have begun with "Star Trek" to be re-done as a TV series as part of Paramount's new TV programming service for individual stations Then it was switched to a theatrical motion picture, but, apparently, when the level of talent available was not sufficient for a theatrical production (both Nimoy and Shatner have had differences with Paramount and Nimoy was tied up on Broadway doing "Equus"), it was switched back to the drawing boards for TV.[27]

This suggests that the Paramount Television Service's lead cheerleader Richard Frank, who was absent from the press conference, hadn't entirely been blowing smoke at the recent NATPE and INTV conventions when he'd said there would still be a new series. Frank later acknowledged that while the concept of Paramount as a supplier of primetime programming for television stations would continue, there would be no *Star Trek II*, and the subtitle *The Motion Picture*—which had been knocking around since the now-unmentioned Philip Kaufman days—was meant to distinguish the film from *Star Trek I*. At the time of the press conference, that show was playing 308 times a week in 134 markets across the United States and had been translated into 42 languages for 131 international markets across 51 foreign countries.[28]

When asked about the fate of *Star Trek II*, Michael Eisner replied, "Our hope now is that *Star Trek—The Motion Picture* will be the first of a series of fantastic Star Trek motion pictures every three years." Never one not to contradictorily blue-sky, Roddenberry added that Star Trek would certainly return to television eventually. Making a case for *Star Trek I*'s relevance at a time when Hal Ashby's *Coming Home* was a big critical and commercial success and Michael Cimino's as-yet-unreleased *The Deer Hunter* was getting early positive buzz, Roddenberry claimed that "A Private Little War" was the episode most frequently screened on college campuses due to it having taken a position against the Vietnam War while that conflict was still raging. (This is difficult to corroborate but seems unlikely, considering it's a middling episode which never made a dent in fan polls or in reported screenings at conventions.)[29]

As for Star Trek not being a television series despite having returned to said drawing boards:

> According to Eisner, the public "inundated" Paramount with demands that "Star Trek" be made for the big screen. He indicated that this was possibly the first time in motion picture history that a project is being produced as the result of fan pressure.[30]

That's questionable, as there's no historical record of a specific campaign that *Star Trek II* be made into a movie rather a television show. Roddenberry's January 6, 1978 "The news is generally good" letter to the fans was confident that the movie would happen, and didn't include any sort of call to action to write Paramount. If it had just been fan pressure—as Eisner put it, "the fans have supported us and consistently written us to pull our act together"— Roddenberry's original *Star Trek II* script may well have been produced back in 1975 when it would have been far less expensive. (And what of Dominique Bluhdorn?) But it was savvy marketing, since whatever the reason Paramount might go broke, it wouldn't be for insufficiently stroking fan egos. A press release handed out at the banquet further said the decision to make the film was "influenced by a persistent campaign waged by fans, popularly known as Trekkies. By letter, phone and in conventions across the country, they mounted a steadily growing movement for the show's return."[31]

The real reason the Robert Wise film or any other major picture has ever been made was because the studio believed the market was ready for it, and Paramount's current regime knew how to exploit the current conditions. Not only was the syndicated *Star Trek I* 77% more popular in 1978 than it had been in 1973, Richard Frank told *Daily Variety* that the last 25 markets to purchase the show had paid 100% more for it than the price when it was first offered for syndication in 1969. Even accounting for nine years of unwhipped inflation, Eisner's Paramount was milking Star Trek in every way legally possible.[32]

Eisner was coy about the movie's budget at the Massive Presser, only saying it would be made "at a cost at least equal to all the original 79 episodes put together." Roddenberry clarified that those episodes averaged at about $188,000 each, making the total cost $14,862,000. Feeling no need to be precious about such things, when asked about the film's budget during the Q&A, Robert Wise replied without missing a beat that it would be "around $15M." This was greeted with cheers and laughter, and Eisner added that he wasn't sure whether Wise meant "around $15M" or "a *round* $15M."[33]

Production was slated to begin in early July 1978, and Wise estimated it would take 50–60 days to shoot, with a projected release in the summer of 1979. (All the figures in that sentence would prove to be gross underestimations.) The film would be shot on Paramount's four biggest soundstages, where security was already tight: Eisner claimed to have taken Diller and Bluhdorn to visit the *Enterprise* sets, where they almost got arrested by the guards. Though certainly apocryphal, it did get a point across to the fans: don't even *think* about trying to sneak in.[34]

One fan who didn't have to sneak in was *Famous Monsters* editor Forrest J. Ackerman, whom Roddenberry took on a tour of the sets later that day. Roddenberry again blustered that the Bridge was now "functional," and that "we've extrapolated as scientifically as we can to produce a working console." Then, as he occasionally would, Roddenberry acknowledged that his puffery was humbug.[35]

> Although the truth probably is that by the 23d century, ships such as the Enterprise will run themselves robotically. But that would eliminate our crew—and who wants to be that technically accurate? We'd put ourselves out of business ... and cheat the public out of a lot of fun and excitement.[36]

Back at the Massive Presser, Jerry Goldsmith had been announced as the composer, while Dennis Lynton Clark was said to be doing a polish on Roddenberry and Livingston's screenplay, which itself was based on a story by Roddenberry and Alan Dean Foster. Those credits would change considerably by the time the Robert Wise film was released, with Livingston taking sole screenplay credit and Foster sole story credit—both to Roddenberry's chagrin—while Clark wouldn't be mentioned at all. He had been brought on by Paramount since he'd worked on the script for Douglas Trumbull's *Silent Running* and thus had actual feature experience, but was let go when he was unable to get the script lean enough for Robert Wise. Joe Jennings, Assistant Art Director for *Star Trek I* and Art Director for *Star Trek II*, would remain on in that capacity for *ST—TMP*. Though not officially working on the Robert Wise film, *Silent Running* director Douglas Trumbull was said to have served as a "special advisor in assembling the special photographic effects team," though it was Robert Abel and Associates who would provide "some of the most spectacular effects on film during the past decade." (As with the writers, the final credits would be quite different.) Some of those optical effects and the miniatures would be shot in 65mm, and the initial release was planned to be in 70mm.[37]

What the film would actually be about was still under wraps, but as always, Roddenberry was happy to talk about the technical side of things, including that the bridge consoles required "over 50 miles of wiring." (In the Autumn 1979 issue of Paramount's official *ST—TMP* newsletter, special effects foreman Alex Weldon would reveal that the final *Enterprise* sets required over 400 miles of wire. That's Entertainment!) According to Fass correspondent Wnoroski in the one-off *Space Trek Special*, Roddenberry promised fans would finally get to see "the often-talked-about but never-before-seen recreation room where crew members can enjoy holographic simulations of different planetary playgrounds." This had actually already been seen in the *Star Trek: Animated* episode "The Practical Joker," and would finally and truly become a thing with the Holodeck in *Star Trek: The Next Generation*. The closest the Robert Wise film would come was the Rec Deck scene between Decker and Robot Ilia in which sound effects editor Colin Waddy layered in the sound of birds, though it's easy to miss if you're not actively listening for it.[38]

An "inside source" told Wnoroski that "there will be a ravishing woman in Spock's life" in the form of the new crew member played by Persis Khambatta, whose "hypnotic power over the opposite sex is something not even the usually emotionless Vulcan can ignore." When asked, Khambatta allegedly said that her character is "a very extraordinary woman who finally reaches Mr. Spock's buried emotions," and when the possibility of a love scene between her and Leonard Nimoy was brought up, she "merely bowed her head and gave cameramen her mysteriously appealing Mona Lisa smile." There are many levels of hooey to unravel, since Spock was a recent addition to the cast and Xon was still being written out at that point. It sounds like a mixture of what was known about the hypersexual (yet safely celibate) character of Ilia thus far, and the mysterious female character in Philip Kaufman's *ST—TMP*, the woman who was going to explore Spock's mind and take him on "an adventure through time and space" in "a love story exploring Spock's human and in-human sides." That's something that only an inside source with access to Kaufman's script could have known, but mostly likely it was all densely raveled hooey.[39]

After the Massive Presser, the Paramount switchboards lit up like a Christmas tree with calls from newspapers and radio stations around the world asking for more information, and requests for interviews with anyone who was willing talk.[40]

The gambit had paid off. Now all they had to do was make the damn movie.

Magicam Can't, but Abel's Able

It couldn't have been more official: *Star Trek—The Motion Picture* first appeared in the "Films in the Future" column of the April 7, 1978, *Daily Variety*, with Dennis Lynton Clark listed as one of the three screenwriters along with Gene Roddenberry and Harold Livingston, and a start date of July 1978. *Starlog* #14 hit the stands on April 13, and though Susan Sackett's "Star Trek Report" was all about the moribund Robert Collins-directed *Star Trek II* feature film, no attempt was made to counteract the Wormhole Effect with a "By the way, this is all out of date" sidebar as had been done in the past. Not all the information was out-of-date, such as having signed Robert Abel and Associates to provide the visual effects, or John Rothwell as unit publicist, both of whom would remain on for the Robert Wise film, though only Rothwell would make it to the end of production. Regarding Rothwell, Sackett wrote that "If you are a fan who has wanted to make some contribution to *Star Trek II*, here is your opportunity," asking fans to send in any articles about Trek found in local newspapers or other publications "for our scrapbooks."[41]

Fanon kept rearing its silly head: Xon had been described in a previous "Star Trek Report" as a "young, 23ish full Vulcan," and a *Starlog* reader pointed out that it couldn't be right: "Has anyone mentioned that a 23-year-old Vulcan would be the equivalent of a 12-year-old human? The approximate ratio of age and life span between Vulcan and human is 2:1, and this predicates the same ratio for physical development and social adaptation…" Sackett smacked them down expertly: "Perhaps this concept was developed in fan literature, but it was not a part of any Star Trek script." And proving that she could do math as well as any nitpicky fan, Sackett pointed out that in Dorothy Fontana's *Star Trek: Animated* episode "Yesteryear"—the only episode of that series accepted by even the most snooty of fans—Spock's age was established as 37, which by that fan's logic would have made him the equivalent of a 18 year-old.[42]

Things continued to percolate behind the scenes, and occasionally in front of them. Though they'd been announced as providing the visual effects for the film in many outlets after the Massive Presser on March 28, including *Variety*'s coverage of the event and their Pix, People, Pickups column on March 30, Robert Abel and Associates felt their involvement had not been sufficiently announced, so they took out a full-page ad in the May 19 *Daily Variety*[43]:

> We're helping send the Enterprise on its greatest adventure.
> All the people at Robert Abel & Associates, including Bob, Con Pederson, and Richard Taylor, are pleased to announce their involvement as *"Creators of Special Visual Effects"* in collaboration with Gene Roddenberry, Robert Wise, and Paramount Pictures Corp. for "STAR TREK"—the Motion Picture.[44]

So that settled that: when the Robert Wise film was released in summer of 1979, its optical effects would be created by Robert Abel and Associates. It couldn't be more announced than that, which meant it was a thing that was definitely going to happen, for sure.

Something not all certain to happen in 1979 was Magicam's effects process being refined enough to shoot on 35mm film. Michael Eisner had said at the August 3, 1977, meeting that he would accept Magicam for the first Star Trek movie if it "looks good at Radio City Music Hall," but as of 1978, Magicam's process still used videotape, which, when transferred to 35mm film, would not look good at Radio City or any other screen larger than a television. And it looked great on those: in March 1978, a commercial Magicam produced for IBM won a special award from the Hollywood Radio & Television Society. But while their director of sales and production Carey Melcher was hopeful that they'd be able to overcome the videotape hurdle by 1979, in the meantime they were happy to still get to build the new models for the Robert Wise film, since the models they'd started on for *Star Trek II* weren't sufficient for 35mm, never mind the planned 70mm release.[45]

Magicam recognized their limitations. Robert Abel and Associates, less so.

To Boldly Pump the Brakes

At Gene Roddenberry's recommendation, Harold Livingston returned to re-rewrite what had once been his script for "In Thy Image" in May 1978 when it proved too difficult a nut for Dennis Lynton Clark to crack. This necessitated the June 14 start date to be pushed back to August 7, which had the benefit of allowing Wise more time to build the crew. Over the next month, Wise brought on the three men who would have the strongest influence on the look of the film: Richard Kline as director of photography, Harold Michelson as art director, and Robert Fletcher as costume designer. Though only Fletcher would be rehired for the second film, it was arguably Michelson's work which lasted

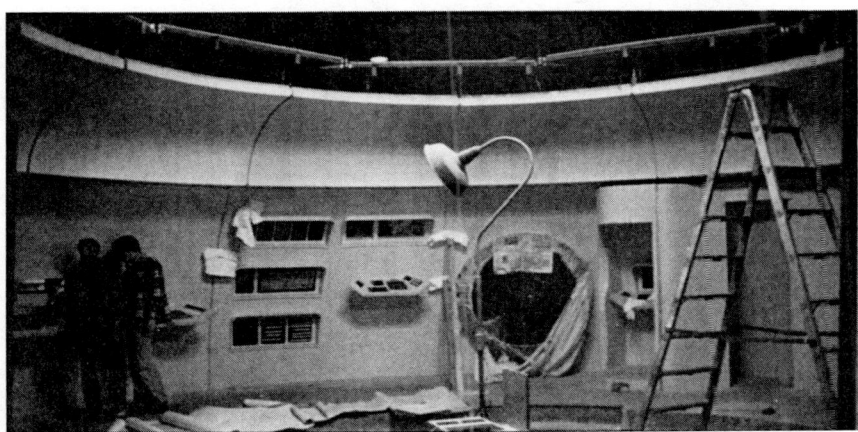

Unidentified people on the Bridge during construction in late 1977 or early 1978. Originally printed in *Fantastic Films* no.3, August 1978 (Susan Sackett).

Unidentified people in Engineering during construction in late 1977 or early 1978. Originally printed in *Fantastic Films* no. 3, August 1978 (Susan Sackett).

longest, having designed sets that would continue to be used—albeit in repainted and often reconfigured forms—for the next few decades.⁴⁶

Photos from before Michelson's arrival were printed in the August 1978 issue of *Fantastic Films*, which featured an interview with Susan Sackett from before the Massive Presser and thus before it was common knowledge that Robert Wise would be directing the film which was still called *Star Trek II*. She revealed that *The Making of Star Trek* author Stephen Whitfield was no longer going to be writing *The Making of Star Trek II*—"he just decided to retire"— and that Sackett herself was going to write it. As for the movie, all she could reveal at the time was that Roddenberry had just completed the third draft, which itself had been rewritten "four or five times," and that "it's very, very exciting, visually as well as in character development." The accompanying photos were taken by Sackett of the new Bridge and Engineering, the latter of which is clearly the same set as the test footage shown in in the 1995 book *The Lost Series* and the 2001 documentary *The Lost Enterprise*. But Sackett's photos showed how much things changed after Robert Wise came on board, including the early presence of a circular hole in the wall which would have held the "large glassy hemisphere" described in *Starlog* #12 back in January.⁴⁷

Fantastic Films was not the only genre magazine whose August 1978 issue previewed the now-moribund *Star Trek II*. The inside cover of that month's *Amazing Science Fiction* featured a Lincoln Enterprises ad headlined "Inside Star Trek II—1978, Star Trek II's Official National Fan Club." For a mere $7.50, one could get a subscription for "an informative and picture laden mini-magazine about the new series and its stars, as it happens, from on-the-spot reporters. Includes editorials, contests, pen pals, synopses ... a real mini-magazine!" Also available was the *Star Trek II Writer's Guide*: "STAR TREK II's official bible by Gene Roddenberry to Star Trek II writers and Directors. A big thirty-eight page professional guide with vital information, background, guidelines, and fascinating details regarding the new Enterprise and its crew ... including the 3 new members!" Next to that ad was a box with the words "NEW MOVIE!" Whether that referred to the Robert Collins film or the Robert Wise film is unclear, then and now. Of the various sci-fi magazines date-stamped August 1978, the only one to have mostly-up-to-date information was *Starlog* #15, which had gone on sale on May 30.⁴⁸

Starlog #16 went on sale on July 18, and in her "Star Trek Report," Susan Sackett answered more fan questions. She wrote that because Roddenberry was busy with the Robert Wise film, Bantam had given him an extension on the novelization of his 1975 *Star Trek II* feature script, the same book she'd said he was "now completing" in June 1977. Another fan asked if the new sets would be constructed to the specifications in Franz Joseph's *Star Trek Blue-*

Advertisement for "Inside Star Trek II" by Lincoln Enterprises. Originally printed in *Amazing Science Fiction* 51, no 4, August 1978.

prints, and like fanon nitpicking about Vulcan aging, Sackett again reminded them the producers were not beholden to things fans made up by themselves. But she did so diplomatically, acknowledging that while Joseph's work was well-done, "we have pointed out in the past that they were prepared entirely by the artist without guidance from Gene Roddenberry or Matt Jeffries, the original designer of the *Enterprise*, and do not necessarily represent our concepts. The new *Enterprise* sets were designed by our art department to best suit the needs of this motion picture, and were not based on Franz Joseph's designs." In the same issue, Philip Kaufman admitted he still had "a certain bitterness" about *ST—TMP* getting pulled out from under him, though he hoped "for the fans, the movie comes out and that it is a good movie. It could still be a grand project."[49]

That grand project finally began shooting on Monday, August 7, 1978. It was scheduled to run for twelve weeks, though by the first week of filming William Shatner decided to keep this 1979 schedule open to account for delays, and with good reason. In a tape recorded by Gene Roddenberry played at the Empathy Midi-Con in Manchester, England on the weekend of October 28, 1978, by which time filming was supposed to be completed, he estimated that the film was "about 45% shot—that is, 45% of our principal photography is finished. The balance of our principal photography should take us through December to complete." Roddenberry talked a great deal about the technical aspects of the film, how everything was bigger and shinier and more expensive than it ever could have been on *Star Trek I*, and indulged in his favorite adjective: "even the corridors are much more exciting, and the reason we can get that excitement is the economics of a motion picture." As for the optical effects, "we think they're going to be very exciting, also some of our model work promises to be extremely exciting."[50]

Exactly when the recording was made is unclear, but it was presumably no later than mid–October, and Roddenberry does not mention that the script did not have a viable third act. After filming on October 31, 1978, the production was shut down for a week so the act in question could be (re)written.[51]

On that same Halloween, the Paramount Television Service as it might have once been was laid to rest. Barry Diller announced in that day's *Daily Variety* that while the Mountain still owned the Hughes Television Network, "it is difficult to operate a network without owning five stations yourself. And we've made the decision not to own stations." Paramount still had plans to produce series and specials for the Hughes stations, but nothing nearly as costly as *Star Trek II* would have been, through Diller displayed the sort of prescience for which Roddenberry was often given credit: "You could project

30, 40 or 70 years a home-entertainment system that would obliterate through technology alone the possibility of going to a theatre, even if you wanted to." At the time of this writing in 2018, it looks like his prediction of home systems outpacing theaters in 40 years was just about right.[52]

Filming resumed on November 7 without a finished third act, and principal photography on the Bridge was completed on November 24. But that was just the question of the *Enterprise* scenes, as most of the rest of the film remained to be shot, including the *Voyager 6* scene in January 1979, which itself would be followed by a quick reshoot on the Bridge in February to account for changes in the script made during the January shoot. Though it would continue to be futzed with in January, the script pages for the *Voyager 6* climax—the payoff, the culmination of the whole film, the closure to everything which proceded it—hadn't been finalized until November 28, which was a month after all filming was supposed to have been wrapped. The scenes set on *Epsilon 9*, the Klingon ship, and the San Francisco tram station had yet to be filmed, and a panic was beginning to set in over Robert Abel's optical effects work, which ran the gamut from "insufficient" to "nonexistent" thus far.[53]

That was Paramount's problem, but it also wasn't Paramount's problem at all, so on Friday, December 8 the Mountain sent a letter to theaters in Chicago and many other markets requesting the exhibitors bid on getting to show *ST—TMP* for a minimum of 16 weeks starting on December 7, 1979. Being asked to blind-bid on a film twelve months in advance for a 16-week run rather than the more standard eight weeks was unprecedented enough, but according to the December 13, 1978, *Variety*, Paramount was asking for a large piece of the still-unbaked-pie[54]:

> Deal is the usual 90–10 breakdown of the boxoffice with the larger percentages of the receipts going to the distributor after deduction of the theatre's weekly house expenses. Letter specifies Paramount will receive no less than 70% of the receipts in the first four weeks, 60% for weeks four through eight, 50% for the ninth, tenth, eleventh and twelfth rounds and 40% for the last four sessions.[55]

The history and politics of blind-bidding is beyond the scope of this book, but the short version is that theater owners were being asked to make a massive commitment to a half-finished film, the production woes of which were already being spoken of in hushed whispers.

If the bid letter was a hard-nosed coach, it was accompanied by a congenial cheerleader in the form of Paramount's press kit for 1979, which bore the *Grease*-aping title *Paramount is the Word*. (*The Greased Ape* was not a 1979 Paramount film, but it sounds like it could have been, doesn't it?) Senior Vice President of Domestic Distribution Frank Mancuso's opening letter reveled in how "Paramount's Mountain of Entertainment for 1978" had "established an industry record of $290 million in domestic film rentals," while promising that each 1979 film "will be keyed to our specialized distribution and marketing plans," and would "be given its identity from a distribution and marketing standpoint" in order to "make every effort to make our customers aware of forthcoming Paramount product." The only product to receive a two-page spread in the spiral-bound, landscape-oriented press kit was *ST—TMP*. On the right-hand page was a Mike Minor *Star Trek II* illustration of the *Enterprise* which would be used for the teaser poster before the final Bob Peak artwork was ready, and on the left page were pictures of the cast (*sans* Persis Khambatta), film credits, and a blurb: "The most anticipated event in motion picture history. The entire original cast in their first motion picture, in spectacular Paramount™ sound and in 70mm and 35mm." Some of that would even come true—the film was released in 35mm, and it featured the *Star Trek I* cast—while the credits would change quite a bit over the next year. "A Robert Wise Film" was listed before "A Gene Roddenberry Production," Roddenberry received co-screenwriting credit with Harold Livingston, Alan Dean Foster wasn't mentioned, and instead of the "Presenting" on the final film, Persis Khambatta merely received "Also Starring" billing.[56]

Only theater owners got the letter Paramount sent out on December 8, 1978, but on December 10 the millions of people who received the Sunday newspaper saw the magazine *Parade*, which featured a cover story about the Robert Wise film by Marguerite Michaels. She had been the first reporter to gain access to the set back in August during the first weeks of filming, at which time Roddenberry told her he was "constantly reworking the script to put in a few more themes *Star Trek* fans will recognize." Michaels also noted that "Trekkies collect every piece of *Star Trek* merchandise—buttons, bubble gum, bumper stickers, model phasers and communicators, starship pendants and rings, books, records, T-shirts."[57]

When Richard Donner's *Superman: The Movie* opened on December 15, 1978, five days after the *Parade* article, many theaters were doing something new: selling movie-related merchandise such as shirts and pins. The tchotchkes were provided by the National Screen Service, the same company which supplied posters, press books, trailers, and other not-for-sale promotional materials to theaters. At Paramount, wheels were turning to make sure Star Trek merchandise was abundant both inside and outside theaters long before the film came out.[58]

1979: Will You Take My $44M Hand?

Star Trek—The Marketing Problem, Part I: The Nerve of Steel

Two days shy of the one-year anniversary of the Massive Presser, the hushed whispers of production woes became a shout: the March 26, 1979, issue of *New West* magazine ran an article by Jeffrey Kaye about Abel's crash and burn with the wonderfully *Variety*-esque headline "Abel Neglex Trex Effex." (As for the best Trek-referencing *Variety* headlines of 1979, it's a tie between "'Trekkies' First in Line for 'Trek' Tix" on November 26 and "Windy City B.O. Is 'Star' Struck: 'Trek' Zowie 600G" on December 12, both in the *Daily* edition.) The breakup had been announced in the trades when Jeffrey Katzenberg confirmed in the March 13 *Daily Variety* that Robert Abel and Associates had split from Paramount because of (let's say it all together now) "creative differences."[1]

A sidebar article in *New West* with the more banal headline "Trekkie Alert" reported that due to the rewrites, "fewer than twenty pages of the original 150-page screenplay will be used." Kaye nevertheless goes on to relay the story from that screenplay, including that "the alien turns out to be the wreckage of NASA's *Voyager VI*, which has been transmogrified into a massive, conscious, intelligent life form." He seems to have worked from a draft from after Leonard Nimoy was signed, for there are no references to Xon, but an early enough draft in which V'ger is specifically looking to capture its creator "Na-sah." This dates back to "Robot's Return" and later Alan Dean Foster's "In Thy Image," though it was versioned out of the shooting script. Keye's summation describes V'ger as merely "[taking] over Ilia's body" as opposed to straight-up murdering her, which suggests it was a draft when there was still a possibility of her returning, and he missed the plot point where Robot Ilia replaced Real Ilia.[2]

Between the secrecy, the production having to all but start from scratch with the visual effects, and photographs from the set being drab people in drab costumes doing drab things in drab surroundings, it was a difficult film to sell. Doing so became the job of Dawn Steel, who started at Paramount in February 1979 as the Director of Merchandising and Licensing.[3]

When Steel was promoted to Vice President of Merchandising and Licensing in July, the Robert Wise film was dropped in her lap. She had to convince major manufacturers to feature the logos, characters, and other visuals on their products without being able to show them any footage from the film, since there was none ready to show. It didn't help that *Star Trek I* was considered a cult television show for children and weirdos which didn't necessarily appeal to a wide audience, even in these post–*Star Wars* times. Word was also getting out that the Robert Wise film was the boondoggle to end all boondoggles, a mantle it would hold until Michael Cimino's *Heaven's Gate* dominated the news the following year. Rumors were already beginning to spread about the Cimino picture; on August 28, 1979, *Variety* noted that while the Wise picture was "estimated by one source close to the film of having little chance of coming in for less than $42,000,000, which would make it by far the most expensive picture ever made entirely in the United States," Cimino's picture was "close on its heels," with current estimates putting "a realistic figure for completion" at upwards of $40M. Also released in the final week of August 1979, *Starlog* #27 ran a four-page article about the sacking of Abel and the hiring of Trumbull and Dykstra which quoted Abel as saying that "his constant problem was that the script was continually being rewritten," while Magicam's Carey Melcher described his firm's involvement with Star Trek as "a political nightmare." Like *New West* before it, *Starlog* casually spoiled the film's big twist: "In the story, the crew of the Enterprise encounters the wreckage of an ancient NASA probe, Voyager VI, which has been transformed into a conscious entity that identifies itself as V'GER. It is interesting to note that this story idea dates all the way back to a proposed TV pilot in 1977." They also found it interesting to note that "Paramount, expressing an almost blind faith in the project, has reportedly now spent more than $30 million on the little film that started as a TV pilot a couple of years ago."[4]

Though a national publication, *Starlog* was not generally read by the boards of Fortune 100 companies, so Steel's work was still cut out for her. Having no steak, she decided to sell the sizzle: she would put on a big production, with all manner of ballyhoo and (live) special effects and, most importantly, Star Trek characters. (The recognizable characters, that is, your Kirk and your Spock and your Scotty, but not your Decker or your Ilia.) With the help of Brenda Mutchnick, who marketed educational films for Paramount, Steel put together a script, hired a director, and figured out the budget. But that was the easy part. The hard part would be not just putting on the presentation, but selling the concept of the presentation itself at a company-wide divisional meeting with Eisner, Diller, and Bluhdorn present. Steel was also aware that other than her fellow executive Maggie Wilde, all the women in the room were administrative assistants. Despite her nervousness, Steel's presentation of the concept was greeted with a smattering of applause, and more importantly, a green light.[5]

The actual presentation was held in Paramount's largest theater, the seats of which were packed with manufacturers of licensed products such as pajamas and hats, the buyers from Sears, Kmart, and JC Penney, and the biggest of the fish, executives from Coca-Cola and McDonald's. Much like Space-Con 3 a few years earlier, the big special effect was a faux-transporter, though Steel's budget was a bit higher.[6]

> The show began. I held my breath as I was beamed onto the stage with lasers. There were gasps and appreciative applause from the audience. I snapped into a running dialogue with a Hal-like computer. Then this dazzling multimedia presentation unfolded. Every minute, the lasers went *tut-a-tttut*, and, zap, there was Leonard Nimoy. Zap, William Shatner. Then James Doohan, who played Scotty. As the entire Star Trek cast was beamed up on the stage the audience just went crazy. Remember, these actors had been off the screen for years. Then I took the mike and went into the audience like Oprah, to do stand-up with Star Trek trivia questions.[7]

It was successful enough that the next day, Eisner told Steel she would be bumped up to Vice President of Production in features once she finished work on Star Trek. And Eisner was as good as his word, for in May of 1980 Steel did receive that promotion, but in mid-to-late 1979 she still had to translate that presentation into getting the *Enterprise*, Spock, and whatever else she could onto toys, Band-Aids, and whatever else they could be gotten onto.[8]

While Steel was able to corral Shatner, Nimoy, McDonald's, and Coca-Cola into the same room for the presentation, getting any significant combination into the same promotion was another matter altogether, especially since the actors refused to appear in commercials. But their non-moving images could still be used, so illustrations of Kirk, Spock, and McCoy as well as Decker and Ilia were used on sets of drinking glasses and plastic tumblers from Coca-Cola, as well as Coke-branded movie posters, all of which were sold in the National Screen Service pop-ups at theaters. For McDonald's, *ST—TMP* became the first film to be tied in with their recently launched Happy Meal line, though they were branded simply as "Star Trek Meals." Rather than Kirk or Spock or any other recognizable characters, the main commercial used an actor dressed as a Klingon and speaking in Klingonese. (The identity of the actor is unknown, though it was not Mark Lenard, who played the Klingon commander in the film.) After showing the commercials to Barry Diller, Steel found herself on a thirty-three-floor elevator descent with Charlie Bluhdorn, who proceeded to recite Steel's accomplishments over the past year, up to and including the laser-soaked presentation and the subsequent McDonald's commercials. She realized she was being observed from above, and those above liked what they were observing.[9]

According to the Paramount Press Book and Merchandising Manual for *Star Trek—The Motion Picture*, 50 million Star Trek Meal sets were distributed to some 4,500 McDonald's outlets. Packages of Cheerios, Trix, Lucky Charms, Cocoa Puffs, and the various General Mills monster-themed cereals were flagged with a mail-in premium offer, and "Scene Cards" were printed on the back. A deal was made with the Campbell Taggart baking company to include trading cards with bread, and for "each loaf to be tagged with the offer." Most relevant to movie theaters, the M&M/Mars-brand candy bars Snickers, 3 Musketeers, M&Ms both plain and peanut, Twix, and Summit were also flagged with a mail-in premium offer. And at the end of the day after all that enriched flour, sugary cereal, and candy—and hopefully at the beginning of the day as well—Crest toothpaste carried an "on-package poster premium offer." For more information on the "over 200 licensed items from 40 manufacturers" which were available in retail outlets, the Press Book encouraged the exhibitor to contact the non-threateningly gender-neutral "D. Steel, Vice President Merchandising and Licensing, Paramount Pictures Corporation."[10]

Considering that her mandate had been to get Star Trek onto all things possible, Steel further knew she had made it when she looked through the February 1980 *New Yorker* and came across a drawing by Robert Mankoff of an ashtray bearing the words "Star Trek: The Ashtray."[11]

Star Trek—The Marketing Problem, Part II: The Purview of John Askew

To think that the first Star Trek movie, or any that followed, existed for any reason other than to turn a profit is the height of naiveté. Profit meant not just people buying tickets to the Robert Wise film—which was important, though Paramount stacked that particular deck by blind-bidding the film so far in advance and so aggressively—but people buying Star Trek-branded products. This was baked into *Star Trek I* from the start: the AMT Corporation was an official merchandising licensee, and designer Matt Jefferies worked with AMT's Stephen Whitfield (who also co-wrote *The Making of Star Trek*, for all things on the mycelial network are connected) to design the first commercially available plastic model kit of the *Enterprise*, which went on sale in January 1967, four months after *Star Trek I* premiered. Those models were later used as background ships, such as the decimated *Constellation* in "The Doomsday Machine" and the *Enterprise* herself in the background of "The Trouble with Tribbles." First published in September 1968, two years after the show premiered, *The Making of Star Trek* included Gene Roddenberry's lyrics for Alexander Courage's theme song—words which were largely unsingable and which the great utopian visionary who predicted a future in which humans stopped being horrible to each other had tacked on so he could get half of Courage's royalties. Roddenberry demanded a lyric royalty on Leonard Nimoy's June 1967 album *Leonard Nimoy Presents Mr. Spock's Music from Outer Space* "since it will undoubtedly contain something of the STAR TREK theme," as well as profit participation and "some voice in the nature and direction of the album," since he'd created the character of Spock. Herb Solow was all for the *Trek I* cast making records, and wrote in a memo to Desilu attorney Ed Perlstein in December 1966 that in addition to hoping they "will make some money out of the exploitation of the music" because of "the amount of consumer publicity we will be receiving," it was all good because "the more times we can get the name STAR TREK in front of the buying public, the better it is for all of us."[12]

To be clear, I am not suggesting that this sort of exploitation of a brand is a bad thing. Merchandising is at worst a necessary evil, and "evil" is a strong word; it exists, it is part of the system, and the pop culture franchise you enjoy enough to read this umpteenth book about it would not be profitable enough to exist without said merchandising. For more on this subject, I again recommend my previous book *Ponyville Confidential*—and I wrote much of that book, as well as this one, in a home which has plenty of Star Trek and My Little Pony merchandise. I believe my emotional well-being is bolstered by representations of these personally beloved pop-culture franchises, and preteen Sherilyn would be envious of many of the items middle-aged Sherilyn owns, including models of both the *Star Trek I* and movie-era *Enterprise*. I'm a hypocrite about many things, but not about this.

Star Trek merchandise became a fertile market in the mid–1970s. Majel Barrett's Lincoln Enterprises sold film clips and other memorabilia, there were ads for all sorts of books and merchandise in the pages of the *Monster Times, Famous Monsters of Filmland*, and *Starlog*, and in May 1975 a store dedicated to all things Star Trek called the Federation Trading Post opened in Berkeley. Though Paramount turned the other way at first, they sued the Post out of business in 1978.[13]

Before Dawn Steel was given the center seat in July 1979, Howard A. Levine was appointed Executive Director of Production and Marketing at Paramount in January, and his first assignment was the coordination and administration of all marketing on the Robert Wise film. Also in January 1979, Paramount presold the deeply unfinished film for seven annual broadcasts on ABC. Because it was a guaranteed money-printing machine which was sure to receive a semi-annual theatrical re-release for the foreseeable future as was the tradition for major films—an edited re-release of Norman Jewison's 1971 *Fiddler on the Roof* played at the MacArthur the week before the Robert Wise film—and home video was still a niche market that could largely be ignored, the first commercial broadcast of *ST—TMP* was to occur no earlier than December 7, 1982. This was a mere three years after its debut, by which time it would have run its initial course in theaters and a television broadcast was unlikely to further dilute its box-office appeal.[14]

Dawn Steel had soon learned that part of the problem with merchandising the film was a lack of material to work with, but even that meager amount posed a security risk. When the *Star Trek II* sets were being built in 1977, a man named John Thomas Askew visited Paramount to discuss creating mylar reflective posters tied in to the show. Walking onto the sets, he saw blueprints sitting on a work bench as is to be expected for a set under construction, and Askew rolled them up with his sample posters. Figuring painters had taken the blueprints, Paramount didn't give the disappearance much thought at the time, and Askew would later blame the victims: "I never thought I had a trade secret. The security was atrocious; the blueprints were just lying around and I took them as a souvenir. We're all collectors." Fans: everything they do is for love, so nothing they ever do is wrong![15]

One fan who suspected that all was not right was Marc Siegall of the Star Trek Association of Irvine, to whom Askew—identifying himself as "Mr. X"—offered to sell the blueprints in late 1977 for the low, low price of $200. (In 2018 dollars, that's approximately $815.) Siegall demurred, and in February 1978 Askew called Siegall again, identifying himself as the prior Mr. X and saying that while "most of his other copies" had been sold off, the remaining ones were now available for the even lower, lower price of $100. (Paramount later said there was no evidence that Askew had duplicated the blueprints.) They met in a mall that afternoon so Siegall could see the print of the overall stage, and after conferring with his fellow Star Trek Association members a few days later, Siegall contacted Paramount, who in turn contacted the FBI. A sting was set up: Siegall would meet Askew at the mall at 1 p.m. on March 2, 1978, to buy the print for the even-lower price of $75, using marked money supplied to him by the Feds. Siegall was instructed to "pass the money slowly" so the exchange could be caught on camera.[16]

The transaction was almost waylaid by Askew bumping the price from $75 back up to $100 because he claimed someone else had offered $200, but he accepted Siegall's offer to send him a check for the additional $25. He made Siegall sign a document promising to not copy or sell the print—nobody fears the first-sale doctrine like a thief!—and when the transaction was completed, the G-Men moved in and read Askew his rights. Prosecuting the case as a felony, the District Attorney's office refused to plea bargain, so Askew pleaded *nolo contendre*, an admission of guilt with no civil liability. On August 4, 1978, Askew was convicted in Los Angeles County Superior Court of violating trade secrets (Sections 499 C and B of the California Penal Code). The maximum penalty for the violation was $5,000 and a ten-year stint in state prison, but due to both his lack of a prior record and because he was a white man who had committed a white-collar crime, Askew received a slap on the wrist: two years' probation with a fine of $750, though the felony conviction remained on his record.[17]

It may come as no surprise that Askew would later try to make Siegall out to be the bad guy: "There was no malicious intent at all. I could have gone out and tried to make a million dollars but I didn't, did I? I just thought the kid would put the things on his wall and that would be the end of it. I had no idea I was dealing with a cultist." He also said, "I learned my lesson about doing a favor"—a favor!—while blaming the George Lucas film: "Ever since 'Star Wars' and the sci-fi trend the studios are acting like the Pentagon: overkill and total paranoia. They're trying to build up some publicity momentum; anything they can get their hands on they'll use." So, you know, he was just a nice guy who got a bum deal from the system when he tried to sell off proprietary material as a "favor" to a "cultist."[18]

Though Askew's jerkitude in this matter is unquestionable, he was not alone in looking askance at Paramount's secrecy. In the March 4, 1979, *Los Angeles Times*, Paul Levine ruminated on why *Time* magazine had been allowed to publish plot details (the refitted *Enterprise* leaves drydock early under the command of Admiral Kirk to face a massive alien cloud) that other outlets were told to keep under wraps, concluding that "this so-called 'secret' information often is leaked selectively to heighten public interest." A Paramount rep agreed that closed sets were a marketing strategy, especially since people already knew so much—"after all, Spock still has pointed ears"—while pointing out the practical necessity[19]:

> Merchandising with a "Star Trek" is a very important asset. Once anything gets out, you'd be surprised in how many places it crops up. It's awful, the thought that we've become monsters, but it's a serious thing. If we didn't prosecute on a thing like this (Askew's theft of Starship Enterprise blueprints), it could multiply and grow and become a real problem.[20]

And Paramount was already dealing with many of those.

Star Trek—The Marketing Problem, Part III: Set Printers to "Tilt"

In her "Star Trek Report" in *Starlog* #21, which went on sale on March 12, 1979, Susan Sackett wrote that according to Richard Weston, "there will be many exciting new items of Star Trek merchandise" tied to the film. Milton Bradley was contracted to build reproductions of props, while Pocket Books was now licensed to publish Gene Roddenberry's novelization, as well as Sackett's own book, the title of which had previously changed from *The Remaking of Star Trek* to *The Making of Star Trek II*, and was now tentatively back to *The Remaking of Star Trek*. Not yet titled were two planned books written by or with Fred and Stan Goldstein, one of which would "cover the history of space flight, from the 20th century through *Star Trek*'s latest model of the *Enterprise*," while the other was to be a collection of lines of dialog from *Star Trek I*.[21]

That series was being eyed for the fledgling home video market's first disc machine, which the April 9, 1979, *New York Times* said was "expected to begin being marketed in the next 12 to 18 months" by RCA. While RCA's Executive Vice President Herbert Schlosser didn't quite grasp how that market would work, declaring "a magnificent production of 'Hamlet' will sell for 10 or 20 years, while a movie like 'Saturday Night Fever' will have to sell while it's hot," his wires were less crossed when he discussed the "huge reservoir of material" they had to draw from: "Can you imagine what it would mean to the 'Star Trek' buffs to have the whole series on disks?" After all, Steve Wozniak did already have most of it on videotape.[22]

Being able to legally watch *Star Trek I* at home on demand without commercials was still a ways off, but nobody doesn't love pinball! According to an April 15, 1979, Bally Manufacturing Corporation press release, a Star Trek pinball machine was "currently in full production" and would feature "all the familiar characters from the long running TV series and incorporates a few new ones from the upcoming Paramount release *Star Trek—The Motion Picture*." Those familiar characters displayed prominently on the backglass in illustrations by Kevin O'Connor were Kirk, Spock, Uhura, and McCoy in action poses on an alien planet. The prominence of Uhura could be seen as mildly progressive for late 1970s pinball culture were it not for how upon closer inspection, her presence mostly seems to be so her breasts would be in the center of the frame. Still, that she's prominent at all is remarkable, as is that other than Kirk, she's the only recognizable character on the backglass to be wielding a phaser. (A woman of color holding a weapon was a rare enough sight in 1970s pop culture outside of blaxploitation films, let alone for a product whose target audience was white teenage males.) Ilia was present on the playfield wearing her *Motion Picture* Starfleet uniform, both seated at a console and floating in space holding a phaser.[23]

Most of the design elements show Bally caught between the different incarnations of Star Trek. The typeface was from *Trek I*, and the *Enterprise* featured the saucer and star drive from *Trek I* but with the raked-back pylons and the narrow nacelles of the *Trek II* redesign. The characters were in Robert Fletcher's uniforms for the Wise film on the backglass; in the center of the playfield as well as on the sides of the machine itself was the *Trek I* design of the *Enterprise* with the cylindrical nacelles, silhouettes of which were printed on the bumpers; and an illustration of Spock in his *Star Trek I* uniform was on the playfield.[24]

Perhaps because Bally's factory was in Ireland, the machine was first released in Europe, and the May 19, 1979, *Cash Box* quoted Bally's Tom Nieman that it was "off to a fast start," having "made a tremendous impact on the European market." The United States market (or at least those who would be marketing it) got their first look in the May 26 *Cash Box*, which featured a two-page glossy insert ad for the machine with a headline of "STAR DATE: 1979. DESTINATION: PROFIT," while the body text promised that "immediate recognition of characters draws players directly to Star Trek." Those players whose quarters would provide said profit got *their* first look at the machine two weeks later in *Starlog* #24, which noted that it utilized "the well-recognized logo from the television show rather than the movie art," but "features the redesigned *Enterprise* on the backglass." A clearer look at that redesigned *Enterprise*, closer to how it would appear in the Robert Wise film, came later in that same issue in the form of the rather nifty Electronic *Enterprise* model from Milton Bradley's South Bend division. It was one of the company's two tie-in offerings alongside a model phaser, and they assured readers "that these are exactly as they will appear in the film—except that the crew's phasers won't say *Star Trek* on the side."[25]

* * *

Gene Roddenberry had long availed himself of the fanzine network, and Paramount soon engaged in what is now referred to as "astroturfing," printing 85,000 copies of a newsletter about the film and mailing them to clubs and conventions around the world. The inaugural Summer 1979 issue was heavy on the Roddenberry-as-visionary angle; he claimed the show's otherworldliness allowed them to do things straight dramas could not, such as "make a statement against involvement in Vietnam" or have a multi-racial crew, "with many key roles played by women." (Well, a single key role in the form of

Uhura, but who's counting?) He also referred to the Robert Wise film as "the most exciting development yet in a career already blessed with its share of excitement," which is Peak Excitable Roddenberry.[26]

The Robert Wise film's credits weren't quite finalized by this point, as Livingston got sole screenplay credit and Roddenberry now shared story credit with Alan Dean Foster, though on the final product Foster would have sole story credit. It was the first appearance of Roddenberry's producer credit coming before Wise, a reverse of their *Paramount is the Word* billing, and the film is referred to twice in the newsletter as "a Gene Roddenberry Production—a Robert Wise Film." The second and final issue of the newsletter was mailed out the week of October 26; it focused primarily on Douglas Trumbull, special effects foreman Alex Weldon, and costumer designer Robert Fletcher, the latter of whom was credited with creating "many of the dozen different alien types seen in the film," and for coming up with "such intriguing names for the aliens as Kazarites, Arcturians, K'normians, Rigelians, Rhaandarites, Zaranites and Aaamazzarites," none of whom are mentioned in the film. If you know where to look, a few are barely on this side of visible in the San Francisco and first Rec Deck scenes; according to Wise, Roddenberry was concerned that the rubber heads wouldn't hold up to close scrutiny, so the aliens were kept in the deep background.[27]

The main utility of the aliens proved to be filler in promotional materials such as the newsletter where there wasn't much else to print, particularly before the backlash against the expense of the film kicked in and the extent of the wasted money and effort became known. The aliens were used in the gatefold for the *ST—TMP* soundtrack LP in late December 1979, and pictures as well as detailed descriptions for each species were printed in *The Making of Star Trek—The Motion Picture*. That February 1980 book, for which Gene Roddenberry was credited as co-author, stated that Fletcher "created many of the dozen different alien types seen in the film, not only naming these creatures but, with the approval and guidance of Gene Roddenberry, providing complete backgrounds for each." When asked why the aliens didn't appear in the movie during his annual call to the Augustrek convention in 1980, Roddenberry blamed the suits as usual: "We had very little to do with the front office publicity. We found ourselves being pulled into the corporate machine. It churns this stuff out. They hired people to make up things about aliens, etc. We who were making the movie never heard of them."[28]

As for the legitimate publishing industry, the April 30, 1979, *Publishers Weekly* contained an ad which was later reprinted in the June 1979 *Star Trek Action Group* newsletter, and which read in part:

> Beginning in August, Pocket Books will launch its Star Trek publishing program, one of the most elaborate and unusual ever. Although the list is still being developed, there are now sixteen separate Star Trek projects in the works under Pocket Books, Wallaby and Wanderer imprints. The titles cover the whole Star Trek galaxy—everything from calendars to blueprints to novels to technical manuals to juvenile books.
>
> Booksellers should know that these are not mere 'movie tie-ins.' Star Trek has already proven its continued saleability in the bookselling market—indeed, these books would be strong sellers to a pre-sold market even without the motion picture.
>
> With STAR TREK—THE MOTION PICTURE, the sky's the limit. Paramount (the studio that broke world-wide industry box-office records in 1978) is now formulating its marketing strategies for this film, and Pocket Books is a significant part of it, working closely with Paramount at every stage.
>
> You'll be seeing and hearing much more about this adventurous Star Trek program in the months to come and about your many profit opportunities.[29]

A more consumer-focused ad appeared in *Starlog* #25, published on July 3, 1979, in the form of a full-page ad for the "Star Trek Publishing Program— a series of painstakingly researched, handsomely designed Star Trek projects that outshines anything ever made available before." (Ya burnt, *Star Fleet Technical Manual*!) Though there would be some slight modifications before the final key art was released, the top of the ad was one of the first public appearances of the new Star Trek font that would remain in use for the films with the *Star Trek I* cast, and would be revived for the titles of *Star Trek: Deep Space Nine* and *Star Trek: Voyager*. Below that in a more traditional, serif-heavy font was the call to "SIGN ON NOW FOR THE 1979–80 VOYAGE OF THE ENTERPRISE." The main copy promised the film "reunites Leonard Nimoy, William Shatner and all the other Star Trek stars, and introduces two new crew members, former Miss India, Persis Khambatta, who portrays Ilia, the exotic navigator from the planet Delta, and Stephen Collins, who plays Commander Willard Decker." In the bottom corner was a mail-in form to be included on the "Pocket Books Enterprise" mailing list, which promised "advance notice of books, projects and events that will keep you light years ahead of your time." (As metaphors go, it's not the most mangled to be used in the marketing of Star Trek.)[30]

Slated for September 1979 publication were *The 1980 Star Trek Calendar* priced to move at $5.95, *The Official USS Enterprise Officer's Date Book* at $6.95, and The *Star Trek Make-Your-Own-Costume Book* at $5.95 for paperback and $9.95 for hardcover. Expected in October were *Star Trek Speaks!* at $2.95, *Star Trek Spaceflight Chronology* at $8.95, *The Star Trek Peel-Off Graphics Book* at $4.95, and *The Star Trek Iron-On Transfer Book*, also at $4.95. November's lone notable was *The Star Trek Make-A-Game Book* for $5.95, while December promised Roddenberry's *Star Trek—The Motion Picture: A Novelization* for $2.50 and *The USS Enterprise Bridge Punch-Out Book* for

Advertisement for "The Star Trek Publishing Program" from Paramount Pictures. Originally printed in *Starlog* no. 25, August 1979.

$4.95. To capitalize on the momentum which would surely still be going at warp speed when the film had been in release for a month, January's offerings were *The Official Blueprints from Star Trek—The Motion Picture* for $5.95, *The Great Star Trek Trivia Book* for $1.95, and *Star Trek—The Motion Picture: A Photonovel* for $2.75. And finally in February would come the book that's such a presence in *this* book's endnotes, *The Making of Star Trek—The Motion Picture*, as well as *The Star Trek Pop-Up Book* and *The USS Enterprise Punch-Out Book*. Whether the latter was a misprint or was intended to be a different book than December's *USS Enterprise Bridge Punch-Out Book* must have seemed unclear at the time, and isn't much less muddy now. But they are two different books, and both were published, which can't be said for everything on this list: the *Iron-On Transfer Book* never materialized, though the great trivia book found life as Rafe Needleman's *Official Star Trek Trivia Book*.[31]

In her "Star Trek Report" in that same *Starlog*, Susan Sackett provided a similar list of proposed publications, with an additional unrealized anomaly: *The Star Trek Frame Blow-Up Book*. More's the pity that it never happened, for it sounds like something young Sherilyn would have loved, considering she spent untold hours in the 1980s pausing her lousy VHS tapes recorded off KMPH to study the images.[32]

The August 16, 1979, *Daily Variety* reported that "Pocket Books will publish 17 different books tied into Paramount Pictures upcoming release of 'Star Trek—The Motion Picture,' including Gene Roddenberry's novel based on the script, picture books, calendars, date books and novelty items." *Cash Box* doubled that estimate on November 17, reporting that "Bantam, Pocket and Ballantine Books" were going to release "as many as 34 related 'Star Trek' books about the television series and the making of the movie." Bookstores which would be carrying at least some of those books were given a mobile display with the Robert Wise film's title in its final font, and which promised "Exciting books, calendars and more from Pocket Books and Wanderer." The covers of Roddenberry's novelization, *The Star Trek Pop-Up Book* and *The Star Trek Peel-Off Graphics Book* were used as insets against stills from the film, one of which was of Kirk and Spock in spacesuits from a scene that had long since been cut.[33]

As if that slate of books didn't show how high expectations were for the Robert Wise film, elsewhere in *Starlog* #25 was a profile of Ray Bradbury in which it was revealed that "despite some redeeming qualities," he felt *Star Wars* "can never compare with *Close Encounters of the Third Kind*, which he regards as the best science-fiction film to date. He qualifies with the phrase 'to date' in order to reserve comment on *Star Trek—The Motion Picture* pending its completion."[34]

To review, the author of *Fahrenheit 451*, *The Martian Chronicles*, and *R is for Rocket* believed ST—TMP could prove to be the best science fiction movie yet. Even if everything had gone right—had production started with a completed script and/or it wasn't constantly being rewritten, or had Abel been able to provide the optical effects as promised, or if Wise had the pre- and post-production time he needed, or maybe if the Sun rose in the West and not in the East—there's still no way it could have lived up to expectations.

Star Trek—The Marketing Problem, Part IV: Brrap Brrap Pew Pew!

While South Bend was correct that the phasers in the Robert Wise film did not have "Star Trek" printed on the side, it may as well have been considering the props are never seen clearly onscreen, or are at least so far in the background as to be functionally nonexistent. The ever-changing script initially called for a phaser to be fired twice: first by a security guard when the plasma-energy probe appears on the Bridge, and later when Kirk is attacked by a swarm of crystals during his and Spock's spacewalk into V'ger. The footage with the security guard was edited out of the final film and has never resurfaced, while the spacewalk sequence as originally scripted was scrapped and reshot from the ground up, with neither Kirk nor phasers. In the final film, the closest look we get at a phaser is in a wide shot at 1:15:19 immediately following Ilia's murder. Prop manufacturer Brick Price later told *Starlog* there were three different kinds of each prop made, and the phaser seen in this shot is most likely the second kind[35]:

> The first version was a highly-detailed, fully-functional prop that could be used in close ups with the principal characters using them. Then there were the non-functioning, not nearly so carefully finished versions, that could be carried around and used in medium shots. Finally there were what we called the $1.98 Specials—which were quick and dirty mock-ups to be used by the extras in the background and were generally considered "disposable."[36]

Hired late into pre-production, Price's company had to make several hundred props for the film. Price himself worked 30 hours straight to deliver a fully operational phaser by the first day of shooting on August 7, 1978, Kirk's first entrance onto the *Enterprise* Bridge, even though there were no phasers in the scene. "Fully operational" meant lights powered by NiCad batteries which took several hours to charge but would only operate for about 15 minutes, though if the batteries were any smaller, they'd only operate for 5 minutes.

As Price related, "one of the problems of building and designing for the 23rd century is that we still have to use 20th century tools and props." That was of no concern to Roddenberry's arbitrary futurism; when Price brought in a prototype phaser, Roddenberry asked if it could be smaller with "a targeting viewscreen with cross hairs that would electronically appear to 'lock on target.'" Price's phasers wouldn't be seen in action with lights and all until the second film, and were replaced by a far superior design in the third film.[37]

For better or worse, phasers were emphasized in the marketing of the Robert Wise film aimed toward children. This could be attributed to the influence of *Star Wars* except that toy guns had always been popular, and that popularity had not yet begun its long-overdue decline by then. In his mid-1976 memo to then-executive producer Jerry Isenberg, Roddenberry decried the "toy packaging which shows Mr. Spock using his phaser to destroy an alien beast which apparently is being killed because it is different and ugly." That particular model would continue to be sold up through the release of the Robert Wise film, by which time Spock had been changed into the new uniform, and both his phaser *and* the alien were removed.[38]

Phasers figured prominently in the McDonald's Star Trek Meals; on one, Kirk and Spock are firing at nothing in particular, and on another box, the phaser is defined as being able to "make whatever it is aimed at disappear." Asked during his call to the August Party convention on August 3, 1979, about what level of influence he had over the merchandising, Roddenberry said that on all future models of phasers, "I wanted a little sign on it for kids that said 'set for stun only,' and a few things like that, and so far I've gotten cooperation." While he was aware that the final live-action shot had been filmed the day before—an angle looking into the Epsilon 9 station from outside, presumably the shot at 6:42—during that same call he claimed to have no idea what the film's budget was at that point, which is arguably the one thing a producer with a credit above the director's credit should know. (It's a safe bet David O. Selznick knew where every penny was going during production on *Gone with the Wind*.)[39]

Roddenberry's stance against violence was among the reasons Susan Sackett had cited in 1976 for why the Dreadnought, Destroyer, and Tug Class ships from Franz Joseph's *Star Fleet Technical Manual* wouldn't be in *Star Trek II*, but South End found a way around that in their Electronic *Enterprise*: the kit's parts "Snap Together to Offer 5 Exciting Starfleet Ships," and two of those ships shown on the box are the Tug and Destroyer Class from the *Manual*. The Dreadnought isn't listed as an option, presumably because it required a third warp nacelle.[40]

Gene Roddenberry's favorite adjective was "exciting," but his utopian pacifism as it evolved in the 1970s was at odds with the unfortunate fact that to many if not most Star Trek fans, excitement equaled action, and action equaled violence. Exploration and peaceful settlements of conflicts are great on paper, but "excitement" is the *Enterprise* firing phasers at a Klingon ship, such as on the sides of the Bally pinball machine. There's a reason why the first computer game, the exuberantly-titled *Spacewar!*—developed at MIT in 1961, a few years before Gene Roddenberry developed Star Trek in Hollywood—was not about the peaceful exploration of space, but about two ships shooting at each other.[41]

After the series premiered in 1966, Star Trek became a common layer of metaphor for computer games. In the May/June 1975 *Creative Computing*, David Ahl recalled playing two very different games by that name on the computers at Carnegie-Mellon and Berkeley by 1968, though what would become the most popular version was written in 1972 by Mike Mayfield for HP's 2000C Timeshare system. It propagated in 1973 when it made its way into the HP contributed program library and thus many HP Data Center machines; as Ahl wrote in 1975, "it is difficult today to find an interactive computer installation that does not have one of these versions of Star Trek available." My father's workplace in the late 1970s and early 1980s had what was called "the computer room," housing big mainframes with reel-to-reels and punch cards and all that jazz, and on more than one occasion when my father was saddled with me he sat me at a terminal to play the COBOL Star Trek game. I couldn't make heads or tails out of it, but hey, it was Star Trek! (I probably wouldn't be good at it now, either—it requires way too much math.)[42]

The ad inside the front cover of the inaugural issue of the BASIC programming magazine *SoftSide* in October 1978 was for Lance Micklus' *Star Trek III*, available on Digital Cassette for the Level II 16K TRS-80 from the TRS-80 Software Exchange in Milford, NH for a mere $14.95. In the game, the player navigates the *Enterprise* through the Omega VI region of the galaxy, known to be patrolled by 20 Klingon ships. The February 1980 issue of the magazine *PROG/80*—edited by *Star Trek III* programmer Micklus—featured an advertisement for *Star Trek III.4*, now with "Improved Klingon Tactics!" In a May 1980 *SoftSide* article, Micklus noted that his was one of many careers changed by Star Trek, and that "had it not been for the sales of *Star Trek III*, I would probably still be working at Vermont Educational Television as an engineer."[43]

In the January 1983 *Starlog*, David Gerrold recalled that at the first showing of the Robert Wise film he attended in 1979 the audience cheered the destruction of the Klingon vessels, and at one of the first showings of the

Nicholas Meyer film in 1982 someone behind him was excited that there was a (simulated) battle right off the bat. Gerrold went on to discuss in his 1983 column how *Star Trek* was possibly the single most popular home computer game ever written, with versions available for practically every model of computer then in existence.[44]

> You can find *Star Trek* computer games on most timesharing systems. It is available on The Source, Micronet, and even the Arpanet. I've found copies of the game in just about every special interest user-group catalog, including the North Star Software Exchange, the CP/M Users Group, Apple Users, TRS-80 Users, and others. All of these games are variations on the same theme: You are the Captain of the good ship *Enterprise*. Your mission is to clean your quadrant of Klingons.[45]

Most of the games, he pointed out, are "challenging, entertaining, and exciting. There's only one thing wrong with them. They're not *Star Trek*." After bringing up many examples from *Star Trek I* about the crew finding non-violent solutions to conflicts, he pulled no punches.[46]

> Look, the *Star Trek* computer games are a lot of fun—but they're missing the point of the original series. They're all about war. They're not about peace at all. Calling them *Star Trek* is not just a lie, it's a perversion of the vision of *Star Trek*.[47]

He wasn't wrong—not that David Gerrold would give a tinker's damn if I did think he was wrong—and it demonstrates the fundamental disconnect between Roddenberry's vision and the demands of a market which was increasingly catering to young men as the blockbuster era got rolling. Gene Roddenberry was like Edith Keeler in "The City on the Edge of Forever": he was right in that peace was the way, but his timing was off.

By virtue of how marketing deals worked, the only officially licensed video game associated with *Star Trek—The Motion Picture* was a cartridge by that name released in the fall of 1982 for the Vectrex Arcade System, a self-contained home console. The game itself was a first-person shoot-'em-up which had less than nothing to do with the story of the Robert Wise film. The player's mission was to "seek out and destroy the enemy Klingon Mothership"; there were Romulan ships because why not, travel through the galaxy was accomplished via black hole, and the player viewed the action "from behind the windshield" of the *Enterprise* from which they fire "lasers" at their enemies. I never owned a Vectrex machine, but I wished I did because it had a Star Trek game, even if it was nothing like Star Trek, what with the firing of lasers behind windshields and all.[48]

The Vectrex game hit the market a few months after the release and near-immediate sanctification of the second Star Trek movie, the popularity of which was due in no small part to the violence and phasers and explosions and people dying in terrible ways, all the things Roddenberry no longer wanted Star Trek to be about. But it's what the general public finds exciting, and that's why even the first Star Trek book with Roddenberry's name attached to it—*The Making of Star Trek*—used a picture of the *Enterprise* firing its phasers from its fifth printing in July 1970 and throughout the 1980s.[49]

This is not to suggest the Robert Wise film would have been liked much more if, for example, V'ger had exploded the Klingon ships instead of imploding them, which had been a deliberate choice to create an effect that had never been seen before.[50]

But it might have been disliked a little less.

Star Trek—The Marketing Problem, Part V: Ready-to-Spacewear, Everywhere

Dawn Steel had been successful at getting Star Trek onto pajamas, but that was almost a given in the post–*Star Wars* merchandising ecology. For good or for ill, the major promotional push for the first Star Trek movie coincided with the end of the disco era and all it represented.

In August 1979, the Macy's on Herald Square in New York opened a Sci-Fi shop in its fourth-floor juniors area. More than half of the items were in spandex, mostly what *Women's Wear Daily* described as "skintight bodywear sculpted into futuristic forms," while even the more mundane t-shirts, jumpsuits, and ski pants tended to be in stretch-knits. Not to be outdone, in November the New York Bloomingdale's opened a Star Trek shop in its second-floor juniors department—though it carried less in terms of spandex and general stretchiness because the department's coordinator had declared spandex disco clothing passé, seeing as how that sort of thing had stopped selling by spring of 1979. The store did carry "functional and futuristic clothing ranging from jumpsuits in parachute nylon to a space suit in cotton based on a design from the U.S. government," and one of the biggest sellers proved to be sweatshirts. The fashion director of Bloomingdale's described the Trek store as selling "not only futuristic designs but clothes with which to stay warm in space."[51]

Robert Fletcher's uniforms for the Robert Wise film were modeled at the Macy's in San Francisco's Union Square on Saturday, December 1, and an ad in the November 30 *San Francisco Chronicle* exhorted kids to "make a stardate with your favorite Star Trek™ characters! Come to Macy's and have them autograph your Star Trek™ p.j.'s and t-shirts." Those favorite Star Trek characters who would somehow autograph pajamas and shirts were "a dreaded Klingon, a Shaman priest, a Vulcan and more," while the kids could "see the new costumes of your favorite heros: Spock, Captain Kirk, Bones,

Scotty and introducing Persis Khambatta." Presumably, this clumsy phrasing meant Robot Ilia's robe would be on display, and the ad's copywriter may have thought that "Persis Khambatta" was the name of a new character. Those authentic costumes were modeled on the 4th floor from 11 a.m. to noon, and again from 1 p.m. to 2 p.m. at the gaudy, rather ironically-named An Elegant Celebration of Christmas across town at the Galleria on Kansas St. It was promised that radio station KSAN would "beam winners of a Star Trek drawing to a special screening" of the Robert Wise film in Los Angeles, though the details of that screening have been scattered like molecules in a malfunctioning transporter.[52]

But other than having to be in New York during the winter, the fans back east had it made, as the actual real-life Persis Khambatta appeared in the New York Bloomingdale's Star Trek Shop on Sunday, December 2 from 1 p.m. to 3 p.m. The magazine *Questar* ran a small piece about her appearance a few months later, noting that "signing autographs and answering questions among actors dressed as the aliens from ST-TMP, she proved to be an even more striking woman with her natural hair than she had in the film without it." The accompanying photo by Tom Sciacca showed Khambatta seated at a table in front of a stack of promotional photos of her as Robot Ilia, her arms outstretched and her palms up in a universal "please step back" gesture.[53]

As with Paramount's push earlier in the year to convince publishers that Star Trek equaled profits, some manufacturers now had to convince retailers. The Los Angeles–based coat and suit company Smart Modes was the exclusive licensee for the Official *ST—TMP* Jacket, and they ran an ad in the November 7 *Women's Wear Daily* suggesting that "when the Star Trek phenomenon sweeps the country make it generate sales for you" with the jacket, which was offered "in sizes to fit all human forms." (Carbon units, Ensign Perez. Us.) Smart Modes re-ran the ad with the same future-tense phrasing in the December 17 issue, by which time the film was well into pulling off the trick of being a massive hit at the box office despite nobody liking it all that much.[54]

The accompanying image in the Smart Modes ad was a head-on picture of the *Enterprise* which was used in much of the marketing—and would be again in 1991 for a box set of the first five films—but it's unclear what the jacket looked like. It probably wasn't the yellow satin number worn by Katzenberg on the flight to the MacArthur Premiere, though even if it was, it was neither the gaudiest nor tardiest outerwear in the game. That honor goes to three items which first appeared the back cover the March 1980 issue of *Starlog*, which went on sale on January 15. The main product was the Official Star Trek Duty Jacket, for which "space-age textiles and electronics have been used to create the most exciting new clothing designs ever offered to science

Advertisement for "The Official Star Trek Duty Jacket" from O'Quinn Studios. Originally printed in *Starlog* no. 32, March 1980.

fiction fans." Featuring a three-quarter angle illustration of the *Enterprise* on the back and a Starfleet insignia on the front, with a colored armband similar to the brown jackets worn in the climax of the Robert Wise film, the shiny silver jacket boasted an "amazing space-age design using metallic, silver fleck polyurethane as the reflective outer shell," and was available in both the Standard model for $40 or a Deluxe LED version for $95. The latter featured a "dazzling array of tiny LEDs (light emitting diodes)" built into the *Enterprise*, and "at your command they can be made to flash and sparkle." Since there was nothing Star Trek fans liked to talk about more than their personal sartorial choices, the ad promised the "stunning, practical windbreaker is a real conversation starter—no one can fail to be amazed and impressed with it."[55]

Also available was the dark navy blue LED Pullover Shirt, which featured the *Enterprise* graphic from the Smart Modes ad, though "secretly mounted across the full width of the saucer portion is a system of LED's which you can turn on and command to flash with dazzling ruby red glints that shine like stars," which is "is certain to make you the center of attention at any event." Larger colored text promised that all eyes would be on the wearer: "THEY LIGHT UP! THEY FLASH! THEY CREATE A SENSATION!" Some of the suggested locales to create a flashing sensation included discos, conventions, science fiction parties, and school activities … but wait, there's more! The audacious outerwear was "fantastic in dark movie theaters or standing in line. Anywhere—everyone will stop and gasp when they see your amazing, magical light display." Which, again, may or may not have been quite the impact the average Star Trek fan was looking to make in the world, and the flashing lights being "fantastic in dark movie theaters" reads doubly strange forty years later when one can rarely go to a movie that doesn't have at least one audience member on their phone.[56]

* * *

The light-up jackets and shirts wouldn't become available until about six weeks after the Robert Wise film premiered, but six weeks *before* the film arrived in theaters, shirts were the linchpin of the National Screen Service's merchandising plan. On October 31, 1979, the second day of the National Association of Theatre Owners (NATO) convention in Los Angeles, the Service's Vice President Stanley Kaplan spoke on a panel about maximizing such merchandising opportunities in theaters, opportunities which were proving more crucial as exhibitor earnings from the box office alone were becoming increasingly marginal. Kaplan told the November 1 *Daily Variety* that over the course of the past two days he had sold 250 Star Trek merchandising packages to theaters where the picture was scheduled to play. Whether these theaters were only those which had blind-bid to open the film on December 7 or if it included the ones which would have to wait until December 21 is unclear, but most likely he sold to any and all theaters that were willing to pony up. The shirts in question were specially designed for this promotion— an exclusivity which Kaplan described as "a breakthrough with important implications for the industry"—and they would retail for between $4 and $6 at a profit margin of 40% to 50% for the theater. He revealed that 25,000 of the shirts were being supplied on the first order alone, presumably meaning that each of those 250 participating theaters would each receive an initial order of 100 shirts each.[57]

This was based on the gamble that people would show up in droves to see the Robert Wise film when it opened—but people first had to know the film was opening at all, and where it could be seen.

Star Trek—The Marketing Problem, Part VI: A Wagon of Trailers Full of Stars

Though Paramount had been supplying theaters with posters and standees since that summer, the trailer was a trickier beast, since it required interesting footage from the film itself. The Mountain's intention was to get a trailer into circulation by the end of September, but they'd intended a lot of things regarding the Robert Wise film. An in-progress teaser trailer was abandoned in early September, and Wise similarly nixed a full-length trailer in mid-production since he found it "very pedestrian and uninteresting, with nothing visually exciting in it." By this point, Douglas Trumbull had produced enough usable footage of the *Enterprise* in drydock to be edited into the revamped trailer, and since Jerry Goldsmith was still composing the score on the piano, Alan S. Howarth's experiments with his home synthesizers to create the sound of the *Enterprise* accelerating to warp seven were used in lieu of music.[58]

Work continued on the trailers (and everything else about the film) throughout October, and in early November, Wise hired Orson Welles do the voiceover for both the teaser trailer and the television commercials. Paramount considered buying both network and local ad time for those commercials, but decided against it because the film wouldn't be opening nationwide on December 7. The Mountain had a list of 40 advertising agencies they usually hired to buy local time, and while the network spots reached more markets overall, they found local agencies could buy ad time more efficiently. (Again, it boiled down to demographics v. raw numbers.) The last picture for which Paramount had bought network time was John Frankenheimer's *Black Sunday* in 1977, while the next time they did so would be for Buzz Kulik's *The Hunter*. Unlike the Robert Wise film, the Buzz Kulik film was expected to be completed well before its August 1980 release date.[59]

The teaser for *ST—TMP* is quite possibly my favorite piece of shortform Star Trek film. Like so much of the advertising it takes on the airs of a portent, suggesting great and important things, but that's difficult to get across when the people making it don't know what those things are supposed to be. So, they went for the ol' razzle-dazzle, starting with the Paramount logo's 22 stars spawning ten more below the mountain to create a circle which itself spawns a tunnel of sparkling stars in layers of white, blue, and red, a sort of Patriotic Star Tunnel—possibly a piece of film left over from the Bicentennial, though I have found no specific evidence of this. The Patriotic Star Tunnel is accompanied by Howarth's ascending synthesizer tone and ending with Welles speaking the film's primary tagline, "The Human Adventure is Just Beginning." (Some posters and marketing materials used the tagline "There Is No

Comparison," but only the distinctly Roddenberry-esque "Human Adventure" made it onscreen, both in the trailers and in the Robert Wise film itself.) Over a gentle wash of synths which create a mood without committing to a melody, the navigational deflector of the *Enterprise* fades into view, followed by Kirk saying "Take us out," and Welles identifying him as "William Shatner as James T. Kirk." This pattern of a close-up of the *Enterprise* model being lit as each performer appears and is named is repeated for Nimoy, Kelley, Doohan, Takei, Barrett, Koenig, Nichols, Collins, and finally Khambatta before the *Enterprise* leaves drydock, all as Howarth's warp sounds continue to rise. This then cuts to a curious animation sequence: a row of glowing green parallel lines in space pulsing with energy, seemingly heading toward something that resembles an edge-on spiral galaxy. Like the Patriotic Star Tunnel, my research did not uncover the provenance of this animated sequence, but I would wager it was purchased from an effects house which sold such dazzling but otherwise nonspecific demonstrations for television commercials, such as Lisberger Studios or possibly even Robert Abel and Associates. Again, this is just speculation, but it's not outside the realm of possibility that in such a time crunch Paramount might have purchased existing Abel footage. It must be noted that they appear to be the same basic optical effects which would be used with different color tinting in the "Suspended in Time" sequence in Robert Greenwald's 1980 Universal film *Xanadu*, which was in production at the time that these trailers were being made. As such, the effect will henceforth be referred to as the Xanadu Lines.[60]

The Xanadu Lines rotate their orientation counter-clockwise to the top of the screen all while changing colors, finally crossing vertically back to the bottom as energy bolts shoot toward the galaxy, causing it to explode into the title of the film. The climbing synth noise resolves into grand organ chords with burbling electronic noise on the edges, and Welles says "*Star Trek—The Motion Picture*, a Gene Roddenberry's production of a Robert Wise film. Coming this Christmas from Paramount." Like so much else about this teaser, what went on in the recording session is unknown, but it would stand to reason that the famously mercurial Welles would object to the grammatically atrocious "*Star Trek—The Motion Picture*, a Gene Roddenberry production— a Robert Wise film," instead insisting on reading it in a way which was not an affront to the English language. But the teaser is a lovely piece of work however it came together, and I can trace my interest in how the Robert Wise film was marketed back to having seen a 16mm print of this teaser at a screening of the Blooper Reel in the late 1980s.

In 1979 there was also the issue of the promotional trailer, typically a one-reeler about twelve minutes long, intended now both to entice those theater owners that hadn't taken the blind-bidding bait and to soothe the nerves of those who had. Normally this reel would have been shown at the NATO convention in late October where Stanley Kaplan had such success selling Star Trek shirts to theaters, but, well, you know.

The reel still wasn't ready by mid-November, since the score was being written and recorded, and Douglas Trumbull's and John Dykstra's effects shops were working the overtime hours that would double the film's budget, but that didn't stop Gene Roddenberry from debuting it at his *World of Star Trek* show in Columbus, Ohio on Sunday, November 18. Though Columbus wouldn't get the film until December 21, Roddenberry told the capacity crowd in the 2,791-seat Ohio Theatre he wanted them to be the first people "outside the Paramount vistas" to see the preview, both because he had "many dear friends" there and it was Majel Barrett's hometown. Roddenberry apologized for the reel's optical effects being largely incomplete and the lack of Jerry Goldsmith's music—Goldmsith's *ST—TMP* music, anyway—while noting with pride that it was being shown against Robert Wise's wishes. The reel was eventually seen by potential exhibitors in an only slightly less-incomplete form about a week and a half later.[61]

Twelve minutes is a lot of time to fill when a picture is moving along right on schedule, let alone when its post-production is so troubled, and even the two-minute teaser and regular trailer have a remarkable amount of filler. This is not a criticism; like so much of the marketing of the Robert Wise film, the filler is an endless source of fascination for me.

The promo reel begins with the Patriotic Star Tunnel minus any sound, followed by a starfield moving from screen left to right. The starfield is accompanied by the cue "Commando Raid" from John Williams' *Black Sunday* score as a narrator who is not Orson Welles sets up the premise.

> 300 years from now, when human technology has reached its millennium ... and universal peace seems at hand ... mankind will face what may be its greatest and final challenge. It will appear in the form of a cloud. Its vastness ... beyond belief. The energy it emits ... overwhelming. And at its center, a mechanical mind which has mastered the art of reason and sent it on a journey across space to seek its creator. Once provoked, it will destroy anything in its path.

That last line introduces footage of the Klingon attack that opens the film—only of the Klingons and their ships, however, and nothing of the aforementioned cloud. After that, it's back to the starfield, followed a shot of a shuttle flying against a blue sky, the *Enterprise*'s cargo bay, and the San Francisco tram station:

> No living organism in the universe can withstand its onslaught. Its ultimate destination: Earth. On Earth, we will learn of its existence just 54 hours before it is scheduled to

reach our planet. And in those hours, the finest minds and the most advanced technology will be needed to face the challenge.

Then comes the first actual English dialog: Kirk informing Scott in the shuttlepod that the *Enterprise* is launching in twelve hours, period. Over footage of the ship in drydock (closer to completion than the footage used in the teaser) and shots of various crewmembers, the narrator continues:

> This is the new voyage of the Enterprise. Futurized beyond our imagination. An intergalactic wonder, the ultimate in astro-navigation. An all-new starship, with an all-new crew, prepared, dedicated, demanding. But as the threat to civilization grows, something more is needed. This is the return of Captain Kirk, Doctor McCoy, Scotty, Sulu, Uhura, Chekov, and Mr. Spock. And joining them on their mission—Commander Will Decker, and Navigator Ilia.

The scene between Kirk and Decker in Engineering is excerpted, as is Kirk ordering Sulu take the ship out of drydock, and the narrator continues:

> Even with logic, teamwork, and 23rd-century technology on their side, the Enterprise has hardly a chance against the vast intelligence and unlimited power of the invading organism known as V'ger. And now, some scenes from Star Trek—The Motion Picture.

The scenes are truncated versions of Kirk's first Captain's Log through Spock's arrival on the ship, ten minutes of screen time in the Robert Wise film shortened to about six in the promo reel. Much of this truncation is due to many of the effects not yet existing, particularly for the wormhole sequence. While the light-streaking for the interiors is mostly in place, the promo reel has no exteriors of the *Enterprise*, and the viewscreen is blank when Decker crosses it, since that effect in particular was one of the very last completed. The sequence in the promo reel also plays oddly because the sound is unfinished, a mix of on-set audio—Decker's yell of "No!" has the echoey, cavernous sound of a live recording that was always intended to be dubbed over—and unsweetened looping in which the cast speaks in a stilted cadence. This unfinished, baffling cut of the Wormhole sequence would often be shown when the cast appeared on television in the weeks to come, since regardless of its incompleteness, it was still the closest thing the Robert Wise film had to an English-language action setpiece. It's all the more valuable now as a look at how much work went into the finished scene; the music used in the promo reel's version of the Wormhole sequence is Williams' "Speed Boat Chase" from *Black Sunday*, and it makes one appreciate the lack of music and the strength of the sound design in the final product. Similarly, the temp track for the corridor scene between Decker and Ilia is Jerry Goldsmith's "It Is All True" from his score for Franklin J. Schaffner's 1977 *Islands in the Stream*, and even though it's the same composer, "Ilia's Theme" in the final film works in all the ways "It Is All True" in the promo reel does not. As Scott would say in the next Star Trek film Jerry Goldsmith would score, it's all about the right tool for the right job.[62]

Our narrator returns at about 10:43 into the 12-minute reel, over the still-iconic shot of the *Enterprise* leaving Earth orbit with the sun rising in the background, and he gets appropriately Biblical.

> This then is the epic journey of the starship Enterprise. Exploring the outer limits of space and time.

This is arguably a riff on 1 John 1:5 from the King James Bible, "This then is the message which we have heard of him, and declare unto you, that God is light, and in him is no darkness at all." While Biblical references were not unheard of in *Star Trek I*—Spock quotes Luke 12:27 in "The Trouble with Tribbles," nobody's idea of Star Trek at its gravest—this was meant to signify that it was an Important Film About Important Things.

After another montage including still more unfinished effects and ending with Spock's line about V'ger being a child, the narrator and the Xanadu Lines return, accompanied by what may be the public debut of Goldsmith's new theme.

> Even after millions of years of evolution, after countless ages of discovery, after centuries of technological achievement, the human adventure is just beginning. Star Trek—The Motion Picture. A Gene Roddenberry production. A Robert Wise Film.

This promo reel was only intended for exhibitors, and the final, honest-to-goodness trailer for the film intended to be seen widely in movie theaters combined elements of both the teaser and the promo. The Patriotic Star Tunnel is replaced by the tagline THE HUMAN ADVENTURE IS JUST BEGINNING in all caps scrolling across the screen from right to left accompanied by a swirling synthesizer growl, which harshly cuts to the Klingon ships firing torpedoes and promptly being destroyed by V'ger. Again over Williams' "Commando Raid," the same narrator as the promo reel intones over footage of the *Enterprise* and the characters in question:

> Travel forward with us 300 years into the future to confront the greatest mystery ever to threaten mankind. We are aboard a huge starship called the Enterprise. This is the return of Captain Kirk.... Mister Spock.... Doctor McCoy.... Scotty ... and joining them on their mission, Commander Will Decker, and Navigator Ilia.

Though shorter than it was in the promo reel, Decker and Ilia's corridor scene is again scored to "It Is All True" from Goldsmith's *Islands in the Stream*. The excerpt from the Wormhole sequence has more complete visual and sound effects, but still feels confusing and incomplete. The narrator returns and again gets Biblical, over the same montage of footage that closed out the promo, including some still-unfinished effects.

This then is the epic journey of the starship Enterprise. Traveling to the outer limits of time and space to challenge a vast, living machine of destruction. The human adventure is just beginning.

The big finale does not involve the Xanadu Lines, but instead thin purple, red, orange, green, and blue lines which emerge from the top of the screen with bursts of electronic noise, expand into a rainbow, and are replaced from above by a vertical wipe with the final Bob Peak *ST—TMP* poster art as grand chords are played on an organ, similar to but not quite the same as the organ music from the teaser. The narrator again concludes as he must because he is not Orson Welles:

Star Trek—The Motion Picture, a Gene Roddenberry production—a Robert Wise film.

None of these trailers mention the film's rating, since it couldn't be rated until a finished print was delivered to the MPAA, and the film didn't begin printing until December 2. After the MPAA announced the "G" rating on December 4, eight 30-second television commercials could finally start running in the markets which would be receiving the film on December 7, all with Orson Welles narratiing and him saying "Rated G," though without his variation on "a Gene Roddenberry production—a Robert Wise film." Each commercial featured 23 seconds of footage, usually shots of visual effects— Spock's vision of the murdered Ilia from his trip into V'ger is in six of the eight spots—followed by the title appearing above the Xanadu Lines, and two pages of credits with about five seconds of silence for the local announcer to specify participating theaters. According to the 2001 DVD and the 2009 Blu-ray, the names of the eight commercials were "Hardware," "Startle Your Senses," "Enterprise," "Cast/Human Adventure," "Spiritual Search," "Spiritual/Startle Your Senses," "Startle/Human Adventure," and "Event/Common Experience," though the last spot was left off the Blu-ray.

Set to Goldsmith's *Motion Picture* cue "Leaving Drydock," the "Hardware" commercial is the most minimalist in terms of narration, with Welles only saying the tagline "The human adventure is just beginning," before returning at the end to announce the title and rating.

"Startle Your Senses" is set to Goldsmith's "Ilia's Theme," and Welles gets a bit more to say:

It will startle your senses, challenge your intellect, and alter your perception of the future ... by taking you there.

"Enterprise" is set to Goldsmith's main theme, and Welles' copy is juicier:

An army of technicians has been working for years to perfect this great starship. When completed, it will be superior to anything in space. But time has run out, and the ship must depart, unfinished, in search of the greatest mystery ever to confront the human race.

"Cast/Human Adventure" also uses Goldsmith's main theme, while Welles' narration insists it's not just about the technology:

> Star Trek—The Motion Picture is all you'd expect, and more. The most surprising thing about it is what happens to the people—Kirk, McCoy, Scotty, Sulu, Uhura, Chekov, Decker, Ilia, and Mr. Spock. The human adventure is just beginning.

(Is that the most surprising thing, though?) "Spiritual Search" uses Goldsmith's "Leaving Drydock," and the narration gets nice and purple:

> A living object of infinite proportions and divine power is searching the universe for its origins, determined to find its creator, and about to encounter a 23rd century starship from Earth called Enterprise. The human adventure is just beginning.

As the name implies, "Spiritual/Startle Your Senses" uses the same copy and reading as "Startle Your Senses," and is also set to "Ilia's Theme," but with mostly different footage. Set to Goldsmith's main theme, "Startle/Human Adventure" again uses the "Startle Your Senses" copy, but Welles gives it a more upbeat reading which includes "the human adventure is just beginning," and his reading of the title and the rating are a bit more lively.

The final commercial "Event/Common Experience"—not included on the same 2009 Blu-ray which claims the film was never rated, though that's probably a coincidence—is the only spot which acknowledges *Star Trek I*'s existence.

> Ten years ago, a television phenomenon became a part of life, shared in 47 different languages, read in 469 publications, and seen by 1.2 billion people. A common experience, remembered around the world. Now Paramount Pictures brings the memory to life.

The commercials were necessary to promote the film to as wide an audience as possible, but there were many people who had never stopped living with that memory, and who couldn't wait for it to come back to life. They already knew where to be, and when.

Star Trek—The Manifest Procession, Part I: New York, New Jersey, Pennsylvania and Florida

On November 16, 1979, an ad in the *New York Daily News* announced tickets would go on sale for the "Reserved Performance Engagement" of *ST—TMP* on Wednesday, November 21 at the Paramount Theatre at 43rd St. and Broadway. The Performance Schedule was listed as beginning daily on

December 7 with 12:00 p.m., 2:30 p.m., 5:00 p.m., 7:30 p.m., and 10 p.m. showings with "an additional 12:15 a.m. showing on the following dates: 12/7, 12/8, 12/14, 12/15, 12/21 thru 1/1." (Take a moment to find a place in your hearts for the Paramount Theatre employees who had to work those quarter-past-midnight showings on Christmas Eve and New Year's Eve—it was surely the last place they wanted to be.) The ad included a mail-in form which asked the patron to fill out their first, second, and third choices for day, date, and performance, with no stated limit on how many tickets they could purchase. At a time when the per capita national average ticket price was $2.56, the option to buy bulk tickets in advance was balanced out not only by the $6 price—about $20 in 2018 dollars, and the Robert Wise film was the first $6 movie ticket in New York since Jack Clayton's similarly advance-seated *The Great Gatsby* in 1974—but also by not knowing what shows they would attend until 7 to 10 days later when their SASE returned containing tickets for which seating was guaranteed but not reserved, and for which there would be no refunds or exchanges. In spite of that uncertainty, it worked: the Paramount Theatre sold $41,604 in combined box office and mail-order tickets in the first five days, and by November 28 all the December 7 showings were sold out, as well as the 7:30 p.m. and 10:30 p.m. showings on December 8.[63]

Advance ticket form for the Reserved Performance Engagement of *Star Trek—The Motion Picture* at the Paramount Theater in December 1979. Originally printed in the *New York Daily News* on November 16, 1979.

A more streamlined ad which didn't allow the customer to specify dates or times started running in the *New York Times* on Saturday, December 1. It was upgraded on Friday, December 7 with an illustration of an eight-pointed star and a wistful suggestion: "This Holiday, Give a Journey Through the Galaxy." The ad ran through New Year's Day, though on Christmas Eve the wording was changed from "Give a Journey" to "Enjoy a Journey"—a reasonable semantic shift considering the shopping season would be over in a matter of hours, though a cynic could parse it as meaning that after two weeks, you couldn't give away tickets to this turkey.⁶⁴

As a result of the November 16 *Daily News* ad, the first line to buy tickets formed outside the Paramount Theatre at 10 p.m. on Tuesday, November 20, 1979, with a Captain Kirk in front. The line was soon two dozen strong, and the Mountain provided the early buyers with Star Trek sleeping bags. By the time the box office opened the following morning, the queue was several hundred people long.⁶⁵

One of first known lines to actually *see* the film after the MacArthur Premiere was not at the Paramount Theatre, but at the nearby Loew's State 1 Theatre at 45th St. and Broadway; exactly when it formed is uncertain, but the Loew's divisional manager had to be rousted from bed at 5:30 a.m. EST to do crowd control, and the line stretched four blocks by the time of the premiere showing at 9 a.m. The first three public showings were in Loew's theaters, the second being at 10 a.m. upstairs from the State 1 at the State 2, and the third was at 10:30 a.m. at the Loew's Orpheum at 86th St. and 3rd Ave. These were all before the noon showing at the Paramount, though everyone in the Paramount line already had their tickets. The State 1 also had the widest range of showtimes on Friday and Saturday, the first at 9 a.m. and the last at 2 a.m. Even assuming the final showing started exactly at 2 a.m.—which it almost certainly did not—the movie would have finished no sooner than 4:15 a.m., less than five hours before the 9 a.m. Saturday showing. If I had a time machine, the first I'd do would be to kill Baby Hitler, and then I'd go to Times Square at 4 a.m. on December 8, 1979, and set up a table with blan-

Showtimes for *Star Trek—The Motion Picture* at the Paramount Theatre and the Loew's State 1, Loew's State 2, and Loew's Orpheum theaters in Manhattan. Originally printed in the *New York Daily News* on December 7, 1979.

kets and hot cocoa for the bleary-eyed patrons exiting the State 1. It just seems like they'd need them.⁶⁶

The Loew's and the Paramount theaters were grand movie palaces with decades of history, but *Star Trek—The Motion Picture* was also the debut film in some new theaters in the state of New York on December 7, 1979. It was the first movie shown at the Sunrise Cinemas in Valley Stream, Long Island, a new multiplex built on the site of the former Sunrise Drive-In, as well as at the not-yet-finished multiplex in the former Pantry Pride Supermarket at the Nanuet Mall South in White Plains. The floors in the Nanuet's 450-seat auditorium were less than a week and a half old, there still wasn't any carpeting, and the other four theaters wouldn't open until Christmas week. All the same, the owners took out a full-page ad in the December 7 *Journal-News* proclaiming the Robert Wise film was opening that day at "Rockland County's Newest and Only 5-Auditorium Complex!" It worked, as over 1,000 people showed up for the three showings, the earliest of which was at 6 p.m., and the *Journal-News* made sure to dispatch a photographer to get a picture of those lines. The Towne Theater in Latham also drew the biggest crowds manager Jerry Hayes had ever witnessed, with all 800 seats selling out. Though the box office didn't open until 6:30 p.m., the audience began lining up outside the Cameo Theater over in Binghamton, at 1 p.m. for the 7 p m. premiere showing, while the line for the 9:45 p.m. showing began shortly after 7 p.m., and a photograph of that line was printed in the following day's *Press and Sun-Bulletin*.⁶⁷

Lines wound through the Arnot Mall in Elmira, where the resident Cinema had six showings starting at noon on Friday and Saturday, including a late show at 11:40 p.m. on both nights. The queue for one showing formed before the previous showing was even half over, which was a new enough phenomenon to be frequently mentioned in local newspaper articles about the opening of the Robert Wise film. The *Star-Gazette* printed a picture of an Arnot Mall Cinema line, and noted that some people were there because it was a good excuse to go out on a Friday, others "out of curiosity over the hoopla," while the "few they call the Trekkies"—which the paper defined as "those who have developed unusual compulsions about the Star Trek television show"—were there "because they couldn't help it."⁶⁸

Showings at the Blue Star Theater down in Watchung, New Jersey began at noon to a half-full house, though one of the attendees was a teenager who was there with his mother, who had a sent a note to her son's teacher explaining his whereabouts. The thrill of getting to see the first show was offset by the Blue Star receiving a faulty print which lacked audible dialog for the first 15 minutes. Most of that dialog was in subtitled Klingonese or Vulcan, but that didn't keep the angry patrons from demanding their money back. Just down Route 22 from the Blue Star, the Somerville Circle wasn't faring much better: though the print's sound was fine, the picture was split in half and flip-flopped, and the manager got booed out of the theater when he asked the patrons to please stay calm. (New Jersey, folks!) The following day the *Courier-News* ran a picture of that soon-to-be-angry crowd before they entered the theater, clustered in front of an awkward lobby standee featuring cutouts of Kirk, Spock, McCoy, Chapel, Scotty, Uhura, and Sulu, themselves awkwardly clustered together like a promo for a local evening news team. Next to it was a large picture of the *Enterprise* in which the ship is tilted at a downward angle. It doesn't look like it's sailing into the cosmos so much as it's about to crash back down to Earth—an appropriate visual accompaniment to the article's headline of "Science Fiction Film Fails to Send New Jersey 'Trekkies' Into Orbit."[69]

As opposed to the single student and his mother at the Blue Star, a group of science students were bused in from Parsippany High for a Friday afternoon show up at the Morris Hills Cinema I, while reservations had already been made for a group of 250 children from Paterson to see it at the Rockaway 6 at the end of the month. The Morris Hills Cinema I was among the few local theaters to hold midnight showings, along with the Rockaway. The latter added a midnight show so late in the game it wasn't listed in the *Daily Record*, though the paper did run a picture of the crowd outside the Morris Hills Cinema I.[70]

Camden County's *Courier-Post* ran a picture of the lines outside the Cherry Hill Cinema, which had also received one of the ungainly news-team standees. But the merchandise was selling briskly, and manager Steven Lauer said he'd never seen such large crowds on an opening day, the first fan having arrived at 8:30 a.m. for the noon show. Lauer expected those kinds of numbers to continue throughout the duration of the sixteen-week run, and in the shorter term he added midnight shows on Friday and Saturday, put his ushers and doormen in Star Trek uniforms, and brought in additional guards.[71]

Only a single person arrived three and half hours early at the Cherry Hill Cinema, but there were 100 blanket-bundled people in line by 7 a.m. at the RKO Stanley Warner Theater in Paramus, New Jersey for the premiere showing at 1 p.m. By half past noon, at least 900 of the theater's 1200 seats were occupied. Though they didn't arrive quite as early, a still-respectable 130 grownups and five children were in the audience for the noon show at the Totowa Cinema up Route 46, the first of six showings that day instead of the Totowa's usual four. As was the case across the country, many fans were playing hooky from work or school to see the first showing; that was part of the thrill of it all, and knowing people were paying up to $6 for that thrill in New York made the Totowa's manager feel comfortable upping his usual matinee price of $1.50 to $2 for children and $3 for adults, and the evening shows up to $4 for adults. The district manager back down at the RKO Stanley Warner didn't feel it was necessary to engage in what in 2018 would be called surge pricing, though he personally sold movie programs to fans in the lobby for $1.50 each. When he opened the doors, people fought over the first copy of the program even though there were plenty to go around, for Star Trek had been defined by nothing if not its scarcity.[72]

This was why the Fox at 16th and Market in Philadelphia had been receiving regular phone calls about the movie for the past two weeks. Some people waited in line all night for the premiere 11:00 a.m. EST showing, though whether that line started forming before the line at the Loew's State 1 in Manhattan is unknown. By the time the Fox opened at 10:30 a.m. the line was two or three people deep and stretched to 17th Street past the local porn theaters. *Philadelphia Inquirer* columnist Murray Dubin noted with some bemusement that the people in line—some smoking "funny-looking cigarettes," and others doing crossword puzzles or drinking unidentified beverages from bottled bags—were focused on the Robert Wise film, and showed no interest in the porn movies.[73]

People who had been waiting for years to see *Star Trek—The Motion Picture* not being lured out of line by *Confessions of Linda Lovelace*, *Hollywood Holly*, or *Gifts of Love*? You've never seen such goings-on![74]

Many theaters were breaking their own rules to accommodate this most-anticipated of films. Though mall theaters generally didn't open until the late afternoon, the first showing at the Sarasota Square 6 in Sarasota, Florida was at 1:30 p.m. EST—and being one of the relatively few multiplexes nationwide to have bid on two prints, it would be showing the Robert Wise film on two of its six screens. Across town, the first showing at the single-screen, non-mall-enclosed Cinema at Bayshore was at 11:30 a.m., and there would be midnight showings on Friday and Saturday.[75]

Down in North Miami Beach, 17 year-old high school senior David Weiss managed a Trek-heavy comic book store called Starship Enterprises. Weiss had noticed business had picked up since the advertising for the Robert Wise film had begun in earnest that summer, and he was confident that the fandom overall would experience an upsurge if the movie did well. In the shorter term, he was among the many fans who attended a special "preview for Trekkies" at 11 a.m. on opening day at the Florida Twin, and then after possibly seeing it once or twice more at one of the several area theaters showing it, Weiss attended the "Star Trek Party" at the Longshot disco in the Holiday

Inn Hialeah. The Longshot's ad in the *Miami News* read "Calling all Trekkies: Celebrate the new movie! Party!" Among the incentives were "Live Entertainment by Clockwork," the opportunity to "Dance and Drink 'til 5 a.m.," as well as "Great Prizes, Surprises and Contests," and of course "Anyone in Costume Admitted Free." Many fans did appear in costume, and also present was one of the standees of the *Enterprise* at the odd downward angle, at least until it was returned to its theater at midnight. But again, it must be stated that a Miami disco of the sort which specified in want ads that the staff "must be young, attractive & personable" was devoting a night to a new, sight-unseen G-rated studio film. This just did not happen in the brief history of that rating, but perhaps it was because of the sophistication of the Trekkers—though definitely not the revoltin' Trekkies. As explained to a *Miami News* reporter by a 20 year-old who saw *Star Wars* in the theater at least two dozen times, bought two phaser replicas for $35 each, owned several costume uniforms and traveled all over the country to conventions, the word Trekkie was "revolting," while Trekker meant "means a more sophisticated science fiction fan." Again, this was from a 20 year-old who saw *Star Wars* in the theater at least two dozen times, bought two phaser replicas for $35 each, owned several costume uniforms and traveled all over the country to conventions. (This writer saw *My Little Pony: The Movie* twelve times in the theater in 2017 yet personally rejects the word "Brony," but that's different. Read *Ponyville Confidential* to find out why!)[76]

Star Trek—The Manifest Procession, Part II: Kentucky, Mississippi and Arkansas

Regardless of the sophistication of the people dancing near it, the *Enterprise* standee was removed from the Longshot while many theaters up and down the Eastern seaboard were beginning their midnight showings. While such a thing was unprecedented in most locales, the nine-screen Showcase Cinemas megaplex in Louisville, Kentucky had no truck with such precedent. They regularly showed all their features in late-or-midnight shows, including the currently re-released Disney film *Sleeping Beauty*—*Fantasia* could often also be found in midnight showings throughout the decade, but that was for a more niche crowd—and their final opening day showing of the Robert Wise film was at half past midnight EST. The first was at 1:45 p.m., the line for which was already winding around the huge building by 12:45 p.m., and easily filled the 1,012-seat auditorium. The first person in line for the 7:05 p.m. showing arrived by 3 p.m., and different showings had different lines, requiring an usher with a megaphone to walk around the building making sure patrons were correctly queued. Upon discovering that the 7:05 p.m. showing only had seats left in the first two rows, several hundred people in its line decided to wait a few more hours for the 9:50 p.m. Meanwhile, someone who did get into the 7:05 p.m. was Teri Howard, one of the charter members of the Star Trek Revival Association of Kentuckiana, aka STRAK. She knew exactly what had happened: the fans wanted Star Trek revived, and through sheer force of their desire, they willed it into existence. "I can't believe it! We did it!"[77]

Over in Owensboro, Kentucky, the more modest Plaza Twin was only showing the Robert Wise film at 7:15 p.m. and 9:30 p.m. CST, and both shows sold out. The management specified in the print ad that the theater didn't open until 6:30 p.m., but people nonetheless started lining up at 6:15 p.m., and once they got inside they were happy to buy merchandise in spite of the ticket prices being bumped up from $3 to $3.50. (Opening that same day on the Twin's other screen, and for the usual $3.00, was Nicholas Meyer's *Time After Time*.)[78]

Further west in Kentucky, the phone had been ringing off the hook at the Columbia II in Paducah, where people had been calling from Indiana and Tennessee to find out if tickets could be reserved. The Robert Wise film wouldn't be shown in Tennessee until December 21, while the Kentucky town of Paducah was much closer for many people in southern Indiana than Warsaw and Lafayette, the northern Indiana cities where it was opening that day. There were only two showings scheduled for Friday and Saturday night at Paducah's 350-seat Columbia II, and hundreds of people had to be turned away. Playing on the theater's other screen was the 1977 Jules Verne adaptation *Where Time Began*, but that was cold comfort to those who didn't get in to the Robert Wise film. (The following week, *Where Time Began* would be replaced by a film alternately known as *Redneck County Rape* or *Massacre at Redneck County*; it had been shot by David Worth, who would later direct *Warrior of the Lost World*.) Those who did make it into the first showing experienced their own frustrations: projection issues stopped the film as soon as it began, and since the Columbia II wasn't equipped for Dolby Stereo, the sound had to be turned up to a hissy high volume to compensate.[79]

Down in Jackson, Mississippi, the Metro Center Cinema was squeezing in as many showings as they could, the first at noon and the last at 12:10 a.m. CST, which proved to be the first time they'd sold out a midnight show. There had been a steady stream of calls, but unlike the beleaguered Columbia II, the Metro could handle it, mostly—people were still turned away, but not as many. In the lobby filled with what the local newspaper described as "boisterous adolescents," a 21 year-old college student who had been a fan since she was 13 and had spent about $200 on Star Trek books and $75 on comics explained to the paper's reporter that she was a Trekker, not a Trekkie: "Trekkies are usually like young girls who go screaming after Shaun Cassidy. Some of us are serious about it." (As it happened, in 1980 Cassidy would record a version of Jerry Goldsmith's "Ilia's Theme" with lyrics by Larry Kusik, though it wouldn't get a proper release in the United States for decades.) Whether Trekkies, Trekkers, or Decline to State, enough fans called the Markham 1 in Little Rock, Arkansas asking about advance tickets that manager Ed Roberts elected to just take the damned phone off the hook. And across the Arkansas River at the McCain Mall Cinema in North Little Rock, where adult tickets were $3, manager Betty Jackson had more than a few people offer her $5.[80]

Star Trek—The Manifest Procession, Part III: Indiana, Illinois, Michigan and Minnesota

The 4-screen Tippecanoe Mall Cinema in Lafayette, Indiana bid on two prints, and the gamble paid off: except for the first two Friday matinees, the eight shows per day on Friday, Saturday, and Sunday all sold out, and a last minute, unpublicized midnight showing on Saturday still sold 180 of the auditorium's 200 seats. The Saturday 5 p.m. EST showing was oversold, an accident on multiple levels since the theater typically didn't sell all available seats in case people wanted to stay and watch a given movie again. Cinema manager Walter Wolverton was pleasantly shocked by how well the Robert Wise film did during their traditionally slow period—so slow that the nearby Cinema West and Lafayette Theaters had gone into hibernation due to a lack of new films, with plans to reopen on December 21—and by Monday, December 10, Wolverton reckoned that at least 5,000 people had seen the Robert Wise film at his theater. While there had been some outliers in recent years such as *Superman*, *Star Wars*, and *Jaws*, this kind of turnout for a brand-new film was simply unheard of at the Tippecanoe. The Vore Cinemas in Warsaw, Indiana only had the one print, and their ads noted that "Due to Contractual Obligations there will be a slight price increase," without specifying what the price increase was.[81]

Up in Battle Creek, Michigan, the line for the film's 7 p.m. EST premiere at Towne Cinema Theatres began forming at 5:30 p.m., an hour before the box office opened, and it stretched far beyond the theater. Upwards of 200 of the people in that line didn't make it into the 370-seat auditorium for the first show, but they did make it into the 9:30 p.m. A photo of the line was printed in the following day's *Enquirer*, and reporter John Sherwood noted with approval that "there were no fanatic trekkies with half-shaven eyebrows and armband insignias," but still hypothesized that "if, in those anticipatory moments as the lights dimmed, someone had yelled 'Fire!' we bet nobody would have left." Among those described as "devout" was a seventeen year-old who "has many of the episodes on videotape," and a ten year-old who had been watching the show since birth. Towne Cinema manager Steve Miller was not quite as sanguine about the madness as some others; between the merch pop-up selling shirts, badges, buttons, and bumper stickers, and the onslaught of phone calls that week from people looking for advance tickets, he told the *Enquirer* that if he didn't have to work there, "I wouldn't be within miles of this place."[82]

Miller wouldn't have found much solace many miles away in Chicago, where theaters in the city and the surrounding suburbs also experienced constant phone calls and long, early lines. Fans started queuing outside the State Lake Theatre in the Loop at 6:30 a.m. CST for the first 9 a.m. show, though only six of them were in uniform, and State Lake manager Pat Burns opened the doors forty minutes early to let in what he noted were very large and enthusiastic but nonetheless "orderly" crowds. He estimated that by 3:30 p.m., about 3,000 people in their twenties had seen the movie, which was about four to five times the State Lake's usual attendance, even for Fridays.[83]

With 2,649 seats and seven showings on Friday, the last one at midnight, the State Lake was equipped to handle the rush. Less so the Parkway Theater over in Moline, Illinois, where a five-deep line of more than 1,100 people started forming at 4 p.m. for the 7:30 p.m. premiere showing, to which only 736 could be admitted. Those who didn't get in stuck around for the 10:00 p.m.—which sold out, much to the amazement of Parkway manager Steve Glueck. Sure, *Buck Rogers in the 25th Century* had done well enough earlier in the year, but he couldn't remember the last time back-to-back showings of the same film had sold out. For that matter, he was still amazed his theater had gotten lucky enough to show the Robert Wise film at all, let alone for a 16-week run; he merely managed the theater, and a booking agent scheduled the films. But Glueck had known it was a big enough deal to make a to-do out of the opening night: he and the other male employees were dressed in blue tuxedoes, while some of the female employees were in long dresses with red corsages, the labor laws in 1979 Illinois allowing him to request such things.[84]

The line stretched around the Parkway, and those first few hundred were doubly lucky in that the building provided some protection from the harsh western winds that chilled the temperature down to zero. But that was of little concern to the hardy Rock Island County residents, some of whom battled the cold by occasionally returning to their vehicles to get liquored up.

Besides, as locals Beth Morford and Christine Burklund told a reporter from the *Daily Dispatch*, not even a blizzard would have kept them away. Inside the theater during the thirty-minute wait for popcorn, a male fan explained to the reporter the difference between a Trekkie and a Trekker: "'A Trekkie is a groupie,' he said disdainfully. 'A Trekker has more of an intellectual concept about what the whole Star Trek notion is all about.'"[85]

A couple dozen fans gathered in the cold outside the Marc Cinema in Green Bay, Wisconsin two hours before the premiere showing at 7 p.m. CST, though they surely would have been there even had the Marc's ad in the *Press-Gazette* not warned that "No one will be admitted once the journey begins." That paper's columnist Warren Gerds sniffed at the concept of waiting in line for the Robert Wise film, declaring that it "isn't that important a movie, despite its pricetag."[86]

Over in the Twin Cities, *Minneapolis Star* columnist Don Morrison took a more religious view of what the whole Star Trek notion was about when he attended the Southtown Theater's premiere showing at 12:30 p.m. CST, describing himself as a "non-initiate" who was lucky to find "an empty pew in the 1,100-seat theater." When he told his seatmate that he was there to review the film, the fellow "beamed like a curate welcoming a prospective convert," and Morrison referred to fans as "votaries" who "evinced the self-possession of long-term believers, keepers of the faith," while the gathered audience was a "convocation," the theater was a "temple," and *Star Trek I* was "the classic canon." (In 1979, the word "canon" would have been intended only as a scriptural reference.) Morrison admitted he "felt enviously excluded by ignorance—as well as unworthy to join in on the brotherhoods' fond whoops of greeting" as each character appeared onscreen.[87]

At the Paramount Theatre in St. Cloud, Minnesota, where the weather was in the mid-teens with brisk winds, the lines didn't start forming until an hour before the first showing at 7 p.m. Anticipating capacity crowds similar to *Star Wars*, the management set up extra concession stands and doubled the staff from the usual four to eight.[88]

Star Trek—The Manifest Procession, Part IV: South Dakota, Nebraska, Kansas, Utah and Arizona

If we follow Don Morrison's metaphor that *ST—TMP* made movie theaters into religious temples, then the West Mall Theater in Sioux Falls, South Dakota was one of the few which boasted an Ark. It was courtesy of local

Elks Club bartender Steve Faye, who attended opening night decked out in a gold Starfleet uniform and carrying business cards reading "Public Information Officer, Headquarters, Star Fleet Command." Moviegoers standing in the long lines in the Mall's Center Court were able to peruse his glass-encased collection, which included replicas of phasers, tricorders, and communicators, models of various ships, and the item Faye was most proud of, a letter of thanks from Gene Roddenberry. (Like Steve Wozniak, Faye had the series on videocassette, though Roddenberry probably didn't thank him for that.) Faye's collection was enough of a draw that it was advertised along with the film itself in the local newspaper, and even the mall's resident Santa was impressed, proudly declaring himself a Trekkie. Faye also had a permanent collection at South Dakota State University—go fighting Jackrabbits!—and planned to donate the contents of his Ark to the Smithsonian. Faye hoped this would lead to him to meeting Gene Roddenberry and thus finagle a cameo in the sequel, because a sequel was something that was definitely going to happen, and when it did Roddenberry would definitely be in charge.[89]

Advertisement for Commander Steve Faye's Nationally Famous Collection of Star Trek items, included in the larger advert for *Star Trek—The Motion Picture* at the West Mall Theater in Sioux Falls, South Dakota. Originally printed in the *Argus Leader* on December 7, 1979.

Down in Lincoln, Nebraska, State Theater manager Jim Mulvaney had his mind blown when the line began forming at 2:15 p.m. CST for the 7:15 p.m. premiere showing. The two kids who arrived first said they were willing to stand in line in order to get the best of the theater's 700 seats, and it just kept growing, longer than Mulvaney had ever seen in Lincoln. The arrival of the ticket seller at 6 p.m. prompted applause from the 100-strong crowd, and the theater chain's city manager Bruce Lee Smith approved the unusual move of opening the doors an hour before the first showing. When that sold out, tickets went on sale for 9:45 p.m., and the fact that people were willing to buy tickets two hours before the show proved to Smith that they were real Star Trek fans. And it's not like Mulvaney didn't know the film was a big deal; when they won the bid to exhibit the Robert Wise film ahead of other local theaters, the State underwent a major renovation to get it ready. But who could have anticipated this? It might even prove to be another *Star Wars*, Smith mused. Time would tell.[90]

Time was the fire in which 20 year-old Kansas City, Missouri resident Bonnie Young burned as she went to the Robert Wise film at a theater in Overland Park: her contractions were just a few minutes apart. She'd waited nine months for the birth of her child, but she'd waited ten years for the birth of the movie based on her favorite television show, and she wasn't going to miss it. She and her spouse Dennis decided to take their chances, and their friends brought sterilized sheets and rubber gloves in case she went into labor during a film which they had no way of knowing would end with a cosmic birth metaphor, one which Dr. McCoy specifically describes as delivering a baby. But they didn't get that far, as at about 90 minutes into the movie Dennis took Bonnie to Kansas City's Menorah Medical Center despite her protests—and to the disappointment of their friends, who were looking forward to the human adventure of delivering the child in the theater. Bonnie gave birth to her son Colin Patrick at about 4 a.m. CST on Saturday, December 8, 1979, around the time that the midnight showings on the West Coast were letting out. The story made the rounds through the UPI, and the *Salina Journal* gave it a headline which rivals "Headless Body Found in Topless Bar" for its sheer beauty: "Debut Interrupts Premiere."[91]

The Century 5 in Salt Lake City, Utah was one of the rare non-coastal theaters to not only show the film on two screens, but to print advance mail-in ticket forms in the local newspaper. Only available through more direct methods were the $15–25 tickets for a 10 p.m. MST benefit screening for the Shriners Children's Hospital, which was promoted as including a buffet to be presented during intermission. What happened when they received the film and discovered it lacked an intermission is unknown.[92]

Unintentional intermissions were the problem for the 10:45 a.m. MST premiere showing at the UA Cinema 6 in Phoenix, where the film broke twice. This was greeted by shouted obscenities from the crowd, who otherwise loved the movie, and also loved buying the posters, programs, and other merchandise on sale. The first in line was 21 year-old Dave McDonald, who arrived at 7:00 a.m. Having seen *Star Wars* at least six times, he reckoned he would see the Robert Wise film upwards of 15 to 20 times—even though, as he told a reporter from the *Arizona Republic*, "I was a little disappointed they didn't hardly use any of their weapons." McDonald didn't shy away from the T-word though another patron of drinking age insisted that he wasn't one, since "Trekkies are people who are addicted to Star Trek. The fans just like it a lot." Also planning to see it a few more times (but without registering her status as a Trekkie or not) was Debby Grimm, who took her two sons out of school to see the movie.[93]

Star Trek—The Manifest Procession, Part V: Washington, Oregon, Nevada and California

After walking over four miles from adjoining Mercer Island because the buses hadn't started running yet, a pair of boys *sans* their mother made it to the John Danz Theater in Bellevue, Washington at 3 a.m. PST. Arriving at a slightly more reasonable time (but still seventeenth in line) was fortysomething Kitty Canterbury, who intended to buy 260 tickets for the evening showing for her fellow fans who weren't able to spend the workday waiting in line. At the 1,307-seat Capitol theater across the border in Victoria, British Columbia, 1,250 people attended the 7 p.m. PST premiere, and the 9:20 p.m. had about 1,000 people. Many theater owners were amazed by these kinds of turnouts, but not Capitol manager John McRae—after all, people had started lining up at 9 a.m. during a re-release of *Old Yeller*, so, whatever.[94]

The line for the 7 p.m. PST premiere at the 500-seat Cinema World theater in Corvallis, Oregon began at 4:30 p.m. with four souls, and was soon hundreds of people long. The doors didn't open until 6:30 p.m., and undeterred by the seasonally chilly, damp fog, a celebratory atmosphere soon took over as people drank beer and wine and ate fast food such as pizza, hamburgers, and tacos from local restaurants. The crowd cheered when the doors opened, and booed at the trailers before the feature started, including the teaser for Buzz Kulik's *The Hunter*.[95]

A more formal celebration was taking place in Portland, Oregon that night, both the biggest *ST—TMP* event outside of the MacArthur Premiere as well as the biggest film party in Portland in recent decades. With assistance from Paramount via local PR firm Thunder Media, Portland radio station KGW held a bombastic, black-tie premiere at the Rose Moyer Theatre. The over 700 attendees included sports figures and local celebrities such as Greg Smith of the Portland Trail Blazers and City Commissioner Frank Ivancie, and all who were invited were asked to dress in 1930s-style Hollywood glamour. After a champagne cocktail reception at Cedarville Park in Gresham, a caravan of limousines took them to the Rose Moyer, which like the MacArthur was outfitted with a red carpet and spotlights.[96]

While the event itself aspired to classiness, the promotion had a more playful bent. Led by KGW disc jockey Glynn Shannon, the DJs had been conducting "ear raids" at Portland shopping centers for the past two weeks in which they gave out pointed Spock ears to the public, 50 of whom would be able to get into the Rose Moyer premiere for free. Being showmen who knew how to sell it hot, Shannon and his fellow spinners of platters that mattered also distributed ears at the November 29 Ice Capades performance, which itself was in its second year of presenting a sci-fi-themed show called "Star Struck."[97]

Though they wouldn't be the first to see the film, the Portlanders did have one advantage over the MacArthur attendees: the Portland screening would be preceded by a laser light show. (If that didn't make up for the absence of William Shatner, nothing would.) Other than wearing the ears distributed by the KGW DJs, most of the Star Trek fans who attended dressed in their street clothes, though one young man was in full alien regalia, while City Commissioner Mildred Schwab got into the spirit of things by dressing sharp *and* wearing pointed ears.[98]

The spirits continued to flow after the Cedarville Park reception, as many people were still drinking when the movie began at 6:00 p.m., and every so often an empty glass could be heard journeying down the sloped theater floor. But the consumption of alcohol where alcohol was not legally permitted to be consumed was the least of local law enforcement's concerns: a bomb threat was called into the Multnomah County sheriff's office at 8:00 p.m., by which time both the film and the spent champagne flutes were rolling. The male caller said the bomb would go off at 8:30 p.m., conveniently after the movie was over, and sheriff's deputies ushered the attendees out of the theater as soon as the lights came up. After checking under the seats and finding nothing but the occasional stray champagne glass, and further determining that the popcorn machine was free of incendiary devices, they reopened the theater in less than 15 minutes. The irony of the Portland bomb hoax was that the MacArthur Premiere the night before was the one attended by nationally-known political figures and celebrities of the sort who more commonly attracted such threats, and yet on that level, it had gone off without any such hiccups.[99]

Down in Reno, Nevada, the Century Screen Complex theater scheduled six showings for opening day, from the premiere at 11:45 a.m. PST to the final some 13 hours later at 12:45 a.m. The line for the 11:45 a.m. showing began at 8:30 a.m. and stretched for nearly a block, which manager Jim Siekman took to be a good sign, as was how all six shows played to near-capacity crowds of people in their 20s and 30s. Some were carrying Star Trek books, others wore sweatshirts depicting their favorite characters, and a few were in uniform complete with pointed ears—though there were no Trekkers explaining to the local press why *those* people weren't sophisticated, intellectual fans such as themselves.[100]

Leslie De Manche of the Los Angeles–based Mann Theaters chain was amazed at how well advance tickets had been selling in spite of how little material there had been from the film, which already had a bigger opening than *Star Wars* or the new gold standard, *Superman: The Movie*. On Thursday night, a dozen fans set up camp outside Mann's Chinese Theatre in Hollywood to ensure being first in line for the premiere showing at 9:30 a.m. PST, which would be the first on the West Coast. The Chinese's last opening-day showing would begin at 1:00 a.m. Saturday morning, giving that venue the second widest range of starting times nationwide after the Loew's State 1 in New York, which still had it beat with its staggering 9 a.m. to 2 a.m. run. Though he did not camp out the night before, among those attending that first showing at the Chinese was David Gerrold, who in addition to appearing onscreen as an *Enterprise* crewmember, wanted his first time seeing the picture to be with a "fannish audience."[101]

A few hours up U.S. 101, the fannish audiences in Santa Maria were in luck. Their town seldom received new movies on opening day, let alone a movie that wasn't playing yet in some states, and the manager of the Santa Maria Theatre further hedged their bets by noting on the marquee that *ST—TMP* featured the "Original Crew." Though the line for the 7 p.m. PST premiere stretched down South Broadway and onto East Main, it still didn't fill all the 1,236 seats. But the early buzz from that first showing was that the film was "pretty good," though just to be on the safe side, by Tuesday the theater noted in their *Santa Maria Times* ad that the film featured the Original Crew.[102]

There was no shortage of Original Crew fans up in Salinas, where about 700 showed up for the 242 tickets available for the three showings at the Northridge Cinema multiplex. The theater staff started working around 2 p.m. to get the Dolby sound working properly before the box office opened at 5 p.m., by which time the line was stretching around both sides of the theater. Tickets for the 5:30 p.m. premiere sold out in 35 minutes, and those who weren't among the line's front 242 waited for tickets to go on sale for the 7:50 p.m. The biggest challenge for manager David Martin and his ushers was trying to get one audience out and the next audience in between shows, and while they'd been quiet and orderly in line outside, once inside the noise began. In addition to the usual cheers when the lights lowered and the curtains opened as well as to the appearance of the familiar faces, one attendee who had clearly taken Star Trek's message of peace and tolerance to heart yelled out, "Kill the Ayatollah!" When leaving the 7:50 p.m. showing, another patron yelled, "The movie sucks, get your money back!" His advice went unheeded by the audience making their way into the theater for the night's third and final showing.[103]

As we've seen, audiences with strong opinions were the order of the day across the country. *San Francisco Examiner* columnist Bill Mandel attended the 10 a.m. premiere showing at the Regency I in San Francisco with what he described not unkindly as "a pack of rabid Trekkies." In preparation for the pack, this was the first film shown at both the Regency I and the neighboring Regency II simultaneously. Well, mostly simultaneously: the first showing at the Regency II would be at noon. Two security guards were hired to keep an eye on the line outside the theater, there were an extra 15 ushers for inside, and four times the usual amount of cola syrup and popcorn was ordered for the patrons. Mandel observed that some were comparing photos of *Star Trek I*'s *Enterprise* to her *Motion Picture* incarnation, and noting the change in the shape, one young man declared, "they've borrowed Klingon engines." That was pure headcanon on his part—but not without precedent, since in the *Trek I* episode "The Enterprise Incident" it was established that the Romulans had begun using Klingon designs—but it again went to show how little Gene Roddenberry understood the fans when he told *Cinefantastique* "nobody's likely to get up there with a ruler and see the difference" in the ship. Of course they would, and once they got over their disappointment about the new designs not following Franz Joseph's books—though some images from *Star Trek Blueprints* do briefly appear on a screen at Spock's station around 1:14:05—they would fill in the blanks on their own. That's just how fandoms express themselves, for better or worse. But unlike so many correspondents, the *Examiner*'s Mandel didn't distance himself from those fans. He wrote that "everything we loved from the TV series is back," and "there were plenty of tears at 'Star Trek: The Motion Picture' Friday, mine among them. I hadn't realized how important the inhabitants of this better dream had become to me."[104]

The Shakedown, Part I: Acceleration

Wasting no time, Paramount ran a two-page "For Your Consideration" ad in the December 7, 1979, *Daily Variety* for "Art Direction, Cinematography, Costume Design, Sound, Film Editing and Music." (The Robert Wise film would go on to be nominated for Best Art Direction, Visual Effects, and Original Score, winning none.) The ad also promoted Academy member screenings on the Paramount lot every night of the week beginning Monday,

December 10, and again on Monday, December 17; it was one of the many ways membership had its privileges, since tickets for the Robert Wise film were $5 in most Los Angeles theaters. It wasn't setting a new local precedent so much as following one, as Francis Ford Coppola's *Apocalypse Now* broke the half-a-sawbuck barrier earlier that year at the Cinerama Dome. The venue had already confirmed that was how much tickets for Steven Spielberg's *1941* would cost when it opened the following week, though the Robert Wise film would never play the theater where Robert Collins began to realize he would never direct his own Star Trek film. In 2018, *ST—TMP*'s reputation is closer to that of *1941* than *Apocalypse Now*, though perhaps owing to having seen them both around the same impressionable age, this writer loves *1941* almost as much as she loves the Robert Wise film. (*Apocalypse Now* came later for me, though I did see it in 70mm when it played every few years at the Castro Theatre in San Francisco in the 1990s and 2000s, until the print started to lose its color.)[105]

Gene Roddenberry's novelization of the Robert Wise film debuted on the *New York Times* Paperback Best Sellers list on Sunday, December 9, 1979, at number nine, between Helen MacInnes' *Prelude to Terror* at eight and M.M. Kaye's *The Far Pavilions* at ten. Come Monday, December 10, Paramount was reporting that the movie version of Roddenberry's book had already grossed $2M in 105 of the 850-odd theaters, which was enough for Distribution and Marketing President Frank Mancuso to call it "historic." $325,076 of that $2M was from 17 theaters in Los Angeles, including breaking house records at Mann's National in Westwood and the Chinese in Hollywood, and Paramount claimed records were being broken all over the country. As *Daily Variety*'s Dale Pollock pointed out, the Mountain needed it, badly: though the studio had "steadfastly refused to confirm any budget figure (and some published reports indicate estimates have moved skyward in an intrastudio p.r. competition), reliable sources indicate a negative cost of around $42,000,000," meaning the film would need to gross "at least $100,000,000 to come into the black in this country, although foreign and ancillary markets look to be tremendous."[106]

The domestic markets weren't looking un-tremendous, and the headline of the Tuesday, December 11 *Daily Variety* read "'Star Trek Sets Three-Day Record." With 852 theaters reporting, the weekend gross came out to $11,815,203, beating both *Jaws 2*'s three-day opening of $9,904,000 in June 1978, and *Superman*'s all-time three-day total of $10,364,384 in December 1978. It was noted that this record-breaking was partially accountable to the increased ticket prices in both Los Angeles and New York, and that the picture's average of $13,868 per theater was still less than other films which had a more modest and selective opening pattern. Still, the numbers were impressive in and of themselves: the picture grossed $1,231,374 throughout 58 locations in Los Angeles, $1,373,848 in 81 theaters in New York, and $432,701 in a mere dozen Chicago theaters. Since the troubled making of the film was of no less interest than the final product, the article included a soon-to-be legendary photo of 2500 film cans containing of 7000 reels of *ST—TMP* at MGM's Stage 12 waiting to be distributed across the country, a collection which still didn't constitute every print of the film in circulation. Jeffrey Katzenberg was proud of that image, telling *Cinefantastique*'s Preston Neal Jones of "an extraordinary photo, which you must get from publicity so you can run it in your magazine: at the MGM lab, where there was a stack of literally hundreds of film cans, all about to be rushed out that same day to all the theaters across the country that had booked *Star Trek*." (The photo did not run in Jones' Winter 1979 *Cinefantastique* article about the film, and Katzenberg's entreaty to do so wouldn't surface until *Return to Tomorrow* in 2014.)[107]

There was a ripple effect at work: the movie business was in what *Variety* referred to as "its seasonal pre-holiday trough," and the domestic box office had already dropped more than 40% from the previous week. Things were expected to pick up a few days before Christmas, hence theaters such as the Cinema West and the Lafayette in Indiana closing until December 21. But until then, the Robert Wise film was draining away what business there was from all the other films, "cutting in noticeably to the holdover business of recent hits and clobbering the others."[108]

Among the clobbering cities was New York, where by Monday, December 10 its gross had reached $1,423,848, with the closest competitor being its fellow event picture *Apocalypse Now* at $280,000. The Robert Wise film grossed $600,000 in a dozen Chicago theaters by December 11, the closest competitor in the Loop being a re-release of the 1971 Jacqueline Bisset vehicle *Secrets* at $51,000 in 20 theaters. In the considerably smaller market of San Francisco, the Robert Wise film grossed $92,000 at the Regency I and II, and the next highest-grosser was *The Pizza Triangle*, itself a re-release of a 1970 film, which grossed $7,200 at the (much smaller) Lumiere. By December 12, the Robert Wise film had grossed $192,000 in Seattle, with the Dudley Moore vehicle *10* next in line with $31,000.[109]

Though the reviews across the board were mixed-to-meh, Charlie Bluhdorn's bottom line was doing well, as on December 10 Gulf and Western's stock slid up ⅜ to 18½. Neither the reviews nor the middling word-of-mouth hurt the momentum after opening weekend: according to Mancuso, the picture grossed $1,295,160 nationwide on Monday, December 10, $1,360,193 on Tuesday,

December 11, and $1,302,304 on Wednesday, December 12, resulting in a six-day domestic gross of $15,884,078. As *Daily Variety* pointed out, this meant the film had a good chance of beating *Jaws 2*'s initial seven-day gross of $16,654,000. For as much as the Robert Wise film is associated with *Star Wars* in the conventional wisdom, both as its *sine qua non* and its competition, at the time *Jaws 2* was the hurdle it had to clear. As it happened, one of the only other new films being released in competition with the Robert Wise film was itself a *Jaws* ripoff called *Killer Fish*. It did not do as well.[110]

That was inside-baseball stuff, however. Outside baseball, on Friday, December 14, Paramount ran two-page ads in Los Angeles, New York, and Chicago newspapers with the key art from the film, and the words "Star Trek—The Phenomenon!" at a diagonal across the pages. (In San Francisco it was a one-page ad, because San Francisco always has been and always will be an afterthought to the movie industry.) Text along the bottom shouted, "LAST WEEKEND MORE THAN 4½ MILLION PEOPLE JOURNEYED TO THE GREATEST MOTION PICTURE EVENT IN HISTORY."[111]

Roddenberry's novelization, which featured no fewer than two descriptions of Kirk getting an erection, was at number five on the *New York Times* Paperback Best Sellers list on Sunday, December 16, 1979. That same day, the Film Advisory Board held their monthly (!) awards luncheon for what they considered to be the best in family entertainment, and the G-rated Robert Wise film was the only movie to receive their Award of Excellence that month. The other recipients were all television specials, including *Perry Como's Christmas in New Mexico* and Don Bluth's animated short *Banjo, the Woodpile Cat*.[112]

Paramount's embarrassment at the film's G-rating would prove so profound that in later decades, the Mountain simply ignored it. The Blu-rays released in 2009 and 2013 list it as "Not Rated," which is a lie, while the DVD of the theatrical cut claims to be PG, which is also a lie. At the time of this writing, the version available to stream on YouTube which Paramount uploaded on June 20, 2012—described as "the original theatrical version of the film as it was initially released in theaters," which leads me to believe it's the original theatrical version which received a G rating on December 4, 1979, and was initially released to theaters on December 7 of that same year—is listed as being rated PG, which is not true. The 2001 *Director's Edition* did receive a PG rating for some reason, but the original theatrical version of the film as it was initially released in theaters was rated G.[113]

As though being honored alongside *Banjo, the Woodpile Cat* wasn't glory enough, the bad fish had been put in its place: by Monday, December 17, 1979, the numbers were in from enough theaters to know the Robert Wise film's initial seven-day gross in 857 theaters across the United States and Canada was at least $17,060,837, thus beating *Jaws 2* in that particular metric. In doing so, the Robert Wise film set an industry record which would hold until the release of the Hal Needham film *Smokey and the Bandit Part II*, which grossed nearly $18M in its opening week in August 1980.[114]

In terms of rentals, meaning the money theaters handed over to the studio, the Robert Wise film made $12M in its first week. The grosses were still behind *Superman*'s all-time record for *non*-opening seven-day gross of $18.2M during the week between Christmas and New Year's Eve in 1978, but the Wise film would only keep expanding, as 154 more prints would debut on December 21 in states which had passed anti-blind-bidding legislation. Never missing an opportunity to be dickish to theater owners in states where it was illegal for the studios to make them exhibit a film without getting a chance to see it first, Paramount's Frank Mancuso pointed out those theaters had already lost two weeks of business, and that it would be like "seeing the World Series delayed two weeks." *Variety* noted that the previous estimate of a domestic gross of at least $100M being necessary to come into the black in the United States was upped to $125M, with $55M in rentals required to just break even, though Mancuso was confident that if the film received positive word-of-mouth, it would show the "legs" necessary to reach those numbers. *Daily Variety*'s Dale Pollock wrote that the picture could be expected to dip slightly that week, but if it "doesn't pull down its heaviest figures between Christmas and New Year's, something is decidedly wrong."[115]

Things were looking decidedly right overseas: the picture grossed $51,387 in two days after its Saturday, December 15 opening at the Empire Theatre Leicester Square in London. It was scheduled to open in 380 theaters throughout the rest of the United Kingdom on December 20, in Australia and New Zealand on December 22, and in South Africa on Wednesday, December 26. (Whether the Robert Wise film played Sun City, the resort which was also first unveiled to the public on December 7, 1979, is unknown.) Come December 21 in the United States, it was looking doubtful whether the film did have the legs; its second-week gross was around $10.5M, a drop of about 38% from its first week take of $17M, and this was before those additional 154 prints went into circulation.[116]

Exactly who was the first wag to dub the first Star Trek movie "The Motionless Picture" is unknown, but the earliest instance I've been able to find was Derek Malcolm in the London *Guardian* on December 20, 1979. It's often attributed to Harlan Ellison because his review in *Starlog* #33 in February 1980 was reprinted in his 1989 book *Harlan Ellison's Watching* as "Star Trek—The Motionless Picture," and because many fans want to credit Ellison with all the clever things. But in *Starlog* it was simply titled "Ellison Reviews Trek" and the review itself doesn't use the word "motionless," so there is no evidence that he originated the *bon mot*.[117]

It was around this time that certain manufacturers began to feel like they'd been had, and in some cases dodged a bullet. Movie poster licensee Lawrence Blum had pre-bought the rights based on the popularity of *Star Trek I*, and he sold 1.2 million posters, 150,000 of which around special two-sided poster which was 3-D on one side and four-color on the other. (This writer owns one of those, and you are jealous.) But the majority of those were pre-orders before the film came out on December 7, and there were no significant orders after the film's expansion on December 21, because by then it was clear that nobody liked it all that much. Blum was grateful he didn't over-print—and there was precedent for larger print runs, since his Star Wars posters sold 5 million, and the iconic Farrah Fawcett poster he helped to market sold twice that—but after nearly taking a bath on Star Trek, he swore to never buy a license without seeing the product first.[118]

The downturn in enthusiasm coincided with the one thing most everybody liked about the film: Jerry Goldsmith's score, which was original scheduled for release by Columbia Records on December 10 as a single-disc LP for $8.98. Unlike the movie, the record's release date was able to be delayed until it was ready to go: the album was reviewed in the December 22, 1979, issue of *Cash Box*, and debuted on their charts at #154 on December 29, 1979. Record stores were being provided with standees, mobiles, posters and other promotional aids for a marketing push for the Goldsmith record which, like Paramount's own push of the Robert Wise film, would continue well into January. On December 23, 1979, around the time Goldsmith's soundtrack was released, Roddenberry's novelization reached no. 3 on the *New York Times* list.[119]

A week after Goldsmith's album, Columbia rush-released two 7" singles of brass-heavy covers of the theme song by jazz artists Bob James and Maynard Ferguson. They are both disco numbers—which isn't a bad thing!—though *Cash Box* bent over backwards to avoid using the increasingly poisonous d-word, writing of Ferguson's single that "jazz and pop stations will go for this, but its also adaptable to dance lists," and that on James' track "Latin-tinged percussives keep an insistent backbeat throughout," nudge nudge wink wink. It's a pity they were both released too late to be played at the Longshot's Star Trek Party.[120]

In spite of its 40% drop in its second week, by December 31 the Robert Wise film did something that would be nigh-unthinkable for a new movie in later decades: it bounced back. In its third week, finally playing in 1005 theaters in the United States and Canada, the picture grossed $13,609,350. Bad reviews and tepid word of mouth should have damaged it, as well as its primary competition no longer being the likes of *Killer Fish* or decade-old Jacqueline Bisset vehicles but now Carl Reiner's brand-new Steve Martin vehicle *The Jerk*—which itself had grossed $20,252,093 since opening on December 14—as well as Gary Nelson's Disney epic *The Black Hole*, Steven Spielberg's comedy spectacular *1941*, and the Important Movie for Grownups Who Like Movies About Important Grown-up Things, aka Robert Benton's *Kramer vs. Kramer*. The Benton film did especially well in Boston, where the *Globe*'s Bruce McCabe wrote that *Kramer*'s success had "gratifying" implications "for the discerning moviegoer," since "a poignant, sensitive film about real, emotional issues" turned out to be "bigger box office than a $42-million space epic crafted to build on a ready-made audience left over from the successful TV series." Ugh, film critics are the worst. (I'm a film critic, so I can say that.)[121]

By the last day of 1979, Roddenberry's novelization had reached no. 1 on the *New York Times* list. As for the movie itself, *Daily Variety* calculated that U.S. box office hit a new record that year of $2.806B, and approximately 1,120,000,000 movie tickets had been purchased. In what may be an example of Zipf's Law in action, three films were responsible for 40% of those ticket sales: *Kramer vs. Kramer* accounted for 7%, *The Jerk* for 10%, and the remaining 23% was *ST—TMP*. Put another way, approximately one out of four of the more than one billion movie tickets purchased in 1979 was for the Robert Wise film.[122]

As a franchise, Star Trek managed to close out the 1970s on top. For its creator and for *Star Trek—The Motion Picture*, there was nowhere to go but down.

1980: The Vulcan Goodbye

The Shakedown, Part II: Deceleration

The descent was not immediate. By January 3, 1980, Paramount was reporting that in its first 26 days of release the Robert Wise film had grossed $53,270,710 in the United States, which translated into $35M in domestic rentals. Non-domestic grosses were at $5,081,416 thus far, and $3,829,439 of that was in the United Kingdom, where it broke previous records held by *Jaws 2* and *Grease*.[1]

As was the custom for major releases, the logo and primary credits for the Robert Wise film had been painted on the side of Mann's National Theatre in Westwood. However, it didn't escape the notice of the Writers Guild of America that while credited screenwriter Harold Livingston's name was on the side, only Wise and Roddenberry were listed on the front-facing marquee. By January 15, the Guild had filed a formal legal protest, and Wise and Roddenberry's names were removed from the marquee. Paramount refused further comment on the matter, though *Daily Variety* noted that the marquee on Mann's Chinese Theatre remained the same.[2]

When the film had been in release for six weeks on Friday, January 13, 1980, Paramount decided to re-up their marketing in Los Angeles and New York, going heavy on the bandwagon. In each city's respective *Times*, the ads for the film read "25 Million People Agree.... Fantastic! Sensational! Mind-boggling! A Winner! Now It's Your Turn!" It was just a string of superlatives credited to nobody in particular, and while Saturday's ad was simpler, it at least had a directive: "See the Movie Event of the Year—25 Million Have!" By Sunday, the ad itself seemed to be getting punch-drunk: "Trek-tacular! America's #1 Film Experience." Again, there was no attribution for the claim, but it wasn't about something quantifiable like weekly box-office receipts, the standard by which the Robert Wise film was no longer at #1. But as "Film Experiences" go, sure, why not say it's at #1? If anything made the numbers seem fishy, it was that when the ad campaign was run again the following week, the boast was still 25 million people, which seemed to imply that nobody had gone to see it in the meantime.[3]

According to ads appearing in the *Los Angeles Times* starting in late January, a six-week seminar on the making of *Star Trek—The Motion Picture* began on Monday, February 4 at Sherwood Oaks Experimental College, with guest speakers including Persis Khambatta, Steven Collins, James Doohan, Alan Dean Foster, Jerry Goldsmith, DeForest Kelley, Richard Kline, Walter Koenig, Jon Povill, and Todd Ramsay. Unfortunately, I was unable to find anything else about this event, but, it must have been ... something.[4]

The Making of Star Trek—The Motion Picture was published by Pocket Books in February 1980, and Roddenberry was credited as co-author with Susan Sackett. By his own admission in his Introduction, that plan for him to co-author was "impossible" due to his obligation to write the novelization and produce the film itself: "In the end, the only choice was for me to supply information and comments (reflected in my name on the book cover) and leave it to author Sackett to be the actual writer." To paraphrase one of the most overrated films of the 1990s, the Great Bird of the Galaxy even managed to sound magnanimous.[5]

In the February 24, 1980, *New York Times*, Fred Bratman observed that while many theater owners felt burned by having to blind-bid on the film—a buyer for a chain of United Artists theaters in Westchester County was quoted that once he saw the movie, "I realized that my company would lose a lot of money"—Paramount's gambit had worked. Even without the rentals, between the $30M in blind-bid guarantees from theater owners and the success of the merchandising campaign, the Robert Wise film had grossed Paramount more than $135M, meaning it had turned a profit. Not as much of a profit as anyone would have liked, to be sure (is it ever?), and over the course of the year the narrative changed to suggest the film hadn't been profitable, or was even an out-and-out flop. And while the studio was still reeling from the negative critical reaction, the work of Eisner, Katzenberg, and Steel nonetheless paid off, hence being rewarded with promotions.[6]

The sixteenth and final week of release of *ST—TMP* to which many theaters had committed to when they accepted the blind bid contract in December 1978 began on March 21, 1980, and the majority of the first-run theaters which were legally able stop showing it were more than happy to. Paramount would later claim it was around this time that the first pirated tapes started to appear, thus proving that their system of lead seals and finger-wagging was workable.[7]

In the meantime, the film had its pay-cable premiere in March 1980 on the "Z" Channel in Los Angeles, as part of a week of what they advertised in the March 9 *Los Angeles Times* as "special screenings" for "the convenience of members of the Academy of Motion Picture Arts and Sciences—so many of whom subscribe to the famous 'Z' Channel." The ad then added, "But you can see these fine films even if you're not an Academy member.... IF you have 'Z.'" (Though even in its seventeenth week of release the general public still couldn't use passes to see the film at the UA theaters in the Los Angeles area, Academy members could get in for free if they showed their membership cards, as was the case with all the nominated films still playing theaters.) While the "Z" Channel prided itself on showing more unusual, less commercial fare—to emphasize dismissed, underrated, and forgotten films, to borrow a phrase—their promotion for that week of films emphasized *ST—TMP*, *The Rose*, and *Being There*, all of which were huge mainstream hits.[8]

One Brief, Shining Sequel Set in … Camelot!

Despite the largely negative critical reception, the Robert Wise film had been successful enough that Gene Roddenberry submitted a 60-page treatment for a sequel on May 23, 1980. Titled *Star Trek III*, for he still thought of the 1960s television series as *Star Trek I* and the Robert Wise film as *Star Trek II*, it involved the *Enterprise* having to fix damage done in 1963 by time-traveling Klingons. (Later in the decade he would decry the first two films' nonexistent over-reliance on "Klingon villainy," but post-1980 Gene Roddenberry was by no means beholden to what 1980 Gene Roddenberry wrote.) This damage results in Earth's population in the 23rd century becoming barbarians who, among other things, rape and eat Spock's mother Amanda, while his father Sarek gets a heroic death when he helps the crew escape from a Klingon attack. The *Enterprise* goes back to 1963, where President Kennedy is still alive because he canceled the Dallas trip. Kirk has to talk Kennedy into giving him a rare isotope the *Enterprise* needs to travel faster than light in order to both go further back in time to stop the Klingon ship as it first appears in 1963, and then return to the 23rd century. To be clear, much like Roddenberry's *Star Trek II* treatments from 1975 and 1976, it was not good.[9]

Even setting aside pacing and aesthetic issues, the primary fan complaint about the Robert Wise film was the lack of emphasis on the characters. Throughout 1980, Roddenberry gave public lip service about how if it had been up to *him*, the Robert Wise film would have been much more character-oriented, and good in all the ways it was considered not-good. During his annual call to the Augustrek convention on August 1, 1980, he assured the audience that "it was the people-to-people that has always characterized Star

Trek, not the special effects," but that once the December 7, 1979, date was locked in he was shut out from all post-production decisions, and that "if Wise and I had discussed it, it never would have been done the way it was." As always, he was the lone hero fighting for the integrity of the property: "I realized the flight over V'ger was too long. That many personal spots were cut. We had to make room for the special effects. That was what I didn't want, but we had no choice." Speaking to *Starlog* a few months later, Roddenberry admitted that during production "the personal stories were excised from the script or the shooting schedule," what he called "the 'talky' things." Perhaps because he was speaking in his office to a journalist and not to a crowd of fans who required appeasement, he declared that "major motion picture spectacle doesn't lend itself easily to Mr. Spock's cute little remarks with Captain Kirk." In his October 1978 recording to the Empathy Midi-con during production on the Robert Wise film, Roddenberry had brushed off complaints from the actors (including Majel Barrett) about not having enough to do: "I think the only way I could have probably satisfied everyone is to have a hundred-hour movie."[10]

These issues went unrectified in Roddenberry's *Star Trek III* treatment, which was not particularly character-oriented but rather spent a lot of underlined ink on the mechanics of time travel and the mind-bending things than can happen when a ship travels faster than light, suggesting that Roddenberry had forgotten anything he might have known about the warp drive system he ostensibly created. *The Making of Star Trek—The Motion Picture*, which had been published a few months earlier and had his name on the cover, went into some detail about how much faster than the speed of light the *Enterprise* can already travel. By that book's math, when the *Enterprise* achieved warp seven—which is a triumphant moment in the Robert Wise film—it was traveling at 343 times the speed of light. But Gene Roddenberry was a Big Idea man; he tended not to get hung up on details such as continuity within the universe he created, so he assumed nobody else did, either.[11]

In March 1981, a rumor soon spread via *Starlog* from a Paramount official "who asked not to be named" about Roddenberry's *Star Trek III* treatment, claiming that "just about the last scene in the story had Spock walking up to Kennedy's limousine and killing him with his phaser," which was not true. However, a *très*-Roddenberry touch—one that the Paramount source, which anecdotal evidence suggests was publicist Eddie Egan, didn't feel was worth mentioning—was that the *Enterprise* returns to the 23rd century with Danse, a teenage girl from a remote Canadian village who becomes McCoy's wife. The source wasn't troubled by McCoy marrying a girl who was a third of his age, nor did he seem to mind Amanda being raped and eaten, but Spock killing Kennedy was an outrage that could not go unraged about, even if it didn't happen in the story.[12]

Roddenberry's *Star Trek III* did not get made, but in a writeup dated May 30, 1980, Jeffrey Katzenberg's story analyst Karl Schanzer—who was good enough at his job that he championed the story which became the 1982 hit *48 Hrs.*—didn't hate it, either.[13]

> I think this story is better than the last. The overall theme is a bit familiar; some of the action has the simplistic feel of TV. But it also has many elements of solid space-opera, and the battle against time itself has a good mythic quality.
>
> The introduction of Kennedy as a character worries me a little, but it also gives a new dimension to the plot. I like the dichotomy of Kirk taking the long historical view while Kennedy is caught up in the events of his time, and I like Kennedy's decision to supply the isotope. But I hope that bringing him in doesn't jar the audience.[14]

Schanzer went on to make specific critiques about the structure—including noting that the character of Danse doesn't serve any purpose, and that the death of a Klingon prisoner from measles in 1963 is a steal from *The War of the Worlds*, in addition to being clumsily foreshadowed—while still concluding that "assuming technical perfection and solid execution, there's no reason why this production shouldn't delight still another generation of Trekkies."[15]

It would not. In Paramount's original contracts with Shatner and Nimoy, they had until six months after the film's release to pick up their option for a sequel, which expired on June 7, 1980. That same month, Merrill Lynch analyst Harry Allen observed that while the current recession wasn't helping matters, Paramount was likely to experience declining profitability due to *ST—TMP* not having been as successful they had hoped. Granted, it was still record-setting when it came out—even the far more beloved *The Empire Strikes Back* only grossed $10,840,307 its opening weekend that month, compared to the Robert Wise film's $11,815,203—and not unsuccessful enough to prevent Jeffrey Katzenberg from being promoted to Paramount's Senior Vice President of Production, while Gene Roddenberry and Susan Sackett were asked to vacate their Paramount offices in July.[16]

Speaking at the University of Central Arkansas on October 6, 1980, Roddenberry told the audience that Paramount executives had called him multiple times over the course of the previous week to talk about producing a new version of the show. As he had in the past, Roddenberry said that he would not do a weekly series, but instead would be willing to do "'six or eight 90-minute or two-hour shows each year." The story was picked up by the UPI, and Paramount neither confirmed nor denied it, though it was almost certainly a fabrication on Roddenberry's part which could not have helped his reputation with the studio.[17]

A Moving Analog Image Transferred from a Magnetic Medium

Paramount Home Video began releasing pre-recorded videotapes in November 1979, and by June 1980 they were offering episodes of *Star Trek I*. During the week of October 24, 1980, *ST—TMP* was released on VHS and Beta for $79.95, or $237 in December 2018 dollars. This price point was intended to gouge video store owners and discourage customers from buying them outright, but the Robert Wise film was nonetheless promoted as a sale item in November 1980. The Big Ben's Records & Tapes chain advertised it in the *Los Angeles Times* as among the pre-recorded movies they offered for cost plus 10%, and it was notably the most expensive at $62.70, with the next closest being *Superman* at $52.18 and *All That Jazz* at $51.79. National Discount Video Centers offered a coupon in the *New York Times* for $1 off the rental of major motion pictures including but not limited to the Robert Wise film, or $5 off the purchase of a pre-recorded movie, without mentioning what the pre-coupon prices were. (Marilyn Chambers in *Insatiable* was $79.95, however.) For their four-store grand opening celebration, Video Depot advertised "Star Trek Movie" in the *Los Angeles Times* as among the "over 2000 movies in stock—for rent or sale," while the least expensive player available was the RCA VET250 for a mere $788 in 1980 dollars, or about $2,300 in December 2018. Most upfront of all was Captain Video, whose ad in that same day's *Times* asked the questions the reader was surely asking: "Where can I rent STAR TREK? Where can I rent CLOSE ENCOUNTERS? Where can I rent CHINA SYNDROME? Where? CAPTAIN VIDEO!"[18]

It again must be stressed that video rentals and especially VCRs themselves were still luxury items. For example, in February 1981 the Video Station in Nashville charged $10 for one tape, $15 for two, and $10 each for tape thereafter for a one- or two-day period, and each tape required a $50 deposit. Adjusted into December 2018 coin, that's approximately $29 plus a deposit of $143 each for just a single rental, or $72 plus a $429 deposit for three pan-and-scan, monaural movies that you'd have to return in a couple of days—and all this at a time when there were dozens of first-run films playing in local theaters at an average ticket price of $2, or approximately $6 now. The Video Station did offer two-for-one specials on Tuesday, Wednesday, and Thursday, and you could also join the Budget Video Club for annual dues of $50 (again, $143 in December 2018), which offered two free rentals after every six paid rentals. (I recall our local video store in Fresno offered a "Lifetime Membership," and even as an eight year-old in 1981 who carried her favorite stuffed animal around and insisted that her mother rent both the Robert Wise film and Robert Altman's *M*A*S*H* on multiple occasions, I suspected a given store's lifetime would be short.) But the business model worked for that moment in time, and the Robert Wise film was itself a model; an article about the Video Station in the *Tennessean* on February 19 began with "Star Trek, the Motion picture playing on your television screen, after midnight when there are few other options for TV viewing? It's no longer the dream of the Trekkies of this world; it can be a reality in the growing number of Middle Tennessee households that have video cassette recorders (VCRs)." And again, the machines themselves cost several hundred 1981 dollars.[19]

Put simply, after it left wide release, *ST—TMP* was only viewable if you could afford to do so. And enough people did, for between October 1980 and September 1982, Paramount moved 50,000 of the $79.95 cassettes, which wasn't too shabby for a film which was already being compared to an unwieldy cetacean.[20]

V'ger's Gait

As the Robert Wise film approached its first birthday, it was becoming a cautionary tale in the worst possible context: being mentioned in the same breath as Michael Cimino's *Heaven's Gate*. On Sunday, November 16, 1980, prior to its scheduled Friday, November 21 release, the *Los Angeles Times* observed that according to *Variety*'s book *Film Facts* the $40M Michael Cimino film was the third most expensive film ever made after 1963's *Cleopatra* and 1979's *Star Trek—The Motion Picture*, both of which cost $44M in their given year's currency.[21]

As we've observed in detail, the Robert Wise film had a successful opening weekend on December 7, 1979; meanwhile, after being roundly thrashed by critics at a New York preview, *Heaven's Gate* was pulled for major re-editing before its November 21, 1980, release. Richard De Atley wrote in that day's *Boston Globe* that *Gate* "appeared likely to follow in the footsteps of other legendary big-budget films that flopped, among them *Cleopatra* which cost $44 million in 1963 and *Star Trek* which cost $40 million last year. Neither film has earned back its investment."[22] Come November 30, Peter H. Brown mused in the *Washington Post* that "*Heaven's Gate* is only the latest in a commercially dismal school of movie whales that have been beached on the marketplace since November of last year: *Star Trek, The Black Hole, 1941, The Blues Brothers,* and *Raise the Titanic*—all in the $30- and $40-million range and none of them yet within sight of showing a profit."[23] This was strictly true only if one looked at the domestic box office returns for the Robert Wise film, but the "beached whale" metaphor was one that would stick, and would be used frequently going forward by Harve Bennett.[24]

Nimoy and Shatner's contract clauses stipulating that filming on a sequel couldn't begin until a year after the release of the first Star Trek movie had expired on December 7, 1980, so that particular coast was clear. Two days later, Paramount Television ran a full-page ad in *Daily Variety* announcing the hiring of Harve Bennett, and by Christmas 1980, Bennett had become the executive producer of the second Star Trek movie.[25]

Whether that movie would be made for theaters or for television was uncertain. All that was certain was that Gene Roddenberry would not be in charge.

Epilogue: Star Trek— The Mathematical Phantom

On January 14, 1981, *Variety* published its annual list of "All-Time Film Rental Champs," on which a given film had to have earned at least $4M in rentals for the distributor. At the top was *Star Wars* with $175,685,000, and the Robert Wise film came in at 17 with $56M, suggesting that based on *Variety*'s own estimate of needing to gross $55M just to break even, the film had indeed done that. And, as the *New York Times* had pointed out a year earlier, the film had already made a profit by February 1980. None of this would change the film's reputation as a beached whale, and of the other films so described by the *Washington Post* in November 1980, the next closest on *Variety*'s list was *The Blues Brothers* at 56 with $31M in rentals.[1]

May 1981 was a big month for the Robert Wise film. Its first priced-to-own video release came that month, but even then it wasn't on the increasingly popular cassette format, but rather the eternally-niche RCA SelectaVision VideoDisc. With a list price of $27.98, the disc sold over 35,700 copies by April 1982, earning an RIAA/Gold Award. But that's still minimal exposure by most any other standard, and after the one-week "Z" Channel run limited to the Los Angeles area in 1980, the Robert Wise film debuted on cable in May 1981 on the Movie Channel, which had 600,000 subscribers nationwide.[2]

That same month, Paramount filed a lawsuit against Aviva Enterprises for breach of written agreement. Aviva was to produce merchandise such as toy phasers, kites, puzzles, luggage, T-shirts, tote bags, jewelry, and rubber stamps, and Paramount was to receive at least $150,000 or 6½% of the net sales of those products; the suit alleged that Paramount had only received $5,000 thus far, and in addition to the remaining $150,000, they also sought $1M in punitive damages. In a shocking turn of events, Aviva denied the charges and claimed that it was Paramount who had breached the agreement. There may have been something to Aviva's claims, as in July 1982, Paramount and Aviva reached an amicable settlement. Or perhaps the Mountain was just tired, so very tired, of the endless uphill climb the film had become.[3]

What they *were* ready to do was sell, sell, sell! After having it yanked out from under him in the past, Richard Frank finally got to peddle Star Trek at the 10th annual INTV convention, which kicked off on January 15, 1983, in Los Angeles. The Robert Wise film was being offered as part of Paramount's Portfolio X package, which a full-page ad in the concurrent issue of *Broadcasting* described as "the hottest lineup of movies ever released—16 of the 20 titles are on Variety's list of all-time rental champions!" (The last two packages had been called Portfolio 8 and 9, hence X.) Among the 20 titles on offer were well-remembered films such as *Airplane!*, *Grease*, and *Ordinary People*, and some that are less so now, such as the Mac Davis vehicle *Cheaper to Keep Her*, the television movie *Midnight Offerings*, and the two-part pilot episode of *Tenspeed and Brown Shoe*. Once again, the Robert Wise film was present on the cusp of changes in how films were exhibited: whereas previous film packages averaged out to allowing 10 runs over seven years, the movies in Portfolio X could only be run six times over the next three years.[4]

Star Trek—The Motion Picture was finally by seen again by anyone who owned a television with rabbit ears when it was broadcast on ABC on February 20, 1983, two and a half months after the three-year waiting period expired on December 7, 1982. It was a longer cut which re-incorporated 12 minutes of what Roddenberry had referred to as the "talky" scenes, and it was well-received by the fans, many of whom were rightfully confused as to why these character moments had been removed in the first place. The inelegantly-titled "Special Longer Version" was released on VHS and Beta in June 1983 for $39.95—or about $100 in December 2018—but it was still too little too late for the Robert Wise film's reputation, especially since the better-loved Nicholas Meyer film had already been released at the same price point in November 1982.[5]

For a movie nobody liked much, and which spawned three more films that the public enjoyed far more upon their initial release, the "Special Longer Version" of the Robert Wise film hung in there in terms of video sales throughout the 1980s. In the final week of 1984, it was no. 20 on *Billboard*'s videocassette sales chart; in 1985, it was again no. 20 of *Billboard*'s top-selling videocassettes of the year; in the final week of 1986, it was at no. 10; in 1987, it was at no. 21; and *Billboard*'s top-selling videocassettes of the year; and in the final week of December 1988, it was again at no. 10 of *Billboard*'s top-selling videocassettes of the year—and this was all *after* it became a presence on broadcast and cable television. (I still remember quite well where the commercial breaks were in the ABC broadcasts.)[6]

* * *

It is human nature to look for patterns in chaos, and no sooner was William Shatner's clunky 1989 *Star Trek V: The Final Frontier* released to tepid audience response did the myth of what is often referred to as the "even-numbered rule" begin. We will never know who the first person was to point it out—almost certainly it was multiple people around the same time—but the earliest reference I've been able to find was in George Anderson's *Pittsburgh Post-Gazette* column on June 20, 1989:

> The "Star Trek" movies are the reverse of Beethoven's symphonies. Somebody once said you need to listen to only his odd-numbered symphonies to hear all the good ones. With the "Star Trek" movies you need to watch only the even-numbered ones to see all the good ones.[7]

While Anderson was probably not the first person to notice that the even-numbered films were more popular, he was probably the last to compare Star Trek to Beethoven. As it happens, Beethoven himself did not believe that his odd-numbered symphonies were inherently superior. According to Frederick J. Crowest's 1908 biography of the composer, when Beethoven's Eighth Symphony debuted in Vienna on February 27, 1814, immediately following a performance of the Seventh, it was met with "little appreciation." This didn't faze Beethoven, who reportedly said regarding the middling response to the Eighth, "That's because it is so much better than the other."[8]

I disagree with the even-numbered rule regarding Star Trek films, partially because it retroactively brands the third film as a bad movie, whereas I consider it to be the best of the six films with the *Star Trek I* cast. Taste is subjective, but my other issue with what I tend to think of as the even-numbered coincidence is that it takes taste out of the equation. For as much as I love the first Star Trek movie, I consider the third movie to be the first to get Star Trek right. All the character moments that everyone complained about not being in the first film—and which are far and few between in the beloved second film, if we're being honest—can be found in abundance in the third film, in which the story is driven by the choices the crew makes to help a friend, and the sometimes tragic consequences of those choices.

In their broad strokes, the first two films tell similar stories: something launched from Earth in the late twentieth century returns in the twenty-third century to wreak havoc. Khan's motivations are much clearer than V'ger's, but in both cases there's a bad thing which attacks them and must be dealt with; the non-violent resolution of the Robert Wise film is much closer in spirit to the Star Trek ethos, but audiences like seeing things go kablooey. In the third film, the characters are motivated by their love for each other—and because it's directed by someone who knows those characters intimately, they all get moments to shine. Nothing in the first two films comes close to bringing me the joy of Uhura's smackdown of Mr. Adventure in the third. That Uhura is written out of the film until the denouement is unfortunate, and the absence of Spock's mother Amanda is inexcusable. Therefore, I am by no means claiming it is a perfect film, but it is the first Star Trek movie in which the action is motivated by who our characters are. V'ger's mission is ultimately too vague to make an impact, and Khan wants revenge, but someone else wanting revenge isn't interesting—cf. *Star Trek: Nemesis*, and the two J.J. Abrams pictures—while helping a friend is, especially when it motivates our heroes to act outside of their comfort zone by sacrificing their careers and their ship. The fourth film is a lot of fun and there are even more great character moments, but they are once more reacting to an external force, as they are again in the fifth.

If there's anything more played out than doing a William Shatner impression, and that's a big "if," it would be an impression of Shatner yelling "Khaaan!" in the second film. Unfortunately, "Khaaan!" is what much of pre–*Next Generation* Star Trek has been reduced to since the 1990s, and sometimes by its gatekeepers. On July 7, 2018—by which time CBS Studios owned the Star Trek copyright, which is another book entirely—the subject line of the official StarTrek.com newsletter was "Everything You Need for KHAAAN!" At first I was worried it meant the second season of *Discovery* was going to the Khan well the way the second Abrams film had, but it turned out to be a reference to the upcoming San Diego Comic-Con. As the chapter titles and section headings of this book demonstrate, I live in a glass house regarding homonym jokes—even involving the word "con"—but I cannot condone such laziness on CBS' part. The most curious thing about the emphasis on "Khaaan!," which makes me cringe the way Darth Vader's "Nooooo!" in *Revenge of the Sith* does so many Star Wars fans, was that the among the small number of Trek fans I knew in the mid-to-late 1980s, the go-to Shatner impression was his final words to Christopher Lloyd in the third film as Kirk is kicking Kruge *in the face*: "I…have had … enough … of *you*!" But that was in an odd-numbered movie, so I guess it's bad.

* * *

I've never read a compelling argument as to *why* the third film was bad beyond it being odd-numbered; it always seems to boil down to the first and fifth films being fatally flawed and therefore the third is too because that's how math works, right? I have always suspected that all other things being equal, if *The Voyage Home* was odd-numbered and *The Search for Spock* was even-numbered the rule would still be considered law, since it's based on the dislike of the first and the fifth films and the veneration of the second. It also brings to mind when I saw *Star Trek: Insurrection* on opening night in 1998; waiting for the theater doors to open, my companion and I were talking about it being written by *Next Generation* producer Michael Piller, and as if on cue the gentleman in front of us turned and said: "Do you think there'll be a lot of Piller Filler?" He proceeded to chuckle at his own cleverness for what I suspected was not the first time, and I said nothing.

In *Star Trek: The Next Generation: The Continuing Mission*, published by Pocket Books in November 1997, the Reeves-Stevenses made what may be the first reference to the even-numbered coincidence in a Paramount-approved publication. They wrote that "conventional wisdom" among fans holds that "the even-numbered films are better than the odd-numbered ones," and they further postulate that "there might be a logical reason for this observation, having to do with the way movie stories are developed and budgets are determined. In a sense, business can be seen to be influencing art."[9]

That potentially logical reason was that the success of the second film resulted in the cast demanding higher salaries to be in the third film, but since sequels generally didn't fare as well at the box office back when dinosaurs roamed the Earth, studios didn't want to increase the budget to compensate. According to the Reeves-Stevenses, that "invariably has the effect of reducing the number of new sets, starships, and special effects seen in the next film." In spite of this invariable effect, there are in fact *more* new sets, starships and optical effects in the third film than there were in the second. There is no recycled effects footage in the third film after the opening recap, but there are six new starships: the *Excelsior*, the *Grissom*, the merchant ship, the Klingon Bird-of-Prey, arguably the post-explosion *Enterprise*, and Spacedock, which itself required several interior miniatures. There were also many new sets, including the Bridges of the *Excelsior*, the merchant ship, and the Bird-of-Prey; multiple interiors on Spacedock and on Earth, as well as the multiple environments on the Genesis Planet, and Mount Seleya on Vulcan. On top of that, the phasers, communicators, and tricorders were redesigned, which is all the more impressive if the production was working with a reduced budget due to the cast demanding higher salaries.

It's true that the third film was not expected to do as well as the second film. Nimoy was quoted in the June 6, 1984, *Variety* that "when we set out to make 'Star Trek III,' the original goal was to do about 25% less business than Part II," but when theater owners were able to screen it in advance in states where blind bidding was outlawed, the owners "wanted it and hundreds of more prints were made. Now we're hoping to equal Part II's performance." Nimoy's film did open larger than its predecessor, earning $16,673,229 in its first three days compared to the Nicholas Meyer film's $14,347,221. However, the Reeves-Stevenses argued that since the second film cost $12M (due in part to the cast demanding higher salaries) and grossed $93M but the third film cost $17M and grossed $85M, the "slight decrease meant it was time to go back to the drawing board, to avoid any chance of additional slippage for the fourth film." That slippage was far less than the anticipated 25% drop in box office, but the Reeves-Stevenses painted it as a victory for creativity, since "key personnel didn't have quite as much negotiating power to ask for increased salaries," which meant "art could now influence business." And because art was finally influencing business as opposed to the other way around as it had on the third film, the fourth film cost $22M and grossed more than $100 million. Hooray, and no wonder people like it better, right? But darn if those greedy actors didn't muck things up again! According to the Reeves-Stevenses, because of the fourth film's "overwhelming success" the cast demanded higher salaries on the fifth film, so as "a cost-cutting measure" Paramount decided to not hire Industrial Light and Magic to do the effects for the first time since the second film. This resulted in the hiring of the less expensive Bran Ferren which in turn resulted in the fifth film's visuals being subpar and that's why the even-numbered films are considered better than the odd-numbered films, question mark?[10]

Let's consider.

Published by Pocket Books in July 1989 while the unloved fifth movie was still in theaters, Lisabeth Shatner's epically-titled *Captain's Log: William Shatner's Personal Account of the Making of Star Trek V: The Final Frontier* never mentions Industrial Light and Magic. Instead, Bran Ferren's outfit was one of several companies asked to produce a demonstration of "a column of light with a figure inside it" for the climax. When none of the other demos were satisfactory, William Shatner was wowed by Ferren's version: "In that moment, I realized he was a creative genius, so we gave him the job." The job in question was to do all the visuals for the picture, not just the ending, and though budget cuts are a major theme in the book—beginning with "some budget disputes with the front office" as early as the scripting stage—there's never a reference to cast salaries being the cause.[11]

In his article about the Shatner film's troubled production in the May 1990 *Cinefex*, Paul Mandell wrote the picture "lost valuable preproduction time" due to a March 1988 Writers Guild strike, and post-production on Leonard Nimoy's non–Trek film *The Good Mother* further pushed principal photography back to October 1988, by which time Shatner's picture had "an unalterable June 1989 release date." (Stop me if any of this sounds familiar.) Meanwhile, executive producer Ralph Winter had wanted to get Industrial Light and Magic for the optical effects, "but with the facility knee-deep in commitments to *Ghostbusters II* and other projects, and with money being tight, Winter had to seek out another facility," which turned out to be Bran Ferren's Associates and Ferren.[12]

In his 1994 book *Star Trek Movie Memories*—published by HarperCollins, so take that as you will—William Shatner wrote that he'd wanted to use ILM, but "we were dismayed to find that most of that firm's best technicians, the A team, were already hard at work on the Spielberg/Lucas collaboration *Indiana Jones and the Last Crusade*," and a "good portion" of the B team "were putting together the effects for *Ghostbusters II*." Shatner realized "the best ILM could offer us simply wasn't their best," hence the production winding up with Bran Ferren doing the optical effects. I know I made a case for not trusting William Shatner's memories back in the Introduction, but that interview had been him speaking off the cuff after 26 years, whereas *Movie Memories* was published five years after the fifth film came out. (And he doesn't make a single reference to burning the sets between movies!) Daren Dochterman repeated the *Movie Memories* story in the group commentary on the *Star Trek V* Blu-ray in 2009, and though the Reeves-Stevenses were there, they did not contradict him or suggest that the real reason ILM wasn't hired because of the cast demanding more money.[13]

The Reeves-Stevenses wrote in *The Art of Star Trek* in 1995, a year after *Movie Memories*, that ILM not being available to do the effects was one of a "series of events that could not have been foreseen" which resulted in a film "that was not as visually exciting as the four that had gone before." These events included a Writers Guild strike cutting into preproduction and "unexpected budget cuts," all of which were discussed in *Cinefex* and *Movie Memories* with no mention of the cast's salary demands being an issue. The Reeves-Stevenses concluded in *The Art of Star Trek* that for all its visual shortcomings, "in terms of engaging and thoughtful themes and true character interactions," the fifth film "remains a strong addition to the STAR TREK saga." But as we've seen, 1995 was a transitional year in the Mountain's relationship with the history of Star Trek.[14]

The Continuing Mission and its codification of the even-numbered rule was published in 1997 after the commercial and critical success of *Star Trek: First Contact*, and Paramount had every reason to hope that there might be as many films with the new crew as there had been with the original. As such, it makes sense that the Mountain would want to put the idea into the æther that the agreed-upon inferiority of the odd-numbered films was due to the greed of the cast. This would be less of a cautionary message to the *Next Generation* cast, who probably weren't in the habit of reading nonfiction books about Star Trek, and more of a pre-emptive PR strike should any of the successive films prove underwhelming—as was the case with 1998's *Insurrection*. It was the ninth Star Trek film produced, and reaction had also been somewhat mixed to *Generations*, which was the seventh film and the first since the Robert Wise film to not have a number in the title.

* * *

There is some indication that the even-numbered silliness is being moved past, and that *Star Trek—Motion Picture* is being reevaluated on its own merits. Some of my research for this book was done looking for contemporaneous coverage of the Robert Wise film on YouTube, so naturally that site suggested many other videos about it. Most appeared to be of the "lol it's so slow and boring" variety, but one caught my eye, by two young men who run a pop-culture channel called the Cinemologists.

They had discovered the film around the same impressionable age as I had—though much later, on VHS in the 1990s after growing up with *The Next Generation*—and like myself, they didn't realize that the film had such a bad reputation until after they'd fallen in love with it.

> But whatever the popular consensus, I strongly suggest that you don't let a fan theory about the parity of integers dissuade you from checking out all the Star Trek movies and deciding for yourself which ones you enjoy the most. Regardless of which ones are the best or worst films in the series, there's a lot to be enjoyed in all of them.[15]

My thoughts exactly. For all its flaws, without *Star Trek—The Motion Picture*, the human adventure that has been the past forty years of Star Trek might have ended before it began.

Chapter Notes

Introduction

1. Susan Adamo, "Log Entries," *Starlog* no. 46 (May 1981), 9.
2. Edward Gross and Mark A. Altman, the *Fifty-Year Mission: The Complete, Uncensored, Unauthorized Oral History of Star Trek: The First 25 Years* (New York: St. Martin's Press, 2016), 389–390.
3. Scott Collura, "The William Shatner Interview Page 2 of 2," *IGN*, last modified August 18, 2017, http://www.ign.com/articles/2017/08/18/the-william-shatner-interview?page=2; Charles Schreger, "'Star Trek': a Stellar Premiere?," *Los Angeles Times*, December 8, 1979; Peter H. Brown, "Embattled Enterprise," *Washington Post*, December 18, 1986.
4. David Alexander, *Star Trek Creator: The Authorized Biography of Gene Roddenberry* (New York: Penguin, 1994), 516–517; Stephen E. Whitfield and Gene Roddenberry, *The Making of Star Trek* (New York: Ballantine, 1968), 36; Larry Nemecek, *The Star Trek: The Next Generation Companion* (New York: Pocket Books, 1992), 28–29.
5. Alexander, 517.
6. Alexander, 517.
7. Alexander, 517.
8. Alexander, 517; *The Making of Star Trek IV*, YouTube video, 3:44, posted by "Zeeb," March 15, 2017, https://www.youtube.com/watch?v=XpFTK9NkcvE; Randy & Jean-Marc Lofficier, "Harve Bennett: Preparing 'Star Trek IV,'" *Starlog* no. 103 (February 1986), 17.
9. Alexander, 518–519.
10. Susan Sackett, *Inside Trek: My Secret Life with Star Trek Creator Gene Roddenberry* (Tulsa, OK: HAWK Publishing, 2002), 88.
11. Susan Sackett, "Star Trek Report: a Fan News Column," *Starlog* no. 7 (August 1977), 31.
12. Susan Sackett and Gene Roddenberry, *The Making of Star Trek—The Motion Picture* (New York: Pocket Books, 1980), 34; Allan Asherman, *The Star Trek Compendium* (New York: Pocket Books, 1986), 152.
13. Nemecek, 2; J.M. Dillard, *Star Trek: Where No One Has Gone Before": A History in Pictures* (New York: Pocket Books, 1994), 62–67; Larry Nemecek, *The Star Trek: The Next Generation Companion* rev. ed. (New York: Pocket Books, 1995), 2.
14. Leonard Nimoy, *I Am Spock* (New York: Hyperion, 1995), 150; Judith and Garfield Reeves-Stevens, *The Art of Star Trek* (New York: Pocket Books, 1995), 55, 155; Herbert F. Solow and Robert H. Justman, *Inside Star Trek: The Real Story* (New York: Pocket Books, 1996), 423.
15. Judith and Garfield Reeves-Stevens, *Star Trek Phase II: The Lost Series* (New York: Pocket Books, 1997), 1, 16–17, 84; Larry Nemecek, *The Star Trek: The Next Generation Companion* rev. ed. (New York: Pocket Books, 2003), 2.

Prologue

1. Susan Sackett, *Inside Trek: My Secret Life with Star Trek Creator Gene Roddenberry* (Tulsa, OK: HAWK Publishing, 2002), 76.
2. "'Star Trek' Preem," *Variety* 296, no. 3 (August 22, 1979), 28; Sackett, *Inside Trek*, 76; Dale Pollock, "'Trek' Beams Up $2 Mil-Plus in 105 Enterprises," *Daily Variety* 186, no. 3 (December 10, 1979), 23.
3. Jeff Maynard, "Interview with Susan Sackett," *Fantastic Films* 1, no. 3 (August 1978), 29; Sackett, *Inside Trek*, 76; Susan Sackett, "Star Trek Report," *Starlog* no. 2 (December 1979), 31.
4. "Four of Eight Pix Rated Come from Majors," *Daily Variety* 185, no. 63 (December 5, 1979), 6; Preston Neal Jones, *Return to Tomorrow: The Filming of Star Trek—The Motion Picture* (Sierra Madre, CA: Creature Features, 2014), 587–589; Bob Thomas, "Big-Gamble 'Star Trek' Film Opens Today," *Great Falls Tribune*, December 7, 1979; "'Star Trek' Sets Three-Day Record," *Daily Variety* 186, no. 4 (December 11, 1979), 29.
5. "'Ark' Raid Tied to Par's Upfront Anti-Piracy Ploys," *Variety* 303, no. 9 (July 1, 1981), 5.

6. Preston Neal Jones, *Return to Tomorrow: The Filming of Star Trek—The Motion Picture* (Sierra Madre, CA: Creature Features, 2014), 591–592; Harlan Lebo, *Citizen Kane: A Filmmaker's Journey* (New York: St. Martin's Press, 2016), 197; Peter Matthews, "Vertigo Rises: the Greatest Film of All Time?", *Sight & Sound*, last modified July 13, 2018, https://www.bfi.org.uk/news-opinion/sight-sound-magazine/polls-surveys/greatest-films-all-time/vertigo-hitchcock-new-number-one; Walter Koenig, *Chekov's Enterprise: A Personal Journal of the Making of Star Trek—The Motion Picture* (New York: Pocket Books, 1980), 45; "Pix, People, Pickups," *Daily Variety* 185, no. 43 (November 2, 1979), 29.

7. Jones, 592; Thomas, "Ballyhooed Movie Opens."

8. Steven Ginsberg, "Full Year Ahead, Par Seeks Bid on 'Star Trek'; 16-Week Deal, Percentages Stun Showmen," *Variety* 293, no. 6 (December 13, 1978), 5; Susan Sackett, "Star Trek Report," *Starlog* no. 21 (April 1979), 24; Aljean Harmetz, "15th State Outlaws Blind Bidding on Films," *New York Times*, June 19, 1979; Sergio Leeman, *Robert Wise on His Films: From Editing Room to Director's Chair* (Los Angeles: Silman-James Press, 1995), 195.

9. Julie Yue, "Memories of a Neighborhood Movie Theater, from When There Was Such a Thing," *Humanities*, last modified December 2014, https://www.neh.gov/humanities/2014/novemberdecember/statement/memories-neighborhood-movie-theater-when-there-was-such-t; "The MacArthur Theater," *Going to the Movies*, n.d., http://www.goingtothemoviesdciff.org/theaters/#/macarthur/; "The Metropolist," *Washington Post*, November 13, 2008; Michael Benson, *Space Odyssey: Stanley Kubrick, Arthur C. Clarke, and the Making of a Masterpiece* (New York: Simon & Schuster, 2018), 413; Alison Castle, *The Stanley Kubrick Archives* (Köln, Germany: Taschen, 2013), 375; Charles Schreger, "Getting Set for the Second Coming of 'Star Trek,'" *Los Angeles Times*, December 7, 1979.

10. Schreger, December 7, 1979; Schreger, December 8, 1979; Dan Chiszar, "'Star Trek': Big Bucks," United Press International, December 6, 1979.

11. "The Macarthur Theater"; Schreger, December 7, 1979.

12. Preston Neal Jones, "Star Trek—The Motion Picture," *Cinefantastique* 9, no. 2 (Winter 1979), 41; Judy Stone, "'Star Trek': the Enterprise Takes Off," *San Francisco Chronicle*, December 5, 1979; Joe Brown, "K-B MacArthur Closes," *Washington Post*, August 26, 1982; "Extra Forces Prepare for the Trekkies," *San Francisco Examiner*, December 6, 1979.

13. Stone.

14. Schreger, December 8, 1979; "The Star Trek Premiere," A *Piece of the Action* no. 78 (November 1979), 1; "History," *National Space Club and Foundation*, n.d., http://www.spaceclub.org/about/history.html.

15. Jurate Kazickas, "Trekking Down to a World Premiere," *Washington Star*, December 7, 1979; Schreger, December 7, 1979; Tia Gindick, "Trekking to a Movie Benefit," *Los Angeles Times*, November 29, 1979; "Star Trek—The Motion Picture," *Star Trek Action Group No. 38* (December 1979), 6.

16. Gene Roddenberry, "Letter to Fans," *Star Trek Action Group* no. 38 (December 1979), 7; "Star Trek—The Motion Picture," *Star Trek Action Group* no. 40 (April 1980), 3; Kazickas.

17. "Star Trek—The Motion Picture," *Star Trek Action Group* no. 39 (February 1980), 3; "A Dream Come True," A *Piece of the Action* no. 80 (January/February 1980), 1.

18. "What's In-Store," *Cash Box* 41, no. 17 (December 22, 1979), 17.

19. Roman Kozak, "Swoosh! 'Star Trek' Promotion Takes Off," *Billboard* 91, no. 49 (December 8, 1979), 74.

20. Gindick; Richard Arnold, email message to author, June 29, 2018; Schreger, December 7, 1979.

21. Susan Sackett, "Star Trek Report," *Starlog* no. 20 (March 1979), 32; Gindick; *RARE 1979 STAR TREK: The Motion Picture PREMIERE!!*, YouTube video, 18:03, posted by "Hezakya Newz & Music," May 29, 2016, https://www.youtube.com/watch?v=aMahpAHN2Xw&; Shirley Maiewski, "A Dream Come True," A *Piece of the Action* no. 80 (January/February 1980), 1; Arnold.

22. Sonni Cooper, "Where's Bill? Call Scotland Yard!" *Star Trek Action Group* no. 41 (June 1980), 6; Roger Piantadosi, "Beaming Up at the Stars," *Washington Post*, December 7, 1979; Susan Adamo, "Log Entries," *Starlog* no. 33 (April 1980), 12; "Reviewers Get Lost Characterizes Policy Re 'Trek' in Chicago," *Variety* 297, no. 6 (December 12, 1979), 3.

23. Piantadosi.

24. Piantadosi; "The WSFA Journal, December 1979," *Washington Science Fiction Association*, n.d., http://www.wsfa.org/journal/j79/c/index.htm.

25. "Star Trek—The Motion Picture," *Star Trek Action Group* no. 38 (December 1979), 6.

26. "The WSFA Journal, September 1979," Washington Science Fiction Association. n.d.,

http://www.wsfa.org/journal/j79/9/index.htm; Kazickas; *RARE 1979 STAR TREK: The Motion Picture PREMIERE!!*

27. Schreger, December 8, 1979; Anthony Timpone, "Starlog Profile: Stephen Collins," *Starlog* no. 104 (March 1986), 60; Piantadosi; *RARE 1979 STAR TREK: The Motion Picture PREMIERE!!*

28. *RARE 1979 STAR TREK: The Motion Picture PREMIERE!!*; Schreger, December 8, 1979.

29. Jones, Winter 1979, 42; *RARE 1979 STAR TREK: The Motion Picture PREMIERE!!*

30. *RARE 1979 STAR TREK: The Motion Picture PREMIERE!!*

31. *RARE 1979 STAR TREK: The Motion Picture PREMIERE!!*

32. *RARE 1979 STAR TREK: The Motion Picture PREMIERE!!*

33. *RARE 1979 STAR TREK: The Motion Picture PREMIERE!!*

34. Schreger, December 8, 1979.

35. Kazickas; Adamo; "Jesco von Puttkamer: 1933–2012," *NASA*, last modified December 27, 2012, https://www.nasa.gov/topics/people/features/von_puttkamer_obit.html; Rudy Maxa, "Take It from a NASA Scientist: Star Trek's High Tech Isn't Child's Play," *Washington Post*, December 16, 1979; Sackett and Rodddenberry, 150–151; "Personal Appearance: Jesco Von Puttkamer, NASA Scientist," *Starlog* no. 3 (January 1977), 27.

36. Gary Arnold, "Star Trek: the Motion Picture," *Washington Post*, December 8, 1979; Adamo; Schreger, December 8, 1979; Sackett and Roddenberry, 26.

1969: The Network's Knife Cares Not for the Show's Cry

1. Herbert F. Solow and Robert H. Justman, *Inside Star Trek: The Real Story* (New York: Pocket Books, 1996), 251.

2. Bill Greeley, "Jerry Lewis Slot for 'Star Trek' After Gap," *Variety* 253, no. 11 (January 29, 1969), 43.

3. "CBS, NBC Fall Sked Makeup Going Calmly This Year, Thanks to ABC," *Variety* 253, no. 13 (February 12, 1969), 41.

4. "'Star Trek' Reentry," *Variety* 254, no. 4 (March 19, 1969), 44; Paramount Television, "Take Off with Star Trek," Advertisement, *Broadcasting* 76 no. 12 (March 24, 1969), 87.

5. "Take Off with Star Trek."

6. Bill Greeley, "'Underground' Syndie at NAB," *Variety* 254, no. 6 (March 26, 1969), 74; "WOR-TV Headed for Big Program Overhaul," *Variety* 254, no. 6 (March 26, 1969), 55; "UHF's Cleve. Breakthrough," *Variety* 254, no. 8 (April 9, 1969), 53.

7. Solow and Justman, 251.

8. "ABC Betting on Summer Firstruns to Build Rating Momentum for Fall," *Variety* 254, no. 5 (March 19, 1969), 51.

9. "Early N.B.C. Forecast on Vote Irks Viewers," *New York Times*, June 4, 1969.

10. "BBC Slots 'Star Trek,'" *Variety* 255, no. 4 (June 11, 1969), 67; "Star Trek: Where No Man Has Gone Before," *BBC Genome*, n.d., http://genome.ch.bbc.co.uk/8c3b788506504b309063
66ab0edfa45f.

11. Paramount Television, "Star Trek is Out of this World," Advertisement, *Variety* 255, no. 9 (July 16, 1969), 49.

12. "Atlanta's 2d UHF to Debut in Aug," *Variety* 255, no. 5 (June 18, 1969), 40; "Breaks Go WKBD's Way in Detroit," *Variety* 256, no. 1 (August 20, 1969), 38; "New Fall Garb for Chi's WGN-TV, but Sports and Kidvid Still Mainstays," *Variety* 256, no. 3 (September 3, 1969), 40; "In St. Louis…," *Variety* 256, no. 3 (September 3, 1969), 50; "In Indianapolis…," *Variety* 256, no. 4 (September 10, 1969), 76; "New Video Season, Indie-Style," *Variety* 256, no. 6 (September 24, 1969), 38; Solow and Justman, 418; "Paramount TV Shuffles Syndie Sales Staffers; John Pearson Resigns," *Variety* 256, no. 8 (October 8, 1969), 48.

13. Bill Greeley, "'Paradise' Limps but Indies Hot," *Variety* 256, no. 6 (September 24, 1969), 39; "'Paradise' Heads for Overhaul as N.Y., L.A. Drop It," *Variety* 256, no. 8 (October 8, 1969), 38; "Indies Vs. News," *Variety* 256, no. 8 (October 8, 1969), 38; Bill Greeley, "Look Out for TV Independents," *Variety* 256, no. 8 (October 8, 1969), 5; "Cronkite at 7 P.M. Holds Off Indies' Rising N.Y. Tide," *Variety* 256, no. 10 (October 22, 1969), 49; "Leider-Headed Warner Bros. TV Tooling Up for Season After Next," *Variety* 256, no. 12 (November 5, 1969), 35; "In Pittsburgh…" *Variety* 257, no. 3 (December 3, 1969), 40.

14. "In London," *Variety* 256, no. 9 (October 15, 1969), 44; "Star Trek: the Corbomite Manoeuvre," *BBC Genome*, n.d., http://genome.ch.bbc.co.uk/a1e62e5e36004d3fb99627134446090c; "Star Trek: Arena," *BBC Genome*, n.d., http://genome.ch.bbc.co.uk/133c4ba85c4b4f3fa616f313dbf81b4e; Hannah Khalil, "46 Years of Colour TV on BBC One," *BBC Blogs*, last modified November 12, 2015, http://www.bbc.co.uk/blogs/aboutthebbc/entries/1546d154-dd8a-4e2b-bbb3-45d395445
596; "'Bonanza' in Blighty," *Variety* 257, no. 5 (December 17, 1969), 34.

15. Bill Greeley, "Webs Gain on New York Indies," *Variety* 257, no. 7 (December 31, 1969), 2; Whitfield and Roddenberry, 37.

1970–1972: What's in Reruns Is Prologue

1. Independent Television Corporation, "The Saint is #1," Advertisement, *Variety* 257, no. 9 (January 14, 1970), 48–49.
2. "Television," *New York Times*, July 1, 1969; "Television," *New York Times*, July 8, 1969; "Television," *New York Times*, July 15, 1969.
3. "In Miami…" *Variety* 258, no. 1 (February 18, 1970), 46; Paramount Television, "Star Trek Ratings Orbit on Any Heading," Advertisement, *Variety* 258, no. 1 (February 18, 1970), 51.
4. "London," *Variety* 258, No. 8 (April 8, 1970), 44; "TV Independents' New Schedules," *Variety* 260, no. 5 (September 16, 1970), 56; Solow and Justman, 418; "Continuing Series in Syndication," *Variety* 260, no. 5 (September 16, 1970), 54, 56.
5. "If the Mind is Free," *Variety* 261, no. 12 (February 3, 1971), 44; "If the Mind is Free" film, 1971, Saint Mary's High School and Center for Learning Records, Special Collections, University of Illinois at Chicago; "What the Kiddies Prefer," *Variety* 261, no. 13 (February 10, 1971), 34.
6. "In Lieu of ABC Evening News," *Variety* 262, no. 1 (February 17, 1971), 36; "Bitter at Brit., Pakistan Slots U.S. TV Series," *Variety* 262, no. 13 (May 12, 1971), 214; "Buffalo," *Variety* 263, no. 5 (June 16, 1971), 44.
7. "ARB's Syndie Ratings Show Limited Circulation; May Be Blow to Barter," *Variety* 263, no. 13 (August 11, 1971), 36.
8. Frank Beerman, "'Star Trek' Conclave in N.Y. Looms as Mix of Campy Set and Sci-Fi Buffs," *Variety* 265, no. 10 (January 19, 1972), 1, 69; Sackett and Roddenberry, 17; "Star Trek Lives! (convention)/1972," Fanlore, last modified March 1, 2017, https://fanlore.org/wiki/Star_Trek_Lives!_%28convention%29/1972; Joan Marie Verba, *Boldly Writing: A Trekker Fan and Zine History, 1967–1987* (Minnetonka, MN: FTL Publications, 2003), 9.
9. Chuck McNaughton, "Editorial," *Monster Times* 1, no. 2 (February 16, 1972), 2.
10. McNaughton.
11. "Star Trek Convention News," *Monster Times* 1, no. 2 (February 16, 1972), 23.
12. "Star Trek Convention News."
13. Chuck McNaughton, "Exclusive 'Rumor' to the Monster Times," *Monster Times* 1, no. 2 (February 16, 1972), 18.

14. McNaughton, "Exclusive 'Rumor' to the Monster Times."
15. McNaughton, "Editorial."
16. "S.T.A.R.," *Star-Borne* 1, no. 1 (May 1972), 1; "StarWatch," *Star-Borne* 1, no. 1 (May 1972), 1; "Par-TV Euro Org Beating the 'Rap' on British Sales," *Variety* 267, no. 4 (June 7, 1972), 40.
17. "StarWatch," *Star-Borne* 1, no. 2 (June 1972), 1.
18. "StarWatch," June 1972; "Roddenberry Cool on NBC-TV Offer to Go Through 'Trek' Pilot," *Variety* 267, no. 8 (July 5, 1972), 29; "TV-Radio Production Centres in the U.S. and Abroad," *Variety* 268, no. 2 (August 23, 1972), 44; "WENY-TV Using Eleven Prime-Access Series," *Variety* 268, no. 6 (September 20, 1972), 41.
19. "Letter from D.C. Fontana," *Star-Borne* 1, no. 3 (September/October 1972), 1; Cecil Smith, "Roddenberry Sires Son of Star Trek," *Los Angeles Times*, February 16, 1973.
20. "Detroit Triple Fan Fair Convention Report," *Star-Borne* 1, no. 4 (November/December 1972), 1; Phil Thomas, "Comic Strips Are Collectors' Items," *Owosso Argus-Press*, April 3, 1965.
21. "Detroit Triple Fan Fair Convention Report"; David Gerrold, *The Trouble with Tribbles* (New York: Ballantine Books, 1973), 127.
22. "Detroit Triple Fan Fair Convention Report"; "StarWatch," *Star-Borne* 1, no. 1 (November/December 1972), 1.
23. "'Genesis II' Set for Filming with Alex Cord as Star," *Los Angeles Times*, December 19, 1972; Smith.

1973–1974: Choose Your Televised Pain

1. Smith.
2. Bill Feret, "The Monster Times Teletype," *Monster Times* 1, no. 19 (February 19, 1973), 25; Jeff Szalay, "Gene Roddenberry: the Years Between, the Years Ahead," *Starlog* no. 51 (October 1981), 40; Alexander, 400.
3. "Step Into a Time Capsule at 9:40," *Los Angeles Times*, March 23, 1973; Cecil Smith, "'Genesis II' Takes Look at AD 2133," *Los Angeles Times*, March 23, 1973.
4. Susan Sackett and Gene Roddenberry, *The Making of Star Trek—The Motion Picture* (New York: Pocket Books, 1980), 57–58.
5. "NY ST Con," *Star-Borne* 1, no. 5 (January/February 1973), 1.
6. "D. C. Fontana Speech," *Star-Borne* 2, no. 6/7 (March/April 1973), 1.

7. "D. C. Fontana Speech."
8. Solow and Justman, 421.
9. "D. C. Fontana Speech."
10. "D. C. Fontana Speech."
11. "D. C. Fontana Speech."
12. "Gene Roddenberry letter to Leonard Nimoy—March 1973," March 27, 1973, *The Trek Files*, last modified November 12, 2018, https://www.facebook.com/TheTrekFiles/photos/ms.c.eJwzNLAwMrQ0tzCwMDMyNDQ20jOECh-hCBAwBcTkGpQ~-~-.bps.a.1082197788621134/1082197808621132/.
13. "Gene Roddenberry letter to Leonard Nimoy—March 1973."
14. "Gene Roddenberry letter to Leonard Nimoy—March 1973."
15. "NBC Axes All 7 Kidvid Frosh, Adds ABCer in New Sat Shake for Fall," *Variety* 270, no. 7 (March 28, 1973), 50; "Inside Stuff—Radio-TV," *Variety* 270, no. 10 (April 18, 1973), 60.
16. J.B. Brancatelli, "The Monster Times Teletype," *Monster Times* 1, no. 22 (May 19, 1973), 26; "Letter from D.C. Fontana," *Star-Borne* 2, no. 9 (August/September 1973), 1.
17. Brancatelli.
18. "TV-Radio Production Centres in the U.S. and Abroad," *Variety* 271, no. 2 (May 30, 1973), 48.
19. "Leonard Nimoy Addresses the Star Trek America Convention (1977)," *Fanlore*, last modified November 4, 2017, https://fanlore.org/wiki/Leonard_Nimoy_Addresses_the_Star_Trek_America_Convention_(1977).
20. "TV-Radio Production Centres in the U.S. and Abroad," *Variety* 271, no. 8 (July 4, 1973), 40.
21. "The Monster Scene," *Monster Times* 1, no. 24 (July 1973), 13.
22. "The Monster Scene," July 1973.
23. "Star Trek KMPH 26," *TV Guide* 21, no. 35 (September 1, 1973), A-50.
24. "Television," *New York Times*, September 8, 1973.
25. Mark Evanier, "Star Trek Lives!", *Monster Times* 1, no. 26 (September 1973), 15.
26. Evanier.
27. Margaret A. Basta, "Editorial," *Star-Borne* 2, no. 10 (September/October 1973), 1.
28. Basta.
29. "New Kidvid Slate Firmed by NBC," *Variety* 278, no.5 (March 12, 1975), 44; Frank Beermann, "'Don't Publicize Losers,' Walters Sez at ABC Daytime Emmy Show," *Variety* 279, no. 2 (May 21, 1975), 48.
30. "'Trek' on 106 TV's," *Variety* 273, no. 6 (December 19, 1973), 30; "New 'Trek' Outlets," *Variety* 274, no. 8 (April 3, 1974), 35; "At Last—The Enterprise is Back," *A Piece of the Action* no. 14 (May 1974), 1.
31. Alan E. Andres, "Gene Roddenberry," *Star-Borne* 3, no. 13 (June 1974), 1.
32. Andres, June 1974.
33. Hal Wilson, "Con," *A Piece of the Action* 2, no. 5 (July 1974), 1.
34. Helen Young, "From D.C. Fontana," *A Piece of the Action* 2, no. 18 (September 1974), 1.
35. Young, September 1974.
36. "Par Unveils Its Double-Camera Magicam System," *Daily Variety* 165, no. 4 (September 11, 1974), 1, 17.
37. Walter Irwin & G.B. Love, *The Best of Trek* (New York: Signet, 1978), 72; "Trek Talk," *Monster Times* 1, no. 36 (October 1974), 25.
38. "Trek Talk," October 1974.
39. Susan Sackett, "Revival News," *A Piece of the Action* 2, no. 19 (October 1974), 1.
40. Mike Mooney, John Knoll, Kevin Kay, Marylou Cook, and Nancy Audete, "An Interview with Gene Roddenberry," *Star Trek Today* 2, no. 1 (June 1976), 9; "'Trek' to 130," *Variety* 276, no. 13 (November 6, 1974), 43; N. Zarar, 'Istanbul," *Variety* 277, no. 1 (November 13, 1974), 61; "Show of Subtle Colors is Tops in Arg.; U.S. Product Thrives," *Variety* 277, no. 2 (November 20, 1974), 30.
41. Mooney, 10–11.
42. Carole Brownell, *Save the Star Trek Cast Mailer*, 1974.
43. Brownell.
44. "Is This the End of the Enterprise?" *Monster Times Collectors' Issue* no. 1 (1973), 14–15; "Trek Talk," *Monster Times* 1, no 37 (December 1974), 25.
45. "Star Trek News," *Star Trek Action Group* no. 11 (December 1974/January 1975), 4.
46. "Star Trek News."

1975: Magicam to Make the Sanest Man Go Mad

1. "TV Syndication," *Variety* 277, no. 11 (January 22, 1975), 70; "TV Syndication," *Variety* 278, no. 3 (February 26,1975), 38.
2. Alan E. Andres, "Revival News," *A Piece of the Action* no. 23 (February 1975), 1; "Notes from Broadcast Markets in the U.S. and Abroad," *Variety* 278, no. 5 (March 12, 1975), 54; "TV 'Star Trek' as Theatrical Feature for Paramount," *Variety* 278, no. 6 (March 19, 1975), 6.
3. Virginia Walker and Helen Young, "Revival News," *A Piece of the Action* no. 24 (March 1975), 1.
4. Gene Roddenberry, "From the Log of the Starship Enterprise," *Archives' Log* 2, no. 5 & 6 (May & June 1975), 3.

5. Roddenberry, May & June 1975, 3.
6. Roddenberry, May & June 1975, 3.
7. Roddenberry, May & June 1975, 3.
8. Steve Ruben, "Star Trek Treks," *Cinefantastique* 5, no. 3 (Winter 1976), 10; Susan Sackett, "One to Beam Up: Jerry Isenberg," *Star Trektennial News* 3, no. 20 (March/April, 1977), 7.
9. Roddenberry, May & June 1975, 4.
10. Roddenberry, May & June 1975, 4.
11. "Star Trek Lives," *Monster Times* 1, no. 42 (July 1975), 24.
12. "Star Trek Lives," *Monster Times*, July 1975.
13. "Star Trek Lives," *Monster Times*, July 1975.
14. "Star Trek Lives," *Monster Times*, July 1975.
15. "Star Trek Lives," *Monster Times*, July 1975.
16. "Star Trek Lives," *Monster Times*, July 1975.
17. Sackett and Roddenberry, 22.
18. Helen Young, "Revival News," *A Piece of the Action* no. 26 (May 1975), 1.
19. Young, May 1975.
20. "'Trek' in 140 Markets," *Variety* 279, no. 9 (July 9, 1975), 49.
21. "Bonanza," *Variety* 279, no. 13 (August 6, 1975), 37.
22. "Welcome Everyone!", *Star Trek Action Group* no. 13 (1975), 1.
23. Sackett and Roddenberry, 96.
24. "Star Trek News," *Star Trek Action Group* no. 13 (1975), 2.
25. Susan Sackett, "Star Trek Report: a Fan News Column," *Starlog* no. 8 (September 1977), 32; Sackett and Roddenberry, 23–24.
26. Sackett and Roddenberry, 24.
27. Sackett, *Inside Trek*, 69.
28. Sackett and Roddenberry, 24.
29. "Star Trek News," *Star Trek Action Group* no. 13; Sackett and Roddenberry, 24; Gene Roddenberry, "Star Trek II Treatment," June 20, 1975, Margaret Herrick Library, Beverly Hills, 953.f-S-1350.
30. Sackett, September 1977; Helen Young, "Revival News," *A Piece of the Action* no. 34 (January 1976), 1.
31. Susan Sackett, "Star Trek II," *Star Trektennial News* no. 13 (May 1976), 3.
32. Sackett, May 1976.
33. Sackett and Roddenberry, 24.
34. "'Star Trek' to Atlanta Meet by 2,000 of Program's Faithful," *Variety* 279, no. 8 (July 9, 1975), 57; "Notes from Broadcast Markets in the U.S. and Abroad," *Variety* 280, no. 4 (September 3, 1975), 44, 68; "TV Syndication," *Variety* 280, no. 11 (October 22, 1975), 148.
35. "New Video Season, Indie-Style"; Michael Monahan, *Shock It to Me: Golden Ghouls of the Golden Gate* (San Francisco: UHF Nocturne, 2011), 66; "Notes from Broadcast Markets in the U.S. and Abroad," *Variety* 280, no. 13 (November 5, 1975), 148; Michael Monahan, email message to author, July 28, 2018.
36. "S.F.'s KQED Hits Peak Ratings; Com'l TV Now Not So Cooperative," *Variety* 281, no. 12 (January 28, 1976), 39, 56.

1976: The War Within the Script, the War Without

1. Jones, 2014, 10–11; Jon Povill, *Star Trek II* (January 19, 1976).
2. *Star Trek Tom Snyder Interview February 1976*, YouTube video, 42:45, posted by "FredsBankInc," Nov 16, 2013, https://www.youtube.com/watch?v=Ozv0iAjIQLo.
3. *Star Trek Tom Snyder Interview February 1976*.
4. Stephen King, *Danse Macabre* (New York: Gallery Books, 2010), 395–396.
5. Bjo Trimble, "Fan Scene," *Starlog* no. 65 (December 1982), 40; Verba, 16.
6. Trimble, 40–41; Verba, 27–28; "Star Trek News," *Star Trek Action Group* no. 13.
7. Irwin and Love, 117.
8. Verba, 27.
9. Irwin and Love, 117–118.
10. Bob Thomas, "Star Trek Fanatics Scare Creator," *San Bernardino Sun-Telegram*, March 23, 1976.
11. Sackett, September 1977; Sackett and Roddenberry, 25.
12. Sackett, "One to Beam Up: Jerry Isenberg," 3–4; "Gene Roddenberry memo to Jerry Eisenberg ca. 1976," 1976, *The Trek Files*, last modified May 22, 2018, https://www.facebook.com/media/set/?set=ms.c.eJwlybkRADAIA7CNcjw24P0XSxFS6iRaRZIDMIJHa~_8eUt~_gu49yXXhvF5u4DNs~-.bps.a.943592839148297&type=1&__tn__=HH-R.
13. Robert Greenberger, "Majel Barrett Roddenberry: a Woman of Enterprise," *Starlog* no. 116 (January 1987), 16–18.
14. "'Star Trektennial' Fan Club, 1966–1976," *Lincoln Enterprises Catalog* no. 6 (May 1976), 1.
15. "Yes—It Lives! Welcome to our 'Star Trektennial' 1966–1976," *Lincoln Enterprises Catalog* no. 6 (May 1976), 2.
16. Jim Meadows, "News of Trekdom," *Star Trek Today* 2, no. 1 (June 1976), 1.
17. Meadows; Sackett and Roddenberry, 25.
18. Meadows.
19. "On and Off Par 'Star Trek' Revival on as a Feature," *Daily Variety* 179, no. 18 (March 29, 1978), 18; Meadows.

20. Meadows.
21. Will Brooker, *Star Wars* (Basingstoke, Hampshire, UK: Palgrave Macmillan, 2009), 92.
22. Susan Sackett, "Star Trek II," *Star Trektennial News* no. 14 (June 1976), 3.
23. Susan Sackett, "Questions," *Star Trektennial News* no. 14 (June 1976), 6.
24. Susan Sackett, "One to Beam Up: Matt Jeffries," *Star Trektennial News* no. 15 (August 1976), 5.
25. Susan Sackett, "Questions," *Star Trektennial News* no. 15 (July 1976), 2.
26. Sackett, "Star Trek II," July 1976.
27. Sackett, "One to Beam Up: Matt Jeffries."
28. Susan Sackett, "Questions," *Star Trektennial News* no. 16 (August 1976), 2–3.
29. Dave Kaufman, "Popular 'Star Trek' Series Spawns Multi-Million-Dollar Paramount Feature Version," *Daily Variety* 172, no. 47 (August 11, 1976), 1; Susan Sackett, "Movie Writers Set," *Star Trektennial News* 2 no. 17 (September-October 1976), 3; Alexander, 429.
30. Bill Irvine, "Screenwriter Allan Scott Talks About Star Trek—The Movie," *Starlog* no. 7 (August 1977), 33; Kaufman; "Star Trek Convention in Oakland (1976)," *San Francisco Bay Area Television Archive*, last modified September 12, 2017, https://diva.sfsu.edu/collections/sfbatv/bundles/209260.
31. Sackett and Roddenberry, 29.
32. "A Busy Week Ahead for Moviegoers," *San Francisco Chronicle*, July 12, 1976; Judy Stone, "The Man Behind 'Star Trek, the Movie,'" *San Francisco Chronicle*, January 7, 1977; Susan Sackett, "One to Beam Up: Phil Kaufman," *Star Trektennial News* 3, no. 21 (May–June 1977), 13; Mick Garris, "Re-Invasion of the Body Snatchers: an Interview with Director Phillip Kaufman," *Starlog* no. 16 (September 1978), 27.
33. Sackett, "One to Beam Up: Phil Kaufman," 14.
34. Sackett, "One to Beam Up: Phil Kaufman," 14.
35. Sackett, "One to Beam Up: Phil Kaufman," 14.
36. Stone.
37. Sackett, "One to Beam Up: Phil Kaufman," 13.
38. Tony Crawley, "The Star Trek Interviews—Part 1," *Starburst* 1, no. 10 (June 1979), 19.
39. Kerry O'Quinn, "The Roots of Starlog," *Starlog* no. 24 (June 1979), 6.
40. David Houston, "Star Trek: Past, Present, and Future," *Starlog* no. 1 (August 1976), 25–26.
41. Kez Howard, "Two Men in One: Gene Roddenberry," *Starlog* no. 2 (November 1976), 10–12; "Star Trek Lives," *Monster Times* I, no. 42 (July 1975), 24.
42. "Log Entries," *Starlog* no. 2 (November 1976), 7–8.
43. Jim Burns, "The Star Trek Movie," *Starlog* no. 2 (November 1976), 13.
44. "Star Trek Fans Torpedo Name for Space Shuttle," *Los Angeles Times*, September 9, 1976.
45. Paramount Pictures, "Welcome Aboard … Space Shuttle Enterprise," Advertisement, *New York Times*, September 21, 1976.
46. "Welcome Aboard .. Space Shuttle Enterprise."
47. Sackett, September 1977; Alexander, 430–431.
48. "Star Trek Movie Update," *Starlog* no. 3 (January 1977), 8, 12; "Personal Appearance: Jesco Von Puttkamer, NASA Scientist"; "Personal Appearance: William Shatner," *Starlog* no. 3 (January 1977), 34–35.
49. Stone; "International Sound Track," *Variety* 285, no. 6 (December 15, 1976), 44; Reeves-Stevens, 1995, 54–59; Anthony D'Alessandro, "Bryan Fuller Unloads Details About Upcoming 'Star Trek Discovery' Series—TCA," *Deadline*, last modified August 10, 2016, http://deadline.com/2016/08/star-trek-discovery-bryan-fuller-cbs-all-access-1201801698/.
50. "Par's Tot 'Trek,'" *Variety* 284, no. 10 (October 13, 1976), 74.
51. "Paramount Names Two to New Executive Posts," *Los Angeles Times*, October 27, 1976; Cecil Smith, "New Appointments in ABC Hierarchy," *Los Angeles Times*, October 26, 1976
52. Michael Eisner and Tony Schwartz, *Work in Progress* (London: Penguin, 1999), 89; Lee Marguiles, "Paramount to Offer Original TV Shows," *Los Angeles Times*, April 1, 1977.
53. Marguiles.

1977: The Battle of the Binary Star Treks

1. "'ll Take 'Trek,'" *Variety* 285, no. 9 (January 19, 1977), 56; Irwin and Love, 151–2.
2. Susan Sackett, "Questions." *Star Trektennial News* 2, no. 18 (November/December 1976), 11.
3. Irwin and Love, 151.
4. "New & Forthcoming Merchandise," *Star Trek Action Group* no. 22 (March 1977), 3; Susan Sackett, "Editor's Log," *Star Trektennial News* 3, no. 24 (November-December 1977), 10; Sackett and Roddenberry, xvi–xvii.
5. Sackett, "One to Beam Up: Jerry Isenberg."

6. Sackett, "One to Beam Up: Jerry Isenberg."
7. Sackett, "One to Beam Up: Jerry Isenberg."
8. Sackett, "The Movie," *Star Trektennial News* 3, no. 19 (January / February 1977), 3.
9. Sackett, "The Movie."
10. Irvine; Solow and Justman, 64.
11. Sackett, "The Movie."
12. Nemecek, 4.
13. Sackett, "The Movie"; Jones, 2014, 12.
14. "File:Spacecon3 schedule.jpg," *Fanlore*, last modified August 2, 2011, https://fanlore.org/wiki/File:Spacecon3_schedule.jpg; "File:Spacecon3-2.jpg," *Fanlore*, last modified August 29, 2017, https://fanlore.org/wiki/File:Spacecon3-2.jpg; Monahan, 2011, 66.
15. "Space-Con (Star Trek and Science Fiction convention)," *Fanlore*, last modified September 17, 2017, https://fanlore.org/wiki/Space-Con_(Star_Trek_and_Science_Fiction_convention).
16. Allen Barra, "Philip Kaufman: Right Stuff! Wrong Package? He's a Fine Filmmaker Without a Real Hit, but 'Rising Sun' May Change That," *Wall Street Journal*, August 1, 1993.
17. "File:Puget1977jan.jpg," *Fanlore*, last modified January 22, 2016, https://fanlore.org/wiki/File:Puget1977jan.jpg; Howard Zimmerman, "Harlan Ellison: Science Fiction's Last Angry Man," *Starlog* no. 8 (September 1977), 25.
18. Susan Sackett, "Star Trek Report: a Fan News Column," *Starlog* no. 7 (August 1977), 30; Ronald L. Soble, "'Star Trek' Still Grounded," April 28, 1977, *Los Angeles Times*.
19. Sackett and Roddenberry, 32–33.
20. Sackett and Roddenberry, 32–33.
21. Susan Sackett, "Star Trek Report: a Fan News Column," *Starlog* no. 6 (June 1977), 58.
22. Soble.
23. Soble; Barra.
24. Stone; Crawley, 19; Jay Scott, "The First/Last Gang Picture Show How the Warriors Beat the Wanderers and Why Kaufman's Bitter," *Globe and Mail*, July 28, 1979.
25. Crawley, 19.
26. Crawley, 19.
27. Crawley, 16; Judy Stone, "Paramount Cans 'Star Trek,'" *San Francisco Chronicle*, June 7, 1977.
28. Crawley, 19.
29. Jones, 2014, 13.
30. Jones, 2014, 13.
31. Sackett, September 1977; "Star Trek—The Motion Picture," *Star Trek Action Group* no. 24 (August 1977), 3.
32. Crawley, 17.
33. Stone; Crawley, 17–18; Garris.
34. "Leonard Nimoy Addresses the Star Trek America Convention (1977)."
35. "Leonard Nimoy Addresses the Star Trek America Convention (1977)."
36. Marguiles.
37. Lee Grant, "Trek from TV to Movie to TV," *Los Angeles Times*, May 25, 1977; Dave Kaufman, "Par Wants 3-Hour Slice of TV," *Daily Variety* 175, no. 57 (May 24, 1977), 1.
38. Grant.
39. Stone, June 9, 1977.
40. Stone, January 7, 1977.
41. Soble; James McBride, "H'wood Hitches to 'Star,' Joins Race to Space," *Variety* 287, no. 6 (June 15, 1977), 1; Bill Greeley, "Paramount, MCA Each Mull '4th Web,'" *Variety* 287, no. 6 (June 15, 1977), 45, 61.
42. Sackett and Roddenberry, 34; "Log Entries," *Starlog* no. 9 (October 1977), 51.
43. Sackett and Roddenberry, 34; Les Brown, "Is a Fourth Network About to Hatch?", *New York Times*, May 8, 1977; "Frank Named President of Paramount TV Distribution," *Los Angeles Times*, October 29, 1977.
44. Sackett, August 1977; Irvine.
45. Irwin and Love, 229.
46. Irwin and Love, 230.
47. Irwin and Love, 230.
48. Irwin and Love, 231.
49. Irwin and Love, 233–234.
50. Irwin and Love, 234.
51. Irwin and Love, 236.
52. Irwin and Love, 238–239.
53. Susan Sackett, "Star Trek Report: a Fan News Column," *Starlog* no. 9 (October 1977), 50.
54. *Star Trek: The Superstars—The Superfans*, directed by Bob Wilkins, written by Bob Wilkins, KTVU, January 30, 1977.
55. *Star Trek: The Superstars—The Superfans*; Lucy Dowling, *Star Wars Year by Year: A Visual Chronicle* (New York: DK, 2010), 48.
56. *William Shatner Interview Bob Wilkins Interviews Hollywood*, YouTube video, 12:36, posted by "Zainin999," Aug 3, 2012, https://www.youtube.com/watch?v=l8kdJ7UFuyk.
57. *William Shatner Interview Bob Wilkins Interviews Hollywood*.
58. *William Shatner Interview Bob Wilkins Interviews Hollywood*.
59. Sackett, September 1977.
60. Sackett, September 1977.
61. "Bulletin," *Starlog* no. 8 (September 1977), 33.
62. Alexander, 437; Susan Sackett, "Letters & Questions????", *Star Trektennial News* 3, no 23 (September-October 1977), 2; Sackett and Roddenberry, 58–59.

63. "STAR TREK Meeting—August 3, 1977," August 5, 1977, the *Trek Files*, last modified August 17, 2018, https://www.facebook.com/pg/TheTrekFiles/photos/?tab=album&album_id=1025809107593336; "Goodwin Leaves Par TV Post for Playboy Vidspot," *Daily Variety* 172, no. 12 (June 22, 1976), 1, 11.

64. "STAR TREK Meeting—August 3, 1977"; "Pix, People, Pickups," *Daily Variety* 175, no. 39 (April 28, 1977), 1, 9; "Goodwin and Livingston Producers of 'Star Trek,'" *Daily Variety* 176, no. 55 (August 22, 1977), 1; "Borgnine Rolling in First Series Part since 'M'hale,'" *Daily Variety* 174, no. 32 (January 18, 1977), 38; Edward Gross, "Star Trek II: the Lost Generation," *Starlog* no. 136 (November 1988), 45; "Goodwin and Livingston Producers of 'Star Trek,'" *Daily Variety* 176, no. 55 (August 22, 1977), 1.

65. Eisner and Schwartz, 90.
66. "STAR TREK Meeting—August 3, 1977."
67. "STAR TREK Meeting—August 3, 1977."
68. "STAR TREK Meeting—August 3, 1977."
69. "STAR TREK Meeting—August 3, 1977."
70. "STAR TREK Meeting—August 3, 1977."
71. "STAR TREK Meeting—August 3, 1977."
72. "STAR TREK Meeting—August 3, 1977."
73. Gross, 48, 57.
74. Reeves-Stevens, 1997, 34.
75. "$30,000 Bite for Par-TV 3-Hr. Spread," *Variety* 288, no. 1 (August 10, 1977), 43; "An NBC Offer for 'Star Trek'?," *Variety* 288, no. 8 (September 28, 1977), 6.
76. Susan Sackett, "The Making of *Star Trek II*: a Conversation with Gene Roddenberry," *Starlog* no. 12 (March 1978), 24–25.
77. Sackett, "The Making of *Star Trek II*: a Conversation with Gene Roddenberry," 25.
78. *Empire of Dreams*, directed by Kevin Burns and Edith Becker (Beverly Hills: 20th Century Fox Home Entertainment, 2004), DVD.
79. Sackett, "The Making of *Star Trek II*: a Conversation with Gene Roddenberry."
80. Sackett, "The Making of *Star Trek II*: a Conversation with Gene Roddenberry."
81. Sackett, "The Making of *Star Trek II*: a Conversation with Gene Roddenberry."
82. Sackett, "The Making of *Star Trek II*: a Conversation with Gene Roddenberry."
83. Susan Sackett, "Star Trek Report," *Starlog* no. 11 (January 1978), 38; Army Archerd, "Just for Variety," *Daily Variety* 176, no. 59 (August 26, 1977), 3.
84. Peter Mikelbank, "The Boss Speaks: 'Star Trek' Lives!", *Washington Post*, August 29, 1977; Marguiles.
85. Marguiles; David Houston, "William Shatner: Moving Right Along," *Starlog* no. 9 (October 1977), 46.
86. Sackett, October 1977; Reeves-Stevens, 1997, 240–243.
87. Army Archerd, "Just for Variety," *Daily Variety* 176, no. 63 (September 1, 1977), 2.
88. Mikelbank; Don Wigal, "Stardate: Supplemental," *Future Fantasy* 1, no. 1 (February 1978), 53; "Leonard Nimoy Addresses the Star Trek America Convention (1977)"; Leonard Nimoy, *I Am Spock* (New York: Hyperion, 1995), 6.
89. "Leonard Nimoy Addresses the Star Trek America Convention (1977)."
90. "Leonard Nimoy Addresses the Star Trek America Convention (1977)"; "William Shatner to Return in New Star Trek Version," *Los Angeles Times*, September 13, 1977; Susan Sackett, 'Star Trek Report," *Starlog* no. 10 (December 1977), 51.
91. "Star Trek II," *Star Trek Action Group* no. 25 (October 1977), 3.
92. Susan Sackett, "Star Trek II," *Star Trektennial News* 3, no. 24 (November-December 1977), 3; Susan Sackett, "Star Trek Report," *Starlog* no. 24 (July 1979), 31; "The Andromeda Backstory," SciFiwww, n.d., https://web.archive.org/web/20050720001221/http://www.scifi.com:80/andromeda/about/index.html.
93. Gary Nardino to Gene Roddenberry, September 15, 1977. https://www.facebook.com/TheTrekFiles/photos/a.957656681075246.1073741855.799697610204488/957656691075245/; Larry Nemecek, *The Star Trek: The Next Generation Companion* rev. ed. (New York: Pocket Books, 1995), 186; Kerry O'Quinn, "Harve Bennett on 'Star Trek IV,'" *Starlog* no. 101 (December 1985), 73.
94. Reeves-Stevens, 1997, 204.
95. Reeves-Stevens, 1997, 42.
96. "New Star Trek Debut Postponed," *Los Angeles Times*, November 9, 1977.
97. "New Star Trek Debut Postponed."
98. Charles Champlin, "Saucer Sorcery," *Los Angeles Times*, November 18, 1977; Gross, 57.
99. Gross, 57.
100. "Shatner Guest Stars," *Long Beach Independent*, November 18, 1977; Lewis Seagal, "Mehta Leads 'Star Wars' at Bowl," *Los Angeles Times*, November 22, 1977.
101. Reeves-Stevens, 1997, 68; "Telewriters," *Daily Variety* 177, no. 56 (November 23, 1977), 12; "Stark Trek!," *Famous Monsters* no. 142 (February 1978), 70.
102. Don Shay, "Star Trek—The Motion Picture," *Cinefantastique* 8, no. 2–3 (Spring 1979), 90.
103. Reeves-Stevens, 1997, 68, 90.
104. Reeves-Stevens, 1997, 69; Susan Sackett, "Star Trek Report," *Starlog* no. 13 (May 1978), 67.
105. Hoyt Bowers, "De Forest Kelley / Series /

Feature Deal Memo," December 8, 1977, Margaret Herrick Library, Beverly Hills, 4.f-7.
106. "The Lost Enterprise: Star Trek—Phase II," *Star Trek—The Motion Picture: The Director's Edition*, DVD (USA: Paramount Pictures, 2001).
107. Dave Kaufman, "Production Start on Par 'Trek' Once Again a Feature, Delayed," *Daily Variety* 178, no. 16 (December 28, 1977), 1.

1978: Into the Luminescent Powerfield I Go

1. Susan Pamela Batho, "Effect of Commercialisation and Direct Intervention by the Owners of Intellectual Copyright: a Case Study: the Australian *Star Trek* Fan Community" (PhD thesis, University of Western Sydney, 2009), 99–100.
2. Batho, 100–101.
3. Batho, 101.
4. Batho, 101.
5. Batho, 101.
6. Sackett and Roddenberry, 48–49.
7. John Dempsey, "Fourth TV Net Again in Focus at Indie Meet," *Variety* 289, no. 12 (January 25, 1978), 65.
8. David Hutchison, "Special Report on the (New) Enterprise," *Starlog* no. 12 (March 1978), 31
9. Hutchison; Koenig, 60–62.
10. Hutchison; Cecil Smith, "A Window Opens on the 'Cosmos,'" *Los Angeles Times*, September 25, 1980.
11. "Trek Update," *Starlog* no. 12 (March 1978), 31.
12. Lee Cole, *Enterprise Flight Manual*, February 1978; Sackett and Roddenberry, 86.
13. Gross, 47.
14. David Houston, "The Model Makers at Magicam: How They Survived 'Star Trek—The Motion Picture,'" *Starlog* no. 27 (October 1979), 26–28.
15. David Houston, "The Magical Techniques of Movie & TV Special Effects: Part XV: Brick Price-The Model Man," *Starlog* no. 20 (March 1979), 70; David Houston, "Andy Probert Talks About the Lost Designs of Star Trek the Motion Picture," *Starlog* no. 32 (March 1980), 27; Andy Probert to Gene Roddenberry, June 19, 1972, https://www.facebook.com/pg/TheTrekFiles/photos/?tab=album&album_id=961499494024298.
16. Gross, 57.
17. Gross, 57.
18. Alexander, 446; Gross, 57; Army Archerd, "Just for Variety," *Daily Variety* 179, no. 55 (May 19, 1978), 3.
19. Gross, 57.
20. Morrie Gelman, "OPT Will Produce Half-Hour Strip," *Daily Variety* 179, no. 4 (March 9, 1978), 18.
21. Charles Schreger, "As Adv. Costs for Launchings Rise, Distribs Turn to Tie-Ins; Array of Recent Arrangements," *Variety* 290, no. 7 (March 22, 1978), 34.
22. Gregg Kilday, "Countdown for Mr. Spock?," *Los Angeles Times*, March 27, 1978.
23. "On and Off Par 'Star Trek' Revival on as a Feature," *Daily Variety* 179, no. 18 (March 29, 1978), 1–18; Susan Sackett, "Star Trek Report," *Starlog* no. 15 (August 1978), 48.
24. "Latest 'Star Trek' Enterprise Keeps the 'Trekkies' Truckin,'" *Daily Variety* 179, no. 19 (March 30, 1978), 3; Sackett, "Star Trek Report," August 1978; Forrest J. Ackerman, "Star Trek 23rd Century Style," *Famous Monsters* no. 145 (July 1978), 34.
25. Reeves-Stevens, 1995, 61; Sackett, "Star Trek Report," August 1978; Gross, 57.
26. "On and Off Par 'Star Trek' Revival on as a Feature," 18; Vernon Scott, "'Star Trek' Crew Has First Reunion," UPI, April 19, 1978.
27. "On and Off Par 'Star Trek' Revival on as a Feature," 18.
28. "Built-In Audience for 'Star Trek' Pic," *Daily Variety* 179, no. 18 (March 29, 1978), 18–19.
29. Sackett, "Star Trek Report," August 1978; Charles Champlin, "Another 'Star' is Born," *Los Angeles Times*, March 31, 1978.
30. "On and Off Par 'Star Trek' Revival on as a Feature," 18.
31. Batho; Sackett, "Star Trek Report," August 1978; Jim Wnoroski, "A Preview of Star Trek: the Movie," *Space Trek Special* (1978), 20–23, 59.
32. "Built-In Audience for 'Star Trek' Pic."
33. Sackett, "Star Trek Report," August 1978; "On and Off Par 'Star Trek' Revival on as a Feature," 18; Champlin, March 31, 1978.
34. "On and Off Par 'Star Trek' Revival on as a Feature," 18; "Latest 'Star Trek' Enterprise Keeps the 'Trekkies' Truckin.'"
35. Ackerman, 35–36.
36. Ackerman, 36.
37. Jones, 2014, 77–78; "On and Off Par 'Star Trek' Revival on as a Feature," 18; Sackett, "Star Trek Report," August 1978.
38. Wnoroski; "Special Effects Are His Specialty from Tara to Outer Space," *Star Trek—The Motion Picture Newsletter*, no. 2 (Autumn 1979), 3; Jones, 2014, 548.
39. Wnoroski; Crawley, 19.
40. Champlin, March 31, 1978.
41. "Films in the Future," *Daily Variety* 179,

no. 25 (April 7, 1978), 10; Susan Sackett, "Star Trek Report," *Starlog* no. 14 (June 1978), 48.

42. Sackett, "Star Trek Report," January 1978; Sackett, "Star Trek Report," June 1978.

43. "Pix, People, Pickups," *Daily Variety* 179, no. 19 (March 30, 1978), 14.

44. Robert Abel & Associates, "We're Helping Send the Enterprise on its Greatest Adventure," Advertisement, *Daily Variety* 179, no. 55 (May 19, 1978), 11.

45. Morrie Gelman, "Ad Prod'n Keeps Magicam Growing," *Daily Variety* 179, no. 20 (March 31, 1978), 3; "STAR TREK Meeting—August 3, 1977"; Susan Sackett, "Star Trek Report," *Starlog* no. 16 (September 1978), 20.

46. Jones, 2014, 78; "Pix, People, Pickups," *Daily Variety* 180, no. 7 (June 14, 1978), 6; "Pix, People, Pickups," *Daily Variety* 180, no. 13 (June 22, 1978), 1; "Pix, People, Pickups," *Daily Variety* 180, no. 15 (June 26, 1978), 13.

47. Maynard, 28–29; Hutchison, 31.

48. Lincoln Enterprises, "Inside Star Trek II—1978," Advertisement, *Amazing Science Fiction* 51, no. 4 (August 1978).

49. Sackett, "Star Trek Report," August 1977: 31; Sackett, "Star Trek Report," September 1978: 21; Garris, 27.

50. Susan Sackett, "Star Trek Report," *Starlog* no. 18 (December 1978), 64–65; Army Archerd, "Just for Variety," *Daily Variety* 180, no. 49 (August 14, 1978), 3; Quarton.

51. Koenig, 176–177.

52. "60 Years of Revolution and Evolution in Film Biz," *Daily Variety* 181, no. 40 (October 31, 1978), 20.

53. Koenig, 176, 218–220; Jones, 2014, 318; Roddenberry and Livingston.

54. Steve Ginsberg, "Full Year Ahead, Par Seeks Bid on 'Star Trek'; 16-Week Deal, Percentages Stun Showmen," *Variety* 293, no. 6 (December 13, 1978), 5.

55. Ginsberg.

56. Paramount Pictures, "Paramount is the Word." Paramount Pictures press release, December 1979.

57. Marguerite Michaels, "A Visit to Star Trek's Movie Launch," *Parade*, December 10, 1978, 4, 6.

58. Aljean Harmetz, "Cinemas Start Sale of Doodads," *New York Times*, December 10, 1978.

1979: Will You Take My $44M Hand?

1. Kaye, 58; "'Trekkies' First in Line for 'Trek' Tix," *Daily Variety* 185, no. 58 (November 26, 1979), 4; "Windy City B.O. Is 'Star' Struck: 'Trek' Zowie 600G," *Daily Variety* 186, no 5 (December 12, 1979), 3; "Abel Splits with Par Over 'Trek' Effects," *Daily Variety* 183, no. 6 (March 13, 1979), 6.

2. Jeffrey Kaye, "Trekkie Alert," *New West* (March 26, 1979), 60; Sackett and Roddenberry, 56–57.

3. "Dawn Steel Added to Par Merchandise, License Staff," *Daily Variety* 182, no. 50 (February 15, 1979), 4.

4. Dawn Steel, *They Can Kill You, But They Can't Eat You: Lessons from the Front* (New York: Pocket Books, 1993), 105; Todd McCarthy, "U.S. Pic Budgets into Megabuck Era," *Variety* 296, no. 4 (August 29, 1979), 20; David Houston, "The Model Makers at Magicam: How They Survived 'Star Trek—The Motion Picture,'" *Starlog* no. 27 (October 1979), 26–30.

5. Steel, 107–109.

6. Steel, 107–109.

7. Steel, 109.

8. Steel, 110; "Dawn Steel Paramount Production Veepee," *Daily Variety* 187, no. 42 (May 2, 1980), 1.

9. Steve Kelley, *Star Trek: The Collectibles* (Iola, WI: Krause Publications, 2008), 129; Christopher Mills, "STAR TREK—THE MOTION PICTURE (1979) Coca-Cola Premium Poster," *space1970*, last modified December 7, 2012, http://space1970.blogspot.com/2012/12/star-trek-motion-picture-1979-coca-cola.html; Steel, 111–112.

10. Paramount Pictures, *Paramount Press Book and Merchandising Manual: Star Trek—The Motion Picture*, 1979.

11. Steel, 113; Robert Mankoff, "New Yorker February 11th, 1980," *Fine Art America*, last modified April 3, 2017, https://fineartamerica.com/featured/new-yorker-february-11th-1980-robert-mankoff.html.

12. Solow and Justman, 173, 184–186.

13. Tom Dalzell, "How Quirky is Berkeley? the Federation Trading Post reunion," *Berkeleyside*, last modified May 14, 2018, https://www.berkeleyside.com/2018/05/14/how-quirky-is-berkeley-the-federation-trading-post-reunion.

14. "Pix, People, Pickups," *Daily Variety* 182, no. 33 (January 23, 1979), 8; Schreger, December 7, 1979; Morrie Gelman, "'Star Trek' Feature Reported Presold by Par to ABC-TV," *Daily Variety* 182, no. 37 (January 29, 1979), 1, 6; Dale Pollock, "ABC Stocks Up on Films for the '80s," *Daily Variety* 186, no. 9 (December 18, 1979), 24.

15. "Blueprints for Sets of New 'Star Trek' Film are a Steal; Thief is Fined," *Variety* 292, no.

4 (August 30, 1978), 1, 92; "'I Learned a Few Things,'" *Los Angeles Times*, March 4, 1979.

16. "'Star Trek' or 'Dragnet'?", *Los Angeles Times*, March 4, 1979; "Blueprints for Sets of New 'Star Trek' Film are a Steal."

17. "'Star Trek' or 'Dragnet'?"; "Blueprints for Sets of New 'Star Trek' Film are a Steal."

18. "'I Learned a Few Things.'"

19. Paul G. Levine, "The Unearthly Silence from the Sci-Fi Sets," *Los Angeles Times*, March 4, 1979.

20. Levine.

21. Sackett, April 1979.

22. Les Brown, "RCA Assembles Fare for First Video Disks," *New York Times*, April 9, 1979.

23. Bally Manufacturing Corporation, "Bally's Star Trek a Space Age Pinball Voyage," Bally Manufacturing Corporation press release, April 15, 1979.

24. Bally Manufacturing Corporation.

25. "Coin Machine," *Cash Box* 41, no. 1 (May 19, 1979), 54; Bally Manufacturing Corporation, "Star Date: 1979. Destination: Profit," Advertisement, *Cash Box* 41, no. 2 (May 26, 1979); "Log Entries," *Starlog* no. 24 (July 1979), 16; "Space-Age Spaceware," *Starlog* no. 24 (July 1979), 30.

26. "Pix, People, Pickups," *Daily Variety* 185, no. 37 (October 26, 1979), 23; Paramount Pictures, *Star Trek—The Motion Picture Newsletter*, no. 1 (Summer 1979), 1.

27. *Star Trek—The Motion Picture Newsletter*, Summer 1979, 1–2, 4; Paramount Pictures, *Star Trek—The Motion Picture Newsletter*, no. 2 (Autumn 1979), 4; Jones, 2014, 239.

28. "Images for Jerry Goldsmith—Star Trek: the Motion Picture," *Discogs*, n.d., https://www.discogs.com/release/3168110-Star-Trek-The-Motion-Picture/images; Sackett and Roddenberry, 129; "Star Trek—The Motion Picture," *Star Trek Action Group* no. 33 (December 1980), 3.

29. "New & Forthcoming Merchandise," *Star Trek Action Group* no. 35 (June 1979), 10.

30. Paramount Pictures, "Sign on Now for the 1979–80 Voyage of the Enterprise," Advertisement, *Starlog* no. 25 (August 1979), 5.

31. "Sign on Now for the 1979–80 Voyage of the Enterprise."

32. Susan Sackett, "Star Trek Report," *Starlog* no. 25 (August 1979), 5.

33. "Pix, People, Pickups," *Daily Variety* 184, no. 51 (August 16, 1979), 1; "'Star Trek' Movie Set for Cross Promotion," *Cash Box* 41, no. 27 (November 17, 1979), 16.

34. Barbara Lewis, "Ray Bradbury: the Martian Chronicler," *Starlog* no. 25 (August 1979), 29.

35. Roddenberry and Livingston, 69, 99; Jones, 2014, 291, 450.

36. David Hutchison, "Star Trek—The Motion Picture Props," *Starlog* no. 47 (June 1981), 57.

37. "Communications," *Starlog* no. 30 (January 1980), 7; Hutchison, June 1981, 57–58; Jones, 2014, 217–218.

38. "Gene Roddenberry memo to Jerry Eisenberg ca. 1976"; Kelley, 171.

39. "The Roddenberry Phone Call," *Fanlore*, last modified September 25, 2016, https://fanlore.org/wiki/The_Roddenberry_Phone_Call.

40. "South Bend USS Enterprise configurations.jpg," *Memory Alpha*, n.d., http://memory-alpha.wikia.com/wiki/Milton_Bradley?file=South_Bend_USS_Enterprise_configurations.jpg.

41. "Spacewar! Video Games Blast Off," *Museum of the Moving Image*, last modified December 12, 2015, http://www.movingimage.us/exhibitions/2012/12/15/detail/spacewar-video-games-blast-off/.

42. David Ahl, "Super Star Trek History," *Creative Computing* 1, no. 4 (May/June 1975), 40.

43. TRS-80 Software Exchange, "Star Trek III," Advertisement, *Softside* 1, no. 1 (October 1978), 2; the Software Exchange, "Star Trek III.4," Advertisement, *PROG/80* 1, no. 6 (February 1980), 27; Lance Micklus, "The $44,000,000 Star Trek! Game," *Softside* 2, no. 8 (May 1980), 18.

44. David Gerrold, "Soaring," *Starlog* no. 67 (February 1983), 56.

45. Gerrold, February 1983, 56.

46. Gerrold, February 1983, 56–57.

47. Gerrold, February 1983, 57.

48. Ronald Rosenberg, "Bradley Plans to Buy into Video Game Field," *Boston Globe*, July 15, 1982.

49. "The Making of Star Trek Cover Gallery," *Memory Alpha*, n.d., http://memory-alpha.wikia.com/wiki/The_Making_of_Star_Trek#Cover_gallery.

50. Jones, 2014, 443.

51. Mary Reinholz, "Bloomingdale's Sets Its Entry in Spacewear Race," *Women's Wear Daily* 139, no. 48 (September 7, 1979), 8; Joyce Wells, "No-Sweat Look Grows, but Peak Not in Sight," *Women's Wear Daily* 139, no. 100 (November 20, 1979), 1.

52. Macy's, "Christmas at Macy's," Advertisement, *San Francisco Chronicle*, November 30, 1979; Macy's, "Christmas at Macy's," Advertisement, *San Francisco Chronicle*, December 1, 1979.

53. Bloomingdale's, "Bloomingdale's Has a Sunday Kind of Love for Christmas," Advertise-

ment, *New York Times*, December 2, 1979; "Panorama," *Questar* 2 no. 3 (June 1980), 12.

54. Smart Modes, "Official Star Trek the Motion Picture Jacket," Advertisement, *Women's Wear Daily*, November 7, 1979; Smart Modes, "Official Star Trek the Motion Picture Jacket," Advertisement, *Women's Wear Daily*, December 17, 1979.

55. O'Quinn Studios, "The Official Star Trek Duty Jacket," Advertisement, *Starlog* no. 32 (March 1980).

56. O'Quinn Studios.

57. Will Tusher, "Profit-Hunting Exhibs Find New Revenue Sources," *Daily Variety* 185, no. 42 (November 1, 1979), 1, 23.

58. Jones, 2014, 486.

59. Geri Fabrikant, "State Laws Foil Film Buys," *Variety* 297, no. 3 (November 21, 1979), 1, 160.

60. Army Archerd, "Just for Variety," *Daily Variety* 186, no. 33 (January 23, 1980), 3.

61. "3,000 'Trekkies' Prevue 'Star Trek'", *Variety* 297, no. 6 (November 28, 1979), 21.

62. Jones, 2014, 540.

63. Paramount Pictures, "Reserved Performance Engagement at the Paramount Theatre," Advertisement, *New York Daily News*, November 16, 1979; Dale Pollock, "Mega-Buck Pix Push Filmbiz into '80S; B.O. Champs A-Changin'," *Daily Variety* 186, no. 19 (January 3, 1980), 2; "3,000 'Trekkies' Prevue 'Star Trek.'"

64. Paramount Pictures, "This Holiday, Give a Journey Through the Galaxy," Advertisement, *New York Times*, December 7, 1979.

65. "'Trekkies' First in Line for 'Trek' Tix," *Daily Variety* 185, no. 58 (November 26, 1979), 4; "3,000 'Trekkies' Prevue 'Star Trek.'"

66. Roger Petterson, "Loyal Trekkies Flock to Movie," Associated Press, December 8, 1979.

67. Sunrise Cinemas, "Gala Opening Today," Advertisement, New York Daily News, December 7, 1979; Paul Carlsen, "Enterprising Rocklanders Jam Opening of 'Star Trek' Movie," *Journal-News*, December 8, 1979; The Movies, "Star Trek—The Motion Picture Starts Today," Advertisement, *Journal-News*, December 7, 1979; Barry Hanson, "'Star Trek' Blasts Off Again," Associated Press, December 8, 1979; "Lengthy Trek," *Press and Sun-Bulletin*, December 8, 1979.

68. Craig Scott, "Curiosity Brings People to 'Star Trek' Premiere," *Star-Gazette*, December 8, 1979.

69. Mike Yablonski, "Science Fiction Film Fails to Send New Jersey 'Trekkies' Into Orbit," *Courier-News*, December 8, 1979.

70. Linda Roman, "Star Trek Fans Trek to Catch Movie Version," *Daily Record*, December 9, 1979.

71. Rita Manno, "A Grand Return for 'Star Trek,'" *Courier-Post*, December 8, 1979.

72. Ellen M. Prendergast, "Trekkies Look to the Stars," *Record*, December 9, 1979.

73. Hanson; Murray Dubin, "The Scene," *Philadelphia Inquirer*, December 10, 1979.

74. Dubin.

75. Bill Rufty, "Trekkie Heaven," *Sarasota Journal*, December 7, 1979.

76. Eliott Rodriguez, "Star Trek's Enterprise Orbits Dade," *Miami News*, December 4, 1979; Longshot, "Star Trek Party," Advertisement, *Miami News*, December 7, 1979; "Trekkies in Their Glory," *Miami News*, December 8, 1979.

77. John C. Long, "Trek Tricks … Despite Crowds, Fans Were Persistent," *Courier-Journal*, December 8, 1979.

78. Jamie Lucke, "Curious, Devoted Flock to Film Version of 'Star Trek,'" *Messenger-Inquirer*, December 9, 1979.

79. Steve Wingfield, "Space … is at a Premium for Trekkers," *Paducah Sun*, December 9, 1979.

80. Judy Putnam, "'Trek' is Rising Star in Local Movie Sky as Fans Crowd Theater," *Clarion-Ledger*, December 9, 1979; Petterson.

81. Larry Schumpert, "Fans Trek to Movie," *Journal and Courier*, December 10, 1979.

82. John Sherwood, "A Guaranteed Sellout Audience," *Battle Creek Enquirer*, December 8, 1979.

83. Storer Rowley, "'Trekkies' Flood Theaters," *Chicago Tribune*, December 7, 1979; Petterson.

84. Janet Helling, "Star Date 12.7.79: 1,100 in Q-C Swarm to 'Star Trek' Opening," *Daily Dispatch*, December 8, 1979.

85. Helling.

86. Warren Gerds, "'Star Trek' Offers Lots of Everything, but Top Acting," *Green Bay Press-Gazette*, December 8, 1979.

87. Don Morrison, "'Trekkies' Are More Fun Than 'Star Trek,'" *Minneapolis Star*, December 10, 1979.

88. Dave Daley, "Trekkies Return: Movie Version of 'Star Trek' Brings Out the Faithful Fans," *Cloud Times*, December 8, 1979.

89. Mary Jo Howe, "Star Trekkies Invade the City," *Argus-Leader*, December 8, 1979.

90. Gene Kelly, "'Star Trek' Lovers Stand in Line for Hours, Willingly, to See Film," *Lincoln Journal Star*, December 8, 1979.

91. "Debut Interrupts Premiere," *Salina Journal*, December 11, 1979.

92. "Star Trek Beams in this Week," *Deseret News*, December 3, 1979.

93. Steve Hallock, "Trekkies," *Arizona Republic*, December 9, 1979.

94. Petterson; "Star Trek Isn't Bad, but It's No Old Yeller," *Victoria Times*, December 17, 1979.

95. Lance Robertson, "'Star Trek' Capacity Crowd in Corvallis Cheers Long-Awaited Movie," *Albany Democrat-Herald*, December 8, 1979; Army Archerd, "Just for Variety," *Daily Variety* 185, no. 55 (November 20, 1979), 3.

96. "'Trek' a la Barnum Is Biggest Film Kickoff for Portland in 20 Yrs," *Variety* 297 no. 6 (December 12, 1979), 3; "Star Trek Nets Threat," *Oregonian*, December 8, 1979.

97. Rod Patterson, "More Ear: UNICEF Gets Proceeds," *Oregonian*, November 25, 1979. John Wendeborn, "'Star Struck': Ice Show Spacy in Best Sense," *Oregonian*, November 28, 1979.

98. "'Trek' a la Barnum Is Biggest Film Kickoff for Portland in 20 Yrs"; Rod Patterson, "More Ear: 'Star Trek' Soundtrack Fairly Tinkles," *Oregonian*, December 16, 1979; "Star Trek Nets Threat."

99. Patterson, "More Ear: 'Star Trek' Soundtrack Fairly Tinkles"; "Star Trek Nets Threat."

100. Martin Griffith, "'Trekkies' Savor the Movie," *Reno Gazette-Journal*, December 8, 1979.

101. Chiszar; Barry Hanson, "'Star Trek' Blasts Off Again," Associated Press, December 8, 1979; "'Star Trek' Into B.O. Stratospherics: $42-M Negative; $100-M to Recoup," *Variety* 297, no. 6 (December 12, 1979), 3; David Gerrold, "Rumblings," *Starlog* no. 33 (April 1980), 24.

102. "Trekkies Turned Out by the Hundreds," *Santa Maria Times*, December 8, 1979.

103. Cyndee Fontana and Tom Watson, "700 Salinas Fans Keep a 'Stardate,'" *Salinas Californian*, December 8, 1979.

104. Bill Mandel, "Beam Me Up!," San Francisco Examiner, December 9, 1979; Stone; Shay, 92.

105. Paramount Pictures, "For Your Consideration," Advertisement, *Daily Variety* 186, no. 2 (December 7, 1979), 18–19; "The 52nd Academy Awards," *Oscars.org*, n.d., https://www.oscars.org/oscars/ceremonies/1980; Dale Pollock, "Mega-Buck Pix Push Filmbiz into '80s; B.O. Champs A-Changin'," *Daily Variety* 186, no. 19 (January 3, 1980), 2; "'Star Trek' Sets Three-Day Record," *Daily Variety* 186, no. 4 (December 11, 1979), 29; "H'w'd-Westwood Ticket Prices Likely $5 for Christmas Films," *Daily Variety* 186, no. 1 (December 6, 1979), 3.

106. "Paperback Best Sellers," *New York Times*, December 9, 1979; Dale Pollock, "'Trek' Beams Up $2 Mil-Plus in 105 Enterprises," *Daily Variety* 186, no. 3 (December 10, 1979), 1, 23.

107. "'Star Trek' Sets Three-Day Record"; Jones, 2014, 591.

108. "Pre-Xmas Slump; 'Trek' Siphons from All," *Variety* 297, no. 6 (December 12, 1979), 3.

109. "'Star Trek' Rockets to $1.4 Mil Gotham Week-End on 81 Screens," *Daily Variety* 186, no. 4 (December 11, 1979), 3; "Windy City B.O. Is 'Star' Struck: 'Trek' Zowie 600G," *Daily Variety* 186, no. 5 (December 12, 1979), 3; "'Trek' Only Bright Spock on S.F. B.O. Scanner During First Flight," *Daily Variety* 186, no. 5 (December 12, 1979), 3; Judy Stone, "'Star Trek': the Enterprise Takes Off," *San Francisco Chronicle*, December 5, 1979; "'Star Trek' Sensash 192G in Seattle; Other Biz Spotty," *Daily Variety* 186, no. 6 (December 13, 1979), 3.

110. "Showbiz Winners Edge Losers on Average Volume," *Daily Variety* 186, no. 4 (December 11, 1979), 4; "'Trek' Rockets Toward New 7-Day B.O. Mark," *Daily Variety* 186, no. 7 (December 14, 1979), 1, 43; "'Star Trek' Sensash 192G in Seattle; Other Biz Spotty."

111. Paramount Pictures, "Star Trek—The Phenomenon!," Advertisement, *Los Angeles Times*, December 14, 1979.

112. "Paperback Best Sellers," *New York Times*, December 16, 1979; "FAB Honors Par's 'Star Trek' Feature," *Daily Variety* 186, no. 9 (December 18, 1979), 27.

113. *Star Trek I: The Motion Picture*, YouTube video, 2:10:18, posted by "YouTube Movies," Jun 20, 2012, https://www.youtube.com/watch?v=8mJNWyluSRs.

114. Dale Pollock, "'Star Trek,' with $17 Mil Domestic Box-Office, Sets New Opening-Week Record," *Daily Variety* 186, no. 8 (December 17, 1979), 1; Aljean Harmetz, "'Smokey II' is Said to Gross $18 Million," *New York Times*, August 23, 1980.

115. Pollock, December 17, 1979, 1, 43.

116. "Par Reports Good B.O. Overseas for 'Trek,'" *Daily Variety* 186, no. 9 (December 18, 1979), 8; "'Trek,' Despite 40% 2D-Wk. Dip, Eyes $27 Mil B.O.," *Daily Variety* 186, no. 12 (December 21, 1979), 1, 24.

117. Derek Malcolm, "Cinema," *Guardian*, December 20, 1979; Harlan Ellison, *Harlan Ellison's Watching* (San Francisco: Underwood-Miller, 1989), 141; Harlan Ellison, "Ellison Reviews Trek," *Starlog* no. 33 (April 1980), 60–63.

118. John Stanley, "Within the Empire of the King of the Movie Posters," *San Francisco Examiner*, July 13, 1980.

119. Roman Kozak, "Swoosh! 'Star Trek' Promotion Takes Off," *Billboard* 91, no. 49 (December 8, 1979), 74; "Album Reviews," *Cash Box* 41, no. 32 (December 22, 1979), 13; "Cash Box Top

Albums / 101 to 200," *Cash Box* 41, no. 33 (December 29, 1979), 117; "Columbia Promoting 'Star Trek' Soundtrack," *Cash Box* 41, no. 32 (December 22, 1979), 14; "What's In-Store," *Cash Box* 41, no. 32 (December 22, 1979), 17; "Paperback Best Sellers," *New York Times*, December 23, 1979.

120. "Singles," *Cash Box* 41, no. 33 (December 29, 1979), 24.

121. Dale Pollock, "Holiday Release Glut Brings Riches to Some, but There's Risks—and Always, Losers," *Daily Variety* 186, no. 17 (December 31, 1979), 1, 2; Bruce McCabe, "Movies," *Boston Globe*, January 4, 1980.

122. "Paperback Best Sellers," *New York Times*, December 30, 1979; A.D. Murphy, "'79 Holds U.S. Box-Office Record," *Daily Variety* 186, no. 23 (January 9, 1980), 1, 8.

1980: The Vulcan Goodbye

1. Pollock, January 3, 1980; "'Trek' Collects $5 Mil Overseas in First Frames," *Daily Variety* 186, no. 20 (January 4, 1980), 1.

2. "The Names Have Been Changed...," *Daily Variety* 186, no. 27 (January 15, 1980), 8.

3. Paramount Pictures, "25 Million People Agree," Advertisement, *New York Times*, January 18, 1980; Paramount Pictures, "See the Movie Event of the Year," Advertisement, *New York Times*, January 19, 1980; Paramount Pictures, "Trek-tacular!", Advertisement, *New York Times*, January 20, 1980; Paramount Pictures, "25 Million People Agree," Advertisement, *New York Times*, January 25, 1980.

4. Sherwood Oaks Experimental College, "Star Trek Seminar: the Making of a Film," Advertisement, *Los Angeles Times*, February 3, 1980.

5. Sackett and Roddenberry, xvi–xvii.

6. Fred Bratman, "Theater Owners Seek End to 'Blind Bidding' on Films," *New York Times*, February 24, 1980.

7. "'Ark' Raid Tied to Par's Upfront Anti-Piracy Ploys."

8. "Z" Channel, "The Oscars are Coming to the 'Z' Channel," Advertisement, *Los Angeles Times*, March 9, 1980.

9. Gene Roddenberry, "Star Trek III Treatment," May 23, 1980, Margaret Herrick Library, Beverly Hills, 952.f-S-1342.

10. "Star Trek—The Motion Picture," *Star Trek Action Group*, December 1980; Karen E. Willson, "An Interview with Gene Roddenberry the Man Behind the Myth," *Starlog* no. 40 (November 1980), 47; Quarton.

11. Sackett and Roddenberry, 89.

12. Susan Adamo, "Log Entries," *Starlog* no. 46 (May 1981), 9; Roddenberry, "Star Trek III Treatment."

13. Stephen Galloway, "Karl Schanzer, Who Inspired Coppola's 'The Conversation,' Dies at 81," *Hollywood Reporter*, last modified June 3, 2014, https://www.hollywoodreporter.com/news/karl-schanzer-who-inspired-coppola-708829.

14. Karl Schanzer, "Star Trek III Analysis," May 30, 1980, Margaret Herrick Library, Beverly Hills, 952.f-S-1342.

15. Schanzer.

16. Army Archerd, "Just for Variety," *Daily Variety* 182, no. 37 (January 29, 1979), 3; Mark Lukasiewicz, "Gulf and Western Industries Interests Investors, Analysts Cool," *Globe and Mail*, June 16, 1980; Aljean Harmetz, "After 2 Good Summers, Film Business Lags," *New York Times*, June 26, 1980; Charles Schreger, "Latest Summer Releases: Ups, Downs," *Los Angeles Times*, July 28, 1980; Willson, 47.

17. "'Star Trek' Producer Gene Roddenberry, the Man Who Put...", *UPI Archive: Domestic News*, October 8, 1980.

18. Charles Schreger, "Software Hard Sell in Chicago," *Los Angeles Times*, June 17, 1980; Big Ben's Records & Tapes, "Pre-Recorded Movies on Video," Advertisement, *Los Angeles Times*, November 4, 1980; National Video Discount Centers, "The One Stop Video Shop," Advertisement, *New York Times*, November 13, 1980; Video Depot, "Video Depot's 4-Store Grand Opening Celebration," Advertisement, *Los Angeles Times*, November 15, 1980; Captain Video, "Where Can I Rent Star Trek?" Advertisement, *Los Angeles Times*, November 15, 1980.

19. Candy McCampbell, "Home Movies Not What They Used to Be," *Tennessean*, February 19, 1981.

20. "Dealers Ecstatic as Par Video Halves Trek 'II' Tape Tab," *Variety* 308, no. 5 (September 1, 1982), 56.

21. William K. Knoedelseder, Jr., "'Heaven's Gate': Everything Hinges on the Box Office," *Los Angeles Times*, November 16, 1980.

22. Richard De Atley, "Studio Recalls $36M Movie," *Boston Globe*, November 21, 1980.

23. Peter H. Brown, "Behind the 'Heaven's Gate' Disaster," *Washington Post*, November 30, 1980.

24. Lawrence Cohn, "Par Backs Nimoy, 'Trek' to Hilt; Talks Going Re Possible Part IV," *Variety* 315, no. 6 (June 6, 1984), 26.

25. Archerd, January 29, 1979; Paramount Pictures, "Paramount Television Welcomes

Harve Bennett," Advertisement, *Daily Variety* 190, no. 2 (December 9, 1980), 28; Lisabeth Shatner, *Captain's Log: William Shatner's Personal Account of the Making of Star Trek V: The Final Frontier* (New York: Pocket Books, 1989), 40.

Epilogue

1. "All-Time Film Rental Champs (of U.S.-Canada Market)," *Variety* 301, no. 11 (January 14, 1981), 28; Bratman.
2. Tom Bierbaum, "Par Releasing Pix on its Own Laser Videodisk Label," *Daily Variety* 191, no. 43 (May 5, 1981), 1; "RCA Videodisks Nab RIAA Gold," *Variety* 306, no. 10 (April 7, 1982), 37; David Crook, "Premiere Partners in Deal with Competitor," *Los Angeles Times*, February 12, 1981.
3. "Par Sues Aviva Re 'Star Trek' Products," *Variety* 303, no. 6 (May 27, 1981), 4; Stone, December 5, 1979; "Par Pix and Aviva Reach Settlement," *Daily Variety* 196, no. 20 (July 2, 1982), 13.
4. "Programs and People in the INTV Screening Rooms," *Broadcasting* 104, no. 3 (January 17, 1983), 70; Paramount Television, "Paramount's Portfolio X," Advertisement, *Broadcasting* 104, no. 3 (January 17, 1983), 4; "Upbeat Outlook for TV's Independents," *Broadcasting* 104, no. 3 (January 17, 1983), 58.
5. Robert Greenberger, "Science Fiction Television in Review 1982–1983," *Starlog* no. 72 (July 1983), 40.
6. "Favorite Videos," *Times Recorder*, December 30, 1984; "The Top Video Cassette Sales in 1985," *Sunday Dispatch*, December 29, 1985; Donna Strickland, "Notebook," *Tampa Tribune*, December 30, 1986; "The Top 50 Videocassette Sales for 1987," *UPI*, December 18, 1987; "Top Video Cassettes," *Miami News*, December 23, 1988.
7. George Anderson, "Reflections On, Off Screen," *Pittsburgh Post-Gazette*, June 20, 1989.
8. Frederick J. Crowest, *Beethoven* (London: J. M. Dent, 1908), 186–188.
9. Judith and Garfield Reeves-Stevens, *Star Trek: The Next Generation: The Continuing Mission* (New York: Pocket Books, 1997), 218.
10. Reeves-Stevens, *The Continuing Mission*, 1997, 218–220; Cohn, 5.
11. Shatner, 75–76, 68.
12. Paul Mandell, "Star Trek V: Sharing the Pain," *Cinefex* no. 42 (May 1990), 48.
13. William Shatner and Chris Kreski, *Star Trek Movie Memories* (New York: HarperCollins, 1994), 298–300; Daren Dochterman, "Audio Commentary," *Star Trek V: The Final Frontier*, directed by William Shatner, Blu-ray (USA: Paramount Pictures, 2009).
14. Reeves-Stevens, 1995, 245.
15. *Star Trek: The Motion Picture (1979) Review*, YouTube video, 22:30, posted by "Cinemology 101," Jul 2, 2015, https://www.youtube.com/watch?v=Z_dqDZgIzY8.

Bibliography

"ABC Betting on Summer Firstruns to Build Rating Momentum for Fall." *Variety* 254, no. 5 (March 19, 1969), 51.

Ackerman, Forrest J. "Star Trek 23rd Century Style." *Famous Monsters* no. 145 (July 1978), 32–37.

Adamo, Susan. "Log Entries." *Starlog* no. 46 (May 1981), 9.

_____. "Log Entries." *Starlog* no. 33 (April 1980), 9–15.

_____. "Log Entries." *Starlog* no. 52 (November 1981), 9–16.

Ahl, David. "Super Star Trek History." *Creative Computing* 1, no. 4 (May/June 1975), 40.

"Album Reviews." *Cash Box* 41, no. 32 (December 22, 1979), 13.

Alexander, David. *Star Trek Creator: The Authorized Biography of Gene Roddenberry.* New York: Penguin, 1994.

"All-Time Film Rental Champs (of U.S.–Canada Market)." *Variety* 301, no. 11 (January 14, 1981), 28, 52, 54, 56, 58, 60, 62, 66.

Anderson, George. "Reflections On, Off Screen." *Pittsburgh Post-Gazette*, June 20, 1989.

Anderson, Martin G. "State Regulation of Motion Picture Distributors." *Pace Law Review* 3, no. 1 (September 1982), 107–133.

Andres, Alan E. "Gene Roddenberry." *Star-Borne* 3, no. 13 (June 1974), 1.

_____. "Revival News," *A Piece of the Action* no. 23 (February 1975), 1.

"The Andromeda Backstory." *SciFi.com*, n.d. https://web.archive.org/web/20050720001221/http://www.scifi.com:80/andromeda/about/index.html.

"ARB's Syndie Ratings Show Limited Circulation; May Be Blow to Barter." *Variety* 263, no. 13 (August 11, 1971), 36.

Archerd, Army. "Just for Variety." *Daily Variety* 176, no. 59 (August 26, 1977), 3.

_____. "Just for Variety." *Daily Variety* 176, no. 63 (September 1, 1977), 2.

_____. "Just for Variety." *Daily Variety* 179, no. 55 (May 19, 1978), 3.

_____. "Just for Variety." *Daily Variety* 180, no. 42 (August 3, 1978), 11.

_____. "Just for Variety." *Daily Variety* 182, no. 37 (January 29, 1979), 3.

_____. "Just for Variety." *Daily Variety* 185, no. 55 (November 20, 1979), 3.

_____. "Just for Variety." *Daily Variety* 186, no. 33 (January 23, 1980), 3.

"'Ark' Raid Tied to Par's Upfront Anti-Piracy Ploys." *Variety* 303, no. 9 (July 1, 1981), 5.

Asherman, Allan. *The Star Trek Compendium.* New York: Pocket Books, 1986.

"At Last—The Enterprise is Back." *A Piece of the Action* no. 14 (May 1974), 1.

"Atlanta's 2d UHF to Debut in Aug." *Variety* 255, no. 5 (June 18, 1969), 40.

Barra, Allen. "Philip Kaufman: Right Stuff! Wrong Package? He's a Fine Filmmaker Without a Real Hit, But 'Rising Sun' May Change That." *Wall Street Journal*, August 1, 1993.

Basta, Margaret A. "Editorial." *Star-Borne* 2, no. 10 (September/October 1973), 1.

Batho, Susan Pamela. "Effect of Commercialisation and Direct Intervention by the Owners of Intellectual Copyright: A Case Study: The Australian *Star Trek* Fan Community." PhD thesis, University of Western Sydney, 2009.

"BBC Slots 'Star Trek.'" *Variety* 255, no. 4 (June 11, 1969), 67.

Beermann, Frank. "'Don't Publicize Losers,' Walters Sez at ABC Daytime Emmy Show." *Variety* 279, no. 2 (May 21, 1975), 48.

_____. "'Star Trek' Conclave in N.Y. Looms as Mix of Campy Set and Sci-Fi Buffs." *Variety* 265, no. 10 (January 19, 1972), 1, 69.

Benson, Michael. *Space Odyssey: Stanley Kubrick, Arthur C. Clarke, and the Making of a Masterpiece.* New York: Simon & Schuster, 2018.

"Bitter at Brit., Pakistan Slots U.S. TV Series." *Variety* 262, no. 13 (May 12, 1971), 214.

"Blind Bidding and the Motion Picture Industry." *Harvard Law Review* 92, no. 5 (March 1979), 1128–1147.

Block, Richard C. "Coming Revolution in UHF to Be Sparked by Programs and Portability." *Variety* 256, no. 4 (September 10, 1969), 55, 104.

"Bonanza." *Variety* 279, no. 13 (August 6, 1975), 37.

"'Bonanza' in Blighty." *Variety* 257, no. 5 (December 17, 1969), 34.

"Borgnine Rolling in First Series Part since 'M'hale.'" *Daily Variety* 174, no. 32 (January 18, 1977), 38.

Bowers, Hoyt. "De Forest Kelley / Series / Feature Deal Memo." December 8, 1977. Margaret Herrick Library, Beverly Hills, 4.f-7.

Brancatelli, J.B. "The Monster Times Teletype." *Monster Times* 1, no. 22 (May 19, 1973), 26.

"Breaks Go WKBD's Way in Detroit." *Variety* 256, no. 1 (August 20, 1969), 38.

Brooker, Will. *Star Wars*. Basingstoke, Hampshire, UK: Palgrave Macmillan, 2009.

Brown, Joe. "K-B MacArthur Closes." *Washington Post*, August 26, 1982.

Brown, Les. "Is a Fourth Network About to Hatch?" *New York Times*, May 8, 1977.

Brown, Peter H. "Behind the 'Heaven's Gate' Disaster." *Washington Post*, November 30, 1980.

_____. "Embattled Enterprise." *Washington Post*, December 18, 1986.

Brownell, Carole. *Save the Star Trek Cast Mailer*. 1974.

"Buffalo." *Variety* 263, no. 5 (June 16, 1971), 40, 44.

"Built-In Audience for 'Star Trek' Pic." *Daily Variety* 179, no. 18 (March 29, 1978), 18–19.

"Bulletin." *Starlog* no. 8 (September 1977), 33.

Burns, Jim. "The Star Trek Movie." *Starlog* no. 2 (November 1976), 13.

Burns, Kevin and Edith Becker, dir. *Empire of Dreams*. 2004; Beverly Hills: 20th Century Fox Home Entertainment, 2004. DVD.

"A Busy Week Ahead for Moviegoers." *San Francisco Chronicle*, July 12, 1976.C-E

Carlsen, Paul. "Enterprising Rocklanders Jam Opening of 'Star Trek' Movie." *Journal-News*, December 8, 1979.

"Cash Box Top Albums / 101 to 200." *Cash Box* 41, no. 33 (December 29, 1979), 117.

Castle, Alison. *The Stanley Kubrick Archives*. Köln, Germany: Taschen, 2013.

"CBS, NBC Fall Sked Makeup Going Calmly This Year, Thanks to ABC." *Variety* 253, no. 13 (February 12, 1969), 31, 41.

Champlin, Charles. "Another 'Star' is Born." *Los Angeles Times*, March 31, 1978.

_____. "Saucer Sorcery." *Los Angeles Times*, November 18, 1977.

Chiszar, Dan. "'Star Trek': Big Bucks." *United Press International*, December 6, 1979.

Cohn, Lawrence. "Par Backs Nimoy, 'Trek' To Hilt; Talks Going Re Possible Part IV." *Variety* 315, no. 6 (June 6, 1984), 5, 26.

Cole, Lee. *Enterprise Flight Manual*. February 1978.

Collura, Scott. "The William Shatner Interview Page 2 of 2." *IGN*. Last modified August 18, 2017. http://www.ign.com/articles/2017/08/18/the-william-shatner-interview?page=2.

"Columbia Promoting 'Star Trek' Soundtrack." *Cash Box* 41, no. 32 (December 22, 1979), 14.

Cooper, Sonni. "Where's Bill? Call Scotland Yard!" *Star Trek Action Group* no. 41 (June 1980), 6.

Crawley, Tony. "The Star Trek Interviews—Part 1." *Starburst* 1, no. 10 (June 1979), 16–21.

"Cronkite at 7 P.M. Holds Off Indies' Rising N.Y. Tide." *Variety* 256, no. 10 (October 22, 1969), 49.

Crook, David. "Premiere Partners in Deal with Competitor." *Los Angeles Times*, February 12, 1981.

Crowest, Frederick J. *Beethoven*. London: J. M. Dent, 1908.

"D. C. Fontana Speech." *Star-Borne* 2, no. 6/7 (March/April 1973), 1.

D'Alessandro, Anthony. "Bryan Fuller Unloads Details About Upcoming 'Star Trek Discovery' Series—TCA." *Deadline*. Last modified August 10, 2016. http://deadline.com/2016/08/star-trek-discovery-bryan-fuller-cbs-all-access-1201801698/.

Daley, Dave. "Trekkies Return: Movie Version of 'Star Trek' Brings Out the Faithful Fans." *Cloud Times*, December 8, 1979.

"Dealers Ecstatic as Par Video Halves Trek 'II' Tape Tab." *Variety* 308, no. 5 (September 1, 1982), 56.

De Atley, Richard. "Studio Recalls $36M Movie." *Boston Globe*, November 21, 1980.

"Debut Interrupts Premiere." *Salina Journal*, December 11, 1979.

Dempsey, John. "Fourth TV Net Again in Focus at Indie Meet." *Variety* 289, no. 12 (January 25, 1978), 1, 65, 66.

"Detroit Triple Fan Fair Convention Report." *Star-Borne* 1, no. 4 (November/December 1972), 1.

Dillard, J.M. *Star Trek, "Where No One Has Gone Before": A History in Pictures*. New York: Pocket Books, 1994.

Dowling, Lucy. *Star Wars Year by Year: A Visual Chronicle*. New York: DK, 2010.

Dubin, Murray. "The Scene." *Philadelphia Inquirer*, December 10, 1979.

"Early N.B.C. Forecast on Vote Irks Viewers." *New York Times*, June 4, 1969.

Eisner, Michael and Tony Schwartz. *Work in Progress*. London: Penguin, 1999.

"11 Take 'Trek.'" *Variety* 285, no. 9 (January 19, 1977), 56.

Ellison, Harlan. *Harlan Ellison's Watching*. San Francisco: Underwood-Miller, 1989.

Evanier, Mark. "Star Trek Lives!" *Monster Times* 1, no. 26 (September 1973), 15.

"FAB Honors Par's 'Star Trek' Feature." *Daily Variety* 186, no. 9 (December 18, 1979), 27.

Fabrikant, Geri. "State Laws Foil Film Buys." *Variety* 297, no. 3 (November 21, 1979), 1, 160.

"Favorite Videos." *Times Recorder*, December 30, 1984.

Feret, Bill. "The Monster Times Teletype." *Monster Times* 1, no. 19 (February 19, 1973), 24–25.

"The 52nd Academy Awards." *Oscars.org*. n.d. https://www.oscars.org/oscars/ceremonies/1980.

"Films in the Future." *Daily Variety* 162, no. 35 (January 25,1974), 20.

_____ *Daily Variety* 165, no. 50 (November 15, 1974), 6.

_____ *Daily Variety* 179, no. 25 (April 7, 1978), 10.

Fontana, Cyndee, and Tom Watson. "700 Salinas Fans Keep A 'Stardate.'" *Salinas Californian*, December 8, 1979.

"Four of Eight Pix Rated Come from Majors." *Daily Variety* 185, no. 63 (December 5, 1979), 6.

"Frank Named President of Paramount TV Distribution." *Los Angeles Times*, October 29, 1977.

Galloway, Stephen. "Karl Schanzer, Who Inspired Coppola's 'The Conversation,' Dies at 81." *Hollywood Reporter*. Last modified June 3, 2014. https://www.hollywoodreporter.com/news/karl-schanzer-who-inspired-coppola-708829.

Garris, Mick. "Re-Invasion of the Body Snatchers: An Interview with Director Phillip Kaufman." *Starlog* no. 16 (September 1978), 26–27, 74.

Gelman, Morrie. "Ad Prod'n Keeps Magicam Growing." *Daily Variety* 179, no. 20 (March 31, 1978), 3.

_____. "OPT Will Produce HalfHour Strip." *Daily Variety* 179, no. 4 (March 9, 1978), 18.

"'Genesis II' Set for Filming with Alex Cord as Star." *Los Angeles Times*, December 19, 1972.

Gerds, Warren. "'Star Trek' Offers Lots of Everything, But Top Acting." *Green Bay Press-Gazette*, December 8, 1979.

Gerrold, David. "Rumblings." *Starlog* no. 33 (April 1980), 24.

_____. "Soaring." *Starlog* no. 67 (February 1983), 56–58.

_____. *The Trouble with Tribbles*. New York: Ballantine Books, 1973.

Gindick, Tia. "Trekking to a Movie Benefit." *Los Angeles Times*, November 29, 1979.

Ginsberg, Steven. "Full Year Ahead, Par Seeks Bid On 'Star Trek'; 16-Week Deal, Percentages Stun Showmen." *Variety* 293, no. 6 (December 13, 1978), 5.

"Goodwin and Livingston Producers of 'Star Trek.'" *Daily Variety* 176, no. 55 (August 22, 1977), 1.

"Goodwin Leaves Par TV Post for Playboy Vidspot." *Daily Variety* 172, no. 12 (June 22, 1976), 1, 11.

Grant, Lee. "Trek from TV to Movie to TV." *Los Angeles Times*, May 25, 1977.

Greeley, Bill. "Jerry Lewis Slot for 'Star Trek' After Gap." *Variety* 253, no. 11 (January 29, 1969), 43.

_____. "Look Out for TV Independents." *Variety* 256, no. 8 (October 8, 1969), 50

_____. "'Paradise' Limps But Indies Hot." *Variety* 256, no. 6 (September 24, 1969), 39.

_____. "Paramount, MCA Each Mull '4th Web.'" *Variety* 287, no. 6 (June 15, 1977), 45, 61.

_____. "'Underground' Syndie at NAB." *Variety* 254, no. 6 (March 26, 1969), 51, 74.

Greenberger, Robert. "Majel Barrett Roddenberry: A Woman of Enterprise." *Starlog* no. 116 (January 1987), 16–18, 64.

Griffith, Martin. "'Trekkies' Savor the Movie." *Reno Gazette-Journal*, December 8, 1979.

Gross, Edward. "Star Trek II: The Lost Generation." *Starlog* no. 136 (November 1988), 45–48, 57.

Gross, Edward, and Mark A. Altman. *The Fifty-Year Mission: The Complete, Uncensored, Unauthorized Oral History of Star Trek: The First 25 Years*. New York: St. Martin's Press, 2016.

Hallock, Steve. "Trekkies." *Arizona Republic*, December 9, 1979.

Hanson, Barry. "'Star Trek' Blasts Off Again." Associated Press, December 8, 1979.

Harmetz, Aljean. "After 2 Good Summers, Film Business Lags." *New York Times*, June 26, 1980.

_____. "Cinemas Start Sale of Doodads." *New York Times*, December 10, 1978.

_____. "15th State Outlaws Blind Bidding on Films." *New York Times*, June 19, 1979.

_____. "'Smokey II' is Said to Gross $18 Million." *New York Times*, August 23, 1980.

Helling, Janet. "Star Date 12.7.79: 1,100 in Q-C Swarm to 'Star Trek' Opening." *Daily Dispatch*, December 8, 1979.

"History." National Space Club and Foundation. n.d. http://www.spaceclub.org/about/history.html.

"Hollywood TV Production Chart." *Daily Variety* 174, no. 63 (March 3, 1977), 20.

Houston, David. "Andy Probert Talks About the Lost Designs of Star Trek The Motion Picture." *Starlog* no. 32 (March 1980), 26–32.

_____. "The Magical Techniques of Movie & TV Special Effects: Part XV: Brick Price-The Model Man." *Starlog* no. 20 (March 1979), 66–71.

_____. "The Model Makers at Magicam: How They Survived 'Star Trek—The Motion Picture,'" *Starlog* no. 27 (October 1979), 26–30.

_____. "Star Trek: Past, Present, and Future." *Starlog* no. 1 (August 1976), 22–26.

_____. "Starlog Interview: Robert Wise." *Starlog* no. 30 (January 1980), 16–21.

_____. "William Shatner: Moving Right Along." *Starlog* no. 9 (October 1977), 46–48.

Howard, Kez. "Two Men in One: Gene Roddenberry." *Starlog* no. 2 (November 1976), 10–12.

Hutchison, David. "Special Report on the (New) Enterprise." *Starlog* no. 12 (March 1978), 31.

"H'w'd-Westwood Ticket Prices Likely $5 for Christmas Films." *Daily Variety* 186, no. 1 (December 6, 1979), 3.

"If the Mind is Free" film. 1971. Saint Mary's High School and Center for Learning Records, Special Collections, University of Illinois at Chicago.

"In Indianapolis…" *Variety* 256, no. 4 (September 10, 1969), 74, 76.

"In Lieu of ABC Evening News." *Variety* 262, no. 1 (February 17, 1971), 36.

"In London…" *Variety* 256, no. 9 (October 15, 1969), 44.

"In Miami…" *Variety* 258, no. 1 (February 18, 1970), 46, 52.

"In Pittsburgh…" *Variety* 257, no. 3 (December 3, 1969), 38, 40.

"In St. Louis…" *Variety* 256, no. 3 (September 3, 1969), 44, 50.

Independent Television Corporation. "The Saint is #1." Advertisement. *Variety* 257, no. 9 (January 14, 1970), 48–49.

"Indies Vs. News." *Variety* 256, no. 8 (October 8, 1969), 38.

"Inside Stuff—Radio-TV." *Variety* 270, no. 10 (April 18, 1973), 60.

"International Sound Track." *Variety* 239, no. 7 (July 7, 1965), 22.

_____ *Variety* 285, no. 6 (December 15, 1976), 44.

Irvine, Bill. "Screenwriter Allan Scott Talks About Star Trek—The Movie." *Starlog* no. 7 (August 1977), 32–33, 52.

Irwin, Walter & G.B. Love. *The Best of Trek*. New York: Signet, 1978.

"Is This the End of the Enterprise?" *Monster Times Collectors' Issue* no. 1 (1973), 14–15.

"Italo B.O. Wilts in Heat; Brooks' 'Frankenstein' Tops." *Variety* 279, no. 6 (June 18, 1975), 33.

"Jesco von Puttkamer: 1933–2012." NASA. Last modified December 27, 2012. https://www.nasa.gov/topics/people/features/von_puttkamer_obit.html.

Jones, Preston Neal. *Return to Tomorrow: The Filming of Star Trek: The Motion Picture*. Sierra Madre, CA: Creature Features, 2014.

_____. "Star Trek—The Motion Picture." *Cinefantastique* 9, no. 2 (Winter 1979), 40–47.

Kaufman, Dave. "Par Wants 3-Hour Slice of TV." *Daily Variety* 175, no. 57 (May 24, 1977), 1, 7.

_____. "Popular 'Star Trek' Series Spawns Multi-Million-Dollar Paramount Feature Version." *Daily Variety* 172, no. 47 (August 11, 1976), 1.

_____. "Production Start On Par 'Trek' Once Again A Feature, Delayed." *Daily Variety* 178, no. 16 (December 28, 1977), 1.

Kazickas, Jurate. "Trekking Down to a World Premiere." *Washington Star*, December 7, 1979.

Kelly, Gene. "'Star Trek' Lovers Stand in Line for Hours, Willingly, to See Film." *Lincoln Journal Star*, December 8, 1979.

Khalil, Hannah. "46 Years of Colour TV on BBC One." BBC Blogs. Last modified November 12, 2015. http://www.bbc.co.uk/blogs/aboutthebbc/entries/1546d154-dd8a-4e2b-bbb3–45d395445596.

Kilday, Gregg. "Countdown for Mr. Spock?" *Los Angeles Times*, March 27, 1978.

King, Stephen. *Danse Macabre*. New York: Gallery Books, 2010.

Knoedelseder, Jr., William K. "'Heaven's Gate': Everything Hinges on the Box Office." *Los Angeles Times*, November 16, 1980.

Koenig, Walter. *Chekov's Enterprise: A Personal Journal of the Making of Star Trek—The Motion Picture*. New York: Pocket Books, 1980.

Kozak, Roman. "Swoosh! 'Star Trek' Promotion Takes Off." *Billboard* 91, no. 49 (December 8, 1979), 74.

"Latest 'Star Trek' Enterprise Keeps the 'Trekkies' Truckin'." *Daily Variety* 179, no. 19 (March 30, 1978), 3.

Lebo, Harlan. *Citizen Kane: A Filmmaker's Journey*. New York: St. Martin's Press, 2016.

Leeman, Sergio. *Robert Wise on His Films: From Editing Room to Director's Chair*. Los Angeles: Silman-James Press, 1995.

"Leider-Headed Warner Bros. TV Tooling Up for Season After Next." *Variety* 256, no. 12 (November 5, 1969), 35, 49.

"Lengthy Trek." *Press and Sun-Bulletin*, December 8, 1979.

"Leonard Nimoy Addresses the Star Trek America Convention (1977)." *Fanlore*. Last modified November 4, 2017. https://fanlore.org/wiki/Leonard_Nimoy_Addresses_the_Star_Trek_America_Convention_(1977).

"Letter from D.C. Fontana." *Star-Borne 1*, no. 3 (September/October 1972), 1.

———. "*Star-Borne 2*, no. 9 (August/September 1973), 1.

Lincoln Enterprises. "Inside Star Trek II—1978." Advertisement. *Amazing Science Fiction* 51, no. 4 (August 1978).

Lofficier, Randy & Jean-Marc. "Harve Bennett: Preparing 'Star Trek IV.'" *Starlog* no. 103 (February 1986), 16–18.

"Log Entries." *Starlog* no. 2 (November 1976), 6–8, 53–56.

———. *Starlog* no. 3 (January 1977), 6–8, 12.

———. *Starlog* no. 9 (October 1977), 6–22, 51.

"London." *Variety* 258, No. 8 (April 8, 1970), 44.

Long, John C. "Trek Tricks ... Despite Crowds, Fans Were Persistent." *Courier-Journal*, December 8, 1979.

Longshot. "Star Trek Party." Advertisement. *Miami News*, December 7, 1979.

"The Lost Enterprise: Star Trek—Phase II." *Star Trek—The Motion Picture: The Director's Edition*. USA: Paramount Pictures, 2001. DVD.

Lucke, Jamie. "Curious, Devoted Flock to Film Version of 'Star Trek.'" *Messenger-Inquirer*, December 9, 1979.

Lukasiewicz, Mark. "Gulf and Western Industries Interests Investors, Analysts Cool." *Globe and Mail*, June 16, 1980.

"The MacArthur Theater." *Going to the Movies*. n.d. http://www.goingtothemovies-dciff.org/theaters/#/macarthur/.

Maiewski, Shirley. "A Dream Come True." *A Piece of the Action* no. 80 (January/February 1980), 1.

Malcolm, Derek. "Cinema." *Guardian*, December 20, 1979.

Mandel, Bill. "Beam Me Up!" *San Francisco Examiner*, December 9, 1979.

Mandell, Paul. "Star Trek V: Sharing the Pain." *Cinefex* no. 42 (May 1990), 46–67.

Mann, Roderick. "This is a Trek Shatner Doesn't Mind." *Los Angeles Times*, December 22, 1981.

Manno, Rita. "A Grand Return for 'Star Trek.'" *Courier-Post*, December 8, 1979.

Marguiles, Lee. "Paramount to Offer Original TV Shows." *Los Angeles Times*, April 1, 1977.

Mason, George. "Production File: Robert Wise—Director." *Star Trek Giant Poster Book*, 1979.

Matthews, Peter. "Vertigo Rises: The Greatest Film of All Time?" *Sight & Sound*. Last modified July 13, 2018. https://www.bfi.org.uk/news-opinion/sight-sound-magazine/polls-surveys/greatest-films-all-time/vertigo-hitchcock-new-number-one.

Maxa, Rudy. "Take It from a NASA Scientist: Star Trek's High Tech Isn't Child's Play." *Washington Post*, December 16, 1979.

Maynard, Jeff. "Interview with Susan Sackett," *Fantastic Films* 1, no. 3 (August 1978), 28–29.

McBride, James. "H'wood Hitches to 'Star,' Joins Race to Space." *Variety* 287, no. 6 (June 15, 1977), 1, 78.

McCabe, Bruce. "Movies." *Boston Globe*, January 4, 1980.

McCampbell, Candy. "Home Movies Not What They Used to Be." *Tennessean*, February 19, 1981.

McCarthy, Todd. "U.S. Pic Budgets into Megabuck Era." *Variety* 296, no. 4 (August 29, 1979), 1, 20.

McNaughton, Chuck. "Editorial." *Monster Times* 1, no. 2 (February 16, 1972), 2

———. "Exclusive 'Rumor' to the Monster Times." *Monster Times* 1, no. 2 (February 16, 1972), 18.

Meadows, Jim. "News of Trekdom." *Star Trek Today* 2, no. 1 (June 1976), 1–4, 31.

"The Metropolist." *Washington Post*, November 13, 2008.

Micklus, Lance. "The $44,000,000 Star Trek Game." *Softside* 2, no.8 (May 1980), 18–32.

Mikelbank, Peter. "The Boss Speaks: 'Star Trek' Lives!" *Washington Post*, August 29, 1977.

Monahan, Michael. *Shock It to Me: Golden Ghouls of the Golden Gate*. San Francisco: UHF Nocturne, 2011.

"The Monster Scene." *Monster Times* 1, no. 24 (July 1973), 13.

Mooney, Mike, John Knoll, Kevin Kay, Marylou Cook, and Nancy Audete. "An Interview with Gene Roddenberry." *Star Trek Today* 2, no. 1 (June 1976), 9–13.

Morrison, Don. "'Trekkies' Are More Fun Than 'Star Trek.'" *Minneapolis Star*, December 10, 1979.

Movies, The. "Star Trek—The Motion Picture Starts Today." Advertisement. *Journal-News*, December 7, 1979.

Murphy, A.D. "'79 Holds U.S. Box-Office Record." *Daily Variety* 186, no. 23 (January 9, 1980), 1, 8.

Murphy, Mary. "Screen Version of Star Trek Due." *Los Angeles Times*, March 19, 1975.

Naha, Ed. "The Re-Making of Star Trek: Part Two." *Starlog* no. 61 (August 1982), 16–20.

"The Names Have Been Changed…" *Daily Variety* 186, no. 27 (January 15, 1980), 8.

Nardino, Gary. Gary Nardino to Gene Roddenberry, September 15, 1977. https://www.facebook.com/TheTrekFiles/photos/a.9576566 81075246.1073741855.799697610204488/957656691075245/.

"NBC Axes All 7 Kidvid Frosh, Adds ABCer in New Sat Shake for Fall." *Variety* 270, no. 7 (March 28, 1973), 50.

"An NBC Offer for 'Star Trek'?" *Variety* 288, no. 8 (September 28, 1977), 6.

"NBC-TV Wraps Up Fall Schedule." *Variety* 254, no. 1 (February 19, 1969), 43, 78.

Nemecek, Larry. *The Star Trek: The Next Generation Companion*. New York: Pocket Books, 1992.

_____. *The Star Trek: The Next Generation Companion*. Rev. ed. New York: Pocket Books, 1995.

_____. *The Star Trek: The Next Generation Companion*. Rev. ed. New York: Pocket Books, 2003.

"New & Forthcoming Merchandise." *Star Trek Action Group* no. 22 (March 1977), 3.

"New 'Trek' Outlets." *Variety* 274, no. 8 (April 3, 1974), 35.

"New Fall Garb for Chi's WGN-TV, But Sports and Kidvid Still Mainstays." *Variety* 256, no. 3 (September 3, 1969), 40.

"New Kidvid Slate Firmed By NBC." *Variety* 278, no.5 (March 12, 1975), 44.

"New Star Trek Debut Postponed." *Los Angeles Times*, November 9, 1977.

"New Video Season, Indie-Style." *Variety* 256, no. 6 (September 24, 1969), 38.

Nimoy, Leonard. *I Am Spock*. New York: Hyperion, 1995.

"Notes from Broadcast Markets in the U.S. and Abroad." *Variety* 278, no. 5 (March 12, 1975), 54.

_____." *Variety* 280, no. 4 (September 3, 1975), 44, 68.

_____." *Variety* 280, no. 13 (November 5, 1975), 56, 148.

"NY ST Con." *Star-Borne* 1, no. 5 (January/February 1973), 1.

Okuda, Michael and Denise, Judith and Garfield Reeves-Stevens, and Daren Dochterman. "Audio Commentary." *Star Trek V: The Final Frontier*. Directed by William Shatner. USA: Paramount Pictures, 2009. Blu-ray.

"On and Off Par 'Star Trek' Revival on as a Feature." *Daily Variety* 179, no. 18 (March 29, 1978), 1, 18.

O'Quinn, Kerry. "Harve Bennett on 'Star Trek IV.'" *Starlog* no. 101 (December 1985), 73.

_____. "The Roots of Starlog." *Starlog* no. 24 (June 1979), 6–7.

O'Quinn Studios. "The Official Star Trek Duty Jacket." Advertisement. *Starlog* no. 32 (March 1980).

"Panorama." *Questar* 2 no. 3 (June 1980), 12.

"Paperback Best Sellers." *New York Times*, December 9, 1979.

_____ *New York Times*, December 16, 1979.

_____ *New York Times*, December 23, 1979.

_____ *New York Times*, December 30, 1979.

"Par Pix and Aviva Reach Settlement." *Daily Variety* 196, no. 20 (July 2, 1982), 13.

"Par Reports Good B.O. Overseas for 'Trek.'" *Daily Variety* 186, no. 9 (December 18, 1979), 8.

"Par Sues Aviva Re 'Star Trek' Products." *Variety* 303, no. 6 (May 27, 1981), 4.

"Par Unveils Its Double-Camera Magicam System." *Daily Variety* 165, no. 4 (September 11, 1974), 1, 17.

"Par-TV Euro Org Beating the 'Rap' On British Sales." *Variety* 267, no. 4 (June 7, 1972), 40.

"'Paradise' Heads for Overhaul as N.Y., L.A. Drop It." *Variety* 256, no. 8 (October 8, 1969), 38.

"Paramount Names Two to New Executive Posts." *Los Angeles Times*, October 27, 1976.

Paramount Pictures. "For Your Consideration." Advertisement. *Daily Variety* 186, no. 2 (December 7, 1979), 18–19.

_____. "Paramount is the Word." Paramount Pictures press release, December 1979.

_____. *Paramount Press Book and Merchandising Manual: Star Trek—The Motion Picture*. 1979.

_____. "Reserved Performance Engagement at the Paramount Theatre." Advertisement. *New York Daily News*, November 16, 1979.

_____. "Star Trek—The Phenomenon!" Advertisement. *Los Angeles Times*, December 14, 1979.

_____. "This Holiday, Give a Journey Through the Galaxy." Advertisement. *New York Times*, December 7, 1979.

_____. "Welcome Aboard … Space Shuttle Enterprise." Advertisement. *New York Times*, September 21, 1976.

Paramount Television. "Paramount Television Welcomes Harve Bennett." Advertisement. *Daily Variety* 190, no. 2 (December 9, 1980), 28.

_____. "Paramount's Portfolio X." Advertisement. *Broadcasting* 104, no. 3 (January 17, 1983), 4.

_____. "Star Trek is Out of this World." Advertisement. *Variety* 255, no. 9 (July 16th, 1969), 49.

_____. "Star Trek Ratings Orbit on any Heading." Advertisement. *Variety* 258, no. 1 (February 18, 1970), 51

_____. "Take Off with Star Trek." Advertisement. *Broadcasting* 76 no. 12 (March 24, 1969), 87.

"Paramount TV Shuffles Syndie Sales Staffers; John Pearson Resigns." *Variety* 256, no. 8 (October 8, 1969), 48.

"Par's Tot 'Trek.'" *Variety* 284, no. 10 (October 13, 1976), 74.

Patterson, Rod. "More Ear: 'Star Trek' Soundtrack Fairly Tinkles." *Oregonian*, December 16, 1979.

_____."More Ear: UNICEF Gets Proceeds." *Oregonian*, November 25, 1979.

"Personal Appearance: Jesco Von Puttkamer, NASA Scientist." *Starlog* no. 3 (January 1977), 27.

"Personal Appearance: William Shatner." *Starlog* no. 3 (January 1977), 34–35.

Petterson, Roger. "Loyal Trekkies Flock to Movie." *Associated Press*, December 8, 1979.

Piantadosi, Roger. "Beaming Up at the Stars." *Washington Post*, December 7, 1979.

"Pix, People, Pickups." *Daily Variety* 175, no. 39 (April 28, 1977), 1, 9.

_____. " *Daily Variety* 179, no. 19 (March 30, 1978), 14.

_____. " *Daily Variety* 180, no. 7 (June 14, 1978), 1, 6.

_____. " *Daily Variety* 180, no. 13 (June 22, 1978), 1, 21.

_____. " *Daily Variety* 180, no. 15 (June 26, 1978), 1, 13.

_____. " *Daily Variety* 185, no. 43 (November 2, 1979), 29.

Pollock, Dale. "ABC Stocks Up On Films for the '80s." *Daily Variety* 186, no. 9 (December 18, 1979), 1, 24.

_____. "Holiday Release Glut Brings Riches to Some, But There's Risks—and Always, Losers." *Daily Variety* 186, no. 17 (December 31, 1979), 1, 2.

_____. "Mega-Buck Pix Push Filmbiz into '80s; B.O. Champs A-Changin.'" *Daily Variety* 186, no. 19 (January 3, 1980), 2.

_____. "'Star Trek,' with $17 Mil Domestic Box-Office, Sets New Opening-Week Record." *Daily Variety* 186, no. 8 (December 17, 1979), 1, 23.

_____. "'Trek' Beams Up $2 Mil-Plus in 105 Enterprises." *Daily Variety* 186, no. 3 (December 10, 1979), 1, 23.

Povill, Jon. "Star Trek II Treatment." January 19, 1976. Margaret Herrick Library, Beverly Hills, 953.f-S-1351.

"Pre-Xmas Slump; 'Trek' Siphons from All." *Variety* 297, no. 6 (December 12, 1979), 3.

Prendergast, Ellen M. "Trekkies Look to the Stars." *Record*, December 9, 1979.

Probert, Andy. Andy Probert to Gene Roddenberry, June 19, 1972. https://www.facebook.com/pg/TheTrekFiles/photos/?tab=album&album_id=961499494024298.

"Programs and People in the INTV Screening Rooms." *Broadcasting* 104, no. 3 (January 17, 1983), 68–70.

Putnam, Judy. "'Trek' is Rising Star in Local Movie Sky as Fans Crowd Theater." *Clarion-Ledger*, December 9, 1979.

Reeves-Stevens, Judith and Garfield. *The Art of Star Trek*. New York: Pocket Books, 1995.

_____. *Star Trek Phase II: The Lost Series*. New York: Pocket Books, 1997.

_____. *Star Trek: The Next Generation: The Continuing Mission*. New York: Pocket Books, 1997.

"Reviewers Get Lost Characterizes Policy Re 'Trek' in Chicago." *Variety* 297, no. 6 (December 12, 1979), 3.

Robert Abel and Associates. "We're Helping Send the Enterprise on its Greatest Adventure." Advertisement. *Daily Variety* 179, no. 55 (May 19, 1978), 11.

Robertson, Lance. "'Star Trek' Capacity Crowd in Corvallis Cheers Long-Awaited Movie." *Albany Democrat-Herald*, December 8, 1979.

"Roddenberry Cool on NBC-TV Offer to Go Through 'Trek' Pilot." *Variety* 267, no. 8 (July 5, 1972), 29.

Roddenberry, Gene. "From the Log of the Starship Enterprise." *Archives' Log* 2, no. 5 & 6 (May & June 1975), 3–4.

_____. "Letter to Fans." *Star Trek Action Group* no. 38 (December 1979), 7.

_____. "Star Trek II Treatment." June 20, 1975. Margaret Herrick Library, Beverly Hills, 953.f-S-1350.

_____. "Star Trek III Treatment." May 23, 1980. Margaret Herrick Library, Beverly Hills, 952.f-S-1342.

_____. "Yes, It Lives!" *A Piece of the Action* no. 25 (April 1975), 1–2.

Roddenberry, Gene and Harold Livingston. *Star Trek—The Motion Picture Shooting Script*. July 19, 1978.

Rodriguez, Eliott. "Star Trek's Enterprise Orbits Dade." *Miami News*, December 4, 1979.

Roeder, Bill. "Periscope." *Newsweek*, May 16, 1977.
Roman, Linda. "Star Trek Fans Trek to Catch Movie Version." *Daily Record*, December 9, 1979.
Rosenberg, Ronald. "Bradley Plans to Buy into Video Game Field." *Boston Globe*, July 15, 1982.
Rowley, Chris. "Star Trek—The Motion Picture." *Star Trek Giant Poster Book*, 1979.
Rowley, Storer. "'Trekkies' Flood Theaters." *Chicago Tribune*, December 7, 1979.
Ruben, Steve. "Star Trek Treks." *Cinefantastique* 5, no. 3 (Winter 1976), ___.
Rufty, Bill. "Trekkie Heaven." *Sarasota Journal*, December 7, 1979.
Sackett, Susan. "Editor's Log." *Star Trektennial News* 3, no. 24 (November/December 1977), 10.
_____. *Inside Trek: My Secret Life with Star Trek Creator Gene Roddenberry*. Tulsa, OK: HAWK Publishing, 2002.
_____. "Letters & Questions????" *Star Trektennial News* 3, no 23 (September-October 1977), 2.
_____. "The Making of *Star Trek II*: A Conversation with Gene Roddenberry." *Starlog* no. 12 (March 1978), 24–29.
_____. "Movie Writers Set." *Star Trektennial News* 2, no. 17 (September-October 1976), 3.
_____. "The Movie." *Star Trektennial News* 3, no. 19 (January / February 1977), 3.
_____. "One to Beam Up: Jerry Isenberg." *Star Trektennial News* 3, no. 20 (March-April, 1977), 3–8.
_____. "One to Beam Up: Matt Jeffries." *Star Trektennial News* no. 15 (July 1976), 5–7.
_____. "One to Beam Up: Phil Kaufman." *Star Trektennial News* 3, no. 21 (May/June, 1977), 13–15.
_____. "Questions." *Star Trektennial News* 2, no. 18 (November/December 1976), 11.
_____. "Questions." *Star Trektennial News* no. 14 (June 1976), 2.
_____. "Questions." *Star Trektennial News* no. 16 (August 1976), 2–3.
_____. "Star Trek II." *Star Trektennial News* 3, no. 24 (November/December 1977), 3.
_____. "Star Trek II." *Star Trektennial News* no. 13 (May 1976), 3.
_____. "Star Trek II." *Star Trektennial News* no. 15 (July 1976), 3.
_____. "Star Trek Report." *Starlog* no. 20 (March 1979), 32–33.
_____. "Star Trek Report." *Starlog* no. 10 (December 1977), 51
_____. "Star Trek Report." *Starlog* no. 11 (January 1978), 38.
_____. "Star Trek Report." *Starlog* no. 12 (March 1978), 30.
_____. "Star Trek Report." *Starlog* no. 13 (May 1978), 67.
_____. "Star Trek Report." *Starlog* no. 14 (June 1978), 48.
_____. "Star Trek Report." *Starlog* no. 15 (August 1978), 48.
_____. "Star Trek Report." *Starlog* no. 16 (September 1978), 20–21.
_____. "Star Trek Report." *Starlog* no. 18 (December 1978), 64–65.
_____. "Star Trek Report." *Starlog* no. 23 (June 1979), 31.
_____. "Star Trek Report." *Starlog* no. 24 (July 1979), 31.
_____. "Star Trek Report." *Starlog* no. 25 (August 1979), 5.
_____. "Star Trek Report." *Starlog* no. 26 (September 1979), 52–53.
_____. "Star Trek Report." *Starlog* no. 29 (December 1979), 31.
_____. "Star Trek Report." *Starlog* no. 6 (June 1977), 58–59.
_____. "Star Trek Report." *Starlog* no. 7 (August 1977), 30–31.
_____. "Star Trek Report." *Starlog* no. 8 (September 1977), 32.
_____. "Star Trek Report." *Starlog* no. 9 (October 1977), 50.
Sackett, Susan and Gene Roddenberry. *The Making of Star Trek—The Motion Picture*. New York: Pocket Books, 1980.
"Sarasota Square 6." *Sarasota Journal*, December 7, 1979.
Schanzer, Karl. "Star Trek III Analysis." May 30, 1980. Margaret Herrick Library, Beverly Hills, 952.f-S-1342.
Schreger, Charles. "As Adv. Costs for Launchings Rise, Distribs Turn to Tie-Ins; Array of Recent Arrangements." *Variety* 290, no. 7 (March 22, 1978), 34.
_____. "Getting Set for the Second Coming of 'Star Trek.'" *Los Angeles Times*, December 7, 1979.
_____. "Latest Summer Releases: Ups, Downs." *Los Angeles Times*, July 28, 1980.
_____. "Software Hard Sell in Chicago." *Los Angeles Times*, June 17, 1980.
_____. "'Star Trek': A Stellar Premiere?" *Los Angeles Times*, December 8, 1979.
Schumpert, Larry. "Fans Trek to Movie." *Journal and Courier*, December 10, 1979.
Scott, Craig. "Curiosity Brings People to 'Star Trek' Premiere." *Star-Gazette*, December 8, 1979.
Scott, Jay. "The First/Last Gang Picture Show How the Warriors Beat the Wanderers and

Bibliography

"Why Kaufman's Bitter." *The Globe and Mail*, July 28, 1979.

Scott, Vernon. "'Star Trek' Crew Has First Reunion." *UPI*, April 19, 1978.

Seagal, Lewis. "Mehta Leads 'Star Wars' at Bowl." *Los Angeles Times*, November 22, 1977.

"S.F.'s KQED Hits Peak Ratings; Com'l TV Now Not So Cooperative." *Variety* 281, no. 12 (January 28, 1976), 39, 56.

"Shatner Guest Stars." *Long Beach Independent*, November 18, 1977.

Shatner, Lisabeth. *Captain's Log: William Shatner's Personal Account of the Making of Star Trek V: The Final Frontier*. New York: Pocket Books, 1989.

Shatner, William and Chris Kreski. *Star Trek Movie Memories*. New York: HarperCollins, 1994.

Shay, Don. "Star Trek—The Motion Picture." *Cinefantastique* 8, no. 2–3 (Spring 1979), 88–95.

Sherwood, John. "A Guaranteed Sellout Audience." *Battle Creek Enquirer*, December 8, 1979.

"Show of Subtle Colors is Tops in Arg.; U.S. Product Thrives." *Variety* 277, no. 2 (November 20, 1974), 30, 41.

"Showbiz Winners Edge Losers on Average Volume." *Daily Variety* 186, no. 4 (December 11, 1979), 4.

"Singles." *Cash Box* 41, no. 33 (December 29, 1979), 24.

"60 Years of Revolution and Evolution in Film Biz." *Daily Variety* 181, no. 40 (October 31, 1978), 14, 16, 18, 20.

Smith, Cecil. "'Genesis II' Takes Look at Ad 2133." *Los Angeles Times*, March 23, 1973.

_____. "New Appointments in ABC Hierarchy." *Los Angeles Times*, October 26, 1976.

_____. "Roddenberry Sires Son of Star Trek." *Los Angeles Times*, February 16, 1973.

_____. "A Window Opens on the 'Cosmos.'" *Los Angeles Times*, September 25, 1980.

Soble, Ronald L. "'Star Trek' Still Grounded." April 28, 1977, Los Angeles Times.

Solow, Herbert F. and Robert H. Justman. *Inside Star Trek: The Real Story*. New York: Pocket Books, 1996.

"Special Effects Are His Specialty from Tara to Outer Space." *Star Trek—The Motion Picture Newsletter*, no. 2 (Autumn 1979), 3.

Stanley, John. "Within the Empire of the King of the Movie Posters." *San Francisco Examiner*, July 13, 1980.

"Star Trek: Arena." *BBC Genome*. n.d. http://genome.ch.bbc.co.uk/133c4ba85c4b4f3fa616f313dbf81b4e.

"Star Trek Beams in this Week." *Deseret News*, December 3, 1979.

"Star Trek Convention in Oakland (1976)." *San Francisco Bay Area Television Archive*. Last modified September 12, 2017. https://diva.sfsu.edu/collections/sfbatv/bundles/209260

"Star Trek Convention News." *Monster Times* 1, no. 2 (February 16, 1972), 23.

"Star Trek Fans Torpedo Name for Space Shuttle." *Los Angeles Times*, September 9, 1976.

"Star Trek II." *Star Trek Action Group* no. 25 (October 1977), 3.

"'Star Trek' Into B.O. Stratospherics: $42-M Negative; $100-M to Recoup." *Variety* 297, no. 6 (December 12, 1979), 3.

"Star Trek Isn't Bad, But It's No Old Yeller." *Victoria Times*, December 17, 1979.

"Star Trek KMPH 26." *TV Guide* 21, no. 35 (September 1, 1973), A-50.

"Star Trek Lives." *Monster Times* 1, no. 42 (July 1975), 24.

"STAR TREK Meeting—August 3, 1977." August 5, 1977. https://www.facebook.com/pg/TheTrekFiles/photos/?tab=album&album_id=1025809107593336.

"Star Trek Movie Update." *Starlog* no. 3 (January 1977), 8, 12.

"Star Trek News." *Star Trek Action Group* no. 11 (December 1974/January 1975), 3–4.

_____ *Star Trek Action Group* no. 13 (1975), 2.

"The Star Trek Premiere." *A Piece of the Action* no. 78 (November 1979), 1.

"'Star Trek' Producer Gene Roddenberry, the Man Who Put…" *UPI Archive: Domestic News*, October 8, 1980.

"'Star Trek' Reentry." *Variety* 254, no. 4 (March 12, 1969), 44

"'Star Trek' Rockets to $1.4 Mil Gotham Week-End On 81 Screens." *Daily Variety* 186, no. 4 (December 11, 1979), 3.

"'Star Trek' Sensash 192G in Seattle; Other Biz Spotty." *Daily Variety* 186, no. 6 (December 13, 1979), 3.

"'Star Trek' Sets Three-Day Record." *Daily Variety* 186, no. 4 (December 11, 1979), 1, 29.

"Star Trek: The Corbomite Manoeuvre." *BBC Genome*. n.d. http://genome.ch.bbc.co.uk/ale62e5e36004d3fb99627134446090c.

Star Trek: The Superstars—The Superfans. Directed by Bob Wilkins. Written by Bob Wilkins. KTVU, January 30, 1977.

"'Star Trek' to Atlanta Meet by 2,000 of Program's Faithful." *Variety* 279, no. 8 (July 9, 1975), 57.

"Star Trek: Where No Man Has Gone Before." *BBC Genome*. n.d. http://genome.ch.bbc.co.uk/8c3b788506504b30906366ab0edfa45f.

"Star Trek—BBC One London—31 August 1974." *BBC Genome.* n.d. https://genome.ch.bbc.co.uk/63e409f29a8a461da62208725e3da72e.

"Star Trek—The Motion Picture." *Star Trek Action Group* no. 24 (August 1977), 3.

_____. *Star Trek Action Group* no. 39 (February 1980), 3.

_____. *Star Trek Action Group* no. 40 (April 1980), 3.

_____. *Star Trek Action Group* no. 38 (December 1979), 6.

"'Star Trektennial' Fan Club, 1966–1976." *Lincoln Enterprises Catalog* no. 6 (May 1976), 1.

"S.T.A.R." *Star-Borne 1*, no. 1 (May 1972), 1.

"Stark Trek!" *Famous Monsters* no. 142 (February 1978), 64–70.

"StarWatch." *Star-Borne* 1, no. 1 (May 1972), 1.

_____ *Star-Borne* 1, no. 2 (June 1972), 1.

_____ *Star-Borne* 1, no. 4 (November/December 1972), 1.

Steel, Dawn. *They Can Kill You, But They Can't Eat You: Lessons from the Front.* New York: Pocket Books, 1993.

"Step into a Time Capsule at 9:30." *Los Angeles Times,* March 23, 1973.

Stone, Judy. "The Man Behind 'Star Trek, the Movie.'" *San Francisco Chronicle,* January 7, 1977.

_____. "Paramount Cans 'Star Trek.'" *San Francisco Chronicle,* June 7, 1977.

_____. "'Star Trek': The Enterprise Takes Off." *San Francisco Chronicle,* December 5, 1979.

Strickland, Donna. "Notebook." *Tampa Tribune,* December 30, 1986.

Sunrise Cinemas. "Gala Opening Today." Advertisement. *New York Daily News,* December 7, 1979.

Szalay, Jeff. "Gene Roddenberry: The Years Between, The Years Ahead." *Starlog* no. 51 (October 1981), 36–42, 60.

"Television." *New York Times,* July 1, 1969.

_____ *New York Times,* July 8, 1969.

_____ *New York Times,* July 15, 1969.

_____ *New York Times,* September 8, 1973.

"Telewriters." *Daily Variety* 177, no. 56 (November 23, 1977), 12.

"$30,000 Bite for Par-TV 3-Hr. Spread." *Variety* 288, no. 1 (August 10, 1977), 43.

Thomas, Bob. "Big-gamble 'Star Trek' Film Opens Today." *Great Falls Tribune,* December 7, 1979

_____. "Star Trek Fanatics Scare Creator." *San Bernardino Sun-Telegram,* March 23, 1976.

Thomas, Phil. "Comic Strips Are Collectors' Items." *Owosso Argus-Press,* April 3, 1965.

Thompson, Howard. "Dull Double Bill." *New York Times,* March 18, 1971.

"3,000 'Trekkies' Prevue 'Star Trek.'" *Variety* 297, no. 6 (November 28, 1979), 21.

Timpone, Anthony. "Starlog Profile: Stephen Collins," *Starlog* no. 104 (March 1986), 59–61.

"The Top 50 Videocassette Sales for 1987." *UPI,* December 18, 1987.

"The Top Video Cassette Sales in 1985." *Sunday Dispatch,* December 29, 1985.

"Top Video Cassettes." *Miami News,* December 23, 1988.

"'Trek,' Despite 40% 2D-Wk. Dip, Eyes $27 Mil B.O." *Daily Variety* 186, no. 12 (December 21, 1979), 1, 24.

"'Trek' a la Barnum Is Biggest Film Kickoff for Portland in 20 Yrs." *Variety* 297, no. 6 (December 12, 1979), 3.

"'Trek' Collects $5 Mil Overseas in First Frames." *Daily Variety* 186, no. 20 (January 4, 1980), 1.

"'Trek' in 140 Markets." *Variety* 279, no. 9 (July 9, 1975), 49, 59.

"'Trek' on 106 TV's." *Variety* 273, no. 6 (December 19, 1973), 30.

"'Trek' Only Bright Spock On S.F. B.O. Scanner During First Flight." *Daily Variety* 186, no. 5 (December 12, 1979), 3.

"'Trek' Rockets Toward New 7-Day B.O. Mark." *Daily Variety* 186, no. 7 (December 14, 1979), 1, 43.

"Trek Talk." *Monster Times* 1, no. 36 (October 1974), 25.

_____ *Monster Times* 1, no. 37 (December 1974), 25.

_____ *Monster Times* 1, no. 38 (January 1975), 25.

"'Trek' to 130." *Variety* 276, no. 13 (November 6, 1974), 43.

"Trek Update." *Starlog* no. 12 (March 1978), 31.

"'Trekkies' First in Line for Trek' Tix." *Daily Variety* 185, no. 58 (November 26, 1979), 4.

"Trekkies in Their Glory." *Miami News,* December 8, 1979.

"Trekkies Turned Out by the Hundreds." *Santa Maria Times,* December 8, 1979.

Trimble, Bjo. "Fan Scene." *Starlog* no. 65 (December 1982), 40–41.

TRS-80 Software Exchange. "Star Trek III." Advertisement. *Softside* 1, no. 1 (October 1978), 2.

Tusher, Will. "Profit-Hunting Exhibs Find New Revenue Sources." *Daily Variety* 185, no. 42 (November 1, 1979), 1, 23.

"TV 'Star Trek' as Theatrical Feature for Paramount." *Variety* 278, no. 6 (March 9, 1975), 6.

"TV Independents' New Schedules." *Variety* 260, No. 5 (September 16, 1970), 54, 56.

"TV Syndication." *Variety* 277, no.11 (January 22, 1975), 70.

_____. *Variety* 278, no.3 (February 26,1975), 38.
_____. *Variety* 280, no. 11 (October 22, 1975), 148.
"TV-Radio Production Centres in the U.S. and Abroad." *Variety* 271, no. 2 (May 30, 1973), 48.
_____. *Variety* 271, no. 8 (July 4, 1973), 40.
_____. *Variety* 268, no. 2 (August 23, 1972), 44.
"UHF's Cleve. Breakthrough." *Variety* 254, no. 8 (April 9, 1969), 53, 64.
Umland, Rebecca and Sam. "Star Trek: The Motion Picture: The Director's Edition." *Video Watchdog* no. 94 (April 2003), 61–63.
"Upbeat Outlook for TV's Independents." *Broadcasting* 104, no. 3 (January 17, 1983), 55–58.
Uram, Marian Sue. "George Takei: Sulu's Log." *Starlog* no. 119 (June 1987), 17–19.
Verba, Joan Marie. *Boldly Writing: A Trekker Fan and Zine History, 1967–1987*. Minnetonka, MN: FTL Publications, 2003.
Walker, Virginia and Helen Young. "Revival News." *A Piece of the Action* no. 24 (March 1975), 1.
Warga, Wayne. "Prepare to Beam Aboard! 'Star Trek' at the Movies." *Los Angeles Times*, October 15, 1978.
"Web Affils are Paramount in Par's Program Venture." *Variety* 288, no. 3 (August 24, 1977), 38, 46.
"Welcome Everyone!" *Star Trek Action Group* no. 13 (1975), 1.
Wendeborn, John. "'Star Struck': Ice Show Spacy in Best Sense," *Oregonian*, November 28, 1979.
"WENY-TV Using Eleven Prime-Access Series." *Variety* 268, no. 6 (September 20, 1972), 41.
"What the Kiddies Prefer." *Variety* 261, no. 13 (February 10, 1971), 34.
"What's In-Store." *Cash Box* 41, no. 32 (December 22, 1979), 17.
Whitfield, Stephen E., and Gene Roddenberry. *The Making of Star Trek*. New York: Ballantine, 1968.

Wigal, Don. "Stardate: Supplemental." *Future Fantasy* 1, no. 1 (February 1978), 53.
Willson, Karen E. "An Interview with Gene Roddenberry the Man Behind the Myth." *Starlog* no. 40 (November 1980), 43–47.
Wilson, Hal. "Con." *A Piece of the Action* 2, no. 5 (July 1974), 1.
"Windy City B.O. Is 'Star' Struck: 'Trek' Zowie 600G." *Daily Variety* 186, no. 5 (December 12, 1979), 3.
Wingfield, Steve. "Space ... is at a Premium for Trekkers." *Paducah Sun*, December 9, 1979.
Wnoroski, Jim. "A Preview of Star Trek. The Movie." *Space Trek Special* (1978), 20–23, 59.
"WOR-TV Headed for Big Program Overhaul." *Variety* 254, no. 6 (March 26, 1969), 55.
"The WSFA Journal, December 1979." *Washington Science Fiction Association*. n.d. http://www.wsfa.org/journal/j79/c/index.htm.
"The WSFA Journal, September 1979." *Washington Science Fiction Association*. n.d. http://www.wsfa.org/journal/j79/9/index.htm.
Yablonski, Mike. "Science Fiction Film Fails to Send New Jersey 'Trekkies' Into Orbit." *Courier-News*, December 8, 1979.
Young, Helen. "From D.C. Fontana." *A Piece of the Action* 2, no. 18 (September 1974), 1.
_____. "Revival News," *A Piece of the Action* no. 26 (May 1975), 1.
_____. "Revival News." *A Piece of the Action* no. 34 (January 1976), 1.
Yue, Julie. "Memories of a Neighborhood Movie Theater, from When There Was Such A Thing." *Humanities*. Last modified December 2014. https://www.neh.gov/humanities/2014/novemberdecember/statement/memories-neighborhood-movie-theater-when-there-was-such-t.
Zarar, N. "Istanbul." *Variety* 277, no. 1 (November 13, 1974), 61.
Zimmerman, Howard. "Harlan Ellison: Science Fiction's Last Angry Man." *Starlog* no. 8 (September 1977), 22–27, 48.

Index

ABC (television network) 32, 42, 74, 84, 86, 94, 96, 104, 115, 132, 186
Abel, Robert 120, 125, 127–128, 140
Access Hollywood 2
Ackerman, Forrest J. 115, 117
Adam, Ken 73, 82
Adam-12 25
The Addams Family (1973 animated television series) 40, 42
Ahl, David 142
Airplane! 186
Alexander, David: *Star Trek Creator: The Authorized Biography of Gene Roddenberry* 3–6
Alien (1979 film) 15
All That Jazz 182
Allen, Harry 181
Altman, Mark A.: *The Fifty-Year Mission: The Complete, Uncensored, Unauthorized Oral History of Star Trek: The First 25 Years* 2–3
The Amazing Chan and the Chan Clan 42
Amazing Science Fiction (magazine) 122–123
AMT Corporation 130
Anderson, George 187
Andrews, Julie 13
The Animal Kingdom (textbook) 68
Apocalypse Now 171–172
Apollo 11 moon landing 27, 30
Apple (computer manufacturer) 15
Apple Users Group 143
ARB 27, 30, 32
Arbitron *see* ARB
Archives' Log 50
Arizona Republic 166
Armen, Margaret 39–40
Arnold, Richard 18
Arnot Mall Cinema (Elmira, NY) 157
ARPANET (computer network) 143
Ashby, Hal 116
Asherman, Alice 16
Asherman, Allan: *The Making of Star Trek II: The Wrath of Khan* 7; *The Star Trek Compendium* 7
Askew, John 130
Askew, John Thomas 130, 132–133
Associated Press 61, 72
Associates and Ferren 190–191
Association of Independent Television Stations (INTV) 110, 116, 186

At the Circus 35
Aviva Enterprises 185
Ayatollah Khomeini 169

Ballantine Books 139
Bally Manufacturing Corporation 134–135, 142
Banjo, the Woodpile Cat 173
Bantam Books 75, 122, 139
Barrett, Majel 17, 21, 35, 37, 40, 62, 115, 131, 149–150, 180
Barrett, Rona 92–93
Barron, Arthur 74
Barry, Marion 16
Bartlett, Hall 14
Barton, Howard 107
BASS 15
Battleforce 19–20
BBC (British television network) 27–28, 31–32, 34, 57
Beethoven, Ludwig van: Seventh and Eighth Symphonies 187
Being There 179
Bellerophon (fanzine) 79
Belli, Melvin 103
Ben Casey (1961 television series) 31
Bennett, Harve 5, 103–104, 184
Benton, Robert 176
Bergier, Jacques: *The Morning of the Magicians* 77
The Best of Trek (book series) 1, 60, 87
Bewitched (1964 television series) 32
Bi-Centennial-10 (1976 convention) 73
Big Ben's Records & Tapes 182
The Big Valley 32
Billboard 186
The Black Hole (1979 film) 95, 176, 183
Black, John D.F. 56, 100
black holes 80, 143
Black Sunday (1977 film) 148, 150–151
blind bidding 13, 125, 130, 148, 150, 159, 162, 166, 174, 178, 189
Block, Dick 26
Bloomingdale's (New York) 144–145
Blue Star Theater (Watchung, NJ) 157–158
The Blues Brothers (1980 film) 183
Bluhdorn, Charlie 3, 22, 85, 115, 117, 129–130, 172

221

Bluhdorn, Dominique 3, 22, 116
Blum, Lawrence 175
Bluth, Don 173
Boggs, Lindy 22
Bonanza 28, 53
Boston Globe 176, 183
Bottoms, Timothy 69
Bowers, Hoyt 107
Boyett, Bob 94
Bradbury, Ray 56, 100, 139–140; *Fahrenheit 451* 140; *The Martian Chronicles* 140; *R Is for Rocket* 140
Brick Price Movie Miniatures 112, 140
Bridge Theater (San Francisco) 67
Bring Me the Head of Alfredo Garcia 69
British Film Institute 12
Broadcasting (magazine) 26, 186
Brown, Peter H. 183
Brownell, Carole 47, 59
Bryant, Chris 7–8, 66–67, 72, 75, 77–82, 94
Buck Rogers in the 25th Century (1979 film) 163
Burke, Howard 61
Burklund, Christine 163
Burns, Pat 163
Burroughs, Edgar Rice: *John Carter of Mars* (book series) 77
Burton, Richard 54
Burtt, Ben 98
Butch Cassidy (1973 animated television series) 42

Cafe Continental 114
Cameo Theater (Binghamton, NY) 157
Campbell Taggart 130
Campbell, William 88
Canadian Broadcasting Corporation 115
Canterbury, Kitty 167
Capital Centre 99
Capitol Theater (Victoria, BC) 167
Captain Video (video store) 182
Carmel, Roger C. 88–89
Carnegie-Mellon 142
Carr, Terry 79
Carrie (1976 film) 69
Carry On (film series) 13
Carter, Jimmy 14–15
Cash Box 135, 139, 175
Cassidy, Shaun 161
Castro Theatre (San Francisco) 171
CBS (television network) 18, 37, 42, 74, 84, 86, 96, 104, 115
CBS News 18
CBS Records 17
CBS Studios 188
Cedarville Park 167–168
Century 5 (Salt Lake City, UT) 166
Century Screen Complex (Reno, NV) 168
Century 22 B (San Jose, CA) 15
Chambers, Marilyn 182
Charles Hansen Music and Books 17
Chasen's 115

Cheaper to Keep Her 186
Cheerios 130
Cherry Hill Cinema (Cherry Hill, NH) 158
Chew, Richard 98
Chicago Tribune 18
The Children of Sanchez 14
The China Syndrome 182
Cimino, Michael 116, 128
Cinefantastique 2, 51, 78, 105, 170, 172
Cinefex 190–191
Cinema at Bayshore (Sarasota, FL) 159
Cinema West (Lafayette, IN) 162, 172
Cinema World (Corvallis, OR) 167
Cinémathèque Française, La 73
Cinemologists 192
Circle Records 16
Citizen Kane 12–13, 21, 23
Clark, Dennis Lynton 117–119, 121
Clarke, Arthur C.: *Childhood's End* 77
Clayton, Jack 155
Cleopatra (1963 film) 183
Clockwork (band) 159
Close Encounters of the Third Kind (1977 movie) 85, 97, 104–107, 109, 115, 139, 182
Coca-Cola 129
Cock Tavern 19
Cockfighter (1974 film) 69
Cocoa Puffs 130
Coke *see* Coca-Cola
Cole, Lee 112
Collins, Joan 89–90
Collins, Robert 82, 95, 104–105, 113–114, 119, 122, 171
Collins, Stephen 20, 137
Columbia Records 17, 175
Columbia II (Paducah, KY) 161
Columbo (television movies) 52
Coming Home (1978 film) 76
Confessions of Linda Lovelace 159
Connelly, Sherilyn: *Ponyville Confidential: The History and Culture of My Little Pony, 1981–2016* 1, 43, 57, 61, 65, 87, 101, 131, 160
Coon, Gene L. 3–4, 39–40
Cooper, Sonni 18
Coppola, Francis Ford 62, 67, 171
Cosmos (1980 television series) 111
Courage, Alexander 131
Courier-News (Bridgewater, NJ) 158
Courier-Post (Camden, NJ) 158
Cox, Jan 19
CP/M Users Group 143
Creative Computing 142
Creature Features (1971 KTVU television series) 57
Credibility Gap 94
Crest toothpaste 130
Crowest, Frederick J.: *Beethoven* 187

Daily Dispatch (Moline, IL) 164
Daily Record (Morristown, NJ) 158
Daily Variety 30, 67, 84, 105, 107, 115, 117, 119–

Index 223

120, 124, 127, 139, 147, 170–171, 173–174, 176–177, 184
Darby, Kim 62
Dark Shadows (1966 television series) 28
A Day at the Races (1937 film) 35
The Day the Earth Stood Still (1951 film) 33, 77
De Atley, Richard 183
The Deer Hunter 116
DeLaurentiis, Dino 79
DeManche, Leslie 169
De Palma, Brian 69
Desilu 26, 29, 131
Detroit Triple Fan Fair (1972) 35
The Dick Van Dyke Show 26, 28–29, 32
Dillard, J.M.: *Star Trek: "Where No One Has Gone Before": A History in Pictures* 7
Diller, Barry 7, 48, 62, 74, 94, 115, 117, 124, 129
Dinah (1974 television series) 53
Disney, Walt 22
Dixon of Dock Green 28
Dochterman, Daren 191
Doctor Who (1963 television series) 27
Dolby Stereo 161, 169
Donner, Richard 126
Don't Look Now (1973 film) 66
Doohan, James 20, 40, 58, 60, 129, 149, 178
Dow, Jim 113
Dragnet (1954 film) 33
Dragnet (1967 television series) 32–33
Dubin, Murray 159
Duck Soup 35
Dykstra, John 22, 128

Ealing Studios 13
Egan, Eddie 2, 180
Eisner, Michael 16, 73–74, 84–85, 93–96, 99, 106, 115–117, 120, 129, 178; *Work in Progress: Risking Failure, Surviving Success* 2
Electronic *Enterprise* 135, 141
Ellison, Harlan 56, 58–59, 79, 100, 174–175; *Harlan Ellison's Watching* 174
Emergency Plus Four (1973 animated television series) 40, 42
EMI-Elstree 64
Empire of Dreams 98
The Empire Strikes Back (1980 film) 111, 113, 181
Empire Theatre Leicester Square 15–16, 174
Enquirer (Battle Creek, MI) 162–163
Enterprise (space shuttle) 72, 75, 78
Enterprise Flight Manual 112
Equicon (1973 convention) 42
Equicon (1974 convention) 44
Equus (1974 Broadway play) 81, 83, 99, 115
Evanier, Mark 42
Evans, Robert 53; *The Kid Stays in the Picture* (1994 book) 53

Famous Monsters of Filmland 105, 115, 117, 131
Famous Music 17
Fantasia (1940 film) 160

Fantastic Films 121–122
Fass, Myron 115, 118
Fawcett, Farrah 175
Faye, Steve 165
FBI 12, 132
Federation Trading Post 131
Fellows, Arthur 93–95
Ferguson, Maynard 175
Ferren, Bran 190–191
Fiddler on the Roof (1971 film) 132
Film Advisory Board 173
Film Facts 183
Filmation 39–40, 43
Fletcher, Robert 121, 135–136, 144
Florida Twin (North Miami Beach) 159
Fontana, Dorothy 4, 34–35, 38–40, 45, 90
Forbidden Planet 77
Ford, Gerald 72
48 Hrs. (1982 film) 181
Foster, Alan Dean 93, 99, 118, 126–127, 136
Four Seasons Hotel (Washington, D.C.) 11, 18
Fox Theater (Philadelphia) 159
Frank, Richard 84, 86, 94, 99, 104, 110, 114, 116–117, 186
Frankenheimer, John 148
Frewer, Matt 103
Friedkin, William 67
Fuller, Bryan 73
Future Cop (1977 series) 94
Futureworld 77–78, 91

Gabriel, Peter 8
Gallagher, Teresa 19
Galleria (San Francisco) 145
Garris, Mick 68
Gautreaux, David 115
General Mills 130
Gerds, Warren 164
Gerrold, David xx, 4, 17, 35, 39–40, 115, 142–143, 169; *The Trouble with Tribbles* 1, 35; *The World of Star Trek* 1, 35
Get Smart (1965 television series) 25
Ghostbusters II (1989 film) 190–191
Gifts of Love 159
Glucek, Steve 163
Glut, Don 115
Godzilla 57, 75
Goldberg, Whoopi 103
Goldenberg, Judy Lee 60
Goldsmith, Jerry 11, 17, 22, 117, 148, 150–153, 162, 178
Goldstein, Fred: *Star Trek Spaceflight Chronology* 134, 137
Goldstein, Stan: *Star Trek Spaceflight Chronology* 134, 137
Gone with the Wind (1939 film) 42, 141
The Good Mother 190
Goodwin, Robert 93–94, 96–97, 101, 112, 114
Google Books 6
Grant, Lee 84
Grease (1978 film) 125, 177, 186

The Great Gatsby (1974 film) 155
The Great Northfield Minnesota Raid 67
The Great Star Trek Trivia Book see Needleman, Rafe: *Official Star Trek Trivia Book*
Greeley, Bill 28
Greenwald, Robert 149
Grimm, Debby 167
Gross, Edward: *The Fifty-Year Mission: The Complete, Uncensored, Unauthorized Oral History of Star Trek: The First 25 Years* 2–3
Guardian (UK newspaper) 174
Guinness, Alec 13
Gulf & Western 26, 172

Hamill, Mark 42, 71
Hamlet (play) 134
Handwork, Nancy 20–21
Happy Meals 129
Hartley, Mariette 38
Harvey, Paul 18
Hastings, Larry G. 15
Hayes, Jerry 157
Heaven Can Wait (1978 film) 114
Hellman, Monte 69
High Adventure 28
Hill, Walter 82
Hillman, Bill 67
Hilton Hotel (Detroit) 35
Hirsch, Paul 98
Hitchock, Alfred 12
Holiday Inn Hialeah 159
Hollywood Bowl 105
Hollywood Holly 159
Holmes, Sherlock 47
Holst, Gustav 105
Horse Feathers 35
Houston, David 70, 86, 115
Houston Coliseum 75
Houstoncon (1974 convention) 45
Howard, Kez 70–71
Howard, Teri 161
Howarth, Alan S. 148–149
Hoyle, Fred: *The Black Cloud* 77
HP Data Center 142
HP 2000C Timeshare system 142
Hughes Television Network 74, 84, 92, 124
The Hunter (1980 film) 148, 167
Hunter, Jeffrey 25
Huntley-Brinkley Report 28
Hutchison, David 110–111
Hyperion 7

I Dream of Jeannie (1965 television series) 25
I Love Lucy 28–29
Ice Capades 168
If the Mind Is Free 31
IGN.com 3
Independent Television Corporation 30
Indiana Jones and the Last Crusade (1989 film) 191
Industrial Light and Magic 98, 190

Insatiable 182
Inside Star Trek (zine) 56
Internet Archive 6
Isenberg, Jerry 62, 66, 68–69, 76–78, 80–81, 83, 90, 141
Islands in the Stream (1977 film) 151
ITV (British television network) 28, 32
Ivancie, Frank 167

Jackson, Betty 162
James, Bob 175
Jaws (1975 film) 83, 162, 173
Jaws 2 171, 173–174, 177
JC Penney 129
Jeannie (1973 animated television series) 40, 42
Jeffries, Matt 64–66, 73, 93, 115, 124
Jennings, Joe 93, 112, 118
The Jerk (1979 film) 176
The Jerry Lewis Show (1967 television series) 25–26
Jewison, Norman 132
Jobs, Steve 15
John Danz Theater (Bellevue, WA) 167
John Thomas Dye School 15
Johnson, Kay 16, 18
Jones, Preston Neal: *Return to Tomorrow: The Filming of Star Trek: The Motion Picture* 1–2, 9, 78, 82, 172
Joseph, Franz: *Star Trek Blueprints* 64–65, 106, 122–124, 170; *Star Fleet Technical Manual* 64–65, 81, 106, 137, 141, 170
Journal-News (Rockland County, NY) 157
Jozak Company 62, 66
JPL 47
Justman, Robert H.: *Inside Star Trek: The Real Story* 2, 8, 26, 31, 39

Kaiser Broadcasting 26–28
Kalish, Ed 14
Kandel, Stephen 40
Kaplan, Stanley 147, 150
Katz, Oscar 39
Katzenberg, Jeffrey 16–17, 39, 93–94, 113, 127, 145, 172, 178, 181
Kaufman, Philip 22, 65, 67–69, 72–74, 77–83, 85–86, 104, 108, 116, 119, 124
Kaye, Jeffrey 127
Kaye, M.M.: *The Far Pavilions* 171
KBAK (television station) 46
KCOP (television station) 86
KDNL (television station) 27
Keegan, Terry 93–95
Kelley, DeForest 17–18, 20, 22, 26, 40, 58–59, 66, 107, 115, 149, 178
Kennedy, Ethel 22
Kennedy, John F. 2–3, 180–181
Kershner, Paul 14
KGW (radio station) 167
"Khaaan!" 188
Khambatta, Persis 9, 20, 115, 118, 126, 137, 145, 149, 178

Index

Killer Fish 173, 176
King, Stephen: *Danse Macabre* 59
King Kong (1976 film) 79
Kippax, Nancy 16
Kline, Richard 121, 178
Kmart 129
KMPH (television station) 41, 139
Knopf, Chris 61
Koenig, Walter 20, 45, 50, 58, 115, 149, 178; *Chekov's Enterprise: A Personal Journal of The Making of Star Trek—The Motion Picture* 1
KPIX Eyewitness News 67
KPTV (television station) 53
KQED (television station) 57
Kramer vs. Kramer 176
KRIS (television station) 53
KRUX (radio station) 16
KSAN (radio station) 145
KTLA (television station) 73–74
KTNT (television station) 31
KTVK (television station) 53
KTVU (television station) 27, 57, 74
Kubrick, Stanley 13
Kulik, Buzz 148, 167
Kung Fu (1972 television series) 46
Kusik, Larry 162
KXTX (television station) 53

Ladd, Alan, Jr. 98
Lafayette Theater (Lafayette, IN) 162, 172
Langlois, Henri 73
Lassie's Rescue Rangers (1973 animated television series) 42
Lauer, Steven 158
Lawrence, D.H.: *Whales Weep Not!* 105
Ledger, Heath 69
Lenard, Mark 47, 88–90, 129
Lent, John 22
Leonard Nimoy Presents Mr. Spock's Music from Outer Space 131
Let the Good Times Roll (1973 film) 62
Levine, Howard A. 131–132
Levine, Paul 133
Lichtenberg, Jacqueline 16
Lincoln Enterprises 63, 122–123, 131
Lippincott, Charles 91
Lisberger Studios 149
Little House on the Prairie (1974 television series) 57
Livingston, Harold 93–94, 101, 103, 105, 118–120, 126, 136, 177
Lloyd, Christopher 188
Locus (fanzine) 63
Loew's Orpheum Theatre (New York) 156
Loew's State 1 Theatre (New York) 156–157, 159, 169
Loew's State 2 Theatre (New York) 156
Logan's Run (1976 film) 77, 91
Logan's Run (1977 television series) 90
London Weekend Television (British television network) 28

Longshot Disco 159–160, 175
Loos, Don 112
Loren, Will 61
Los Angeles Convention Center 86
Los Angeles County Superior Court 133
Los Angeles Times 37, 74, 81, 84, 101, 104, 114, 113, 178, 179, 182–183
Lost in Space (1965 television series) 28, 31
Love, American Style (1969 television series) 53
Lucas, George 64, 67, 71, 83, 85, 97–98, 191
Lucas, Marcia 98
Lucky Charms 130

M&M/Mars (candy manufacturer) 130
M&Ms 130
MacArthur Theater (Washington, D.C.) 11–16, 18–20, 22–23, 132, 167–168; projectionist 12
MacInnes, Helen: *Prelude to Terror* 171
Macy's (New York) 144
Macy's (San Francisco) 144
Maggio, Phil 14
Magicam (model building shop) 63, 106, 112–113, 128
Magicam (optical effects process) 45, 49, 52, 63, 71, 106, 111, 119–120
MAGNUM 16
Magnum, P.I. (1980 television series) 103
Maiewski, Shirley 16–18, 46
Making of *Star Trek—The Motion Picture* Seminar 178
The Making of Star Trek II (unwritten book) 76, 122, 134
Malcolm, Derek 174
Malone, Adrian 111
The Man Who Fell to Earth 77
The Man Who Shot Liberty Valance 2
Mancuso, Frank 125, 171–174
Mandel, Bill 170
Mandell, Paul 190
Manilow, Barry 102–103
Mankoff, Robert 130
Mann Theaters 169
Mann's Chinese Theatre (Los Angeles) 16, 169, 171, 177
Mann's National Theatre (Los Angeles) 15, 171, 177
Mann's Westwood *see* Mann's National Theatre
Mantz, Scott 2–3
Marc Cinema (Green Bay, WI) 164
March of Dimes 90
Margaret Herrick Library 6, 8, 58, 80
Markham 1 (Little Rock, AR) 162
Martin, David 169
Martin, Steve 176
Marx Brothers 35
M*A*S*H (1970 film) 183
Massacre at Redneck County see Redneck County Rape
Match of the Day 28
Mayfield, Mike 142

Mayflower Hotel (Washington, D.C.) 18
McCabe, Bruce 176
McCain Mall Cinema (North Little Rock, AR) 162
McDonald, Dave 166
McDonald's 129–130, 141
McHale's Navy (1962 series) 28, 32
McHale's Navy: Animated (unproduced television series) 40
McKean, Michael 94
McNaughton, Chuck 33–34
McQuarrie, Ralph 73, 82, 113
McRae, John 167
Meadows, Jim 63–64
Mehta, Zubin 105
Melcher, Carey 120, 128
Melton, Bob 16
Menorah Medical Center 166
Merrill Lynch 181
Metro Center Cinema (Jackson, MS) 161–162
Metro-Goldwyn-Mayer 11–12, 16, 172
Metromedia 96
Miami-Dade Community College 45
Miami News 160
Michaels, Marguerite 126
Michelson, Harold 121–122
Michigan State University 54
Micklus, Lance 142
Micronet (computer network) 143
Midnight Offerings 186
Mifune, Toshiro 81
Miller, Steve 163
Milton Bradley 134–135
Minneapolis Star 164
Minor, Mike 115, 126
Mitchell, Margaret: *Gone with the Wind* (1936 novel) 42
The Mod Squad (1968 television series) 53
Monster Times 32–34, 37–38, 40–42, 46, 48, 51, 70, 131
Montalban, Ricardo 88
Moore, Dudley 172
Morford, Beth 163
Morris Hills Cinema I (Parsippany, NJ) 158
Morrison, Don 164
The Movie Channel 185
MPAA 11–12, 153
Mulligan's Stew 97
Multnomah County Sheriff 168
Mulvaney, Jim 165
Murphy, Eddie 103
Music from Outer Space—A *Star Wars* Concert 105
Mutchnick, Brenda 128
My Favorite Martians (1973 animated television series) 42
My Friend Tony 25
My Little Margie 31
My Little Pony 131
My Little Pony: Friendship Is Magic 65

My Little Pony: The Movie (2017 film) 160
mycelial network 42, 86, 130

Nanuet Movies 5 (Nanuet, NY) 157
Nardino, Gary 86, 93, 102–103
NASA 22, 36, 38, 47, 72–73, 127–128
National Association of Broadcasters 26
National Association of Television Program Executives (NATPE) 114, 116
National Association of Theatre Owners (NATO) 147, 150
National Discount Video Centers 182
National Rocket Club *see* National Space Club
National Screen Service 126, 129, 147
National Space Club 15–16, 22
National Telefilm Associates 53
NBC (television network) 8, 25–31, 33–35, 37, 39, 41–43, 57, 63, 70, 74, 94, 96–97, 104, 115
Needleman, Rafe: *Official Star Trek Trivia Book* 139
Nelson, Gary 95, 176
Nemecek, Larry: *The Star Trek: The Next Generation Companion* (1992) 7; *The Star Trek: The Next Generation Companion* (1995) 7; *The Star Trek: The Next Generation Companion* (2003) 8
Neptune (planet) 38
Never Say Goodbye 13
New West (magazine) 127–128
New York Daily News 154–156
New York Post 41
New York Times 27, 72, 78, 134, 155, 171, 173, 175–176, 178, 182, 185
New York Times Paperback Best Sellers list 171, 173, 176
New Yorker (magazine) 130
News and Comment 18
Newspapers.com 6
Newsroom (1968 television series) 57
Nichols, Nichelle 17, 20, 40, 50, 115, 149
Nieman, Tom 135
Nielsen ratings 30, 57
Nimoy, Leonard 5, 21–22, 26, 31, 39–40, 43–44, 47, 50–51, 66, 73, 81, 83, 89–90, 95, 99–102, 107, 112, 114–115, 118, 127, 129, 131, 137, 149, 181, 184, 189–190; *I Am Not Spock* 101; *I Am Spock* 7
The 1980 Star Trek Calendar 137
1941 (1979 film) 171, 176, 183
Niven, Larry 115
North Star Software Exchange 143
Northridge Cinema (Salinas, CA) 169
Norway Productions 49
NSI (Nielsen Station Index) 53
The Nude Bomb 25

Oates, Warren 69
O'Connor, Kevin 134
The Official Blueprints from Star Trek—The Motion Picture 139
Official Star Trek Duty Jackets 145–146

Index

Official Star Trek LED Pullover Shirt 146–147
The Official USS Enterprise Officer's Date Book 137
Ohio Theatre (Columbus, OH) 150
Old Yeller 167
Oliver's Story 114
Olympic Hotel (Seattle) 79
Operation Prime Time 86
O'Quinn Studios 146
Ordinary People 186
Our Lady of Victory School 19
The Outsider (1968 television series) 25

Pacific Theatres' Cinerama Dome (Los Angeles) 104, 171
Pakistan Television Corporation 32
Pantry Pride Supermarket 157
Parade (magazine) 126
Paramount Building E 53, 79
Paramount Home Video 182–183
Paramount Is the Word 125–126, 136
Paramount Pictures 2–4, 6–8, 11–14, 16, 18–19, 21–22, 39, 45, 48–56, 58–68, 71–73, 77–83, 85–86, 90–93, 95, 97, 99, 101–102, 106, 108, 111–120, 125–139, 145, 148–150, 154, 167, 170–171, 173–175, 177–178, 180–182, 185, 189–191
Paramount Pictures (as "the Mountain") 12, 16, 18, 27, 61, 83–84, 86, 96–97, 113, 124–125, 148, 156, 171, 173, 185, 191
Paramount Press Book and Merchandising Manual 130
Paramount Television 25–27, 30, 33–35, 39, 44, 46–47, 73–75, 84–86, 92–96, 101, 104, 110, 116–117, 124, 132, 184, 186
Paramount Television Service (unlaunched television network) 91–92, 95–97, 99–100, 104, 109–110, 112, 114–116, 124
Paramount Theatre (New York) 154–157
Paramount Theatre (St. Cloud, MN) 164
Parkway Theater (Moline, IL) 163–164
Parsippany High School 158
Patriotic Star Tunnel 148–150, 152
Pauwels, Louis: *The Morning of the Magicians* 77
Peak, Bob 153
Peckinpah, Sam 69
Pederson, Con 120
Peeples, Samuel 40, 77
The People (1972 television movie) 62
Perlstein, Ed 131
Perry Como's Christmas in New Mexico 173
Philadelphia Inquirer 159
Picker, David V. 66
A Piece of the Action (fanzine) 44–46, 49, 53, 56, 60, 76
Piller, Michael 188–189
Pines, Elyse 32
Pinewood Studios 82
Pittsburgh Post-Gazette 187
The Pizza Triangle 172

Planet of the Apes (1969–1973 film series) 35, 37, 39–40, 46, 70
Planet of the Apes (1974 television series) 37
The Planets (orchestral suite) 105
Playboy Enterprises 93–94
Plaza Twin (Owensboro, KY) 161
Pocket Books 7–9, 134, 137, 139, 178, 189–189
Pollock, Dale 171, 174
Pope John Paul II 14
Portfolio X 186
posters 17, 126, 129–130, 132, 148, 153, 166, 175
Povill, Jon 58, 82, 100, 105–106, 109, 178
Powell, Darla 20
Press-Gazette (Green Bay, WI) 164
Price, Brick 140–141
Probert, Andrew 113
ProQuest 6
Publishers Weekly 136
Puget Sound Star Trekkers Convention II (1977 convention) 79

Questar 145

R & R Lighting 14
Radio City Music Hall 12, 16, 120
Raise the Titanic (1980 film) 183
Rampa, T. Lobsang: *The Third Eye* 77
Ramsay, Todd 11, 14, 178
Rand, Ayn: *The Virtue of Selfishness* 77
Ray Syufy company 15
RCA Americom satellite 74
RCA VET250 182
Redford, Robert 54
Redneck County Rape 161
Reeves-Stevens, Garfield: *The Art of Star Trek* 7–8, 73, 191; *Star Trek Phase II: The Lost Series* 8, 96, 103, 105, 109, 122; *Star Trek: The Next Generation: The Continuing Mission* 189–191
Reeves-Stevens, Judith: *The Art of Star Trek* 7–8, 73, 191; *Star Trek Phase II: The Lost Series* 8, 96, 103, 105, 109, 122; *Star Trek: The Next Generation: The Continuing Mission* 189–191
Regency I (San Francisco, Ca.) 170, 172
Regency II (San Francisco, Ca.) 170, 172
Reiner, Carl 176
The Remaking of Star Trek (unwritten book) 76, 134
Rensselaer Polytechnic Institute 49
Rice University 49
RKO 12
RKO Stanley Warner Theater (Paramus, NJ) 158–159
Robbins, Harold (literary giant) 86
Robert Abel and Associates 18, 113, 118–120, 125, 127–128, 140, 149
Roberts, Ed 162
Rockaway 6 (Rockaway, NJ) 158
Rocky (1976 film) 67
Roddenberry, Eugene 15, 17

Index

Roddenberry, Gene ix, 2, 6–8, 11, 13, 15–18, 22, 25, 28, 31–32, 34–35, 39–40, 42–50, 52–53, 56, 59, 61, 63–66, 72–73, 77–78, 80–81, 83, 85–87, 89–90, 92, 104–107, 113–114, 119–120, 122, 126, 135–136, 165, 170, 178, 181, 184, 186; call to August Party convention (1979) 136, 179–180; call to Augustrek convention (1980) 136, 179–180; credit on *Star Trek—The Motion Picture* 13, 118, 126, 136, 149, 152–153, 177; *Gene Roddenberry's Andromeda* (2000 television series) 102; *Genesis II* (unsold 1973 pilot) 36–38, 93, 102; hiring Philip Kaufman 67–69; *Inside Star Trek* (1976 record) 50; on Klingon overemphasis 3–6; letter to fanzines about *Star Trek—The Motion Picture* 108–109, 116; at the MacArthur Premiere 21; *The Making of Star Trek—The Motion Picture* 1, 7, 38, 54–57, 63, 67, 76, 80, 122, 130–131, 136, 139, 144, 178, 180; on making the *Enterprise* "state of the art" 110–113; mother 17; music royalties 131; novelization (*Star Trek—The Motion Picture*) 6, 55, 134, 137, 139, 171, 173, 175–176, 178; novelization (unproduced 1975 *Star Trek II* film story) 6, 75, 122; Paramount meeting (August 3, 1977) 93–97; *Planet Earth* (unsold 1974 pilot) 102; *Pretty Maids All in a Row* (1971 Roger Vadim film) 37, 39, 62; *The Questor Tapes* (unsold 1974 pilot) 70; recorded message for Empathy Midi-con (1978) 124, 180; as a "Renaissance man" 70–71; Robert Redford and Richard Burton rumor 54; on Star Trek merchandise 62; at the *Star Trek—The Motion Picture* press conference 116–118; *Star Trek II* (unproduced 1975 film story) 50–51, 53–56, 58–60, 63, 179; *Star Trek II* (unproduced 1976 film story) 58, 179; *Star Trek III* (unproduced 1980 film story) 2–3, 179–181; Susan Sackett interview (August 1977) 97–99; on violence 65, 141–144; *World of Star Trek* (touring show) 75–76, 99–101, 150
Rodman, Howard 61
Roeg, Nicholas 66
Rogue One: A Star Wars Story (2016 film) 76
The Rose (1979 film) 179
Rose Bowl 17
Rose Moyer Theatre (Portland, OR) 167–168
Rothwell, John 119
Rotsler, William 115
Rugg, Jim 93
Russin, Joe 57

Sackett, Susan ix, 2, 6–7, 11, 18, 38, 46, 54–57, 62, 64–69, 75–80, 86–87, 92–93, 97–98, 100–102, 106–107, 110, 119–122, 124, 134, 139, 141, 178, 181; *Inside Trek: My Secret Life with Star Trek Creator Gene Roddenberry* 2; *The Making of Star Trek—The Motion Picture* 1, 7, 38, 54–57, 63, 67, 76, 80, 136, 139, 178, 180
Safeway 19
The Saint (1962 television series) 25, 30
St. Mary's Center for Learning 31
Salina Journal (Salina, KS) 166
Samuel Goldwyn Studios 14
San Diego Comic-Con 188
San Francisco Chronicle 67, 69, 82, 85, 144
San Francisco Civic Auditorium 79
San Francisco Examiner 170
Sangamon State University 46
Santa Maria Theatre (Santa Maria, CA) 169
Santa Maria Times 169
Sarasota Square 6 (Sarasota, FL) 159
Sargent, Joseph 64
Saturday Night Fever 134
Save the Star Trek Cast (S.T.S.T.C.) 47–48, 59; fan poll 59–61
Schaffner, Franklin J. 151
Schanzer, Karl 181
Scheimer, Lou 40, 43
Schlosser, Herbert 134
Schroeder, Patricia 22
Schuster, Al 32, 35, 38
Schwab, Mildred 168
Sciacca, Tom 145
Science Fiction Today and Tomorrow 77
Scott, Alan 7–8, 66–67, 72, 75, 77–82, 94
Sears 129
Selleck, Tom 103
Selznick, David O. 43, 141
Shannon, Glynn 167–168
The Shape of Things to Come see *Things to Come* (1936 film)
Shatner, Lisabeth: *Captain's Log: William Shatner's Personal Account of the Making of Star Trek V: The Final Frontier* 190
Shatner, William 3, 9, 18, 21–22, 26, 40, 42, 46, 50–51, 54, 62, 66, 73, 86, 89–92, 95, 100–102, 104–105, 114–115, 124, 129, 137, 149, 168, 181, 184, 186, 188, 190–191; *Star Trek Movie Memories* 191
Shay, Don 105
Shearer, Harry 94
Sherwood Oaks Experimental College 178
Showcase Cinemas (Louisville, KY) 160
Shriners Children's Hospital 166
Siegall, Marc 132–133
Siekman, Jim 168
Silent Running 45, 77, 118
Silverberg, Robert 56, 100
Silverman, Fred 37, 74
Siskel, Gene 18
Sleeping Beauty (1959 film) 160
Smart Modes 145
Smith, Bruce Lee 165–166
Smith, Cecil 38
Smith, Greg 167
Smithsonian National Air and Space Museum 15–18, 22, 52, 165
Smokey and the Bandit Part II 178
Snickers 130
Soble, Ronald 81, 84
Softside 142
Solaris (1972 film) 67, 77–78

Index

Solow, Herbert 39, 131; *Inside Star Trek: The Real Story* 2, 8, 26, 31, 39
Somerville Circle Theater (Somerville, NJ) 158
The Sound of Music (1965 film) 13
The Source (computer network) 143
South Bend (Milton Bradley division) 135, 140
South Dakota State University 165
Southtown Theater (Minneapolis, MN) 164
Space-Con 2 (1976 convention) 67
Space-Con 3 (1977 convention) 79, 129
Space-Con 4 (1977 convention) 86
Space Trek Special 118
Spacewar! (1961 video game) 142
Spielberg, Steven 67, 85, 109, 171, 176, 191
Spinrad, Norman 102
Stapledon, Olaf: *The Starmaker* 77; *Last and First Men* 77
STAR! 13
Star-Borne 34–35, 38–39, 43–44
Star-Gazette (Elmira, NY) 157
Star Trek (COBOL game) 142
Star Trek (early computer games) 142
Star Trek (1966 television series) see *Star Trek I*
Star Trek (1973 animated television series) see *Star Trek: Animated*
Star Trek (1979 pinball machine) 134–135, 142
Star Trek (2009 film) 5, 52, 188
Star Trek (unpublished magazine) 70
Star Trek Action Group (club) 19, 48
Star Trek Action Group (fanzine) 19, 48, 54, 102, 136–137
Star Trek America (1977 convention) 83, 101
Star Trek: Animated 8–9, 39–44, 47, 50, 52, 58, 73–75, 88, 93, 103, 118, 120
Star Trek Association for Revival (S.T.A.R.) 34
Star Trek Association of Irvine 132
Star Trek Beyond 5, 52
Star Trek Blooper Reel 35, 149
Star Trek: Deep Space Nine (1993 television series) 111, 137
Star Trek: Discovery 52, 73, 76, 111, 188
The Star Trek Dream (1975 television special) 57, 79
The Star Trek Frame Blow-Up Book (unwritten book) 139
Star Trek: First Contact (1996 film) 191
Star Trek: Insurrection (1998 film) 188–189
Star Trek Into Darkness 5, 52, 188
The Star Trek Iron-On Transfer Book (unwritten book) 137
Star Trek Lives! (1972 Convention) 32
Star Trek Lives! (1973 Convention) 38
Star Trek Lives! (1976 Convention) 60
The Star Trek Make-A-Game Book 137
The Star Trek Make-Your-Own-Costume Book 137
Star Trek Meals 129–130, 141
Star Trek: Nemesis (2002 film) 188

The Star Trek Peel-Off Graphics Book 137
Star Trek: Phase II see *Star Trek II* (unmade television series)
Star Trek: Planet of the Titans see *Star Trek—The Motion Picture* (unmade Philip Kaufman film)
The Star Trek Pop-Up Book 139
Star Trek Publishing Program 137–139
Star Trek Revival Association of Kentuckiana (STRAK) 161
Star Trek Speaks! 137
Star Trek: The God Thing see *Star Trek II* (unproduced 1975 film story)
Star Trek—The Motion Picture (newsletter) 118, 135–136
Star Trek—The Motion Picture (original motion picture soundtrack) 17, 136, 175
Star Trek—The Motion Picture (Robert Wise film) 1–3, 9–10; 25, 33, 38, 43–45, 47, 51, 63–64, 68, 71, 86, 90, 94, 95, 99, 102, 104, 106, 107, 109, 111–113, 119–122, 124–126, 133, 142, 144 170, 179–180, 185–188; ABC television broadcast 132, 186; Academy member screenings 170–171, 179; advance tickets 154–156, 162–163, 166, 169; advertising 148–149, 153, 159, 165; beached whale comparisons 183–184; box office (domestic) 171–176; box office (foreign) 175; *Cinemologists* review 192; clothing 144–147; Director's Edition 8–9, 173; Film Advisory Board award 173; For Your Consideration ad 170; G rating by MPAA 11, 173; *Heaven's Gate* comparisons 183–184; MacArthur Premiere 11–23, 132, 145, 156, 167–168; merchandising and licensing 126–130; 175; national premiere (Indiana, Illinois, Michigan, and Minnesota) 162–164; national premiere (Kentucky, Mississippi, and Arkansas) 160–162; national premiere (New York, New Jersey, Pennsylvania, and Florida) 154–160; national premiere (South Dakota, Nebraska, Kansas, Utah, and Arizona) 164–167; national premiere (Washington, Oregon, Nevada, and California) 167–170; newsletter 118, 135–136; phasers (prop) 140–141; phasers (toy) 135; pinball machine 134–135; press conference (March 28, 1978) 114–119; principal photography 124–125, publishing program 134–139; reviews 18, 172, 174–176; soundtrack LP 17, 136, 175; trailers and television ads 148–154; VHS and Beta release ("Special Longer Version") 186; VHS and Beta release (theatrical version) 182–183; video games 143–144; videodisc release of the theatrical version 185; "Z" channel premiere 178–179
Star Trek—The Motion Picture (unmade Philip Kaufman film) 6–8, 22, 65, 67–69, 72–73, 74, 77–87, 97, 103, 108, 113, 119, 124
Star Trek—The Motion Picture (Vectrex game) 143
Star Trek—The Motion Picture: A Novelization 137

Star Trek—The Motion Picture: A Photonovel 139
Star Trek: The Next Generation 4–6, 52, 73, 78, 103, 118, 188, 191–192
"Star Trek—The Phenomenon!" advertisements 173
Star Trek—The Superstars and the Superfans (1977 television special) 79
Star Trek Today 46, 63
Star Trek: Voyager (1995 television series) 137
Star Trek Welcommittee 18, 44, 46
Star Trek I (1966 television series) 1, 8–9, 15, 19, 21–22, 25–34, 36–39, 41, 43–44, 46, 49, 52–53, 56–57, 61–65, 68, 70, 73, 77, 85, 87–89, 91, 102–103, 105–107, 116–118, 124, 126, 128, 130–131, 134–135, 137, 139, 142–143, 152, 154, 157, 164, 170, 175, 179
Star Trek II (sailboat) 6
Star Trek II: The Wrath of Khan (Nicholas Meyer film) 2–5, 7–9, 10, 83, 87, 99, 103–104, 121, 141–143, 186–190
Star Trek II Writers/Directors Guide 106, 122
Star Trek III (BASIC game) 142
Star Trek III: The Search for Spock 3–5, 8–10, 73, 90, 99, 112, 115, 141, 187–190
Star Trek III.4 (BASIC game) 142
Star Trek IV: The Voyage Home 5, 9–10, 90, 99, 103, 188, 190
Star Trek V: The Final Frontier 3, 9, 99, 186–188, 190–191
Star Trek VI: The Undiscovered Country 3, 5, 9
Star Trektennial News 51, 56, 62–68, 75–78, 80, 93, 97, 102
Star Wars 64, 70, 76, 86, 111, 144, 175, 188
Star Wars (1977 film) 15, 71, 73, 83–86, 91, 97–98, 104–107, 109, 115, 128, 133, 139, 141, 160, 162, 164, 166, 169, 173, 185
Star Wars: Episode III—Revenge of the Sith 188
Star Wars: The Force Awakens (2015 film) 76
Star Wars: The Last Jedi (2017 film) 76
Starburst (UK magazine) 69, 82–83
Starlog 2, 5–6, 18, 67–68, 70–73, 77, 80, 86, 91–92, 96–97, 100, 102, 104, 106–107, 110–111, 115, 119, 122, 128, 131, 134–135, 137–140, 142–143, 145–146, 174–175, 180
Starship Enterprises (store) 159
State Lake Theatre (Chicago) 163
State Theater (Lincoln, NE) 165–166
Statler Hilton Hotel (New York) 32, 73
Steel, Dawn 127–132, 144, 178; *They Can Kill You, But They Can't Eat You: Lessons from the Front* 2
Stone, Judy 82, 85
Strange Paradise 28
Sturgeon, Ted 56, 100
Summit (candy bar) 130
Sun City (South African resort) 174
SunRise (newspaper) 46–47
Sunrise Cinemas (Valley Stream, NY) 157
Sunrise Drive-In (Valley Stream, NY) 157

Super Friends (1973 animated television series) 42
Superior Carpets 14
Superman: The Movie (1978 film) 126, 162, 169, 171, 174, 182
Synder, Tom 58

Takei, George 20, 40–41, 50, 54, 60, 67, 102, 115, 149
The Taking of Pelham One Two Three (1974 film) 64
Tarkovsky, Andrei 67
Tarzan 47
Taylor, Jud 63–64
Taylor, Richard 113, 120
TelCom Associates 31
10 (1979 film) 172
Tennessean (Nashville, TN) 183
Tenspeed and Brown Shoe 186
TerraCon (1977 convention) 102
Testimony of Two Men (1977 television miniseries) 86, 91
Theiss, William Ware 41
Things to Come (1936 film) 77–78
This Is Your Life (1971 television series) 32
Thomas, Bob 61
Thomas, Lowell 57
Thorne, Worley 105
3 Musketeers (candy bar) 130
Thunder Media 167
Time After Time (1979 film) 161
The Time Machine (1960 film) 77
Tippecanoe Mall Cinema (Lafayette, IN) 162
Toland, Gregg 13
Tomorrow with Tom Snyder (1973 television series) 58–59
Totowa Cinema (Totowa, NJ) 158–159
Towne Cinema Theatres (Battle Creek, MI) 162–163
Towne Theater (Latham, NY) 157
Trek: The Magazine for Star Trek Fans 60–61, 87–90
Trekkies (fandom) 21–22, 42, 53, 68, 79, 85, 102, 117, 126–127, 158–160, 165, 170, 181, 183; as derogatory term 16, 33, 42, 70, 79, 81, 84, 157, 159–160, 162–164, 166–167; as Star Trekkers 47–48, 68; as STrekfandom 34; as Trek'ophiles 49
Trimble, Bjo 16–18, 26, 59, 77; The Star Trek Concordance 77
Trix 130
TRS-80 Users Group 143
Trumbull, Douglas 22, 45, 111, 118, 128, 136, 148, 150
Turkish National Television 46
TV Guide (magazine) 35
T.V. Viewer's Committee 41
Twentieth-Century Fox 98
Twix 130
2001: A Space Odyssey 13, 45, 68, 73, 77, 83

Index 231

UA Cinema 6 (Phoenix, AZ) 166
United Artists theaters (Los Angeles) 179
United Artists theaters (Westchester County, New York) 178
United Press International (UPI) 166, 181
University of California, Berkeley 142
University of Central Arkansas 181
University of Illinois at Chicago 31
University of Illinois at Springfield *see* Sangamon State University
University of Massachusetts at Amherst 17
University of Nebraska 64
University of New Hampshire 44
Uptown Theater (Washington, D.C.) 13
The USS Enterprise Bridge Punch-Out Book 137–139
USS Enterprise Punch-Out Book 139

Vadim, Roger 37, 39, 62
Variety 25–28, 30–32, 34, 40, 46, 49, 53, 84–85, 96, 110, 125, 127–128, 172, 174, 185, 189
Variety Archives 6
Vectrex Arcade System 143
Vermont Educational Television
Verne, Jules 161
Vertigo 12
Video Depot 182
Video Station 182
Village of the Damned (1960 film) 77
Virginia Association for Star Trek (VAST) 19–21
Von Braun, Werner 22
Von Däniken, Erich 59
Von Puttkamer, Jesco 22, 73
Vore Cinemas (Warsaw, IN) 162

Waddy, Colin 118
Waldorf Hotel (New York) 45
Walk Proud (1979 film) 82
Wallaby Books 137
WALT (television station) 31
Wanderer Books 137, 139
The Wanderers (1979 film) 82
The War of the Worlds (unproduced 1974 television series) 45
Warner Bros. 36, 39
The Warriors (1979 film) 82
Washington D.C. Mayor's Command Post 14
Washington Post 99–101, 183, 185
Washington Science Fiction Association 19
WATL (television station) 27
WATU (television station) 46
WBMG (television station) 53
WCKT (television station) 30
WDAY (television station) 46
WDCA (television station) 74
Weiss, David 159
Weldon, Alex 118, 136
Welles, Orson 12–13, 148–150, 153–154
Wells, H.G.: *The War of the Worlds* 105, 181
Wenk, Barbara 16

WENY (television station) 34
West Mall Theater (Sioux Falls, SD) 164–165
Westercon (1977 convention) 91
Weston, Richard 114, 134
Wexler, Anne 22
WFLD (television station) 74
WGN (television station) 27, 31
WGR (television station) 32
WHAG (television station) 46
WHBQ (television station) 46
WHEC (television station) 53
When Worlds Collide (1951 film) 77
Where Time Began 161
The White Dawn 67, 69, 73
Whitfield, Stephen 1, 76, 122, 130
Whitfield, Stephen 1, 76, 122, 130–131, 144
Whitney, Grace Lee 20, 115
WICZ (television station) 53
Wilde, Maggie 129
Wilkins, Bob 57, 79, 90–91
William Morris Agency 102
William Shatner Fan Fellowship 180
Williams, Andy 25
Williams, John 98, 150–152
Williams, Robin 103
Windom, William 88
Winston, Joan 32
Winter, Ralph 190–191
Wise, Millicent 20–21
Wise, Robert 11–14, 20, 33, 67, 113, 117, 120–122, 136, 140, 148, 150, 177, 130
WJAR (television station) 46
WJCL (television station) 46
WJZ (television station) 46
WKBD (television station) 27, 31, 74
WKBF (television station) 26–27, 31
WKBG (television station) 27, 31
WKBN (television station) 46
WKBS (television station) 27, 31, 34, 74
WKEH (television station) 32
WLVI (television station) 74
WLWI (television station) 53
WMAQ (television station) 31
WNBC (television station) 28
WNEW (television station) 28–29
Wnoroski, Jim 115, 118
WNYS (television station) 53
WOI (television station) 53
Wolf, Sherman 18–19
Wolverton, Walter 162
Women's Wear Daily 144–145
WOR (television station) 26, 28
Wormhole Effect 71, 86, 91–92, 97, 100–101, 106, 110–112, 119
Worth, David 161
Wozniak, Steve 15, 134, 165
WPGH (television station) 28
WPIX (television station) 28–29, 31, 73
WQAD (television station) 53
Wright, Steve 14
Writers Guild of America 177

WTCN (television station) 31
WTTG (television station) 27
WTTV (television station) 27
WTVR (television station) 46
Wyatt, Jane 89–90

Xanadu (1980 film) 149
Xanadu Lines 149, 152–153

Yablans, Frank 45, 48
Young, Bonnie 166

Young, Colin Patrick 166
Young, Dennis 166
Young, Helen 45

"Z" Channel 178–179, 185
Zimbert, Richard 63
Zink, John J. 13
Zipf's Law 176